Contributions to Management Science

More information about this series at http://www.springer.com/series/1505

Hasan Dinçer • Ümit Hacioğlu
Editors

Risk Management, Strategic Thinking and Leadership in the Financial Services Industry

A Proactive Approach to Strategic Thinking

Springer

Editors
Hasan Dinçer
Istanbul Medipol University
Kavacik, Istanbul
Turkey

Ümit Hacioğlu
Istanbul Medipol University
Kavacik, Istanbul
Turkey

The views expressed in this book are those of the authors, but not necessarily of the publisher and editors.

ISSN 1431-1941 ISSN 2197-716X (electronic)
Contributions to Management Science
ISBN 978-3-319-47171-6 ISBN 978-3-319-47172-3 (eBook)
DOI 10.1007/978-3-319-47172-3

Library of Congress Control Number: 2016960761

Printed on acid-free paper

This Springer imprint is published by Springer Nature
The registered company is Springer International Publishing AG
The registered company address is: Gewerbestrasse 11, 6330 Cham, Switzerland

Foreword

Risk is part of our lives. We take risks to grow and to develop. For financial institutions, risk is an indispensable part of their life because they cannot survive without taking risk. At this point, the management of risk becomes the main issue. Risks should be managed in order to minimize the threats of risks and maximize their benefits. Risk management is defined as *the process of identification and mitigation of uncertainty in decisions related to investments and controlling threats to an organization's capital and earnings*.

Risk management culture focuses on each person's habit of management of risk. The risk management culture is the situation of *looking for risks when making operational decisions*. Strategic thinking, on the other hand, is the *ability to come up with effective plans pursuant to the objectives of the organization*, whereas leadership is defined as *the inspiration of subordinates to achieve a goal*. Financial Services Industry encompasses the money and capital markets, as well as the foreign exchange markets. This book gathers researchers and market professionals across the globe to understand the Risk Management Culture, Strategic Thinking, and Leadership in the Financial Services Industry.

Risk Measurement and Management culture on the global basis dates back to 1988. This was the year when Basel Committee for Bank Supervision (BCBS), after the failure of Herstatt Bank, led the development of *risk-based capital standard* for credit risk of the internationally active banks of G-10. Basel Capital Adequacy Accord (Basel I) has been phased in by 1993 and became a world standard in a short time. The Accord, due mainly to financial innovation, has been amended in 1996 (effective January 1, 1998) to take a separate account of market risk besides the credit risk. Yet, BCBS started to communicate with the Banking industry as early as 1999 for Basel II due mainly to discrepancies in the measurement of credit risk of Basel I and the need for the inclusion of risk-based capital standards for operational risk. The standard method of Basel II was effective in the EU by January 2007 and the advanced methods by January 2008. In the meantime, by 2007 and 2008 the world witnessed a global financial crisis. Basel III is an answer to this financial crisis. Regulatory standards concerning banks' capital adequacy and liquidity risks are developed by BCBS in June 2011 and January 2013, respectively. There are five major issues in Basel III in addition to these minimum capital and minimum liquidity standards, which are maximum leverage, governance, and remuneration. Capital Requirements Directive (CRD) IV, which is the parallel implementation of the Basel rules to the EU legislation, applies from January 1, 2014, and will be fully applicable by 2019 to banks and investment funds, whereas insurance funds and collective investment funds are covered by Solvency II.

The book welcomes five sections and 25 chapters from authors around the globe. In the first section, Economic Outlook and Expectations for the Financial Services Industry is elaborated. Here, the first two chapters focus on the Global Economic Outlook as well as Sustainable and Inclusive Finance in Turkey. The remaining chapters intricate the Monetary Policy, Banking, and Foreign Exchange Markets. The second section concentrates on Managing Risk in the Capital Markets. Here, the emphasis is on the computation of operational risk, liquidity risk, credit derivatives risk, and financial risk. Section three centers on Volatility, Hedging, and Strategy in Risky Environment. Here, Extreme Value Theory, VaR Performance of EMEs during FED's Tapering, Jumps and Earnings Announcement, Hedging Scenarios, and Option Scenarios are detailed. Section IV spotlights Risk-based Audit and Structured Finance. The chapters in this section examine Risk-based Internal Audit, Accounting Perspectives for Future, Reporting Trends, and Risk Assessment. The last section is on Culture and Leadership in Risk Management. In this section, the chapters concentrate on the role of Risk Management Culture in Strategic Planning, Agile Intrapreneurship in Volatile Business Environment, Emerging Trends in the Post-Regulatory Environment, The effect of National Culture, and Contemporary Leadership Styles.

In order to understand the Risk Management Culture in the Financial Services Industry, the book is the right one, coming at the right time. The editors of the book, Dr. Hacıoglu and Dr. Dincer, have done an extraordinary job in collecting views of the academics and professionals all across the world. This book is an insightful guide to understanding the challenges of Risk Management Culture, Strategic Thinking, and Leadership in the Financial Services Industry.

I recommend this book to all readers who are interested in the Risk notion and Financial Services Industry.

European Union Institute
Marmara University
Kadıköy, Istanbul
Turkey

İmre Ersoy

Preface

Integrated risk management systems with its applications became important key topic for the financial services industry in the last two decades. Apparently, the lessons learned from the latest global financial crisis also played a major role in understanding the pioneering role of effective risk management systems on strategic business operations. With respect to the major studies in the field, it is possible to mention that comprehensive risk governance systems have not been sufficiently examined based on its ties with corporate culture, strategic thinking, and leadership in the global financial institutions.

Another major experience on the global financial crisis is attached to that a profound effect of corporate culture on risk management attitude increases the value for shareholders in the global financial system. Additionally, the major empirical studies in the field also point out the role of effective risk management systems in sustainable business performance during volatile business conditions. Adaptive risk management systems with innovative solutions at these risky conditions have broader ties with economic capital allocation and increase the core value of the business. Especially, in the banking industry, strategic investment decisions are affected by systemic risks during volatile conditions. Hence, an appropriate interdisciplinary approach to risk management systems should be covering theories and practices for a new design, strategic thinking, proactive culture, and the role of leadership.

In this novel book, a broad overview of risk-based empirical studies has been attached to strategic thinking, design, culture, and leadership in the financial services industry. It also aims to develop an interdisciplinary approach for the development of risk management practices with a broader context behind the new design and theory.

This book is composed of five contributory sections. The first section evaluates the 2008–2009 financial crises in historical context and the economic outlook and assesses the expectations for the financial services industry. The distinguished parts of the first section cover the topics on the global economic outlook, sustainable and inclusive finance in Turkey, monetary policy divergence and central banking in the new era, in looking into the foreign exchange risk management, the link between dollarization and its determinants in Turkey, and finally enhancing the risk management functions in banking: capital allocation and banking regulations.

This book continues with section two by assessing basic topics of managing risks in capital markets. In section two, the calibration of market risk measures during period of economic downturn: market risks and measures, computation of operational value at risk using the severity distribution model based on Bayesian method with Gibbs sampler, liquidity risk and optimal redemption policies for illiquid investments, credit derivatives, their risks and role in global financial crisis, and an approach to measure financial risk relative indices: a case study of Indonesian insurance companies are some titles covered inside. The next section covers empirical studies on volatility, hedging, and strategy in risky environment. Titles of this section are the extreme value theory in finance: a way to forecast unexpected circumstances, the value at risk performance of emerging market equity portfolios during the fed's tapering, jumps and earnings announcement: empirical evidence from emerging markets using high-frequency data, hedging scenarios under competition: exploring the impact of competitors' hedging practices, and option strategies and exotic options: tools for hedging or source of financial instability?

The fourth section of this book demonstrates the link between the risk-based audit and the structured finance with the titles of risk-based internal audit, the recent financial crisis and the structured finance, compliance and reporting trends with essential strategies, developing a risk management framework, and risk assessment for non-profit organizations.

Finally, the last section builds on the culture and leadership in risk management. Risk management culture with its role in strategic planning, agile intrapreneurship in volatile business environment: changing roles of financial managers and risk takers according to Schumpeterian approach, emerging trends in the post-regulatory environment: the importance of instilling trust, the effect of national culture on corporate financial decisions, contemporary leadership styles, and Schumpeterian creative destruction in volatile business environment are the titles covered in this section.

The authors of the chapters in this publication have contributed to the success of our work by the inclusion of their respective studies with case studies. This book gathers colleagues and professionals across the globe from multicultural communities to design and implement innovative practices for the entire global society of finance and banking. The authors of the chapters in this premium reference source in the field with the contribution of scholars and researchers overseas from different disciplines examined the related topics of risk management by assessing critical case studies in the financial services industry.

Consequently, we believe this book with its scope and success makes it even more attractive for readers and scholars in this field.

Istanbul, Turkey
August 2016

Hasan Dinçer
Ümit Hacioğlu

Acknowledgment

We have many colleagues and partners to thank for their impressive contribution to this publication. First, we would like to praise the people at Springer International Publishing AG: Dr. Prashanth Mahagaonkar, who has the attitude and substance of a genius: he continually and convincingly conveyed a spirit of adventure in regard to our research at each stage of our book development process; Sivachandran Ravanan, our book project coordinator, without his persistent help this publication would not have been possible; and others who assisted us in making critical decisions about the structure of the book and provided useful feedback on stylistic issues.

We would like to express our appreciations to the Editorial Advisory Board Members. The members who helped with the book included Dursun Delen, Ekrem Tatoglu, Bahcesehir University, Istanbul Turkey. Idil Kaya, Ihsan Isik, Martie Gillen, Michael S. Gutter, Nicholas Apergis, Ozlem Olgu, Ulas Akkucuk, and Zeynep Copur. The excellent advice from these members helped us to enrich the book.

We would also like to thank all of the authors of the individual chapters for their excellent contributions.

We would particularly like to thank the Center for Strategic Studies in Business and Finance for the highest level of contribution in the editorial process.

The final words of thanks belong to our families and parents separately: Dr. Hacioğlu would like to thank his wife Burcu and his son Fatih Efe as well as his parents; Dr. Dincer would like to thank his wife Safiye as well as his parents. They deserve thanks for their enthusiasm, appreciation, help, and love. Their pride in our accomplishments makes it even more rewarding to the editors.

Istanbul Medipol University
Istanbul, Turkey
August 2016

Hasan Dinçer
Ümit Hacioğlu

The Editors would like to acknowledge the following international advisory board members

Contents

Part I
Economic Outlook and Expectations for the Financial Services Industry

Global Economic Outlook

Gökçe Çiçek Ceyhun

Abstract As it is well known the international economic landscape has undergone a change and individual countries have slackened by virtue of economic recession after 2008 global financial crisis. In spite of declination in business activities in many industrial countries since 2008, the global economic recovery is developing and it is estimated to be sustained for keeping up with the international trade. In contravention of many years that passed after economic turmoil which has cost millions of jobs, the economists have been still preoccupying with crisis effects on global economic outlook. This chapter draws attention to some of the economic reports that should be taken into consideration for financial services industry. Moreover the current and expected economic situation is discussed by reviewing reports.

1 Introduction

> I think the US economy is leading global economic growth. The economic growth in the US is much more broadly based than before. So I have full confidence in the US economy's growth (Haruhiko Kuroda).

Maybe this quotation can give an idea relating with global economic outlook of today and future. Due to the fact that 2008 global financial crisis has started at US and the impacts of the turmoil have expanded all over the world swiftly, actually it's not an exaggeration to tell that US economy is determiner of world global economic growth.

The global economy is at the end balancing the recent global financial crisis and Great Recession. One of the major factor that supporting stronger economic growth is lower global commodity prices. Moreover lower fuel prices for households and

G.Ç. Ceyhun (✉)
Department of Maritime Business Administration, Maritime Faculty, Kocaeli University, Kocaeli, Turkey
e-mail: gokceceyhun@hotmail.com

H. Dinçer, Ü. Hacioğlu (eds.), *Risk Management, Strategic Thinking and Leadership in the Financial Services Industry*, Contributions to Management Science, DOI 10.1007/978-3-319-47172-3_1

lower input prices for industry may are providing a boost for aggregating global growth and global demand. The global economy is passing from the Great Recession period to a new stage which hosts more steady growth. However there are still economic weakness together with new risks (Global Economic Outlook 2015-2020).

On the other hand global trade is growing slower for the last five years and it seems to have slackened after global financial crisis. On account of the fact that powerful trade and global growth go hand in hand, the developments in the economic satiation is vital for all. International trade intensifies international competition, keeps the domestic companies strong and extends variety for business and consumers. That's why the economic outlook of world trade can be identified as pioneer of global output (OECD Economic Outlook 2015).

In order to gain momentum the global economy is still struggling and while high income countries are trying to remove the traces of global financial crisis, emerging economies are not dynamic as in the past. This conjuncture is giving chance to countries for reforming their economies (Global Economic Prospects 2015).

In this chapter current and expected global economic outlook has been examined with economic reports by analyzing global outlook, regional outlook, emerging economies and advanced economies.

2 Literature Review

2.1 *Global Outlook*

In the past years, the world economy has witnessed a great variety of positive and negative macroeconomic cases. Actually, the changes in the economic outlook have raised financial stability risks. Sharp drop in oil prices and commodity prices are continued to grow and interest rates supported growth in 2016. Brave monetary policy precautions have been taken in euro area and Japan in order to reverse pressures of disinflation. Credit spreads have constricted in the euro area, equity prices have advanced, yen and euro have decreased their value significantly. On the other hand the appreciation of U.S. dollar has reflected several monetary policies. The rapid change of real exchange rates have reflected global economic growth (Global Financial Stability Report 2015).

The global economy has staggered in 2015 with decreasing commodity prices, ascending financial market volatility and low aggregate demand. The growth rates of aggregate demand and gross fixed capital formation remained same in 2015. It is estimated that the world economy will grow by 2.9 % in 2016 and 3.2 % in 2017 (see Fig. 1). The US monetary policy stance is anticipated to reduce uncertainties of policy and to impede extreme volatility of asset prices and exchange rates (World Economic Situation and Prospects 2016).

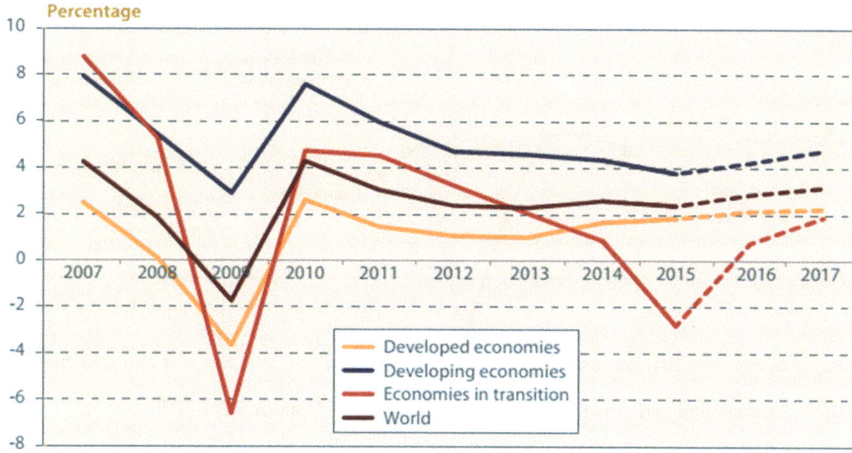

Fig. 1 Growth of world gross product and gross domestic product by country grouping, 2007–2017. Source: United Nations, World Economic Situation and Prospects (2016)

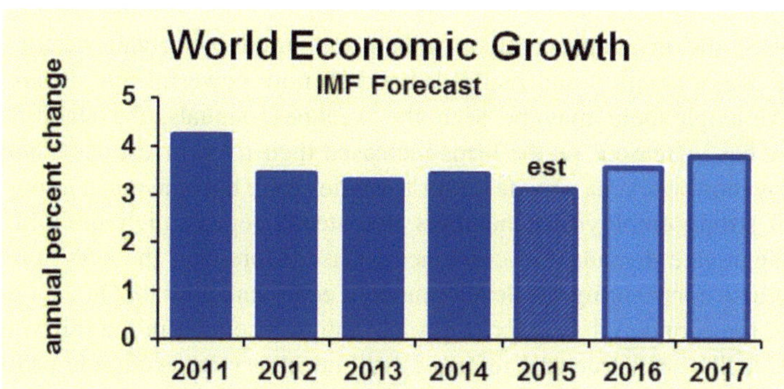

Fig. 2 World economic growth. Source: Conerly (2015)

According to World Economic Outlook Report that was published by International Monetary Fund (IMF), it is anticipated that the world overall will expand 3.6 % inflation in 2016. On the other hand emerging economies and advanced economies will contribute the economic development (Conerly 2015) (Fig. 2).

Moreover according to "Global Economic Outlook 2015-2020" Report that was released by ATKearney Global Business Policy Council, it is expected that there will be a return to annual global growth about 3–4 % between 2015 and 2020 (see Fig. 3).

The historical growth is an unweighted average of the three sources' GDP data at constant prices and exchange rates. This outlook contains not only stagnant markets but also bright spots. Despite the high sustained growth rate, it still does not recover the lost during 2008 and 2013 period (Global Economic Outlook 2015-2020).

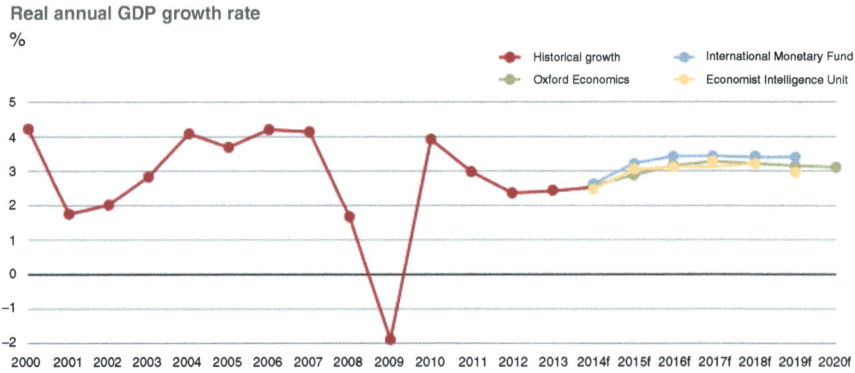

Fig. 3 Estimated global growth. Source: Global Economic Outlook 2015-2020

2.2 *Global Outlook of Developed Economies: USA, Japan, Euro Zone*

In the US, the economic outlook which supported by private sector growth, financial sector stability and rising demand is more powerful than it has been in years. Although there may be seen the weakness signals, the stability of US economy has increased. As the firms increased their fixed investments and started to employ more workers, private sector activities have become much stronger. As a result of strong employment numbers and steady repairs of household balance sheets, aggregate demand has continued to rise. Moreover, the stability of fiscal policy is also contributing the development of economic growth. On the other hand in Japan, the economy has surprisingly fell into a recession in the third quarter of 2014. Actually new structural reform is still necessary for economic prospects of Japan. Prime Minister Shinzo Abe has offered some reforms as containing corporate governance, the promotion of entrepreneurship, and deregulation in National Strategic Special Zones. However, political resistance to these difficult structural reforms must be overcome. On the other side, there is still weak growth economic outlook in the Eurozone. The latest currency deprecation could defuse the problems of competitiveness. Besides mild deflation and low inflation are still constituting an impediment for economic recovery. Since the crisis Greece and Spain have performed a variety of structural reforms, but dissatisfaction of economic recovery has remained same. The political leaders of Euro zone should implement new reforms in order to growth economic outlook (Global Economic Outlook 2015-2020).

Apart from these explanations, developed economies pursued to rely on adaptable monetary policy in 2015. This adaptable monetary policy helped to stop fusion of financial sector and prevented a prolonged recession. Unfortunately this situation could not been effective as anticipated for investment and economic growth. From historical point of view short term and long term interest rates of developed

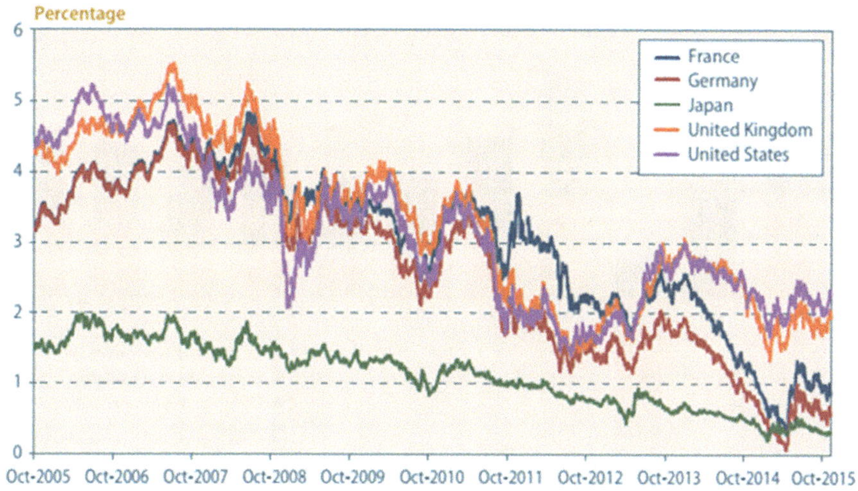

Fig. 4 Ten-year government bond yields in selected developed economies, October 2005–October 2015. Source: World Economic Situation and Prospects (2016)

economies are still depressed. Ten-year government bond yields for France, Germany, Japan, the United States and the United Kingdom has shown in Fig. 4. As the labor market of US has sustained to develop progressively, the FED (Federal Reserve System) has become closer to its first interest rate as in 2006. FED rate is now anticipated to occur same as in 2015. Conversely other banks of developed countries are still loosening their monetary policy. The ECB (European Central Bank) maintains its expanded asset purchase program since March 2015 and it is anticipated to be implemented until the end of March 2017. This program provided recovery of the euro zone. On the other hand, The Bank of Japan has continued the pace of asset purchases under its quantitative and qualitative monetary easing program (QQME). The financial authorities have decided to implement this program until inflation is stable at 2 % (World Economic Situation and Prospects 2016).

2.3 *Global Outlook of Emerging National Economies: Brazil, Russia, India, China and South Africa*

The generation of economic power among the developing countries is inverting the distribution for international governance of political power. The most outstanding emerging powers in the world are the BRIC countries; Brazil, Russia, India and China. According to December 2009 report of Goldman Sachs these countries projected to overtake the Group of Seven (G-7) economies by 2032. It is estimated

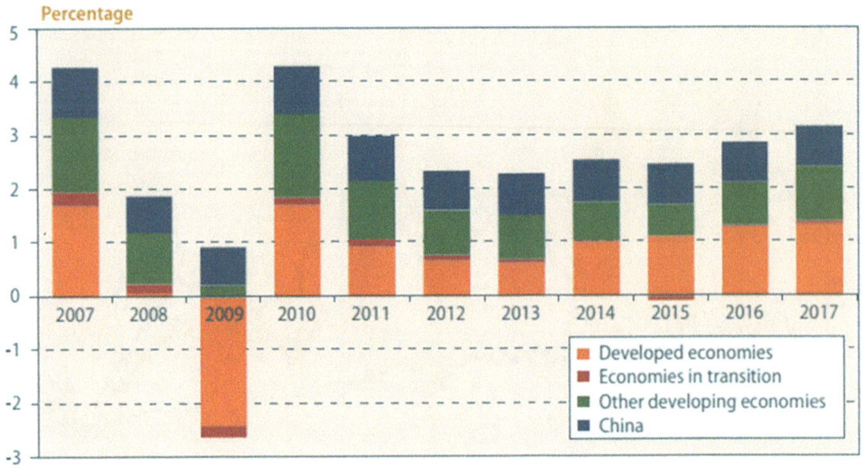

Fig. 5 Contribution to global growth, 2007–2017. Source: World Economic Situation and Prospects (2016)

that collective political and military exploit of the BRIC countries will be commensurate with their economic power in the coming decades (Toh 2010).

Developing countries produced much of the global output growth, since the inception of global financial crisis (see Fig. 5). Particularly, China has become the locomotive country of global economic growth during 2011 and 2012. China has maintained strong demand of commodities and boosted export growth in the rest of the world. With a much anticipated slowdown in China and persistently weak economic performances in other large developing and transition economies—notably Brazil and the Russian Federation—the developed economies are expected to contribute more to global growth in the near term, provided they manage to mitigate deflationary risks and stimulate investment and aggregate demand.

Moreover falling into decrease of commodity price should help reduce macroeconomic suspense and stimulate economic growth in number of developing economies. It is expected that developing countries will grow by 4.3 % in 2016 and 4.8 % in 2017 (World Economic Situation and Prospects 2016).

On the other side Germany has become the largest surplus country in the world, as current account of China has narrowed. Germany's intra-euro area trade surplus has narrowed sharply since 2007, but its extra-euro area surplus has continued to widen, as shown in Fig. 6. The growing external surplus of Germany partly explains the widening current-account surplus of the euro area as a whole, which also reflects the rapid adjustment of the external positions of Greece, Ireland, Italy, Portugal and Spain (World Economic Situation and Prospects 2016).

Against the backdrop of weakening growth, rising financial market volatility, sharp exchange-rate depreciations and increasing portfolio capital outflows, monetary policies in developing and transition economies have shown some divergence in 2015 (Fig. 7).

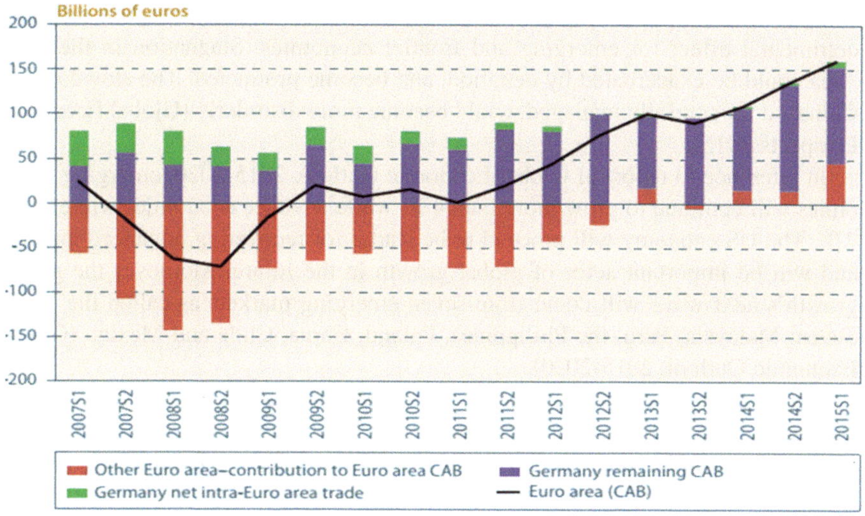

Fig. 6 Euro area current-account balance (*CAB*). Source: World Economic Situation and Prospects (2016)

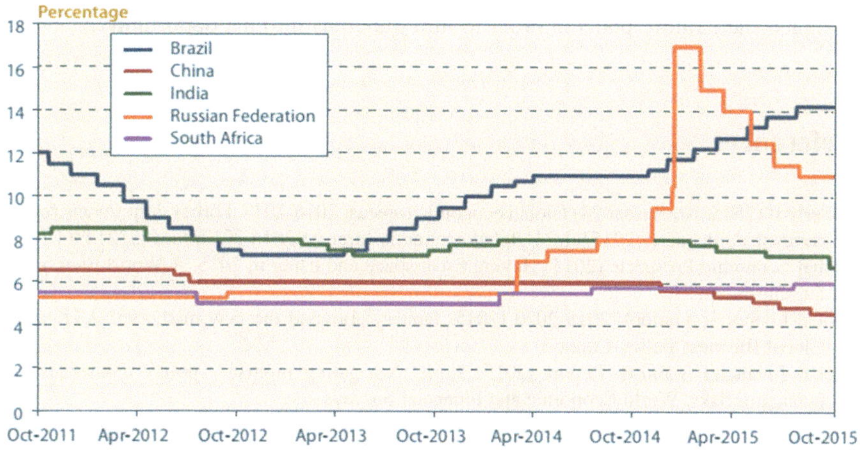

Fig. 7 Central bank policy rates in the BRICS, October 2011–October 2015. Source: World Economic Situation and Prospects (2016)

3 Conclusion

According to the future global economic scenario there will be consolidation for recovery in major global economies, demand in China will be rebalanced, developing countries will pass a smooth transition and commodity prices will be smoother. Besides, these presuppositions includes some risks. Changes in economic growth and policy prospects in financial markets could produce tighter credit conditions and a new financial volatility. These developments could result in detrimental effect for emerging and frontier economies. Stagnation in the Euro Area could be exacerbated by deflation, and become protracted. The slowdown in China, so far carefully managed, could become more disorderly (Global Economic Prospects 2015).

In reference to report of Global Economic Outlook 2015-2020, emerging economies will continue to grow more than 4 %, while advance economies will exceed 2 %. The US economy will proceed to be leader for recovering advanced markets and will be important actor of global growth in the future. Moreover the global growth's next wave will come from seven emerging markets as called the 2020-Seven: Malaysia, Peru, the Philippines, Poland, China, Chile and Mexico (Global Economic Outlook 2015-2020).

During the future period, weakness of the global trade growth will be the same. Because of the tightened monetary policy of high income economies, financial conditions could become more volatile. The failure of recovery in high income economies and slowing down of large emerging markets may cause deeper structural weakness (Global Economic Prospects 2015).

Actually the current economic conjuncture provides a new point of view for all countries. The recessions and incoming crises may be a challenge for some countries as it was in the past. The longsighted economy policymakers have already designed their future plans in order to turn the crisis into the opportunity.

References

Conerly B (2015, November 24) Global economic forecast 2016-2017. Forbes. http://www.forbes.com/sites/billconerly/2015/11/24/global-economic-forecast-2016-2017/#6e14282143f4

Global Economic Prospects (2015) Having fiscal space and using it, 2015. A World Bank group flagship report

Global Economic Outlook 2015-2020 (2015, January) Beyond the new mediocre? ATKearney Global Business Policy Council

Global Financial Stability Report (2015, April) Navigating monetary policy challenges and managing risks. World Economic and Financial Surveys

OECD Economic Outlook (2015) OECD Economic Outlook, Volume 2015 Issue 2. OECD Publishing, Paris. doi:10.1787/eco_outlook-v2015-2-en

Toh LCCHJ (2010) Brazil, Russia, India and China (BRIC): reshaping the world order in the 21st century. Lucent: A Journal of National Security Studies

United Nations (2016) World economic situation and prospects. United Nations, New York

Gökçe Çiçek Ceyhun is an Assistant Professor Doctor of Maritime Business Administration department at Maritime Faculty of Kocaeli University. Dr.Ceyhun has Phd in Maritime Business Administration from Dokuz Eylül University, a Msc in Management and Organization from Celal Bayar University and Bsc in Business Administration from Dokuz Eylül University. Her research interests are maritime boundaries, maritime security, smuggling of migrants, transportation corridors, human resources in maritime sector, maritime economics, supply chain management, stress management, fatigue, job satisfaction, turnover, work engagement and organizational ethic.

Sustainable and Inclusive Finance in Turkey

Sibel Yılmaz Türkmen and Gülcan Çağıl

Abstract For strong and sustainable growth finance must be inclusive. Individuals and companies should have equal opportunity on accessing markets and resources. Financial inclusion does not mean pushing access for the sake of access, and it certainly does not mean making everybody borrow. For inclusive economic development, inclusive finance is a necessary criteria. Growth becomes inclusive if it is supported by structural reforms. The main purpose of this chapter is to explore the terms of sustainable and inclusive finance and assess the underlying role in the developing countries especially in Turkey and to reveal the current situation and further possibilities.

1 Introduction

In the traditional view, the ultimate goal of companies is to use resources efficiently and to maximize risk adjusted return on capital. This view has been challenged by many management scholars who argue that companies have a wider responsibility that goes beyond profit maximization. In this context, the concept of sustainable development has gained increasing attention and relevance in the last decade (Hahn and Figge 2011; Jensen and Meckling 1976; Hanley 2000; Fatemi and Fooladi 2013).

The fast depletion of natural resources and the increase in social tension linked to industrial growth and globalization, has led to a growing awareness of the urgent need for sustainable business models. Maintaining a business—as—usual model

S.Y. Türkmen (✉)
Faculty of Business Administration, Marmara University, Ressam Namık Ismail Sk./1 34180, Bahçelievler, Istanbul, Turkey
e-mail: sibelyilmaz@marmara.edu.tr

G. Çağıl (✉)
School of Banking and Insurance, Marmara University, Göztepe Campus, Kadıköy, Istanbul, Turkey
e-mail: gulcancagil@marmara.edu.tr

H. Dinçer, Ü. Hacioğlu (eds.), *Risk Management, Strategic Thinking and Leadership in the Financial Services Industry*, Contributions to Management Science, DOI 10.1007/978-3-319-47172-3_2

carries with it significant environmental and social risks and technological developments which make communication much easier and information more accessible to a wide range of stakeholders, are increasingly putting businesses on the spot. Businesses have a strong interest to ensure that such risks do not occur, and to manage existing projects with an approach that focuses on multi-stakeholder engagement in which finance sector can play a crucial role (SFF 2014).

The term sustainable development had the potential to stimulate discursive engagement with respect to the future development of society within an ethical framework based around the values of inclusivity, diversity, and integration (Fergus and Rowney 2005).

Financial inclusion plays major role in inclusive growth of the country (Shah and Dubhashi 2015). The concept of inclusive growth does not only represent an economic growth in a way that will benefit certain segments of the society but everyone in society, especially the poor. One of the underlying causes of prosperity and economic growth differences between countries is the institutional structure. Inclusive institutions reduce the power of the elites in society and create an environment that encourages investment which paves the way for economic growth.

Inclusive growth in the economy can only be achieved when all the weaker sections of the society including agriculture and small scale industries are nurtured and brought on par with other sections of the society in terms of economic development (Swamy 2010).

The policy debate has been shifting from the finance-growth nexus to the finance-inequality relationship (Asongu and De Moor 2015). Importance of financial inclusion arises from the problem of financial exclusion of nearly three billion people from the formal financial services across the world. In the developed countries, the formal financial sector serves most of the population, whereas a large segment of the society, in developing countries, mainly the low-income group, has modest access to financial services, either formally or informally (Swamy 2010). An "inclusive financial sector" offers the majority of the population, on a sustainable basis, access to a range of financial services suited to their needs. Building an inclusive financial sector turns the tide on access: inclusion of the majority of the population rather than exclusion (Imboden 2005).

Although there is a broad definition about inclusive finance, in the basic and clear form, financial inclusion was defined as "Financial inclusion is the process that ensures the ease of access, availability, and usage of formal financial system for all members of an economy" (Park and Mercado 2015). According to the another definition, financial inclusion means that "formal financial services—such as deposit and savings accounts, payment services, loans, and insurance—are available to consumers and that they are actively and effectively using these services to meet their specific needs" (Klapper et al. 2016).

Financial inclusion does not mean pushing access for the sake of access, and it certainly does not mean making everybody borrow (Miller 2014, p. 9). Financial inclusion, at a minimum, may be interpreted to mean the ability of every individual to access basic financial services which include savings, loans and insurance in a

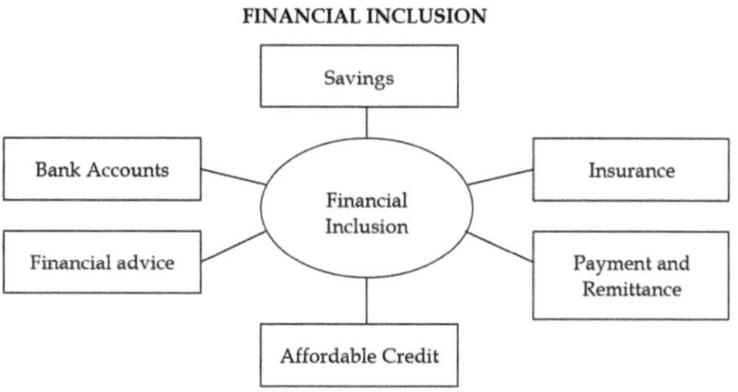

Fig. 1 Financial inclusion. *Source*: RBI, Report of the Committee on Financial Inclusion (2008)

manner that is reasonably convenient and flexible in terms of access and design and reliable in the sense that the savings are safe and that insurance claims will be paid with certainty. Empirical evidence shows that inclusive financial systems significantly raise growth, alleviate poverty and expand economic opportunity (Mor and Ananth 2007). Financial inclusion means delivery of banking services and credit at an affordable cost to the vast sections of disadvantaged and low income groups. As seen in the Fig. 1, the various financial services include savings, loans, insurance, payments, remittance facilities and financial counseling/advisory services by the formal financial system (RBI 2008).

The perfect financial inclusion may therefore be described by the capacity to access and use appropriate financial services proposed by mainstream providers. Meanwhile, there may be an adequate "second best choice" to get appropriate services proposed by alternative providers that comply with rules and regulations and do not exploit low income people (EC 2008). The importance of financial inclusion can be revealed from the following (Shah and Dubhashi 2015):

1. It is a necessary condition for sustaining equitable growth.
2. It protects the poor people from the clutches of usurious money lenders.
3. It will make possible for the governments to make payments under the social security schemes through bank accounts of the beneficiaries, by electronic transfers. This will minimize transaction costs including leakages.
4. It provides an avenue for bringing the savings of the poor into the formal financial intermediation system and channel them into investment.
5. The large number of low cost deposits will offer banks an opportunity to reduce their dependence on bulk deposits and help them to better manage both liquidity risks and asset liability mismatches.

The rest of the paper is organized as follows. Section two overviews existing literature, section three explains the role and importance of inclusive finance in developing countries especially in Turkey and final section provides concluding remarks.

2 Review of Literature

There are many studies available on the financial inclusion in the literature. Zwedu (2014) intended to explore the link among financial inclusion, regulation and inclusive growth in Ethiopia. The study found out that despite huge progress, financial inclusion is still very low. Sarker et al. (2015) recommended some policy measures to overcome the challenges of financial inclusion with regards to the banking sector's initiatives in financing agriculture in Bangladesh.

Garg and Pandey (2007) suggested that in order to reduce poverty and propel India towards sustainable human well-being a comprehensive financial system based on the bank-money lender linkages is required. Mor and Ananth (2007) aimed to express a point of view on the financial system design principles essential to achieve the goal of financial inclusion. Dixit and Ghosh (2013) made analysis of natural hierarchical grouping cluster considering parameters like GDP per capita, literacy rate, unemployment rate and index of financial inclusion on few of Indian states. Shyni and Mavoothu (2014) explained how financial inclusion can help in the inclusive growth of the economy.

Swamy (2010) evaluated using appropriate statistical techniques the impact of financial inclusion efforts on the inclusive growth in the case of a developing economy like India by considering the data for the period from 1975 to 2007 and found that bank led financial inclusion has definitive advantages for inclusive growth in developing economies. Lavoie et al. (2011) investigated the replication of microcredit methodologies as one of the financial inclusion strategies in Brazil and it is expected that the results lead to increase the expansion of microcredit operations across Brazil.

Block et al. (2013) presented a system dynamics model which they were developing for analyzing the relationship between economic growth and consumer debt from a financial and distribution political perspective. Neupane (2015) studied the relation between financial access and poverty incidence in Nepal. Inoue and Hamori (2016) found out financial access has a statistically significant and robust effect on increasing economic growth in Sub-Saharan Africa. Yorulmaz (2013) examined a multidimensional measurement of financial inclusion to gauge the extent of financial system across time in Turkey.

3 Inclusive Finance in Developing Countries

In most countries around the world, there is growing inequality. In some important countries, the increase in inequality has been particularly large. This is of macro-economic importance, because those at the top consume a smaller fraction of their incomes than do those at the bottom and middle (Stiglitz 2016).

In mature economies, rates of exclusion tend to be low—for example only an estimated 4 % of the population in Germany and 9 % in the United States go without basic access to services. But in the world's smaller and less mature economies, financial exclusion rates reach exorbitant levels; approximately 80 % of the financially excluded live in Latin America, Asia or Africa. In this sense, financial inclusion poses policy challenges on a scale and with an urgency that is unique for developing countries. Therefore, financial inclusion became an important policy issue especially in the emerging market economies (Yorulmaz 2013).

In the wake of the global financial crisis, many developed and developing country governments are prioritizing stability at the individual financial institutions and systemic level by strengthening financial regulation. Even though the latter is important to make financial systems more robust, its contribution to inclusive growth might be insufficient, especially in poor countries (Zwedu 2014). The financial crisis has raised deep questions about the role of the financial sector and its impact on growth and income distribution. The crisis has also stimulated reforms to help the sector contribute to growth that is strong, sustainable and inclusive (OECD 2015).

Internationally, the financial inclusion has been viewed in a much wider perspective. Having a current account/savings account on its own, is not regarded as an accurate indicator of financial inclusion. Financial inclusion efforts should offer at a minimum, access to a range of financial services including savings, long and short term credit, insurance, pensions, mortgages, money transfers, etc. and all this at a reasonable cost (Shah and Dubhashi 2015).

Developing countries need to design appropriate strategies for increasing access to financial services by all segments of the population. They must also turn their strategies into effective policy measures and implementation plans. This means that multiple stakeholders must work together to design these strategies and determine the best ways to organize their implementation. Such an effort entails the co-operation of the range of governments, financial institutions, civil society organizations, development partners, and the private sector. And it requires all stakeholders to ensure that adequate attention is focused on financial inclusion over the long term (UN 2006).

As seen in the Table 1 financial inclusion has risen significantly in recent years in developing countries and among people living at the base of the economic pyramid. Account ownership among the poorest 40% has more than doubled in a range of countries with widely varying population sizes and GDPs (UNSGSA 2015).

The United Nations General Assembly adopted the 2030 Agenda for sustainable development. The agenda comprise seventeen sustainable development goals to apply all countries include developing countries. The goals do not only aim to reach financial inclusion but also access to financial services enables to fight against poverty (Klapper et al. 2016). Therefore reaching the goal of inclusive economic development requires reliable financial inclusion data which cover the major components of sustainable financial inclusion development (GPFI 2016).

Access to financial services is key to growth and sustainability in developing countries and emerging economies. In addition access to financial services for large segments of the population is crucial to reduce of poverty and income inequality in

Table 1 Financial inclusion indicators for some developing countries

Countries	Accounts poorest 40%		Adult population (millions)	GDP per capita
	2011	2014		
Nigeria	13 %	43 %	96.6 M	$5423
Botswana	16 %	37 %	1.3 M	$15,247
Mexico	12 %	29 %	87.5 M	$16,291
Indonesia	10 %	22 %	177.7 M	$9254
Zambia	8 %	21 %	7.8 M	$3800
Gabon	9 %	20 %	1.0 M	$18,646
Viet Nam	9 %	19 %	69.3 M	$5125
Peru	5 %	18 %	21.6 M	$11,396
Togo	5 %	12 %	4.0 M	$1346
Argentina[a]	19 %	44 %	31.4 M	–

Source: UNSGSA Annual Report to the Secretary General September (2015)
[a]Recent GDP is not available for Argentina. Adult population and GDP are from 2013; GDP is per capita PPP

developing countries. However access to financial services for the poor majority population still remains limited (Sjauw-Koen-Fa and Vereijken 2005).

Almost 70 % of the adult population in developing countries lack access to basic formal financial services, such as savings or checking accounts based on the 2009 Financial Access report by the World Bank Group. According to the report the largest share of the unbanked live in Sub-Saharan Africa and South Asia, as well as East Asia, Middle East and North Africa, Latin America and Eastern Europe and Central Asia (Stein 2010).

It is known that mainly five challenges prevent financial access for people in developing countries which are lack of financial literacy, lack of valid identification documents, issue of consumer protection and regulation, the rural poor environment situation and opening a transaction account (http://blogs.worldbank.org, 2015).

There are several reasons to prevent access to financial services in developing countries. For example high levels of government debt lead to limited access of credit to firms and individuals. Lack of access to financial services is a disadvantage for individuals, especially for the poor, women, rural populations, as well as for firms such as small and medium enterprises (SMEs) (UNCTAD 2015). SMEs are important drivers to create jobs, employment, innovations and GDP growth in developing countries but many developing countries don't have strong regulation to access to financial services for SMEs (Stein 2010). Moreover many financial intermediaries, such as commercial banks, generally don't accept to serve SMEs due to the high cost of small transactions.

Governments try to increase access to financial services through direct lending to the banks to expand their branch networks in rural areas take the economy to a higher level (Shafi and Medabesh 2012). Banks especially commercial banks are not adequately providing SMEs with capital in developing countries. Therefore there are many alternatives to banking in developing countries such as postal operators, microfinance institutions, mobile banking and money transfer between developing and low-developed countries (www.microworld.org, 2016).

3.1 Inclusive Finance in Turkey

Turkey is a small emerging market, frequently referred as a "satellite" market, compared to the economies of Brazil, Russia, India, and China (BRIC). Even though Turkey is not among larger emerging markets, it draws attention from the global investment community for two reasons: First, it has demonstrated steady growth over the past decade. The real GDP per capita in US$ at constant prices since 2000, reached 8,492 in 2012 from 6,119 in 2000. Second, Turkey is the largest EM to join the European Union. Turkey is also an accidental member of OECD like Mexico, and a member of G20 (Ararat et al. 2014).

With almost 75 million residents (World Bank data as of 2013), Turkey is one of the largest upper middle-income countries with a vast potential to expand financial inclusion. Turkey currently holds the G20 presidency and has declared financial inclusion to be one of its priorities as a powerful driver of inclusive growth. It has traditionally been an important bridge between Europe and Asia and between the developed and developing world, which provides it with a unique opportunity to both learn from varied experiences with financial inclusion initiatives and to share its experience with countries that are less advanced (Tomilova 2015).

The global crisis in 2008 had major negative effects on all countries around the globe. These negative effects included severe recessions across many countries and an episode of acute financial distress in international capital markets, along with the bail-out of banks by national governments accompanied by the threat of total collapse of large financial institutions. Turkey was one of the hardest-hit countries by the crisis, yet Turkish banks were relatively less affected by the global crisis compared to their peers in advanced and other emerging market economies. The favorable position of the Turkish banking sector after the crisis was largely owed to the fact that a comprehensive reform package had already been implemented as part of the transition program for strengthening the Turkish economy, which was adopted subsequent to the financial crisis in 2001 (Ganioğlu and Us 2014).

A key sustainability issue in Turkey is small to medium size firms' access to finance. SMEs in Turkey play a crucial role in economic development. SMEs account for 76.7 % of employment, almost 40 % of investments, 26.5 % of total value-added to the economy, and 25 % of bank credit. Analysis of firm dynamics in Turkey however shows that SMEs are the slowest growing group in the economy. Moreover, SMEs are growing at a slower rate in Turkey than in several comparator countries in the Eastern Europe and Central Asia region. Turkish firms are more dependent on bank financing to fund their investments in fixed assets than are their peers in other countries. This is especially true for medium-size firms where bank financing accounts for 47 % of total funding (Seker and Correa 2010; Ararat

Table 2 Turkey's financial sector

	Compound annual growth rate (CAGR) 2008–2015	Share 2015
Banking	18	65
Central Bank	22	13
Insurance and pension	20	3
Other	15	19
Other includes: BIST capitalization, securities, consumer finance, real estate investments, investment trusts, asset management and venture capital investment trust assets.		

Source: Investment Support and Promotion Agency of Turkey (2016)

et al. 2014). 44.2 % of firms in Turkey using banks to finance investment in 2013 according to World Bank Development Indicator.

As seen in the Table 2 banking dominates the Turkish financial sector, accounting for over 70% of overall financial services, while insurance services and other financial activities also show significant growth potential. There are 53 banks in Turkey (34 deposit banks, 13 development and investment banks, 6 participation banks). Out of 53 banks, 21 hold significant foreign capital (30 % of total assets are held by foreign investors. Turkey's economic growth has resulted in income growth and a growing robust middle class with increasing purchasing power. Also the increase in different loan product categories offered by banks supported the increase in consumer loans. Within this scope, the introduction of mortgage loans, which constitute more than 37 % of total consumer loans, reached to more than TL 143 billion with a CAGR of 27 % from 2005 to 2015 (ISPAT 2016).

In terms of the financial sector itself, initiatives have developed over the past few years to scale up sustainability within the banking sector, and the investor community; the dialogue between these different initiatives are still at initial stage, and the inclusion of insurance, as an important segment of the finance industry, in the sustainability debate, is yet to be done (SFF 2014).

Commercial bank branches per 100,000 adults are 19.8 in 2014 and ATMs per 100,000 adults increased from 28.52 in 2004 to 77.08 in 2014 (data.worldbank.org). Efforts to develop a more inclusive financial system have been successful, and currently more than 85 % of the population has some form of saving and deposit accounts after these laws and legislates in Turkey (Yorulmaz 2013).

As a result of broad-based industrial development and massive job creation throughout the country, growth became more inclusive in the 2000s (Fig. 2). As seen in the graphs income inequality, poverty and material deprivation all declined and income gaps between regions have narrowed (OECD 2014).

Turkish government introduced financial legislation for a more inclusive financial system. The Consumer Protection Law of 1995 included explicitly to financial services, and various consumer protection regulations within the framework of the financial sector. In 2003, The By–Laws on Rules and Procedures for Early Repayment Discount for Consumer Credits and Calculation of Annual Cost Rate was introduced (Yorulmaz 2013).

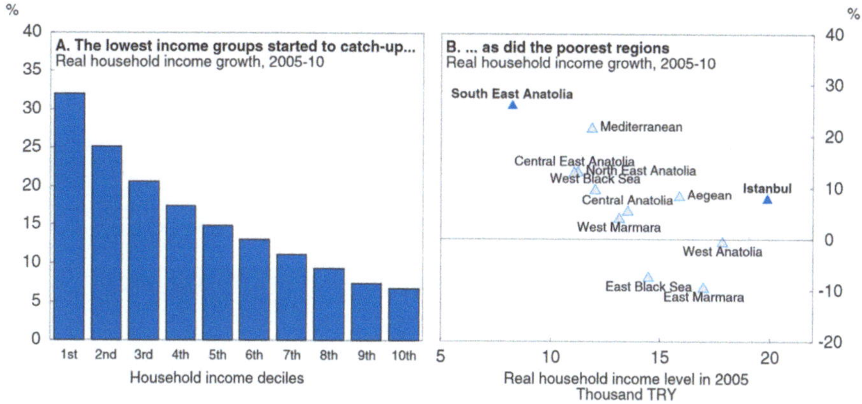

Fig. 2 Growth has been quite inclusive during the 2000s. *Source*: OECD Economic Surveys Turkey (2014)

Financial education increases awareness of opportunities, ability of navigate financial markets; consumer protection laws and regulations support responsible finance and levels of trust may help to explain financial inclusion (Miller 2014). Financial education thus is seen as critical to advancing financial inclusion and consumer protection (Nair and Tankha 2015).

Microfinance and microcredit are "inclusive finance" strategies that represent two of these ways. Microfinance is related to the access and use of financial services by a low-income population, mainly those typically excluded from the traditional financial system. Microcredit programs that extend small loans to poor people for self-employment projects that generate income (Woller and Woodworth 2001; Dichter and Harper 2007; Lavoie et al. 2011). While microfinance is more effective in reducing financial exclusion, financial inclusion is more efficient on reducing poverty through the provision of financial services. Financial inclusion shows the inclusiveness of an economy and microfinance is a powerful tool for achieving higher levels of financial inclusion in economies. Therefore, the way to reach high level of financial inclusion is mostly using microfinance in Turkey (Yorulmaz 2013).

Turkish Grameen Microfinance Program (TGMP) is a private nonprofit microfinance organization founded in 2003. Their mission is to create a poverty-free Turkey where all low-income people have the opportunity to improve their economic welfare through affordable financial services. They operate in 68 provinces in 107 branches across Turkey and have provided small business loans to over 60,000 female borrowers.

Women still largely encounter difficulties in ensuring their own economic sustainability and in accessing financial instruments for entrepreneurship. Job-holder women are still faced with challenges when trying to develop and maintain a business life that include both availability of finance and financial know-how. The low rate of financial literacy rate among women hampers their

Table 3 Key financial inclusion data for Turkey and peer comparisons (2011–2014)

Indicator	Turkey, 2014 (data for 2011 in brackets)	Europe and Central Asia, 2014 (data for 2011 in brackets)	Upper middle income, 2014 (data for 2011 in brackets)
Account (% age 15+)	56.7 (57.6)	51.4 (44.9)	70.5 (57.2)
Account, female (% age 15+)	44.5 (32.7)	47.4 (40.0)	67.3 (53.1)
Account, young adults (% ages 15 – 24)	41.6 (43.8)	35.6 (31.9)	58.1 (51.7)
Saved at a financial institution in the past year (% age 15+)	9.1 (4.2)	8.4 (7.0)	32.2 (24.2)
Loan from a financial institution in the past year (% age 15+)	20.0 (4.6)	12.4 (7.7)	10.4 (7.8)

Source: World Bank; Tomilova 2015

access to finance by creating barriers in terms of procuring funding, managing their business and availing themselves of opportunities (SFF 2014, p. 4).

As seen in the Table 3 the account ownership among women and youth (financial inclusion priorities under the Turkish G20 Presidency) could be further improved—for both of these categories, it is about 25 % lower than the average figure of 56.7 % (Tomilova 2015).

A recent enabling regulatory change is the adoption of a dedicated payments law in 2013 and the issuance of its implementing regulations in June 2014. The law has created two new types of licensing categories referred to as payment institutions and electronic money institutions, which are authorized to provide payment services and issue electronic money, respectively. Both types of institutions will come under direct supervision by the Banking Regulation and Supervision Authority. Electronic money institutions are more promising from a financial inclusion perspective, as they allow customers to open electronic wallets as an alternative to traditional bank accounts (Staschen 2015).

4 Conclusion

Efficient and sustainable financial systems are crucial for developing economies to achieve long-term balanced development. Governments, regulators and international financial institutions have known that access to financial services can play a key role to decrease the poverty and provide financial sustainable economy.

Financial sustainability can not be considered a one-dimensional phenomenon. To contribute to the current debate about sustainable finance is important for all stakeholders. Collaborative work should be initiated in order to spread the sustainability of the financial sector and the real sector activities. Inclusive growth benefits all fractions of the society during an economic growth. Societies need sustained growth with inclusiveness. Growth is inclusive if it comes from structural reforms.

To reduce the number of poor people, to achieve human development and in order to increase the involvement of the private sector, Turkey's adoption of a market operation that supports inclusive business models is seen beneficial. In Turkey, making inclusive market functional is not only the responsibility of the private sector. Both the state through legal regulations, development partners with technical knowledge and funding, as well as civil society organizations with advocacy and awareness raising activities should be actively involved in this process. Companies adopting inclusive business models achieve positive results such as increasing profitability, creating new markets, supporting entrepreneurship, increasing the quality and quantity of employment and strengthening the value chain.

References

Ararat M, Süel E, Yurtoğlu BB (2014) 2014 sustainable ınvestment in Turkey: the case in context—an update. Sabancı University Corporate Governance Forum of Turkey
Asongu S, De Moor L (2015) Recent advances in finance for ınclusive development: a survey, AGDI working paper, WP/15/005
Block J, Hu B, Pickl S (2013) Inclusive growth and sustainable finance—a system dynamics model. In: 31st ınternational conference of the system dynamics society, Cambridge, Massachusett
Dichter TW, Harper M (2007) What's wrong with microfinance? Practical Action Publishing, London
Dixit R, Ghosh M (2013) Financial inclusion growth of India—a study of Indian states. Int J Bus Manag Res 3(1):147–156
EC—European Commission (2008) Financial services provision and prevention of financial exclusion, March
Fatemi AM, Fooladi IJ (2013) Sustainable finance: a new paradigm. Glob Financ J 24:101–113
Fergus AHT, Rowney JIA (2005) Sustainable development: lost meaning and opportunity? J Bus Ethics 60(1):17–27
Ganioğlu A, Us V (2014) The structure of the Turkish banking sector before and after the global crisis, Central Bank of the Republic of Turkey, Working paper no 14/29
Garg AK, Pandey N (2007) Making money work for the poor in India: ınclusive finance through bank-moneylender linkages, Working Paper
GPFI (2016) G20 financial inclusion ındicators. Global Partnership for Financial Inclusion. http://www.gpfi.org/sites/default/files/G20%20Set%20of%20Financial%20Inclusion%20Indicators.pdf
Hahn T, Figge F (2011) Beyond the bounded ınstrumentality in current corporate sustainability research: toward an ınclusive notion of profitability. J Bus Ethics 10(3):325–345
Hanley N (2000) Macroeconomic measures of sustainability. J Econ Surv 14(1):1–30
Imboden K (2005) Building ınclusive financial sectors: the road to growth and poverty reduction. J Int Aff 58(2):65–86
Inoue T, Hamori S (2016) Financial access and economic growth: evidence from sub-saharan Africa. Emerg Mark Financ Trade 52:743–753
Investment Support and Promotion Agency of Turkey—ISPAT (2016) Financial services sector in Turkey

Jensen M, Meckling W (1976) Theory of the firm: managerial behavior, agency costs and ownership structure. J Financ Econ 3(4):305–360
Klapper L, El-Zoghbi M, Hess J (2016) Achieving the sustainable development goals: the role of financial ınclusion. CGAP: 1–20
Lavoie F, Pozzebon M, Gonzales L (2011) Challenges for ınclusive finance expansion: the case of CrediAmigo, a Brazilian MFI. Int Manag 15(3):57–69
Miller M (2014) Financial ınclusion, Global financial development report 2014. World Bank:1–47
Mor N, Ananth B (2007) Inclusive financial systems some design principles and a case study. Econ Polit Week Mar 31:1121–1126
Nair T, Tankha A (2015) Inclusive finance ındia report 2014. Oxford University Press, India
Neupane HP (2015) Advancing ınclusive financial system in the next decade: a case of Nepal, Chapter 5, Ed: Min.B. Shrestha, Kuala Lumpur, Malaysia
OECD (2014) OECD economic surveys Turkey 2014
OECD (2015) Finance and ınclusive growth. OECD economic policy paper, June No 14
Park CY, Mercado RV Jr (2015) Financial ınclusion, poverty, and ıncome ınequality in developing Asia, ADB economics working paper series no 426, pp 1–25
RBI (2008) Report of the Comittee on Financial Inclusion, January
Sarker S, Ghosh SK, Mollika P (2015) Role of banking sector to ınclusive growth through inclusive finance in Bangladesh. Stud Bus Econ 10(2):145–159
Seker M, Correa PG (2010) Obstacles to growth for small and medium enterprises in Turkey, Policy Research working paper 5323, World Bank
SFF (2014) Sustainable finance forum. Proc Forum, 16 May, pp 1–6
Shafi M, Medabesh AH (2012) Financial ınclusion in developing countries: evidences from an Indian State. Int Bus Res 5(8):116–122
Shah P, Dubhashi M (2015) Review paper on financial ınclusion—the means of ınclusive growth. Chanakya Int J Bus Res 1(1):37–48
Shyni VK, Mavoothu D (2014) Financial Inclusion—the way towards ınclusive growth. Int J Adv Res 2(2):649–655
Sjauw-Koen-Fa A, Vereijken I (2005) Access to financial services in developing countries. Rabobank Nederland, September, pp 1–32
Staschen S (2015) Payment innovations in Turkey: not (yet) reaching the unbanked, CGAP. 21 Aug 2015. https://www.cgap.org/blog/payment-innovations-turkey-not-yet-reaching-unbanked. 5 Aug 2016
Stein P (2010) Inclusive finance. Korea-World Bank High Level Conference on Post-Crisis Growth and Development, Korea, pp 1–37
Stiglitz, J.K. (2016). An agenda for sustainable and ınclusive growth for emerging markets, J Policy Model: 6295
Swamy V (2010) Bank-based financial ıntermediation for financial ınclusion and ınclusive growth. Banks Bank Syst 5(4):63–73
Tomilova O (2015) Progress and opportunities for financial ınclusion in Turkey, CGAP, 12 August 2015. https://www.cgap.org/blog/progress-and-opportunities-financial-inclusion-turkey. 5 Aug 2016
UNCTAD (2015) Access to services a driver for the post-2015 development agenda. Policy Brief No 35: 1–4
United Nations(2006) Building ınclusive financial sectors for development, May, New York
UNSGSA (2015) Financial inclusion—creating an ınclusive world, Annual report to the Secretary General
Woller GM, Woodworth W (2001) Microcredit as a grass-roots policy for ınternational development. Policy Stud J 29(2):267–287
Yorulmaz R (2013) Construction of a regional financial ınclusion ındex in Turkey, BDDK Bankacılık ve Finansal Piyasalar, Cilt:7. Sayı 1:79–101
Zwedu GA (2014) Financial ınclusion, Regulation and ınclusive growth in Ethiopia. ODI, November, Working paper 408

http://blogs.worldbank.org/voices/five-challenges-prevent-financial-access-people-developing-countries, 2015. 12 Jun 2016
http://data.worldbank.org/indicator. 12 Jun 2016
http://www.microworld.org/en/news-from-the-field/article/financial-inclusion-challenge-developing-and-developed-countries. 12 Jun 2016
http://www.tgmp.net/en/sayfa/who-are-we-/117/0. 18 Jun 2016
http://www.mod.gov.tr/Lists/OECDEconomicSurveyofTurkey/Attachments/1/OECD%20Economic%20Survey%20of%20Turkey%202014.pdf. 25 May 2016

Sibel Yılmaz Türkmen Associate Professor Sibel Yilmaz Turkmen is currently a faculty member in the Faculty of Business Administration at Marmara University, Istanbul-Turkey. Dr. Turkmen gained her bachelor's degree from Istanbul University, the Faculty of Business Administration in 1999. She received her master's degree (MA) and Doctorate (Ph.D.) in Accounting and Finance, in 2001 and 2006, respectively, both from Marmara University. She teaches finance courses at graduate and undergraduate levels and her research interests are in the areas of corporate finance, financial markets and institutions and international finance.

Gülcan Çağıl Associate Professor Cagil graduated from Faculty of Business Administration at Istanbul University in 1999. Dr. Cagil got her master's degree in Banking in 2001 and also her Doctorate (Ph.D.) degree in Banking in 2006, both from The Instutute of Banking and Insurance at Marmara University in Istanbul, Turkey. Dr. Gulcan Cagil is currently a member of School of Banking and Insurance at Marmara University

Monetary Policy Divergence and Central Banking in the New Era

Bilal Bagis

Abstract After the Great Recession of 2008–2009, advanced economies of the West predominantly went by the Keynesian expansionary policies. Nowadays, though, the monetary policies are diverging. Central banks are diverging on their policies as the global economies continue their significant downward convergence trend. More than 40 central banks have eased their monetary policy in 2015. The ECB, the PBOC and the BOJ are expected to ease further looking forward. Central Banks of many other emerging markets and those of advanced economies such as the USA and the UK are expected to tighten. Uncertainties about the future decrease risk appetite. Capital outflows from emerging markets and fall in trade volumes follow.

1 Introduction

Growth rates among the world economies are in a downhill rivalité trend. Both the Emerging Markets (EMs) and the Advanced Economies (ACs) are likely to converge to the same low growth rates looking forward, Pimco (2015). This is, in particular, due to the major slowdown in the EMs. Even China has much lower growth rates, today. To be more precise, growth rates are still high; but the rate of growth is falling. Japan and the Eurozone are also in recession and need more stimulus packages to avoid the deflationary spirals. In the US and the other EMs, growth rates are still below the potential rates. Geopolitical risks, meanwhile, are still high and less likely to fall in near future.

As the real economies are converging down, there is strong evidence for convergence among the financial markets of the West as well. This is crystal clear particularly for the European economies. It is, after all, one of the key elements of the currency union, Bagis (2016). This financial market liberalization has brought in

B. Bagis (✉)
Faculty of Economics and Administrative Sciences, Department of Economics, Istanbul 29 Mayis University, Umraniye Campus, Umraniye 34662, Istanbul, Turkey
e-mail: bbagis@29mayis.edu.tr

H. Dinçer, Ü. Hacioğlu (eds.), *Risk Management, Strategic Thinking and Leadership in the Financial Services Industry*, Contributions to Management Science, DOI 10.1007/978-3-319-47172-3_3

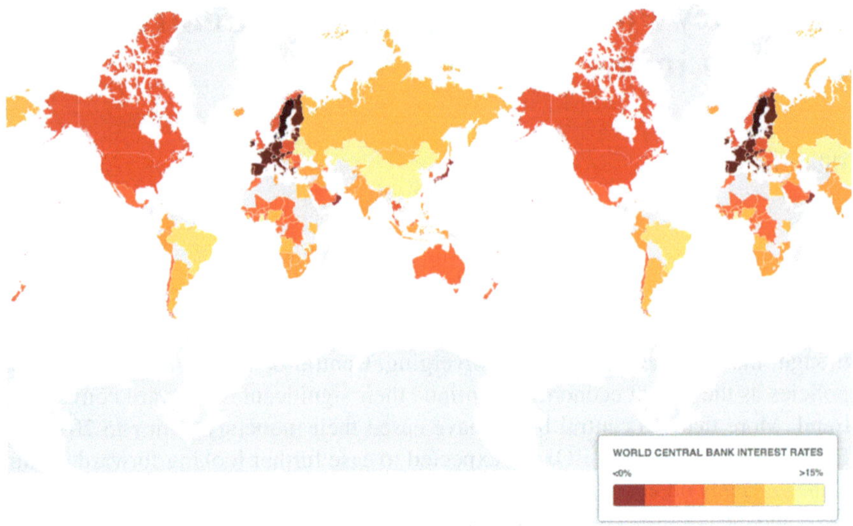

Fig. 1 The policy interest rates around the world. Source, telegraph.co.uk (Telegraph, 2016)

free capital movement; and capital movements usually result in spillover effects to the emerging market economies. Meanwhile, there is currently a significant and increasing variance within the monetary policy cycles of the major economies.

Growth variations are diverging more across regions and unions rather than depending on the level of development. In particular, the USA and the UK are growing faster; while the EU, Japan and China are coping with structural issues and the resulting recessions (Fig. 1).

The American economy is doing quite well these days and the world's most prominent central bank, the Fed, has stopped its bond-buying program. As of December 2015, it has decided to even raise its policy rate. On the other hand, the ECB and the BOJ are imposing negative rates to stimulate their economic activity. Meanwhile, argumentally the third most effective central bank, the People's Bank of China (PBOC), has also recently increased its expansionary stance. As the world's major economies shift their monetary policies, though, just few of the emerging market economies have taken suitable measures to diminish vulnerability of their economies to the external shocks.

The IMF projections and relevant studies point to 3 different trends across the globe.

First of all, there is the group of Emerging Markets where growth rates are lower than the pre-2008 levels; yet these economies are still growing much faster than their Advanced Economy (AC) counterparts. They mostly respond to the policy shifts in the ACs. Secondly, in the UK and the US recovery is continued. They currently normalize their policies. The only risk factor is foreign demand, from the Europe and China. And finally, Europe, China and Japan still struggle with the crisis. Deflation risk is still alive and growth rates are down.

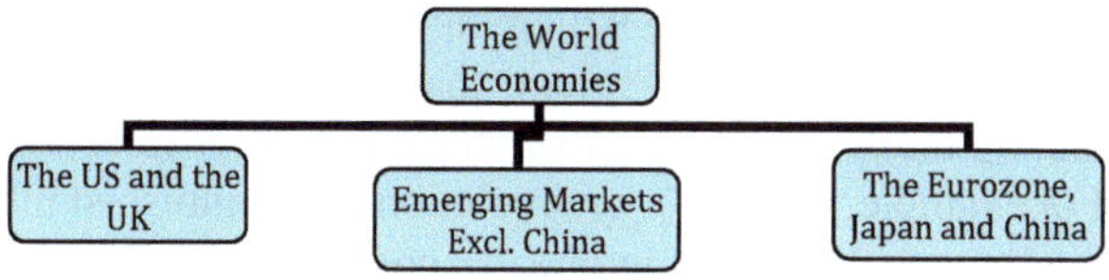

Fig. 2 The recent trend among the world economies. The Author's graph

There are currently concrete divergences across the world economies, both in terms of growth and the monetary policies implemented. Even just focusing on the advanced economies, you would realize that: on one hand, you have the US and UK that are growing acceptably and tightening their monetary policy; and on the other hand, there is the Euro Area and Japan with weak economy and hence following expansionary policies (Fig. 2).

A multi-speed world is the core concept behind the Pimco's New-Neutral argument. In their December 2015 cyclical outlook, Pimco (2015) stated that they expect the central banks policies to vary as the global economies continue to converge. Most resources demonstrate that even the Fed has accepted and has already started to act according to this "new normal". The Fed is said to have already taken the new "neutral" real interest rate into account.

1.1 The World Economy: A New Normal?

As the monetary policies are diverging, one might wonder how the current economic activity and growth rates are across the world. The US economy has been doing relatively well, with growth rates ranging between 1.5 % and 2.5 %. On the other hand, despite the recent improvements in Japan and Europe, most of the significant economies such as the BRICs, Europe and Japan have had new recessions post-2009.

Post the 2008 crisis, the world economies have discovered themselves in a New Normal. This new Normal may be characterized as a new potential level of output, inflation; as well as a new era for financial markets, key economic policies, and the asset market movements. As Pimco has rightly pointed out, the world economies are going through a series of changes and hence are likely to crave for the previous growth figures of the pre-2008 period.

The economic activity across the globe is currently slowing down. The world economy was growing at an average of over 5 % before the 2008 crisis. Post-the-2008 crisis, though, that rate has fallen to around (and in some cases below) 3 %. Even among the BRICs countries, growth rates are falling. More effective policies need to be targeted at sustainable growth rates. Yet, even these growth forecasts might be expected to further slow down from a cut back on QE in the US, which might also trigger a capital outflow from developing economies.

While Europe is still struggling with the recessionary trend, economic indicators from the US economy prove that the USA is currently the strongest economy among the ACs. The positive outlook is likely to continue for a foreseeable future. For example, shale energy revolution has diminished reliance on oil imports and the continuous deleveraging process post the 2008–2009 crisis has decreased the debt burden. Meanwhile, QEs have helped the asset markets recuperate and therefore helped improve the borrowing constrants. The construction sector, in line with improvements in the housing sector, has also contributed to dragging the unemployment rates down.

The more dynamic American economy, with its live labor markets, is gradually recovering from the Great Recession. The European economy, on the other hand, is still stagnant in its recessionary case. Unfortunately, it does not seem very likely to recover very soon. Some parameters, such as extremely low inflation rate, even point to further deterioration. The Eurozone economies are facing serious structural issues. Most of these issues are fundamental and related to the way the Euro system is designed.

Asian economies are also suffering. Most are slowing down, and are likely to remain weakly growing in near future. Export and investment oriented growth strategy of China has failed due to low demand from the rest of the world, and inefficient use of the expansionary monetary policy. The Japanese economy is also struggling to get out of the trap it has been stuck since the mid-1990s. Eastern Asian and Pacific countries have had really high growth rates during the past few decades. Post the 1997 Asian crisis, and except China, they have had relatively low private sector and public leverage.

The Asian economies had traditionally focused on export oriented growth strategy; increased their savings and created huge FX reserves. They increased their savings, and invested that money into the American financial markets. This huge capital inflow has elevated the demand for dollar, lowered the interest rates and strengthened the domestic demand in the US. Post the Great Recession, though, one thing the EMs have been doing very well is to appeal to the macroprudential regulations to deal with the unprecedented monetary expansion process in the advanced economies. That way, the EMs were able to eliminate part of the spillover effects of the QEs implemented by major economies.

The Eurozone economies are suffering from problems in the banking system. Talks of a move towards banking union are common recently. Troubles are prone to carry on at some extend, hence the lower growth forecasts. In the Eurozone, growth projections for 2016 are 1.4 %; a further 1.7 % in 2017 and 1.8 % in 2018. Growth and inflation figures are expected to rise as more QE comes in.

The Chinese economy has recently been slowing down and that makes many economists think that we ought to anticipate a substantial monetary easing from the PBOC in near future. The economy is expected to grow at about 6 % and the inflation rate is likely to be around 0 %. China's current economic outlook may be summarized with a gradual slowdown, structural transformation, a highly leveraged economy, a recent exchange rate regime shift during the summer of 2015 and occasional asset bubbles and equity market corrections.

Meanwhile in China, personal consumption expenditures are below 40 % of GDP (its western counterparts are at or close to 70 %). Despite these unprecedented figures, the savings and accumulated deposits are not sufficient to finance the planned growth model. Low inflation (due mainly to negative PPI) might be a problem. China is also affecting the real economy of EMs as it is already one the biggest trade partners and commodity consumers, it affects the global risk appetite with its huge economy and also affects the world economies via its already international currency, yuan.

Japan, likewise, needs to focus on inflationary policies to deal with the ongoing deflation risk. The economy still suffers from the 2014 VAT hike, the neighboring Asian currencies are devaluing, China is slowing down and they still have a relatively low inflation rate. Japan was an important source of the 1997 financial crisis and is still in recession since the mid-1990s. Japan, is nowadays engaging in an unprecedent scale of QQE policies (along with 2 other branches of the famous Abenomics). These expansionary policies are likely to continue and the economy is also expected to recover slightly. Inflation rate is around 1 % and is expected to stay below the 2 % threshold.

The economic slowdown (hard landing) in China, the Fed decision to raise policy rates (policy normalization) and commodity prices (along with lifting sanctions against Iran and the geopolitical tension in the Middle East) were three key aspects that could possibly best define the 2016. The list could of course be extended further to include: below potential global growth rates and trade volumes, rising volatility in financial markets as the Chinese economy is slowing down and the commodity prices (such as low oil prices) are down, and most importantly, global monetary policy divergence is still alive and capital is streaming out of the EMs.

The global risk-appetite is regressing, and the Chinese slowdown spreads out to the western economies as well. Low commodity prices bear a significant risk factor for exporting countries. And they therefore cause an extra risk factor and volatilities. All of these events have significant contagion impacts over the rest of the world economy.

1.2 The Inflation Outlook

Inflation rates are currently very low globally. Even future inflation expectations are still extremely low in many advanced economies and are likely go down further. Both low commodity prices and supply surpluses are primary reasons that have drawn the inflation rates down. One might wonder why the low inflation rates should matter in the first place. At its core, very low or negative inflation expectations mean higher real interest rates. Higher real rates dissuade consumption and demand. As policy options are limited in many cases, the concern is that central banks will not be able to respond.

Inflation rates in both the US and the UK are not much likely reach the 2 % targets. The 2 % target is considered as an optimal inflation rate by many central banks and prominent economists. In the Eurozone, as opposed to the US, inflation expectations are much lower: still positive at some 1 %, but much lower than the over 1.5 % in the US. Inflation outlook is likely to improve as the base effect (pass-through) of oil prices and (in the case of the US) the base effect of highly valued dollar is likely to fade away.

In troublesome economies such as Brazil, Russia and even in Turkey inflation rates are relatively high, and recessions and shifts in monetary policy are expected to bring the inflation rates down. A recession, for instance would bring the demand down; and hence, the inflation rate will head down. In most EMs where inflation is above the target, though, tighter monetary policy is expected to bring inflation rate down.

The recent slowdown in China has put a downward pressure on commodity prices. As demand for housing has declined; for instance, steel, cement and glass prices have been falling, The Economist (2016). Falling producer prices (because of overcapacity), and decreasing commodity prices have lowered the inflation rate. PPI (producer price index) is down to −5.9 % (the lowest since 2009) in China and increases the deflation risk. Another critical example is the declining new home prices. Headline inflation is expected to fall to 1.5–2.5 % in China. The PBOC is therefore expected to respond aggressively to stimulate the economic activity.

In the Eurozone, in the meantime, headline inflation was −0.2 % in February-2016 and the annual inflation expectation is down to 0.1 % for 2016. At around −0.2 %, the annual inflation rate is at its historic low levels, and much below the ECB target at 2 %. At its current level, inflation rate is at the 5 year low level. Even the 5-year forward expectations are below the 2 % target. Low energy and food prices, as well as low capacity utilization rate, contribute to the low inflation rate and expectations. The extremely low inflation rate brought in a new monetary easing via a much lower negative rate and an increase in the scale of the ongoing QE program. All of these occasions possess impacts over the risk perception of investors and the global economic growth prospects.

2 Policy Implementation

After the Great Recession, advanced economies of the West mostly went by the Keynesian expansionary policies. Nowadays, though, the monetary policies are diverging. But it is more as if the ECB, BOJ and the PBOC are replacing the Fed and the BOE (and even the BOC) to keep the global liquidity high. In particular, the Jackson Hole meeting of August 2014 marks a key period of clear policy divergence across the world economies. Post the meeting, Central Banks in the US and the UK are currently tightening; while, the ECB, the BOJ and the PBOC (as well as some other European central banks) are expected to expand further.

The BOJ and the ECB are running expansionary monetary policies currently and the Fed and the BOE are contracting by interest rate hikes. The PBOC is on its way to expand further. The ECB and the BOJ (in a similar manner to their Swedish,

Danish and the Swiss counterparts) keep cutting their policy rates down the negative territory. The policy implementations and the changing interest rates are causing are higher monetary policy divergence.

2.1 Policy Options

In theory, policy options during a recession such as the latest Great Recession include but not all: the currency flexibility (flexible exchange rate), monetary easing, fiscal stimulus, and various consumption pattern improvements. Post the 2008 crisis, all of the big central banks (the Fed, the ECB, the BOE and the BOJ) except the PBOC have decreased their policy rates to "close to zero-lower-bound". China, on the other hand, still has the highest nominal interest rates among the big economies. The PBOC has not hesitated to even tighten its money supply. This particularly obvious policy divergence offers the 'currency wars' argument.

Here, it is probably important to keep in mind that the unconventional monetary policy—in the form of balance sheet expansion—is a substitute for lower policy rates. Meanwhile, considering the fragile (export-dependent) Asian economies; currency devaluation seems to be a good option as a solution to the current weak activity. Yet devaluations have side effects such as a currency war that brings down the other currencies as well and lowers commodity prices as demand falls. Falling oil prices, for instance, in turn decreases the EM currencies' relative value. It also negatively changes the risk appetite and therefore raises financial market volatilities.

One disadvantage of the expansionary policies is that, at some point, economic growth may become directly related to the loans growth and hence the idea of hormone-fed growth. IMF has long been warning about credit growth rates in emerging markets such as Turkey and China. Especially in China, aggregate credit amounts to over \$20tn, a few times the size of the Chinese GDP. They have more than doubled in the past 5 years.

2.2 Monetary Policy Divergence

The Lehman effect over the global financial system is still not erased completely. As was mentioned above, most of the world economies are still below their pre-2008 potential production level. Whilst the monetary policy so far implemented have in general been effective; in special cases, such as the Eurozone and the Japan, it has proven insufficient. Many central banks are still dealing with the adverse outcomes of the 2008–2009 crisis. According to Pimco (2015), more than 40 central banks have so far gone for easy monetary policies during the year of 2015. The ECB, the BOJ and even the PBOC are very likely to keep their expansionary monetary policies going further (Fig. 3).

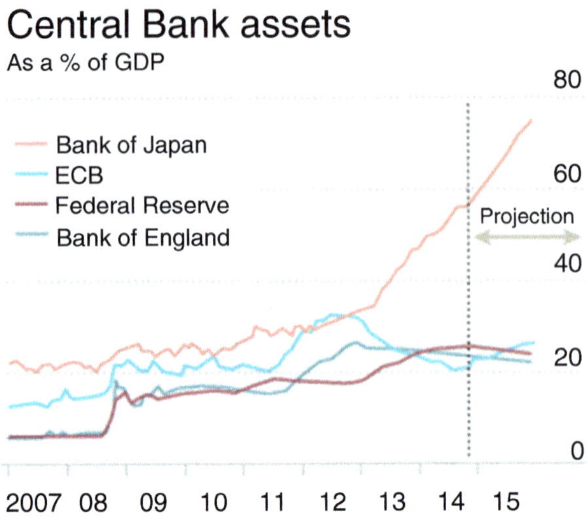

Fig. 3 The world central bank balance sheets. Source, FT.com. As is clear from the graph; post the 2012, Japan has had one of the largest QEs in history

The year of 2016 witnessed a new round of stock price collapse. Ongoing recessions in various big economies and declining trade brought the marketplace anticipation for brand spanking new expansionary policies up. Yet, in particular in the case of China, there is this concern that the central banks are more and more into a tit-for-tat policy action. The biggest danger in this case is the PBOC and the very high possibility of a huge currency devaluation by the Chinese authorities. Indeed, the recent monetary easing policies by the BOJ and the ECB have increased the possibility of such currency devaluation cycle.

In the emerging market countries such as Russia, Brazil and Turkey, where inflation is above the target, tighter monetary policy is expected to bring the inflation rates down. Even IMF suggests that the emerging market economies should focus on tighter measures to deal with, among others, the capital outflows. The Fed is expected to hike its policy rate (tighten) gradually. The BOE and high inflation countries such as Brazil and South Africa are also expected to tighten right after the Fed. The other central banks such as the PBOC, the BOJ and most notably the ECB are all very likely to ease further. They could do it either by expanding the QE or cutting further their policy interest rates.

Advanced economy central banks are diverging. The Fed has raised its policy rate for the first time in 10 years in December 2015 and is planning to gradually increase it further. Japan and the Eurozone are still easing their policies, even further below the negative territory. The fact that not all of the advanced economies are tightening, helps make sure the monetary tightening could have minimal outcomes over the rest of the world.

2.2.1 Tightening Countries Such as the US and the UK

The Fed is currently in a process of tightening. The Fed tightening and rate hike is expected to be slow and gradual. The BOE is also expected to keep the rates high and tighten in line with the Fed. Growth and inflation figures are expected to rise as the economy recovers further in both the US and the UK. As the Fed is tightening, mortgage rates and the long-term rates are also increasing. Increasing bond yields mean more capital outflow out of the EMs and towards the US. This adverse capital move (opposite the post 2008 period) could potentially cause malocclusions in the financial markets.

One thing is for sure: the current Fed governor Yellen is dovish. She is likely to favor keeping the nominal rates low; yet there is a hawkish stance in the Fed in general. She has also explicitly stated her intention towards a gradual nature of exit; in a way "*walking on egg shells*" when reversing their QE policies. The Fed finally raised its policy rate, for the first time in about 10 years, in December 2015. They are expected to raise the short-term rates by 1 % in 2016, another 1 % in 2017 and to 3.25 %. This is, indeed, consistent with the assumption that the neutral (or the equilibrium) policy rate is at 2–3 % nominal and 0–1 % real. Yet, since that decision was expected much earlier, the historic rate rise did not affect the markets much. The Fed, meanwhile, based their decision on the favorable data from American economy.

In the US, especially after the recent policy rate hike; both the mortgage rates and the long-term bond yields are recorded to rise. As nominal rates go up in the US, more and more capital flows into the US from the EMs, in order to benefit from those high rates. This is the fundamental reason behind the recent financial market volatilities.

This gradual upward trend is partly about the movement of the neutral real policy rate. The neutral real rate is proven to have changed recently (see the PIMCO's new neutral argument as opposed to the constant real rate argument of Fama, a classic economist), Pimco (2015). It is considered to be around 0 % currently and moving up very slowly. The equilibrium real policy rate (or the "neutral" real policy rate) was at 2 % before the global financial crisis of 2008. The "equilibrium" real policy rate, mentioned here, is the neutral rate 'r*' that shows up in the Taylor rule.

The BOE, on the other hand, follows the targets set by the British parliament. They currently seek to achieve the 2 % inflation target, and that only. The UK economy is also doing relatively better. The BOE, therefore, is expected to tighten, in order to deal with side effects of the Fed policy and to achieve its inflation target. Tightening is expected to follow that in the US; yet, while the Fed adjusts its LSAPs once, the BOE follows a more active policy and adjusts its asset purchase policies frequently.

The following statement is useful as a measure of the monetary easing used in the UK in the past. The effect of LSAPs on the long-term yields has been small in Japan, due to small scale of purchases and shorter maturities of the assets bought. In the UK, however, it was as high as that in the US, due to the similar scale and maturity of assets purchased. For instance, during the first few years of the post Great Recession period, LSAPs-nominal GDP ratios were 4 % in Japan as opposed to 12 % in the US and 14 % in the UK.

2.2.2 Expanding Countries

Many advanced economies responded to the Great Recession of 2008–2009 with monetary easing. For instance, during the first few years, as the monetary base was increased, balance sheet of the Fed expanded by sixfold (to $3.2 trillion from $500 billion). Nowadays, both the ECB and the BOJ are expanding their money supply. And the PBOC is on its way to be added to that list. The tendency towards further easing is predominantly caused by concerns over very low inflation. Policymakers in China, Japan and Europe are worried that extremely low inflation rates will feed into expectations and the inflation expectations will head further down.

Meanwhile, although not as good as it was hoped for, the QE programs are proven to have worked in the US, the UK and in Japan. The markets seem to have also positively responded to the easing policies. The problem, here, is whether further weakening in yen and euro will cause any problems for the US and China (as an appreciation). After all, export sectors both in the US and China are currently a headache.

The ECB had to appeal to the QE measures to deal with the deflationary trend and the low growth figures. This was in line with the expansionary policy trend in Japan. One key pitfall of the European economy is that the labor markets are not that dynamic, as they are in the US. Because of the stickiness in the labor markets, for instance, the recovery is taking much longer than it should in general. The QE programs implemented by the ECB are more colorful than those in its other counterparts. Mr. Draghi has once defined it as a program covering "*all assets but gold*". The ECB defines their unconventional measures both as a sign that it is "*committed to do whatever it takes*" to stimulate its economy and also to encourage investment into riskier assets. One of the main channels of influence in the European QE case is the portfolio rebalancing effect.

The previous QE program in the Eurozone was expected to end officially in September 2016. Yet, the extremely low inflation rate made a new expansionary measure necessary. In mid-March 2016, considering the stagnant Eurozone economy, the ECB announced a new range of monetary expansion. They downed the main policy rate (the benchmark refinance rate) to 0 % (from previous 0.05 %), the deposit rates to −0.40 % (from earlier -0.30 %) and announced that they will expand its QE program up to $80bn (up from the previous $60bn) per month. The QE program is expected to continue until at least March 2017.

On the other hand; after the Asian crisis, most of the Asian countries started accumulating huge reserves. Later on, this made it possible to use monetary policy effectively, if needed. Wise monetary policy of the post-Asian-crisis is no different than the Great Moderation period in the G7 countries. Indeed, in most of the Asian economies, further expansionary policies are expected looking forward. These expansionary policies should be considered via decrease in interest rates or depreciation in the local currency, Eichengreen (2016).

For example; at the end of January 2016; the BOJ, at its first interest rate move in past 5 years (since October 2010), cut its policy interest rate to −0.1 % (previously +0.1 %). Many considered it as a surprise; yet, it is consistent with their ongoing easing process to hit the 2 % inflation target. The BOJ, therefore, now charges 0.1 % fee on deposits withhold at its reserves. The goal is to boost lending on the financial institutions side and hence more borrowing on the real sectors side. And that way, they intend to take the economy out of the deflationary boundaries. They have also delayed the expected date to achieve their inflation target of 2 %. The 2 % inflation target if one of the key goals of Abenomics.

The BOJ has been expanding its monetary base at the rate of 80 trillion yen per annum, since October 2014. They have also announced that, further downing into the negative territory is still on the table, if necessary. This is just another example of monetary policy divergence across the globe. The BOJ has separated from the Fed and instead approached expanding regions. The BOJ decision follows the same move made by the ECB in June 2014; and is in the same way aimed at having the commercial banks use their excessive reserves, held at the BOJ, as loans to the real sector and businesses.

The BOJ is buying long-term government debts, as well as private assets such as real estate trusts. Mr. Kuroda and his team are determined to do '*whatever it takes to achieve the inflation target*'. The BOJ is expected to keep expanding its monetary base by 80tn yen (equivalent to $705bn or 16 per cent of gross domestic product) in near future. The BOJ balance sheet will therefore soon reach 80 % of GDP and at that level, it will be far bigger than the size of the balance sheet of its other counterparts: namely the Fed, the BOE and the ECB. They also plan to expand maturity of the asset holdings, more towards 10 years.

The PBOC is also easing its monetary policy, by cutting the deposit rates or the required reserve rates. For instance, through the end of January 2016, the PBOC launched its largest easing policy in past 3 years. Alternative to that huge monetary expansion was accepting a deflationary case and a recession. But China preferred monetary easing to deflation. Indeed, post-the 2008 crisis, and in an effort to deal with weaknesses in its exports and investment sectors, Chinese authorities paved the way for an excessive easing policy. They have increased investment and eased the credit policies. The recent easing cycle of the PBOC is candidate for one of the greatest monetary expansions.

China has, during the past 8 years, been in a process of monetary easing and cutting policy rates in an effort to keep the growth rate at its previously high levels. In 2009, the Chinese government injected about $600bn into its slowing economy in an effort to stimulate the economy. The PBOC increased the money supply by more than the total amount in previous 4 years. It worked out and temporarily increased the economic activity. At the end of January 2016, the PBOC announced that it plans to increase monetary base by another 600bn yuan (a little over $90bn).

This latest attempt is meant to deal with any possible liquidity crunches in the near future, to stabilize the interest rates (by controlling the liquidity needs of the market), and is also meant to diminish the pressure to decrease the reserve requirement ratio (another expansionary policy measure). This is, meanwhile, in addition to the ongoing expansionary measures.

Unlike most of the developed world economies, China is not yet out of its conventional policy measures to deal with cyclical volatilities. Policy rates are not yet at the zero-lower bound. They therefore still have a huge room for maneuver to deal with cyclical volatilities. This provides a room for more effective monetary policy use compared to any fiscal expansion policy. Yet, monetary expansions have caused a lot of problems as well. Mostly, due to the inefficient injection of the new money supply; it caused higher leverage and hence has increased the financial risk of the local governments and private corporations. The misdirected loans created housing bubble and soared the debt overhung.[1]

As the Chinese economy has slowed down, expansionary policies from the policymakers are more likely looking forward (in particular in 2016 and 2017). Chinese official have already declared their willingness to expand the monetary and fiscal policies to boost the economic activity. Indeed, even in most of the other Asian economies, further future expansionary policies are expected. These expansionary policies should be considered as part of an effort to boost the economic activity via decrease in interest rates or a depreciation in the local currency.

Monetary easing policies have also lead to the discussion of currency war. The idea is that when one of the countries goes for an expansionary policy, the others follow to devalue their currencies respectively. As an example; America and China are two big trade partners. Once one of them devalue and make their currency relatively cheap, the other may retaliate and devalue their own currencies to make their goods more attractive. Countries may, looking forward, work on making their own currencies more attractive to gain the exorbitant priviledge as well. The US dollar is the dominant global currency today. Yet, Chinese may try to make renminbi the global currency and hence benefit from the "*exorbitant privilege*" (Fig. 4).

The PBOC, in particular, should be expected to assume the role the Fed took in a foreseeable future. The Fed provided an unprecedented amount of QE after the crash of the Lehman Brothers. The PBOC could and indeed should go for a similar measure to stimulate the economic activity in China. They have indeed signaled that they would not hesitate to take on such a role. Yet, the risk of causing uncertainties is out there. If the dollar loses its reserve currency role, financial markets may have difficulty finding the next best safe heaven to insure against a new financial turmoil.

[1]It was the greatest ever monetary expansion in the world economy history according to some: https://www.foreignaffairs.com/articles/china/2016-01-11/end-chinas-rise

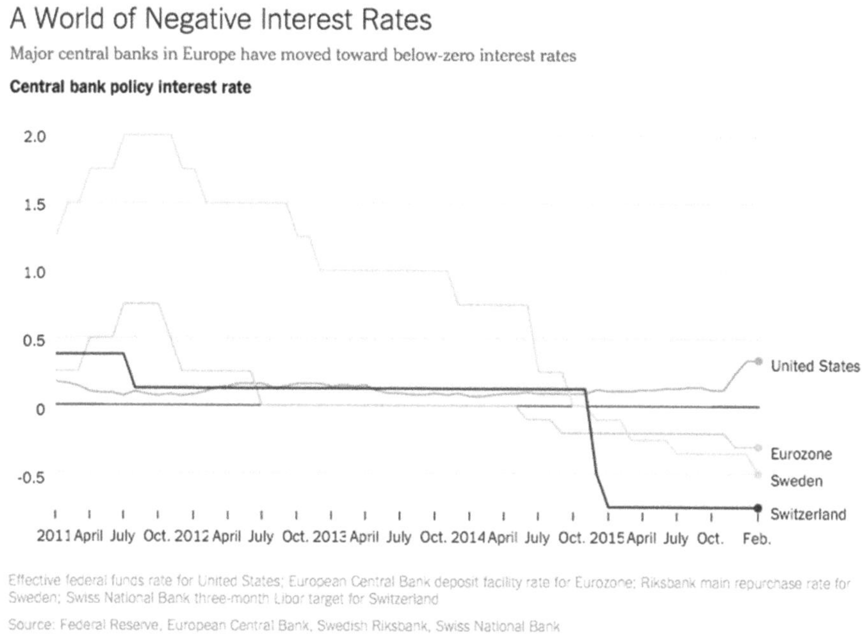

Fig. 4 Interest rates and monetary policy divergence. Source, the Fed

2.2.3 Implications for the EMs

Not all of the EMs demonstrate the same characteristics. Given the interest rate hikes in the US and after the recent oil price slump, most of the oil producing EMs had to tighten their monetary policy. These contractionary policies are implemented in an effort to stop devaluation in their currencies and keep the resulting inflation rate down. Examples include, but not all, the Latin American oil producers Brazil, Mexico; as well as African oil exporters Nigeria and Angola. They keep interest rates high to attract capital and hence foreign currency inflows.

Some of the EM economies usually run huge CA deficits and are therefore more vulnerable to external shocks. The Fed rate hike, negative policy rates and further easing policies as well as economic weakness in China are all crucial factors that determine the fate of the financial markets in the EMs. They frequently face boom and bust cycles; the high growth rates are usually followed by sharp collapses. Fragile 5 economies of the investment bank Morgan Stanley (namely Turkey, Brazil, South Africa, Indonesia and India) are a good example. These varying responses lead to a necessary divergence even among the different EMs as well.

Although most EM currencies have weakened recently, the corresponding economies' outlooks differ substantially. Economies with current account surpluses and relatively strong growth prospects are usually more resilient to tighter policies in the ACs. In contrast, the currencies mostly at risk of a further sell-off are those in countries with larger current account deficits and weak growth prospects, such as

Brazil, Turkey and South Africa, Eichengreen and Bordo (2002). EM assets are likely be driven by the forces of diverging monetary policies in core markets. As the US takes back the lead of the global business cycle, EM economies will face gradually higher Fed rates and a stronger USD.

3 Central Banking in the New Era

In the Eurozone and Japan, the standard monetary policy has run its course. To make a difference, central banks need to turn unconventional. At the end of January 2016, the BOJ announced that they would implement negative rates on bank deposits withheld at the central bank. This policy followed similar measures in the Eurozone and some other smaller European economies such as Sweden, Denmark and Switzerland. Before that, the ECB was giving strong signals of a new round of expansionary policy. Negative rates basically mean that when a bank keeps extra cash on its account at the central bank it will then have to pay the central bank a certain percentage to keep their reserves there. Banks are encouraged to lend money out, rather than keeping them at the central bank.

Negative rate policy, along with the recent monetary policy divergence trend across the globe has reminded us of the recent changing trends of central banking itself. Broadly speaking, the recent central banking trends may be summarized within two following classifications:

The first group of the central banks are changing just the tools they use. They, either return to or are trying to get back to the conventional tools and the active use of the interest rate channel (as in the case of the Fed), or focus on unconventional policies: including using QEs and negative rates. The second group is changing the focus of the Central Banks fundamentally, towards developmental central banking (as in the case of Argentina) or more towards the recent popular nominal GDP Targeting (that was even discussed at the Fed).

Nominal GDP targeting and the developmental central banking trends are less popular. The usual focus today is over negative nominal interest rates. Further easing, beyond the ZLB and implementing negatives rates is the new trend among the advanced economies in particular. Central banks in Japan, Eurozone, Sweden, Switzerland and Denmark have all gone for negative rates. Recently there have been talks of possibility of even the Fed switching to negative interest rate policy. Although Yellen has already announced that the Fed has not ruled out that option; implementing negative rates is not very likely in the US. As pointed out by a recent PIMCO quarterly outlook, the possibility of implementing negative rates is very low due to the unintended side effects of such an expansion.

Meanwhile, there is a bigger tendency and more willingness, at the Fed and the BOE, to reverse the monetary easing and increase the interest rates. Yet, even in those economies, the short-term rates are currently still stable at or close to the Zero-Lower-Bound. More importantly, the Fed is still following its post-1980s trend of the neo-liberal inflation focus.

4 Concluding Remarks

Monetary policy divergence is the new normal of the modern financial system. This is despite the fact that the world economies are increasingly converging (Pimco 2015; Clarida and Balls 2015). The divergence is both among today's advanced economies and the emerging economies. The divergence is not independent of the global growth and inflation projections, as well as the nature of the unconventional policies. Frankly, the QE policies of the post-2008 had similar implications as those of the post-1980s financial liberalization period. Both were claimed to have resulted in a significant spillover effects over the EMs. Hence, macroeconomic instability and more fragile financial markets were inevitable. Some even argue they have caused an illusive growth in the EMs via huge capital and liquidity inflows.

The theory goes that, the ultra loose monetary policy (and extremely cheap loans) of the past 30 years, mainly in the US, have caused bubbles in various markets both in the US and its big trading partners such as China. Low inflation rates and very low nominal rates have created a vision of '*Alice in the Wonderland*' across the world economies. In an effort to deal with these macro volatilities and financial bubbles, policymakers implemented macro-prudential policy measures and expansionary monetary policy. That trend might change now as the policy divergence is becoming crystal clear.

Post-the Great Recession, markets have welcomed all the proactive monetary policy actions and for the most part positively responded to any expansionary measures. Central bankers, for the most part, have done their job to simulate the stagnant World economy. Policymakers have cut policy rates for over 600 times and expanded their balance sheets by over $10tn, since 2008. Meanwhile, ever since the Fed's first QE, the spillover effects have been at the heart of the discussions. Yet, tapering might indeed have caused more volatility across the world economies. In particular, EMs and the most fragile EMs suffered the most from the end of the long expansionary program. EM currencies lost value as capital outflew. And capital outflows, decreased the value of the EM currencies further. As EM currencies lost their value, risk premium went up and the debt burdens went up. Nowadays the same discussion is still alive. But this time the discussion is within the context of policy divergence.

Policy responses across the world economies, to the policy divergence, is changing as well. Just as they did to the earlier expansionary policies from the ECB, the markets seem to positively respond to the BOJ's easing policy. The only problem is whether further weakening in yen and euro will cause any problems for the US (via dollar appreciation) and China (yuan appreciation as a result of dollar appreciation). Export sectors in both the US and China are currently a headache for both economies. Central banks (in particular those in major world economies) should beware of the spillover effects of their policies, hence policy coordination among major central banks is of essence.

Inflation expectations is another crucial topic here. As once pointed out by Mr. Draghi, of the ECB, there is significant positive relationship between "*the size of a central bank balance sheet and the inflation expectations*". Maybe increasing balance sheets in the Eurozone, Japan and even in China (economies that are dealing with a major deflation risk) will help raise inflation expectations.

Policymakers and central banks in particular, usually face with the dilemma of choosing between the continuity of the power they hold and the economic outcome and efficacy of their policies in the global financial markets (as well as the internationalization of their currency). Expanding countries fall more into the group choosing economic outcomes to the power and influence. The currently tightening ones, on the other hand, are the ones that are doing relatively well; and hence are more focused on getting bigger and gaining more effective international roles.

Monetary policies across the world economies are currently diverging. The world financial markets are at an all-new normal today. Despite the growing synchronization, economies are becoming more diverse in terms of the policy implications. As pointed out by El-Erian (2016) and the ECB president Mario Draghi, central banks have even recently been the single and ultimate source of expansionary policies after the onset of the Great Recession. This makes the policy divergence much more important than it has been contemplated upon.

An important risk factor here is that, in case of an expansionary policy, change in the value of a major currency may cause uncertainties and side effects on various other markets such as the commodities. For instance, devaluation in yuan may be directly reflected as a fall in oil prices. It would therefore decrease the risk appetite in the global financial markets and in particular towards the EMs.

References

Bagis B (2016) "Döviz Kuru Sistemleri" (in Turkish). In: Eroglu N, Dincer H, Hacioglu U (eds) Uluslarası Finans: Teori ve Politika. Ankara, Orion Kitabevi

Clarida R, Balls A (2015) December 2015 cyclical outlook. PIMCO.com. Retrieved 13 Feb 2016

Eichengreen B (2016) China's exchange-rate trap. https://www.project-syndicate.org/commentary/china-renminbi-crisis-capital-controls-by-barry-eichengreen-2016-02?utm_source=project-syndicate.org&utm_medium=email&utm_campaign=authnote. Retrieved 10 Feb 2016

Eichengreen B, Bordo M (2002) Crises now and then: what lessons from the last era of financial globalization? NBER working paper no 8716

El-Erian MA (2016) The only game in town: central banks, instability, and avoiding the next collapse. Random House, New York

Pimco (2015) December cyclical outlook. https://www.pimco.com/insights/economic-and-market-commentary/global-central-bank-focus/r-new-neutral. Retrieved 27 Feb 2016

Telegraph (2016) Why negative interest rates Herald new danger for the world. Retrieved from: http://www.telegraph.co.uk/finance/economics/12149894/Mapped-Why-negative-interest-rates-herald-new-danger-for-the-world.html

The Economist (2016) China's excess industrial capacity harms its economy. http://www.economist.com/news/business/21693573-chinas-excess-industrial-capacity-harms-its-economy-and-riles-its-trading-partners-march?fsrc=scn%2Ftw%2Fte%2Fpe%2Fed%2Fthemarchofthezombies. Retrieved 3 Mar 2016

Bilal Bagis is Assistant Professor of Economics at Istanbul 29 Mayis University Department of Economics. Dr. Bagis has a multidisciplinary B.Sc. from ITU (2006), a theoretically focused M.A. in Economics from Sabanci University (2009) and a Ph.D. degree in Economics from the University of California (2014). Dr. Bagis is grateful to the Turkish Government, Tubitak, UC Regents, Fulbright, TEV, ITU and Sabanci University for all the awards, scholarships and financial support they have provided throughout his education. He has had Asst. Prof., lecturer, consultant, strategist and teaching assistant experiences both in Turkey and the USA. His research interests lie in international finance, monetary economics, and macroeconomics. He has taught various graduate and undergraduate level Statistics, Econometrics, Mathematics, Finance and Macroeconomics courses at prestigious universities. Since his return back to academia, in 2015, he has had numerous domestic and international presentations and publications.

In Looking into the Foreign Exchange Risk Management

Asim K. Karmakar and Sovik Mukherjee

Danger can never be overcome without taking risks.
—Latin Proverb

Abstract Businesses that trade internationally or have undertaken ventures overseas are likely to be exposed to foreign exchange risk on account of unpredictability in the currency markets. The usual source of exposure to foreign exchange risk arises from having to make overseas payments for your imports priced in a foreign currency or receiving foreign currency receipts for your exports. If the sum that a company expects to receive falls because of a change in the exchange rate, then it will find that its profits are squeezed even if costs remain unchanged. This paper basically deals with the measurement and management of the financial impact of international operations, particularly with reference to exchange rate risks. Exchange rate risks are classified under the broad headings : economic, transaction, and translation risks. Section 3 takes up the issue of measurement of economic, transaction and translation exposure. Control of the impact is assumed to operate through the application of hedging techniques, the most important of which are described in some detail in Section 4. A recent chronicle of foreign exchange risk management in the Indian context has been discussed in Section 5. This paper ends with a conclusion.

1 Introduction

Expansion into foreign markets offer new prospects but also gives rise to more complicated risks, particularly financial ones, and it is the task of the accountants and corporate treasurers to give advice on how to reduce these risks. In other words,

A.K. Karmakar (✉) • S. Mukherjee
Department of Economics, Jadavpur University, 188, Raja S.C. Mallick Road.,
Kolkata 700032, West Bengal, India
e-mail: iasimkkarmakar@gmail.com; sovik1992@gmail.com

H. Dinçer, Ü. Hacioğlu (eds.), *Risk Management, Strategic Thinking and Leadership in the Financial Services Industry*, Contributions to Management Science, DOI 10.1007/978-3-319-47172-3_4

exchange rate movements can affect the size of payments both to and from overseas. We define 'exposure' as the extent to which a company is affected by exchange rate changes. Unanticipated exchange rate changes has serious implications for the business houses.

Suppose, if the sum that a company is supposed to receive falls because of a change in the exchange rate, then it will find that its profits are squeezed even if costs remain unaffected. It may be equally likely that an exchange rate movement leads to a rise in the prices the company has to pay for overseas components, and this would also lead to a fall in the profit margin if selling prices are fixed. What makes this particularly perturbing is that the direction of change in the exchange rate is uncertain, and an individual company has no control over it. Moreover, the company also faces additional costs if it chooses to eliminate the uncertainty associated with such fluctuations by shielding its exchange rate exposure in the financial markets. Putting it in simple terms, exchange rate changes are of great significance to a company as it affects their overall profitability.

Now, coming to the issue of mitigation of these risks. Companies face a trade off between risk and control. Particularly, in the context of foreign risk, this trade off can be made functional. The exporter may come across a transaction risk which can be guarded against by dealing in a variety of currencies to generate a portfolio diversification effect. At the opposite end of the control spectrum, the company owning investments abroad has to take on the additional risk with regards to the valuation of the assets. Therefore, it is the prerogative of all business houses to decide the degree of protection they want against foreign exchange risk. As we know, hedging refers to any facility having the objective of reducing risk. In foreign exchange risk management parlance, hedging refers to the coordinated buying and selling of currencies with the objective of minimizing the exchange rate risk. If hedging is used to reduce risk, then the any international company exposed to such risks is expected to face some sort of a dilemma. Should the hedging strategy be comprehensive to cover all risk, or should it be selective? The moment you try to hedge against a risk, an associated cost crops up; so, choosing to hedge only key contracts or exposure above a specified value, there is the prospect of saving money. The extent to which hedging instruments are used, and whether companies should merely seek to reduce risk or should engage in currency speculation is a matter of debate.

This paper basically deals with the measurement and management of the financial impact of international operations, with specific reference to exchange rate risks. Exchange rate risks are classified under the broad headings of economic, transaction, and translation risks. Section 3 takes up the issue of measurement of economic, transaction and translation exposure. Control of the impact is assumed to operate through the application of hedging techniques, the most important of which are described in some detail in Section 4. A recent chronicle of foreign exchange risk management in the Indian context has been discussed in Section 5. This paper ends with a conclusion.

2 The Financial Risks of International Trade and Investment

It is a challenging assignment to predict exchange rates with perfect accuracy but the firms can atleast measure the degree to which they are being exposed to fluctuations in the exchange rate depending on the types of exchange rate risk a firm faces. It is common practice to summarize the financial risks of foreign trade or investment under three broad headings viz. Economic, Transaction and Translation risk.

2.1 Economic Risk

With the advent of globalization, capital moves quickly to take advantage of the fluctuations in exchange rates. Economic risk crops up when there is a risk of variation between the actual and forecasted cash flows as a consequence of volatile exchange rate movements. This is important because, according to finance theory, the present value of a company's future cash flows can be used to determine its market value. Stock markets world-wide are continually revising their valuation of quoted stocks; the overall market value of a company is the value per single unit of equity multiplied by the number of equity shares in issue. The current value of each share is determined by discounting the future cash flows that will accrue to that particular share. In this context, the general rule is that, a rise in the value of forecasted cash flows leads to a rise in the value of the company. But, when a business house is subject to a high degree of economic risk, that is, unstable foreign currencies, in due course will make the share price of the corporate house concerned more volatile (Jorion, 1988).

To understand the significance of economic risk, lets look at two real life examples. After the exclusion of the Sterling from the European Exchange Rate Mechanism (ERM) in September 1992, the pound relatively weakened, which dramatically improved trading conditions for the British exporters. Also, according to an extract of the report published by Dorling Kindersley (India), the East Asian crisis in the late 1990s had a damaging effect on the economic problems of the Asian countries. During this period, the value of the Japanese Yen declined drastically, which ruthlessly affected the cash flows of the companies having trade relations with Japan (Damodaran, 2006). This ultimately led to a fall in the market value of those companies.

For example, suppose that an Indian company exports 75 % of its turnover to USA, and the US Dollar is depreciating relative to the Indian Rupee. There is a risk that even if US sales grow rapidly over the next five years, profit and cash flow will not, because the Rupee value of those earnings is actually diminishing. This external factor to the Indian company nevertheless affects the company's market value. Therefore, the technique is to carry out the buying and selling activities in a variety of currencies which leads to diversification of the portfolio. In other words, this implies may be in one currency a business house benefits while in another it suffers losses. So, in the long run the gains will act to counterbalance the losses and minimize the economic risk on the whole.

2.2 Transaction Risk

Transaction risk describes a risk that arises when most goods and services are sold on credit. If the deal is takes place in a currency other than that of the seller's currency, then the seller may find that the sum he is expected to receive varies from what he actually receives due to changes in exchange rates. Whether foreign currency receipts valued in terms of local currency falls or the local value of foreign currency payments rises between the fixing of a contract and the date of payment or receipt is not known. So, this uncertainty actually gives rise to transaction risk. A brief illustration given below shows how the risk arises.

Suppose, ABC Limited is a renowned Indian industrial equipment manufacturer. Suppose that they receive a contract from a US wholesaler for 200 tractors, at a price of 46,000 US$ each. The exchange rate on the date of issue of the invoice is 1 US$ = 60 Rupees (INR). The invoice is paid six months later, when the exchange rate is 1 US$ = 50 Rupees (INR).

When the deal was struck, the rupee value of the invoice is:

$$46,000 \times 200 \times 60 = 5520,00,000 \text{ Rupees (INR)}$$

Six months later, when the actual payment is made, the sum received amounts to:

$$46,000 \times 200 \times 50 = 4600,00,000 \text{ Rupees (INR)}$$

The second outcome is lower as compared to the first. Thus, it is clear that there is a difference between what the company expected and what it actually received. Transaction risk affects the profit and loss account, and it is a manifestation of the impact of short-term movements in the exchange rates. Say for example, in 1998, sports retailer JJB Sports in their annual report had testified a decline in their profits to the tune of 103,000 US$ as a result of random exchange rate movements. For this reason, transaction risk needs to be frequently hedged. The different forms of hedging are discussed in subsequent sections of this paper.

2.3 Translation Risk

When the profit earned abroad by a business house is used to buy foreign assets, then at the end of the accounting year, when the financial statements are prepared, the value of those foreign assets needs to be translated into domestic currency of the company. Purely on account of exchange rate changes, the valuation of these foreign assets might change from year to year. This sort of a balance sheet exchange rate risk is referred to as translation risk. This particular risk relates exchange rate movements to the valuation of foreign assets in the parent company's balance sheet. If the risk relates to a change in values, it follows that the values may either go up or down. As pointed out by the definition, the variation in value relates to both assets and liabilities, and so a fall in the value of a liability might be considered as good, whereas a fall in the value of an asset might be viewed as bad.

Suppose, XYZ is a renowned Indian construction company. We have considered a hypothetical example, where in the year 2015, the company's annual report states that a 50,000 US$ rise in the company's net debt, caused purely by exchange rate movements. From this example, it is clear that liabilities are being valued more purely on account of exchange rate movements than they ought to be. Such changes in valuation are therefore an unrealised loss/gain (as the case maybe). Thus, the magnitude of the exposure to translation risk is determined by the difference between the value of overseas assets and liabilities.

Now, the question which arises is how to take guard against translation risk. One of the ways to reduce translation risk is to tie in foreign held assets with liabilities denominated in the same currency, so that the overall balance sheet impact of changes in exchange rates is eliminated. This type of hedging is known as matching, and later in the paper, it has been explained.

3 Measuring Economic, Transaction and Translation Exposure

3.1 Measuring Economic Exposure

To measure the extent of economic exposure, we are going to discuss two specific approaches. The approaches have been given in details below.

(a) Forecasting: Calculating economic exposure through this measure involves categorizing the firm's cash flows into income statement items, and then evaluating how the earnings that have been forecasted in the income statement changes in response to alternative baseline exchange rate scenarios. In general, firms having more foreign costs than revenues will be unfavorably affected by stronger foreign currencies.

(b) Regression Analysis: This method requires the use of regression analysis to historical cash flow and exchange rate data. The model we are suggesting here is,

$$PCF_t = a_0 + a_1 e_t + u_t$$

where, PCF_t = percentage change in inflation-adjusted cash flows measured in the firm's domestic currency over period t
e_t = percentage change in the currency exchange rate over period t
u_t gives the error term of the model which follows standard OLS assumptions. This regression model can be extended to incorporate multiple currencies by including them as other independent variables, or by making use of a composite currency index. By changing the dependent variable, the impact of exchange rates on the firm's value (as measured by its stock price), earnings, exports, sales, etc. may also be assessed. The novelty of this simple approach is the fact that even if additional explanatory variables are included the sole effect of exchange rate changes can be estimated using a_1.

3.2 Measuring Transaction Exposure

To appraise an MNC's exposure, in general, the modus operandi is to consider each currency's position together with the currency's variability and the correlations among the currencies. The standard deviation statistics on historical data serves as a measure of the currency's variability. It is perfectly possible for the currency variability levels to change over time. The correlation coefficients have been used to measure the correlations among currency movements, that is, the degree to which two currencies move in relation to each other.

Consider an MNC, which is expected to receive payments in two foreign currencies say m and n. This MNC, therefore, is expected to receive cash flows from the two-currency portfolio. If one wishes to measure the deviation in the value of the portfolio than what is expected, standard deviation (as measured by quarterly percentage changes) of the portfolio is a must. To assess the exposure of an MNC to multiple currencies, variability of each currency coupled with the correlation between the currencies need to be considered.

Therefore, the risk associated with a two-currency portfolio can be estimated as:

$$\sigma = \sqrt{p_m^2 \sigma_m^2 + p_n^2 \sigma_n^2 + 2 p_m p_n \sigma_m \sigma_n \rho_{mn}} \tag{1}$$

where,

p_m denotes the proportion of total portfolio value in terms of currency m; p_n denotes the proportion of total portfolio value in terms of currency n; σ_m gives us the standard deviation of quarterly percentage changes in currency m whereas σ_n is the standard deviation of quarterly percentage changes in currency n; Now, ρ_{mn} gives the correlation coefficient of the quarterly percentage changes between currency m and n.

The analysis remains the same for the multi-currency framework and σ can be defined as-

$$\sigma = \sqrt{\Sigma_{i=1}^{n} p_i^2 \sigma_i^2 + 2\, \Sigma_{i=1}^{n} \Sigma_{i=1}^{n} p_i p_j \sigma_i \sigma_j \rho_{ij}} \tag{2}$$

where, i not equal to j. The standard deviation equation takes care of all these elements. The value of the portfolio can be easily calculated from the data provided by the MNC for which we are estimating the risk. Empirically, using the monthly/quarterly/yearly percentage changes in each currency one can calculate σ and comment on the risk associated with the two-currency portfolio and then move onto time series analayis by highlighting the variability in the movement of σ over time. To calculate the correlations among exchange rate movements, we have used quarterly exchange rate data for some of India's major trading partners. We have compiled the data from World Bank Data Bank and OECD's reported exchange rate statistics. The results shown in Table 1 have been obtained using the statistical package Stata 12. Looking at the first column of the following table, it is clear that exchange rate movements are going to have across-the-board implications for the corporate houses located not only in India but also in the countries whose currency correlations have been calculated here. It is important to note that countries who are not engaged in major trading relations, their currency correlations are on the lower side.

The currency correlation results show that the Indian Rupee is highly correlated with the US Dollar, British Pound, Euro and the Chinese Renminbi. By and large, currency correlations are positive and tend to move in the same direction. But, this positive correlation may not always occur on a daily basis, but apparently holds over longer periods of time.

3.3 *Measuring Translation Exposure*

Accounting rules vary from country to country in respect of the way in which balance sheet values should be arrived at for the purpose of year-end translation. There are two fundamental methods regarding the exchange rate that should be used for the purposes of translation. These are explained below.

(a) Closing Rate Method: All financial statements are translated using the 'current'exchange rate, that is, the exchange rate prevailing at the time of

Table 1 Correlations among exchange rate movements

	The rupee	US dollar	British pound	Euro	Chinese renminbi
The Rupee	1				
US Dollar	0.83	1			
British Pound	0.57	0.64	1		
Euro	0.71	0.48	0.67	1	
Chinese Renminbi	0.91	0.61	0.35	0.22	1

preparation of the balance sheet. Starting from assets and liabilities, dividends and equity accounts are all valued at the current exchange rate

(b) Temporal Method: The rate used is the one prevailing at the time the asset/liability was acquired. In other words, certain assets and liabilities are translated at exchange rates consistent with the timing of the item's creation. Also, it assumes that a number of line items for instance inventories and plant and equipment are restated to reflect market value of that particular asset.

4 Hedging Foreign Exchange Risk: The Details of Risk Management

Once a firm recognizes its exposure it deploys the resources for managing it effectively. In Fig. 1 below, the step by step procedure for effective risk management has been highlighted (Sivakumar and Sarkar, 2008). Accordingly, the figure clearly demonstrates which step should be followed by what.

Now, we move onto discuss the hedging techniques available to a firm. In seeking to protect itself from transaction risk, a company may employ a variety of hedging techniques, either in isolation or in combination. These are detailed below.

4.1 Invoice Currency

At the simplest level, an exporter can pass the risk of a change in the exchange rate over to the foreign buyer, by invoicing in the exporter's own currency. As expected, it is possible that the buyer will not deal with the currency risk without some compensation, maybe in the form of discounted prices. Even this simple form of hedging therefore has a cost.

Fig. 1 Framework for risk management

4.2 Matching

Transaction risk only arises when there is a mismatch in respect of the net value of receipts or payments in foreign currencies. This means, that if, for example, a Singapore-based company knows that it needs to make a payment of 20,000 US$ in three month's time it faces the risk that the value of the payment when expressed in terms of Singapore Dollars may change over the three-month period, and may increase. If, however, the company organizes its operations such that it has invoiced a foreign buyer in US Dollars, and is due to receive 20,000 US$ in three months' time, then there is no net exposure to the risk. The risk has been fully hedged. Matching can be applied to receipts and payments to or from both external or internal suppliers or customers. It is therefore, particularly useful for large group organizations where there is a large volume of inter-group sales in a variety of different currencies. Practically, such matching may be quite difficult to organize, as it requires that both the time-scale and the value of deals get matched. Where the match is not perfect, any outstanding net exposure can then be hedged using external markets.

Matching is also used to reduce translation risk exposures, by means of matching of assets and liabilities in a common currency. For example, by borrowing dollars, a business house ensures that if the sterling value of dollar assets reduces because of changes in the dollar-sterling rate, they will also benefit from a fall in the sterling value of the dollar borrowings. If the assets and liabilities are of similar size, the net exchange rate impact on the balance sheet is then zero.

4.3 Netting

This is effectively an extension of matching, but applied only to sales between companies that are part of the same group. For example, suppose that an Indian pharmaceutical company, say, XY limited supplies a Dutch group member of the pharmaceutical division of XY. Some weeks later, there is a reverse sale, from the Dutch company to the Indian company. It makes sense for the two transactions to be netted off, with only one payment of the net amount being made. Such an arrangement is known as bilateral netting. In particularly large concerns, the process may be extended to become multilateral netting. Suppose that we increase the number of deals taking place within XY limited. A third Dutch member company supplies an Indian subsidiary in XY's coating division. This significantly reduces the number of payments required which results in lower banking and dealing costs, so that investors in the group are in a position to take advantage from higher reported profits.

The Electrolux Group is one example of a company which uses multilateral netting to reduce dealing costs. By centralizing transactions, the company is always aware of the scale, direction of its currency risk, and control of that risk is thus made easier.

4.4 Leading and Lagging

Suppose, an importer makes a payment in a currency that is expected to strengthen. It is in his benefit to buy the foreign currency immediately. The converse is true when there is an expectation regarding the depreciation of the currency of payment in relative terms. Leading or lagging is the process of managing the timing of purchase of a foreign currency payable, to take advantage of expected changes in the exchange rate. While, leading implies buying earlier, and paying the associated bill earlier, lagging is just the opposite.

4.5 Forward Contract

So far, in discussing changes in exchange rates, it has been assumed that it is possible to forecast the exchange rate in say, three months' time. This idea is not so spectacular as it may at first appear, because markets do exist to trade in currencies at an agreed rate, at a future point in time. These are the forward markets and they perform a useful function in serving the needs of both speculators and hedgers. A company needs to be reasonably certain of the trading margin on a deal, particularly if the market is highly competitive and margins are narrow. The forward markets grant the opportunity for buyers and sellers of currencies to be certain of the value of a transaction. So how does the forward market work?

Not surprisingly, a price needs to be paid for the certainty associated with a forward deal. The annual percentage cost of each forward rate is usually quoted alongside the rate. The exchange rates quoted are determined by the relative interest rates in the respective countries.

The idea is to present a simple example to show the relationship between spot rate and the forward rate. Exchange rates cannot be forecasted with flawless accuracy but a particular firm can measure the risk of being exposed to exchange rate fluctuations. Since future exchange rates are uncertain, involvement in international financial markets involves a high degree of risk as one can never know for sure what the spot rate will be one month or one year ahead. To increase the potential gains, accurate forecasting is an absolute necessity. The question which arises is how to go for a good forecast? The idea is, for being considered as a good forecast, a forecast should be on the correct side of the forward rate. We consider a hypothetical example,

Current spot rate:	60 Rupees (INR) = 1 US$
Current 12-month forward rate:	55 Rupees (INR) = 1 US$
Mr X forecasts:	46 Rupees (INR) = 1 US$
Mr Y forecasts:	56 Rupees (INR) = 1 US$
Future spot rate realized in 12 months:	53 Rupees (INR) = 1 US$

An Indian firm has 2 million US$ receipts due in 12 months and makse use of the forecasts to come to a decision whether to cover the dollar receivable with a forward contract or wait for 12 months and sell in the spot market 12 months hence. In terms of the forecasting errors, Mr X's prediction of 46 Rupees (INR) = 1 US$ yields an error of 13.2 % against a realized future spot rate of 53 Rupees (INR). Mr. Y's forecast is much closer to the realized spot rate, with an error of 11.3 %. Here lies the puzzle. While Y's forecast is closer to the rate eventually realized, this however is not the important feature of a good forecast. According to our proposed example, Mr Y predicts a future spot rate in excess of the forward rate, so if the firm sticks to Mr Y's prediction, the firm would wait and sell the dollars in the spot market in 12 months i.e., a long position in dollars. Since, the future spot rate is 53 Rupees (INR) = 1 US$ is less than the current forward rate at which the dollars can be sold (55 Rupees (INR) = 1 US$), the firm would actually gain by going for a long position.

Following Mr X's forecast of a future spot rate below the forward rate, the Indian firm would sell dollars in the forward market (or go for a short position in dollars). The firm would then sell the dollars at the current forward rate of 55 Rupees (INR) per dollar rather than wait and receive only 53 Rupees (INR) per dollar in the spot market in the near future. In this case, the forward contract yields much more. So, the moral of the story is that a forecast should be on the correct side of the forward rate; or else a small forecasting error will not be advantageous. Going by two different predictions would lead to two different standpoints. The question which crops up is that should the firm adopt a long or a short position in the FOREX market. The speculators want a forecast that will give them the direction in which the future spot rate will progress and accordingly they would position themselves.

An understanding of whether the currency due to be paid or received is expected to weaken or strengthen is vital to the development of a coherent hedging policy. To analyse it from the standpoint of the trading agents, we first look into the case of importers. An importer may consider hedging to be unnecessary when the the currency payable is weakening. Conversely, if a currency payable is strengthening, a forward contract to buy that currency will be useful to check the increase in value of the sum owed. For exporters, the opposite happens. In practice, many MNCs have in-house forecasting units whose task is to predict future exchange rates.

One of the disastrous effects of hedging using the forward market is that it 'locks the company in' to the forward rate, and if sales are being made in a currency which is declining in value, i.e., depreciating, then even though the hedge protects the value of the receipts, it cannot protect against the depreciation, which will be built in to the forward rate.

4.6 Options

An option is very much similar to a forward contract, in so far as it represents an agreement to buy or sell currency at some time in the future. The dissimilarity with forward market is that an option does not have to be exercised, whereas a forward contract is binding. The purchaser of an option must therefore make a decision as to whether or not to exercise a specific option.

An option which grants a privilege to buy a fixed amount of currency at a present price is a call option while one that confers a right to sell is a put option. The option works by the parties agreeing an exercise price; this is the exchange rate agreed for the currency if the option is to be exercised. There is a charge made for the option itself (the option premium), and this is paid upfront regardless of whether the option is exercised. The result is that the maximum cost of the hedge is the premium cost.

Options are particularly attractive in situation in which there is some uncertainty regarding a transaction. The potential deal can be hedged at a cost equal to the premium charged, and then if the deal stalls, no more expense is incurred and the company is not locked into a currency deal as would be the case with a forward contract. Alternatively, if the transaction does go ahead, the company has the opportunity to exercise or not exercise the option depending on the prevailing spot rate.

If the option is a call option, then the risk is that the option exercise price will exceed the spot price for that particular currency. When this is the case, it is preferable to buy the currency in the spot market rather than exercise the option. In contrast, if the option is a put option, then the concern is that the spot rate will be below the option exercise price. In this instance, it is again preferable to deal in the spot market rather than exercising the option.

4.7 Swaps

A simple currency swap takes the form of an agreement to exchange payments in one currency for payments in another. Frequently, swap are arranged because a company wishes to expand in a country in which there are foreign exchange restrictions, or the local currency is non-convertible. Assume, that a Swedish MNC wishes to invest in construction of a manufacturing plant in Poland, but does not wish to directly exchange Swedish Krona for Polish Zloty. Polish banks are likely to be in need of hard currencies and so a swap should be relatively simple to arrange.

The swap works by means of the Swedish company depositing Krona in a Swedish bank, to the credit of the Polish bank. Simultaneously, the Polish bank places Zloties on deposit in Poland, in the name of the Swedish company. Over the period of the loan, the Swedish company pays interest on the loan in the Polish currency direct to the Polish bank, and the Polish bank makes interest payments in Krona to the Swedish bank. When the swap period expires, the respective currencies are repaid by the two parties.

The effect of the swap is to eliminate the long-term currency risk because the investment has effectively been financed by a Krona investment. There remains, however, a currency risk relating to the interest payments, and it is advisable to hedge these separately, if possible. Swap are particularly attractively forms of hedge because they represent a form of off-the balance-sheet finance, and offers access to capital funds in countries where currency controls may be very tight and exchange rates volatile.

4.8 Currency Futures

Currency futures have declined in popularity in recent years, and are now traded on only a limited number of exchanges. Presently, International Money Market based in Chicago is the the main market where futures are traded.

A future is an obligation to buy or sell a fixed quantity of a commodity at some future point in time. The original futures markets dealt in commodities such as grain or soya beans, but the financial futures markets developed, when it was recognized that currencies or interest rates are simply special types of commodities. The buyer of a futures contract is required to make a deposit equal to between 1 and 5 % of the contract value. While, it is on deposit this sum cannot earn any interest, and so the lost interest forms part of the cost of this type of hedging instrument.

Currency futures are sold in blocks, for example, we consider a hypothetical example where US Dollar futures are traded in 25,000 US$ blocks. This means that to hedge a transaction of, say, 30,000 US$, a single future contract needs to be bought. Consequently, this would leave 5000 US$ unprotected, and a different form of hedge would be needed to protect this balance. The fixed contract sums are an important disadvantage of futures deals.

If a currency is strengthening, the value of a futures contract denominated in that currency will rise. This means that if an importer faces a bill in the strengthening currency, if the position is unhedged the value of the bill will increase over time. If, however, a futures contract has been purchased, the gain in value of the contract will serve to offset the 'loss' from the increased bill value. It is very unlikely that the futures gain will exactly offset the exchange rate loss, but the mechanism does offer some protection.

5 Risk in Foreign Currency Borrowing: Indian Perspective

Borrowings in foreign currency by corporate borrowers in India and other emerging economies is very common given the fact that these business houses want to benefit from the lower rate of interest and longer terms of credit. But, in terms of high currency volatality such borrowings are not always helpful. During good times, domestic borrowers could have the triple benefits of (i) lower interest rates, (ii) longer maturity and finally, (iii) capital gains due to appreciation of domestic currency. This happens when the local currency appreciates due to unexpected capital inflows and the debt service liability is falling in domestic currency terms.

The global financial crisis in 2008 showed how the opposite happens, when domestic currency starts depreciating due to reversal of capital flows during crisis situations. An abrupt depreciation in the domestic currency coupled with increase in debt service liability would eventually lead to wearing away of the profit margin and market-to-market implications for the corporate (Gupta, 2013).

Given this background, it is felt that one of the major factors behind the faster recovery of the Indian economy, post the 2008 global financial crisis was the low level of corporate external debt. And as a result, the significant weakening in the value of the rupee did not have major consequences for the corporate balance-sheets. A corporate body needs to be vigilant when going for a contractual foreign currency borrowing, in particular when natural hedging is not available. This sort of a natural hedge automatically happens when a foreign currency borrower also has an export market for its products. Therefore, export receivables would offset, at least to a certain extent, the currency risk inherent in debt service payments. This transpires because fall in the value of the rupee that leads to higher debt service payments gets partly compensated by the increase in the value of rupee receivables through exports. It might so happen, that the currency of export receivables and currency of borrowings is different. Under such a scenario, the prudent approach for corporations is to enter currency swaps to redenominate asset and liability in the same currency to create natural hedge. Sadly, too many Indian corporations with little foreign currency gains leave foreign currency borrowings unhedged, so as to profit from the low international interest rates. This is a risky venture for reasons cited above and should be avoided.

One imminent hazard for a company, is that, a country in which it owns the assets may institute currency exchange controls. Many emerging and developing countries, including India, have introduced a system of currency exchange controls which puts a ceiling on the use of local and foreign currencies. Developing countries very often have far less hard (convertible) currencies than they need. Therefore, rationing is the procedure which is followed. Anybody wanting hard currencies are required to apply to a government agency, specifying how much of it is wanted and the use to which it will be put to.

In the recent past, phases of exchange rate stability have spread complacency among investors. The Indian corporations have always kept away from hedging their exposures. This can be attributed to the traditional outlook they have, that is, importers had no doubt that the Reserve Bank of India (RBI) would intervene to halt any rupee decline whereas exporters believed that the Rupee has always been over rated and that there is no way that it shall appreciate from the present value. In general, due to corporate reluctance coupled with the lack of information and technology and considering hedging as unwanted cost centres, companies involved in hedging have mostly followed the traditionalist path to hedge their exposures, that is, by entering into forward contracts (FC) with banks, which have been the Authorized Dealers (AD) in foreign exchange market in India. The restricted use and the lack of interest shown in the available instruments explained in Section 4 has not really led to the development of the external sector.

In the coming decades, companies need to understand the importance of foreign exchange risk management given the global integration of the financial markets. However, it is still not clear as to how many companies are working towards building capacity to deal with this changing scenario. The problem gets motivated by the fact that in the Indian context, the market for derivatives other than forward contracts is very unsophisticated. Introduction of innovative products and technology in the domestic securities market is the need of the hour. Also, the route taken by the foreign exchange market has to be in line with the public policy objectives for sustainable growth in the long run.

6 Conclusion

The aim of the chapter is to look in detail at the additional financial risks faced by companies that choose to trade internationally. The risks can be compartmentalized under the headings of transaction, translation and economic risk, but the type of risk faced by the business firm is to some extent dependent on the nature of the international involvement. Companies are primarily concerned about the effect of changing exchange rates on cash flows, and a variety of hedging techniques are employed to reduce exposure to exchange rate volatility. The extent to which hedging instruments are applied and whether companies should merely seek to reduce risk or should engage in currency speculation is a matter of debate. There seems little willingness on the part of corporate houses to disclose to shareholders the features of their foreign exchange management policy, although pressures are increasing in this regard.

On the whole, the conclusion must be that internationalization serves to considerably increase the financial risks faced by companies in determining corporate strategy, there, management need to be aware of these risks, and confident in their ability to manage them. Then, armed with the funds for expansion, and the knowledge to limit financial risks they can address the next area of functional management—how to find a market for their products abroad. International marketing coupled with foreign exchange risk management should be the thrust area in this era of globalization.

References

Damodaran A (2006) *The dark side of valuation*. Pearson Education India

Gupta A (2013) *Risk management and simulation*. CRC Press, New York

Jorion P (1988) On jump processes in the foreign exchange and stock markets. *Review of Financial Studies*, 1(4), 427–445

Sivakumar A, Sarkar R (2008) Corporate hedging for foreign exchange risk in India. Industrial and Management Engineering Department, Indian Institute of Technology, Kanpur

Asim K. Karmakar is an Assistant Professor of Economics, Department of Economics, Jadavpur University, Kolkata, India. Dr. Karmakar has an MA degree in Economics from Rabindra Bharati University (1987) and a PhD in Economics from Jadavpur University (1998). His research interests lie in the analysis of Balance of Payments in the Indian context, issues pertaining to the Indian Economy (like food security, rural livelihoods, etc.), analysis of contagious financial crises. He has taught Indian Economics at both undergraduate and postgraduate levels and Macroeconomics at the undergraduate level. He is a Life Member of the Indian Society of Labour Economics. He is presently the Executive Member of both the Indian Economic Association (IEA) and The Indian Econometric Society (TIES); formerly the Managing Editor (2011–2014) of the Quarterly Referred Journal *Artha Beekshan* of Bengal Economic Association. He has completed three minor research projects sponsored by the Centre of Advanced Studies (CAS), Jadavpur University and University Grants Commission (UGC, India). He has contributed many research papers in reputed journals at home and abroad.

Sovik Mukherjee is a Research Scholar of Economics, Department of Economics, Jadavpur University, Kolkata, India. Mr. Mukherjee has a BA degree in Economics from Jadavpur University (2013), an MA degree in Economics from Jadavpur University (2015) and currently pursuing MPhil in Economics from Jadavpur University. His research interests lie in the area of public economics and taxation, economics of corruption, health economics, international finance and the econometric analysis of financial crises. He is a Life Member of the Indian Economic Association (IEA) and the Bengal Economic Association (BEA). He has completed a consultancy research project sponsored by the State Bank of India, LHO, Kolkata, India.

The Link Between Dollarization and Its Determinants in Turkey

Ozlem Tasseven

Abstract Dollarization which is mostly observed in developing countries has been a widely disputed topic in the literature. It occurs due to high inflation and macroeconomic instabilities. In the previous studies the effects, causes and determinants of dollarization were analyzed using the econometric techniques such as co-integration, vector error correction model and vector autoregressive models for multivariate time series methods. We investigate the relationship between dollarization and its determinants such as interest rate differential, Istanbul stock exchange index, central bank reserve ratio, expected inflation, expected depreciation and volatility index using data between 2001 and 2014 for Turkish economy using Geweke linear feedback, causality tests in frequency domain and the wavelet comovement analysis.

1 Introduction

Heavy dollarization is observed in countries which suffer from high and volatile inflation and high rate of domestic currency depreciation. In countries with high inflation rates and depreciation of domestic currencies, foreign currency captures the store of value function of the domestic currency. Domestic currency losses no longer fulfills its function of acting as a unit of account and a medium of exchange in ongoing high inflation environment. Achievement of functions of money with another currency is observed as currency substitution or dollarization. According to portfolio models of asset demand, currency substitution depends on the opportunity costs of holding domestic currency and other assets (Vegia 2006).

Dollarization occurs as a result of macroeconomic instability. It explains the vulnerabilities and currency crises in such parts of the world including Latin

O. Tasseven (✉)
Faculty of Business Administration, Department of Economics and Finance, Dogus University, Acıbadem, Kadikoy 34722, Istanbul, Turkey
e-mail: otasseven@dogus.edu.tr

H. Dinçer, Ü. Hacioğlu (eds.), *Risk Management, Strategic Thinking and Leadership in the Financial Services Industry*, Contributions to Management Science, DOI 10.1007/978-3-319-47172-3_5

America, parts of East Asia and East Europe. While the financial systems remain underdeveloped in many developing countries, signs of progress in financial deepening are emerging. Dollarization can impose difficulties on policy makers by reducing the effectiveness of monetary policy (Giovannini and Turtelboom 1994). It constraints the ability of Central Banks to act as a lender of last resort, avoids liquidity management of banks and decreases the financial stability. It negatively affects banks' balance sheets. Miles (1978), Girton and Roper (1981), Ortiz (1983), Thomas (1985), Giovannini (1991), Giovannini and Turtelboom (1994), Guidotti (1993), Kruger and Ha (1995), McKinnon (1985), Calvo and Vegh (1992) analyzed the effects of dollarization on monetary policy.

Dollarization can cause ineffectiveness of economic policies by exposing the balance sheets of public and private sector to foreign exchange rate risk when there is currency mismatches between assets and liabilities as well as weakening the structural fiscal balance. Furthermore, dollarization weakens the ability of governments to handle the debt issues and thus causes macroeconomic and output fluctuations. By allowing residents to have foreign currency deposits, encouragement of transacting their savings through financial system is maintained, rather than transferring the savings abroad or holding the savings in non-financial assets (Mecagni et al. 2015).

Currency substitution in developed and developing countries shows different processes. In developed countries, the demand for foreign currency, based on foreign trade, and sometimes on portfolio diversification has been intended for maximizing financial returns. In developing countries, foreign currency is demanded in order to avoid the inflation tax, as well as performing operations in the country along with these two cases. Successive crises experienced in banking and financial systems are assumed to be related to financial dollarization. Financial dollarization is observed when the assets and liabilities of economic units are denominated in foreign currency. Studies carried out in recent years, have shown that particularly liability dollarization, increases financial fragility. These fragilities play an important role in spreading crisis which started with 1994–1995 Tequila crisis, and the Asian crisis in 1997 (Galindo and Liederman 2005).

This chapter uses theoretically strong methods to examine the relationship between dollarization and its determinants for Turkey. These methods are the Geweke linear feedback, causality tests in frequency domain developed by Breitung and Candelon (2006) and the wavelet comovement analysis developed by Rua (2010). Frequency domain causality analysis investigates the causality relationship in both low and high frequencies without the need of a selection of maximum lag. Whether one variable causes the other or there is bi-directional causality over the whole period is determined. The wavelet comovement analysis considers both time and frequency domains. The advantage of using wavelet analysis is that the variables can be observed at different frequencies and though time simultaneously (Gencay et al. 2001).

The objective of this chapter is to investigate the relationship between dollarization and its determinants such as interest rate differential, Istanbul stock exchange index, central bank reserve ratio, expected inflation, expected depreciation and volatility index using data between 2001 and 2014 for Turkish economy. Section 2 reviews the studies on dollarization in the literature. Section 3 describes the methodologies used in the chapter briefly which are the frequency domain causality analysis and wavelet comovement methods. Section 4 presents the empirical findings and finally Sect. 5 concludes.

2 Studies on Dollarization: A Literature Overview

Dollarization and currency substitution can be seen more in the countries where there is a high and inconsistent inflation, where exchange rate depreciates often and where there is a largely public deficit. Studies on dollarization show that dollarization proceeds rapidly in countries with poorly developed capital markets and limited choices for domestic investments. Several Latin American countries including as Argentina, Bolivia and Peru have experienced high dollarization. Once a country experiences hyper-inflation or high and volatile inflation rates, dollarization tends to be irreversible due to the anxiety caused by past experiences. This irreversibility is known as the "ratchet effect" (Kamin and Ericsson 1993). Policies adopted to affect money supply and similar monetary variables may not have the desired results (Miles 1978). The main reason for failing to de-dollarize the economy is that people may not find the reversal credible. In order to reduce dollarization, the use of foreign macroeconomic policies should be strengthened and financial system should be adjusted to increase the attractiveness of local currency. In order to achieve irreversibility, the economy the macroeconomic stability should be restated, companies should take measures to prevent currency mismatches, market based strategies should be considered, investment opportunities in domestic currency should be encouraged so that the dependability of the residents will be restored.

In the literature currency substitution for Turkey is analyzed by several authors including Selcuk (1994, 1997), Akçay et al. (1997), Akıncı (2003), Bahmani-Oskooee and Karacal (2006), Yazgan and Zer-Toker (2010), Domac and Oskooee (2002), Civcir (2003). Turkey experienced high and chronic inflation in during nearly 30 years before 2001. Therefore, the credibility of Turkish lira was lost for a long time. Currency substitution can be seen as a response of economic agents to inflation uncertainty. Akçay et al. (1997) and Domac and Oskooee (2002) find that as currency substitution increases, the volatility of the exchange rate increases as well. Bahmani-Oskooee and Domac (2002) state that in order to limit dollarization the effects of increasing the volatility of exchange rate without raising that of inflation would be effective under inflation targeting regime in Turkey (Table 1).

Table 1 Literature review on dollarization

Author	Subject	Variables	Methods	Findings
Kamin and Ericsson (1993)	The effect of macroeconomic and political uncertainty on dollarization in Argentina	Peso money demand, inflation, economic and political risks	Cointegration and error correction model estimation	a negative ratchet effect from inflation on the demand for pesos The dollarization level remained high in Argentina
Mecagni et al. (2015)	The deposit dollarization in sub-Saharan Africa	Inflation, foreign exchange, variables reflecting institutional characteristics	Panel unit root tests, panel regression	inflation and exchange rate depreciation are found to be the main drivers of dollarization
Bacha et al. (2007)	the effect of dollarization on real interest rate in Brazil	the real interest rate, dollarization	Two-step estimation generating instrument variable in the first step for panel data	dollarization has a negative impact on the real interest rate
Selcuk (1994)	the responses of currency substitution to shocks in certain policy variables in the Turkish economy during 1986–1992	current account deficit, depreciation of domestic, currency substitution	Vector autoregression model estimation, dynamic impulse response estimation	policy makers should decide whether to have less current account deficit or conduct more independent monetary policy
Akçay et al. (1997)	The dollarization in Turkey	Dollarization, volatility of exchange rate	generalized autoregressive conditional heteroscedasticity (GARCH) method	Increase in dollarization can cause increase in volatility of exchange rate
Domac and Oskooee (2002)	the role of currency substitution in the dynamics of inflation in Turkey	Inflation, economic instability, institutional weaknesses, reserve requirements, surrender requirements	generalized impulse response analysis, variance decomposition	high inflation and economic instability are the main reasons of currency substitution in Turkey
Selcuk (1997)	currency substitution in the Turkish economy for the period 1985–1993	Currency substitution, exchange rate between the Turkish lira and the US dollar	Generalized method of moments	the elasticity of substitution between the Turkish lira and the US dollar is found to be high and statistically significant

3 Data and Methodology

The data used in the analysis covers the period between 2001 August and 2014 December. The total sample data is divided into three groups. The first group called "Global Liquidity Abundance" period, the second group called "The Great Recession" period and the third group called "Current Period" cover 2001 August–2007 December, 2008 January–2011 December, 2012 January–2014 December respectively.[1]

The data is obtained from the Central Bank of Republic of Turkey's electronic data distribution system. The monetary variable we consider (M2Y) is the broadly defined monetary balances in natural logarithms which is the sum of currency in circulation and demand, time and foreign currency deposits in the banking system. Currency substitution ratio (FCD) is defined as the logarithm of the ratio of foreign currency deposits to broad monetary aggregate. Interest rate differential (INTD) refers to the percentage of interest rate differential between 3-month TL deposits and 3-month foreign currency deposits. Istanbul stock exchange index (BIST) is defined as the logarithm of the stocks of companies which are included in BIST. Central bank reserve ratio (RES) is the ratio of the level of central bank reserves to monetary aggregate, M2Y. Expected inflation (INFE) is the median of the end of the current month consumer price index obtained from Central Bank Expectation Questionnaire. Expected depreciation (EXPD) is the median of the end of the current month nominal exchange rate obtained from Central Bank Expectation Questionnaire. VIX index (VIX) shows Chicago Board Options Exchange Volatility Index, which shows the market's expectation of 30-day volatility.

Geweke (1982) linear measure of feedback is important in the sense that it provides detailed information on how one variable has the capability of explaining the percentage of another variable's variance over different frequency bands. Hence, we observe how much the variation in dollarization is explained by several key variables for the Turkish economy.

On the other hand the well-known time domain Granger causality test indicates whether the past changes in x (y) have an impact on current changes in y (x) over a specified time period (Granger 1969). Nevertheless, these test results only provide causality for a discrete time dimension.

Through using a Fourier transformation to VAR (p) model for x and y series, the Geweke's measure of linear feedback from y to x at frequency ω is defined as[2]:

[1]To conserve space we only report the figures for the whole period, but stil keep the interpretation of the results for the sub-samples. The remaining figures are available from the author upon request.

[2]For details of the computation of the measure, see Geweke (1982) and Breitung and Candelon (2006).

$$M_{y\to x}(\omega) = \log\left[\frac{2\pi f_x(\omega)}{|\psi_{11}(e^{-i\omega})|^2}\right] = \log\left|1 + \frac{|\psi_{12}(e^{-i\omega})|^2}{|\psi_{11}(e^{-i\omega})|^2}\right| \tag{1}$$

If $|\psi_{12}(e^{-i\omega})|^2 = 0$, then the Geweke's measure will be zero, then y will not Granger cause x at frequency ω. This analysis is further extended to the continuous case by Breitung and Candelon (2006) who present this test by reformulating the relationship between x and y in the VAR equation:

$$x_t = \alpha_1 x_{t-1} + \cdots + \alpha_p x_{t-p} + \beta_1 y_{t-1} + \cdots + \beta_p y_{t-p} + \varepsilon_{1t} \tag{2}$$

The null hypothesis tested by Geweke, $M_{y\to x}(\omega) = 0$, corresponds to the null hypothesis of $H_0 : R(\omega)\beta = 0$ where β is the vector of the coefficients of y and $R(\omega) = \begin{bmatrix} \cos(\omega)\cos(2\omega)\ldots\cos(p\omega) \\ \sin(\omega)\sin(2\omega)\ldots\sin(p\omega) \end{bmatrix}$.

Breitung and Candelon (2006) use an F-statistics so that they can test causality in frequency domain. Therefore, it is obvious that a continuous time dimension will produce a superior analysis of causality with the frequency domain. This is due to the F test which provides us whether this statistically significant causality running from one variable to the other (or bi-variate case).

The last analysis we conduct is the recent wavelet comovement analysis developed by Rua (2010) which is shown to be superior to all the other comovement analysis.[3] Wavelet comovement technique combines the time dimension with the frequency dimension through waves that form a shape which signals for the statistically significant correlation coefficients over the specific interval. In this analysis the pink (light blue) shaded areas constitute the positive (negative) correlation coefficients. Nonetheless, due to the Brownian motion process in the continuous frequency domain, it is not possible to apply any significance tests for the correlation coefficients. Hence, we follow Rua (2010) and assume that any coefficient over 0.75 denotes statistical significance.

4 Empirical Findings

In order to incorporate both the frequency and time domains, Geweke measure of linear feedback and frequency domain Granger causality tests are conducted.

[3]Please see Rua (2010) for details.

4.1 Geweke (1982) Measure of Linear Feedback

Figure 1 shows the percentage of variation in currency substitution ratio that is explained by its determinants. These are interest rate differential, central bank reserve ratio, BIST 100 index, expected inflation, expected depreciation and VIX index for the whole period (2001 August–2014 December). When Fig. 1a is investigated, it is seen that the highest percentage of variance explained by INTD is found in high frequency. When INTD changes, investors react and they adjust their portfolio accordingly in the short run. Figure 1b shows that the highest percentage of variance is explained in the long term by RES, which is compatible with smooth movements in the international reserves. Figure 1c shows that the highest percentage of variance is explained in the long term by BIST 100. This is due to the high share of foreign investors in BIST 100 index. The share of foreign investors in Istanbul Stock Exchange has increased from % 30 in 2001 to % 70s in 2014. During 2000-2014 it was around %50–%60. Therefore, the foreign investors could not alter their positions quick enough in Istanbul Stock Exchange. The highest percentage of variance explained by INFE is found in short and long term. Central Bank has established implicit inflation targeting since 2001 and explicit inflation targeting since 2006. In the beginning, inflation targeting has caused some form of confusion for the households and investors as they started to adjust their expectations. The rather low percentage of variation explained by EXPD is probably due to the twin peaks we observe for inflation in Geweke test. VIX index shows high level of variation in FCD in long term. This is probably due to the low weight assigned to Turkish Lira by foreign investors.

Considering the sub-sample for the global liquidity abundance period between 2001 and 2007, we observe that the exchange rate depreciation explains a higher degree of variation in FCD in low and medium frequencies. During the Great Recession, with the liquidity trap in the whole world and also the low inflation levels, we reach a supporting result. EXPD is able to explain most of the variation in FCD in almost all frequencies. This shows that during the financial crises periods the explanatory power of exchange rate differential increases, which is caused by the decrease in the interest rate differential and also by the increase in the ability of forecasting expected inflation. During the current period (2012–2014), the investors prefer a shorter horizon, so the percentage of variation explained by INTD as well as BIST and INFE in FCD declines to medium term from long term. The main reason for this switch is probably the lower levels of global liquidity compared to the previous period.

4.2 Frequency Domain Granger Causality

This section includes the comments for the results of the frequency domain, Granger causality analysis for the whole period and the respective sub-periods. It

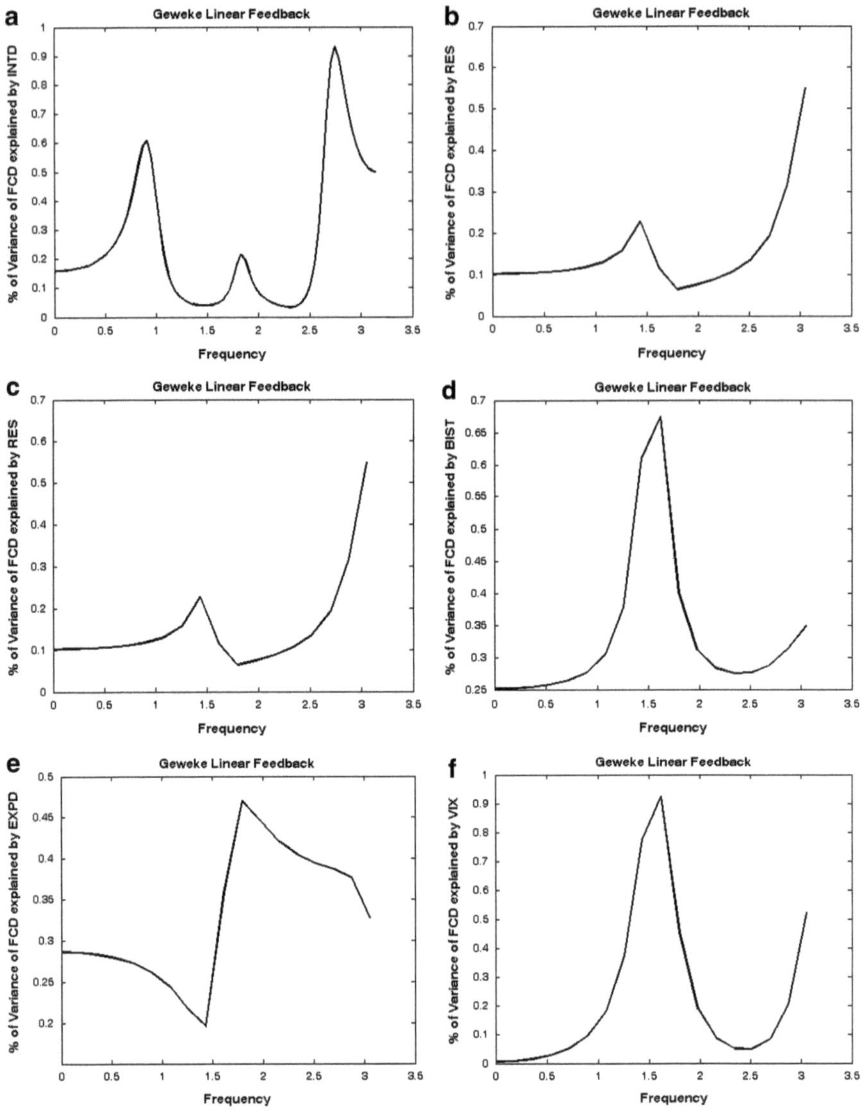

Fig. 1 Geweke linear feedback

is observed that using the frequency analysis provides clearer and more accurate relationships between variables over the all the frequencies with statistical significance compared to the time dimension Granger Causality which provides a result for just one point in time.

When the whole sample period is considered, it can be seen in Fig. 2 that in the short term INTD causes FCD. This is reasonable because the change in the spread between two countries leads to a relative change in the same direction in currency

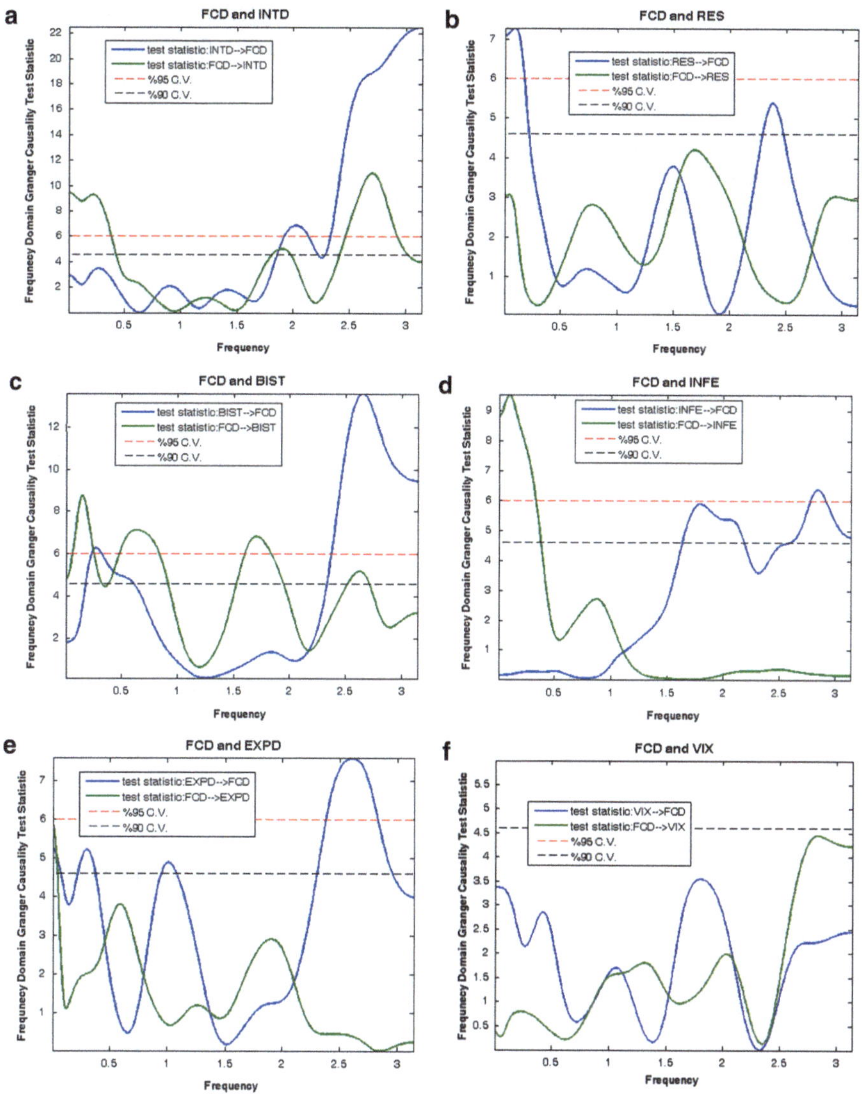

Fig. 2 Frequency domain Granger causality test results

substitution. RES causes FCD at low frequency and this shows a smooth long term relationship between these variables. In the short term BIST causes FCD which is due to the capital inflows into Istanbul Stock Exchange and most of this inflow is from the foreign investors. Once the international reserves increase most of the small Turkish investors prefer to substitute Turkish lira for US dollar.

In the long term FCD causes INFE because the switch form Turkish lira to the dollar leads to a relative depreciation in Turkish lira. Therefore, the inflation expectations are caused by a switch form Turkish lira to the dollar, which is a financial instrument in Turkish market. In the short term EXPD causes FCD, which is in line with the theoretical expectations. When there is the expectation that Turkish lira will depreciate, the agents switch to dollar. In the short term INTD causes FCD. The differences in interest rates between Turkey and United States increase during the Great Recession and this leads to an increase in dollarization and contraction in the Turkish economy. In the long term it is found that the direction of causality is from FCD to BIST. During the Great Recession foreign investors sold some portion of their stocks that they held and switched to dollars. In the long term EXPD causes FCD because during the Great Recession it's rather hard to form expectations for the shorter maturities.

In the long term BIST causes FCD in the current period because foreign investors demand stocks through bringing dollars and converting them into Turkish lira. Then they use the Turkish lira to buy stocks. Consequently, the only thing that is left in the market is the foreign currency which is probably kept in the international reserves of Central Bank. This is why this relationship is significant in the long term.

4.3 Comovement Analysis

The final part in the econometric analysis focuses on explaining the empirical results obtained by employing the Rua (2010) wavelet comovement methodology. It is important to note once again that Rua (2010) considers the correlation coefficients which are greater than 0.75 and smaller than −0.75 as statistically significant.

Figure 3 displays the wavelet comovement analysis with respective correlation coefficients for FCD and its determinants for the whole period. FCD exhibits significant comovement with INTD in high frequency and significant comovement with INTD in medium frequency between 2009 and 2011. These findings mean that FCD and INTD have a statistically significant and positive relationship, with an increase in the spread causing more dollarization and vice versa. It is also found that FCD and RES experience a statistically significant comovement till the Great Recession at high frequency.

When the Global Liquidity Abundance period is examined for FCD and its determinants, a significant positive comovement between FCD and INTD in the short term especially in 2005 is found. On the other hand, for the Great Recession period coefficients of correlation become negative at low frequencies and in the current period the coefficients again change into positive magnitude. During the Great Recession, this contrasting finding probably is due to the increase in dollarization with the expectation of future depreciation in Turkish lira and this demand for dollar reduces the international reserves further as capital flight has already started this vicious cycle. During the Great Recession the BIST 100 hasn't decreased to its 2001 Turkish financial crisis levels because there is a shorter term positive relationship depending on the theory that foreigners are unable to

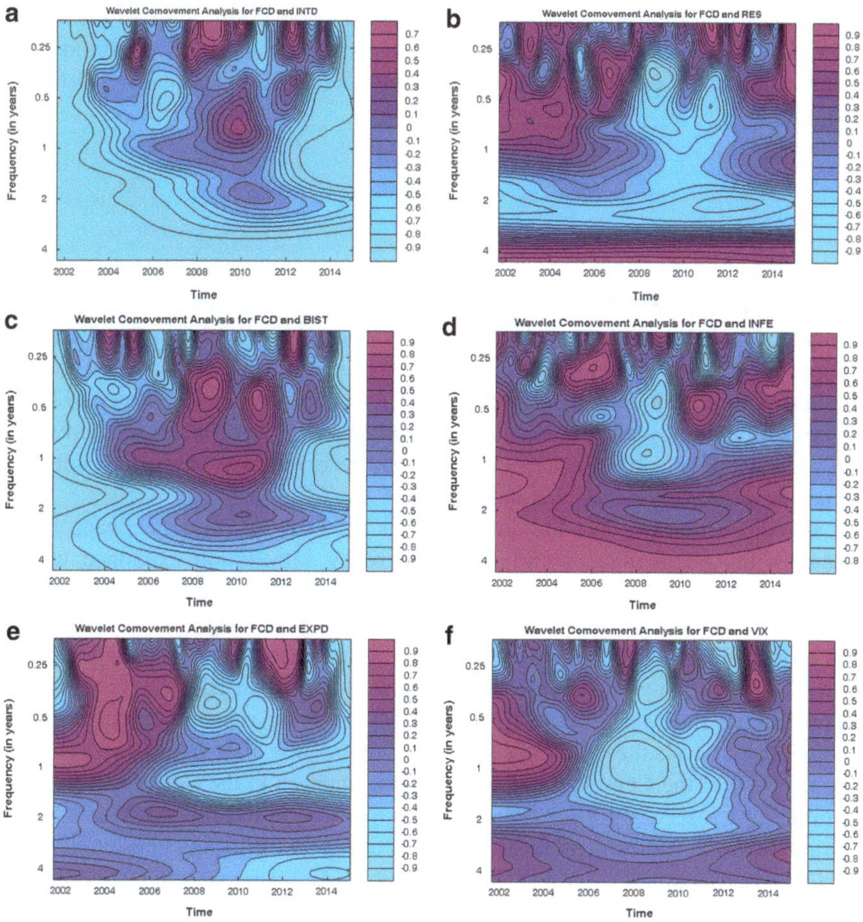

Fig. 3 Wavelet comovement methodology results

sell a huge portion of their stock portfolio. In the mean time, the small Turkish investors demand foreign currency, especially dollars. This is the possible reason for obtaining a statistically significant positive correlation between FCD and BIST during Great Recession period.

The general outlook for the comovement between FCD and INFE is in line with the theoretical approach. Any type of currency substitution will mean that inflation expectations will be affected in the negative manner; however the only part where we observe a statistically significant comovement is during the Great Recession when expectations are completely affected in an adverse manner. We observe a positive correlation for the comovement between FCD and EXPD especially during the first half of the whole period and after the Great Recession whereas this relationship is reversed during the Global financial crisis. In terms of theory, this is appropriate because during the periods of stabilization one should form expectations in a rational manner and a future depreciation in domestic currency should start the currency substitution. However during the turmoil periods, this relationship could easily be broken due to high levels of imperfect information in the market.

5 Conclusion

This chapter analyzes the relationship between currency substitution and its determinants for the emerging market of Turkey using Geweke linear feedback, the frequency domain Granger Causality and wavelet comovement analysis. We use a monthly data set with our endogenous variable (foreign currency deposits/ M2Y) as a proxy for currency substitution and remaining exogenous variables as interest rate differential, BIST 100 index, central bank reserve ratio, expected inflation, expected depreciation and VIX index.

The first empirical test that we employ is the Geweke linear feedback which provides the percentage of variance of currency substitution explained by our exogenous variables. The interest rate differential (BIST 100 and central bank reserve ratio) has the power to explain the highest percentage of variance in the short (long) term for dollarization. This means that changes in the spread immediately cause a change in dollarization whereas a change in BIST 100 and central bank reserve ratio takes more time to affect currency substitution. In terms of theoretical analysis these findings signal the importance of an interest rate change, the key tool of the Central Bank. It looks as if changes in the stock exchange and central bank reserve ratio are transmitted into currency substitution over a longer period due to the adjustment of expectations of the investors and households.

Our empirical findings from frequency domain Granger causality analysis show that in the short term interest rate differential, BIST 100 index and expected depreciation cause currency substitution whereas central bank reserve ratio causes currency substitution which causes expected inflation in the long term. An increase in spread leads to a possible increase in dollarization with capital inflow into Turkey. On the other hand, an increase in stock demand means a portfolio flow into Turkey which probably ends up in international reserves of the Central Bank or in public's holdings of foreign currency. This indeed is well documented in the findings in which an increase in the stock exchange leads to an increase in consumer sentiment (Gunes and Uzun 2010), directing savings towards alternative financial assets like dollar and euro.[4] As dollarization increases, the domestic currency depreciates which leads to the revision of inflationary expectations upwards. During

[4]Turkish people have the perception that foreign currency is a financial asset which has been well documented in the 2001 economic crisis. Although, this belief has somewhat changed during the period 2002–2007, once the depreciation of Turkish currency especially against the dolar has started, even small domestic investors prefer to switch to foreign Exchange, nomatter what the amount is.

the Great recession, our empirical findings show that the direction of causality is from currency substitution to BIST 100 index in the long run and expected deprecation causes currency substitution. In the current period, BIST 100 index is found to cause currency substitution. Once the foreigners who are dominant investors in BIST 100 leave, the amount of foreign exchange in Turkey decreases. Although small Turkish investors would like to use this opportunity to invest in foreign exchange, there isn't sufficient amount of liquidity on the market for them. Hence, their willingness to cause dollarization is not realized or they are only able to form their foreign exchange portfolios after the high levels of domestic currency depreciation has occurred.

The wavelet comovement methodology results demonstrate that when the whole sample is considered, currency substitution shows significant correlation with interest rate differential and central bank reserve ratio at high frequency. We found that there is a negative correlation between currency substitution and expected inflation and there is a positive correlation between currency substitution and expected depreciation, especially during the first half of the whole period. It is observed that the relationship between currency substitution and its determinants is rather weak at low frequencies during the global liquidity abundance period. However, the coefficients change into positive in the current period. From a theoretical standpoint, these findings are all compatible with what the orthodox theory proposes.

References

Akçay OC, Alper CE, Karasulu M (1997) Currency substitution and exchange rate instability: the Turkish case. Eur Econ Rev 41:827–835. doi:10.1016/S0014-2921(97)00040-8

Akıncı O (2003) Modeling the demand for currency issued in Turkey. Central Bank Rev 1:1–25. ISSN 1303-0701

Bacha EL, Holland M, Goncalves FM (2007) Is Brazil different? Risk, dollarization, and interest rates in emerging markets, International Monetary Fund working paper, WP/07/294

Bahmani-Oskooee M, Domac I (2002) On the link between dollarization and inflation: evidence from Turkey. The Central Bank of the Republic of Turkey, Discussion paper

Bahmani-Oskooee M, Karacal M (2006) The demand for money in Turkey and currency substitution. Appl Econ Lett 13:635–42. doi:10.1080/13504850500358819

Breitung J, Candelon B (2006) Testing for short and long-run causality: a frequency domain approach. J Econ 132:363–378. doi:10.1016/j.jeconom.2005.02.004

Calvo GA, Vegh CA (1992) Currency substitution in developing countries: an introduction. Revista de Analisis Economico 7(1):3–28

Civcir I (2003) Dollarization and its long-run determinants in Turkey. Middle East Econ Ser 6

Domac I, Oskooee MB (2002) On the link between dollarization and inflation: evidence from Turkey. Research and Monetary Policy Department, Central Bank of the Republic of Turkey discussion papers no 1217

Galindo A, ve Leiderman L (2005) Living with dollarization and the route to de-dollarization, Inter-American Development Bank, Research Department working paper no 526

Gencay R, Selcuk F, Witcher B (2001) Differentiating intraday seasonalities through wavelet multi-scaling. Phys A 289:543–556. doi:10.1016/S0378-4371(00)00463-5

Geweke J (1982) Measurement of linear dependence and feedback between multiple time series. J Am Stat Assoc 77:304–324. doi:10.1080/01621459.1982.10477803
Giovannini A (1991) Currency substitution and monetary policy. In: Wihlborg C et al (eds) Financial regulation and monetary arrangements after 1992. North Holland, Amsterdam, pp 203–216
Giovannini A, Turtelboom B (1994) Currency substitution. In: Van der Ploeg F (ed) The handbook of international macroeconomics. Blackwell, Malden, MA, pp 390–436
Girton L, Roper D (1981) Theory and implications of currency substitution. J Money Credit Bank 13(1):13–30. doi:10.2307/1991805
Granger CWJ (1969) Investigating causal relations by econometric models and cross-spectral methods. Econometrica 37(3):424–438. doi:10.2307/1912791
Guidotti PE (1993) Currency substitution and financial innovation. J Money Credit Bank 25 (1):109–124. doi:10.2307/2077823
Gunes H, Uzun S (2010) Differences in expectation formation of consumers in emerging and industrialized markets. Paper presented at 69th International Atlantic Economic Society Conference, March, Prague
Kamin SB, Ericsson NR (1993) Dollarization in Argentina, Board of Governors of the Federal Reserve System, International finance discussion papers, 460
Kruger R, Ha J (1995) Measurement of cocirculation of currencies, IMF working paper no 95/34
McKinnon R (1985) Two concepts of international currency substitution. In: Connolly MD, McDermott J (eds) The economics of the Caribbean Basin. Praeger, New York, pp 101–113
Mecagni M, Corrales JS, Dridi J, Garcia-Verdu R, Imam P, Matz J, Macario C, Narita F, Pani M, Rosales M, Weber S, Yehove E (2015) Dollarization in Sub-Saharan Africa, experience and lessons. International Monetary Fund, African Department. ISBN: 978-1-49836-847-6. doi:10.1093/jae/ejv020
Miles MA (1978) Currency substitution, flexible exchange rates and monetary independence. Am Econ Rev 68(3):428–436
Ortiz G (1983) Currency substitution in Mexico: the dollarization problem. J Money Credit Bank 15:174–185. doi:10.2307/1992398
Rua A (2010) Measuring comovement in the time–frequency space. J Macroecon 32:685–691. doi:10.1016/j.jmacro.2009.12.005
Selcuk F (1994) Currency substitution in Turkey. Appl Econ 26(5):509–522. doi:10.1080/00036849400000019
Selcuk F (1997) GMM estimation of currency substitution in a high inflation economy. Appl Econ Lett 4(4):225–228. doi:10.1080/758518499
Thomas LR (1985) Portfolio theory and currency substitution. J Money Credit Bank 17 (3):347–357. doi:10.2307/1992629
Vegia F (2006) Currency substitution, portfolio diversification and money demand. Can J Econ 39 (3):719–743. doi:10.1111/j.1540-5982.2006.00366.x
Yazgan ME, Zer-Toker I (2010) Currency substitution, policy rule and pass-through: evidence from Turkey. Appl Econ 42(18):2365–2378. doi:10.1080/00036840701858018

Özlem Taşseven is an Associate Professor of Quantitative Methods at Doğuş University Department of Economics and Finance, İstanbul-Turkey. Dr. Taşseven has a BS in Statistics Department from Middle East Technical University (1995), a master degree in economics from Middle East Technical University (2000), a Ph.D. in economics from Newcastle University (2007) in United Kingdom. Her PhD thesis was on "Money Demand and Currency Substitution in Turkey". Her research interests are econometric analysis of Turkish economy, applied macroeconomics and finance, research methods, time series, panel data analyses, statistics, operations research and industrial concentration. She has taught statistics, econometrics, microeconomics, macroeconomics and research methods courses at both undergraduate and graduate levels. She has been a reviewer for Doğuş University Journal and Banking & Finance Letters.

Enhancing the Risk Management Functions in Banking: Capital Allocation and Banking Regulations

Serpil Kuzucu and Narman Kuzucu

Abstract This chapter reviews capital allocation in the banking sector. Capital is crucial if banks are to be protected from banking risks. In order to ensure financial stability in the banking sector, banking regulators demand that banks hold sufficient capital to support their risks. The Basel Capital Accords, which aim to enhance the risk management functions of banks and to strengthen the stability of the international banking system, have introduced a common regulation framework for the capital allocation. They are international guidelines to encourage convergence toward common standards in the banking sector. The Basel Capital Accords have evolved over time because of the growth of international risks.

1 Introduction

One of the crucial objectives of a bank is to allocate its capital optimally within its business units. Capital allocation is an important part of the risk management process. Risk management aims to ensure the survival of the bank. Risk management is mainly concerned with defining the optimal amount of capital the bank should hold if it is to be protected from financial risks. Banks face different types of risk in the course of their operations. These risks have potentially negative effects on the banking industry. The key risks that banks face are credit risk, market risk, liquidity risk, operational risk, business risk, legal risk, reputational risk, and systemic risk.

Banks need to hold capital in order to protect themselves against financial risks and failures. Banks decide how much capital is required to cover the potential losses

S. Kuzucu (✉)
Institute of Banking and Insurance, Marmara University, Kadıköy, İstanbul, Turkey
e-mail: kuzucuserpil@gmail.com

N. Kuzucu
Faculty of Economics and Administrative Sciences, Beykent University, Ayazaga Maslak Campus, Sarıyer, Istanbul, Turkey
e-mail: narmankuzucu@gmail.com

H. Dinçer, Ü. Hacioğlu (eds.), *Risk Management, Strategic Thinking and Leadership in the Financial Services Industry*, Contributions to Management Science, DOI 10.1007/978-3-319-47172-3_6

deriving from these risks. A bank's capital allocation decisions depend on many variables, such as the riskiness of its assets, financial conditions, its banking operations and its long-term business strategies. When capital is allocated effectively in the banking sector, economies can grow in a manner that is sustainable and stable over the long term.

The financial environment has become more volatile with increasing globalization and financial integration. Banks face more risks because of the increasing interconnectedness of financial markets. Because banks have the highest leverage of firms in any industry, the banking sector is more critical to financial stability than other sectors. Governments also get involved in the financial system, in order to ensure that there is financial stability and to protect banks' investors and customers. Bank deposits are often insured by governments, so that governments operate as the final guarantor if there is a bank failure. Besides these safety nets, national governments are concerned with banking regulations and supervision. Banking regulators monitor banking activities and systemic risks in order to ensure financial stability in the banking sector. Regulators attempt to ensure the safety and soundness of the banking system. In order to protect banks from bankruptcy and the costs of financial distress, regulators impose minimum capital requirements on banks. The purpose of minimum capital requirements is to prevent a bank's financial problems from spreading and threatening financial stability.

This chapter is structured as follows. The next section discusses the role of capital in the banking sector. The loss absorption function of capital and the key banking risks are reviewed. Section 3 defines economic capital and regulatory capital. Section 4 reviews the banking regulations on capital requirements. The Basel Capital Accords are discussed. Section 5 presents a literature review on the economic impacts of capital requirements. The costs and benefits of higher capital requirements are reviewed. The final section concludes the chapter.

2 The Role of Capital; Key Banking Risks

Capital in banks plays a critical role in the safety and soundness of the banking system. Capital is held to protect depositors. Furthermore, bank capital builds and maintains confidence in the banking sector. The main role of bank capital is to absorbe large unexpected losses. Capital in banks is a substitute for the transfer of risk, and is a buffer to protect a bank against costly unexpected shocks. Capital protects the safety of the bank (Schroeck 2002, p. 141). Banks face various kinds of risks that may cause bank losses. Credit risk, market risk, operational risk, liquidity risk, reputational risk, business risk, and systemic risk are the key risks for banks.

The most important risk that banks face is credit risk, because the business of financial institutions is largely, extending credit to clients. The Basel Committee on Banking Supervision (BCBS) (1999) defined credit risk as the potential that a bank borrower or counterparty will fail to meet its obligations in accordance with the agreed terms. Credit risk arises from an unexpected deterioration in the credit quality of a counterparty (Saita 2007, p. 68). For most banks, loans are the largest source of credit risk.

Market risk is the risk of losses from balance sheet and off-balance-sheet positions arising from the movements of market prices (Bessis 2015, p. 189). Market risk involves other risks, such as the risk of changes in interest rates and exchange rates. Ultimately, market risk arises from changing market conditions. Market risk exposure relates not only to the assets and liabilities on the balance sheet but also to off-balance sheet positions such as securitized products and derivatives.

The main cause of many risks for financial institutions is mismatching. If financial institutions were able to match their assets and liabilities (for instance, maturities, interest rate and currencies) perfectly, then the only risk they faced would be credit risk. Nevertheless, it is not practicable for a bank to match all its assets and liabilities.

Liquidity risk is the risk that an entity does not meet its commitments on time because sufficient liquid assets are not available. Banks and financial institutions collect deposits or funds and place them in investments and loans with different maturities. Liquidity risk and the cost of liquidity arise from the gaps between maturities.

Operational risk is defined as the risk of loss resulting from inadequate or failed internal processes, people, and systems, or from external events (BCBS 2005, p. 140). Losses from operational risk arise from a range of operational weaknesses including inadequate systems, management failure, faulty controls, fraud, human error, natural and man-made catastrophes (e.g., earthquakes, terrorism) and other non-financial risks (Crouhy et al. 2014, p. 35).

Credit risk, market risk, liquidity risk, and operational risk are the most important risks in the banking sector. Business risk, which is related to a bank's long-term business strategy, reputational risk, which damages corporate trust, and systemic risk can also cause losses in banks. The danger of systemic risk has been shown in the global financial crisis. Systemic risk is the risk that one financial institution affects its counterparties with a domino effect and threatens the stability of the financial system as a whole.

3 Regulatory Capital Versus Economic Capital in Banking

In order to maintain safety and soundness in the banking industry, regulators demand that banks have enough capital for the risks that they run. Regulatory capital can be defined as the minimum amount of capital that the regulators require a bank to maintain. Banks must maintain regulatory capital in order to be protected from financial risks and failures. The Basel Committee on Banking Supervision (BCBS) has developed international regulatory capital standards through a number of capital accords. Although the Basel Capital Accords are international guidelines, the regulators of the member countries implement the framework. The Basel Capital Accords are reviewed in the following section.

Economic capital is also related to the risks faced by a bank. Economic capital acts as a buffer that provides protection against all the risks faced by a bank. The BCBS (2008) defines economic capital as the methods and practices that allow a bank to attribute capital to cover the economic effects of its risk-taking activities. Although economic capital is conceptually similar to regulatory capital, it differs from regulatory capital in the sense that economic capital is calculated internally by the bank itself, and the calculation methodology and risk parameters may be different from those of the regulator's framework. Regulatory capital is mandatory capital, and it is calculated according to the rules and methodologies of the regulators. However, economic capital is an estimate of the necessary capital and is used internally by the bank to run its business and manage its own risks. The estimate of the economic capital can be different from the minimum required regulatory capital, because the bank may include risks that are not considered in calculating the regulatory capital, or may use different methodologies to estimate the economic capital.

Economic capital is the amount of capital that a bank needs to be able to absorb unexpected losses up to a certain time horizon at a given confidence level. Most banks calculate economic capital on a monthly or quarterly basis, and the confidence level depends on the risk appetite of the bank. In the measurement of economic capital, risks from certain activities or exposures are identified, and those risks are measured and quantified. After the aggregation of the risks, capital is allocated to them. A wide range of risk measures is used. Standard deviation, Value at Risk (VaR), Expected Shortfall (ES), and spectral and distorted risk measures are commonly used to measure risks. In practice, VaR and ES are the two most widely used risk measures, with VaR being the most widely used in banking. VaR is more easily explained and understood, but it may not always satisfy the subadditivity condition and this leads to a lack of coherence. ES is coherent and it makes capital allocation and internal limit setting consistent with the overall portfolio measure of risk. However, it is not easily interpreted. Economic capital measures are used in decision making areas such as profitability, pricing and portfolio optimization. Economic capital measures also influence senior management decisions (BCBS 2009, pp. 8–21).

4 Banking Regulations on Capital Requirement

The Basel Committee on Banking Supervision issues regulatory documents concerning the minimum adequate capital for banks. The Basel Committee on Banking Supervision was founded in 1974 by the governors of the central banks of the Group of Ten (G10) countries, following the breakdown of the Bretton Woods system. The globalization and internationalization of banking forced national regulators to consider a common regulatory framework for the banking sector. Capital adequacy is the primary focus of the Committee. The Committee aims to strengthen the stability of the international banking system and decrease the competitive inequality among international banks.

The Basel I Accord was published in 1988 and only includes credit risk in the determination of regulatory capital. Basel I was revised in 1996, when market risk was included. The Committee introduced Basel II in 2004. Basel II comprises three pillars -minimum capital requirements, a supervisory review process, and market discipline. Operational risk was included in the risk calculation. Risk measurement methods were enhanced with Basel II. Following the global financial crisis, Basel III was introduced, in 2010. Basel III covers a comprehensive set of reforms to Basel II.

The Basel Capital Accords are international guidelines to encourage convergence across the world towards common standards in the banking sector. Although they are not legally binding, the Basel Capital Accords have been adopted by the regulators of many countries. However, the implementation of international banking standards has some limitations in the real world. First, it takes several years for countries to make changes to their local legislative and regulatory frameworks. Secondly, some countries are not applying the Basel standards to the whole banking industry: they may exempt small banks from adopting the standards. Thirdly, the national regulators and individual banks implement the standards with a considerable degree of interpretation. For example, when the European Capital Requirements Directive IV transposed Basel III into EU law, European banks were exempted from deducting investments in insurance entities from their core capital (Crouhy et al. 2014, pp. 67, 68).

4.1 Basel I

The Basel Committee on Banking Supervision decided to work on convergence in the measurement of capital adequacy because of the growing international risks of the 1980s. The Latin American debt crisis in the early 1980s increased concern about the deteriorating capital ratios of the main international banks. The Committee prepared a weighted approach to the measurement of risk both on and off the banks' balance sheets. The aim of the Committee was to strengthen the stability of the international banking system and to remove the competitive inequality caused by differences in the national capital requirements. The Basel Capital Accord was approved by the G10 governors and released to banks in 1988. The 1988 Accord was introduced to all countries that had active international banks (BCBS 2015, p. 2).

Banks are required to maintain a capital amount equal to at least 8 percent (which is called the Cooke ratio) of their total risk-weighted assets. Regulatory capital consists of two components, Tier 1 capital (core capital) and Tier 2 capital (supplementary capital). Tier 1 capital includes equity capital (stock issues) and disclosed reserves. According to the Basel Accord, at least 50 % of a bank's capital must be contained in equity capital and disclosed reserves (Tier 1 capital). Tier 2 capital includes undisclosed reserves, revaluation reserves, general provisions/ general loan-loss reserves, hybrid debt capital instruments, and subordinated term debt. Each type of bank asset has a risk weight that reflects its riskiness. There are five risk weights, which are 0, 10, 20, 50 and 100 %. Basel I addressed only credit risk.

Basel I has been adopted in more than 100 countries, and Basel II has not yet replaced Basel I in many countries. Europe adopted Basel II in 2008. On the other hand, the United States has not yet adopted Basel II. Larger banks in the United States will move directly to adopting Basel III (Crouhy et al. 2014, p. 72). Although Basel I was successful in forcing banks to maintain higher capital ratios, it has been argued that Basel I encouraged banks to use regulatory capital arbitrage techniques, particularly securitization (Jablecki 2009, 16). Regulatory capital arbitrage techniques enable banks to lower their capital requirements while keeping the risk level unchanged. Capital arbitrage lowers the efficiency of the Basel Capital Accords (Balthazar 2006, pp. 35-36).

Besides the negative effects of regulatory capital arbitrage, there are other deficiencies in the Basel I framework. Risk sensitivity does not exist in Basel I. The risk weights do not adequately reflect the riskiness of bank assets. There is also a "one size fits all" approach: the requirements are the same for all banks, despite the differences in their risk levels, sophistication, and activity types. It is also argued that Basel I focused primarily on credit risk and ignored the other risks that are faced by banks. Although market risks arising from banks' exposures to foreign exchange, traded debt securities, equities, commodities and options were incorporated into the capital requirement measurement by the Market Risk Amendment in 1996, there are still other risks like operational risk, reputation risk, strategic risk, and so on (Balthazar 2006, pp. 35-36).

4.2 Basel II

Despite the deficiencies of Basel I, it was beneficial to the banking industry because it raise the capital amounts in the banking sector. In order to develop a more sophisticated regulatory framework, the Basel Committee started on Basel II. The Basel Committee issued a proposal in 1999 to replace Basel I. The final proposal was published in 2004. BCBS (2015) states that Basel II aims to improve the way in which regulatory capital requirements reflect underlying risks, and to deal better with the financial innovations. The Basel II regulation framework comprises three pillars, minimum capital requirements, a supervisory review process and market discipline.

The definition of capital is the same under Basel II as it was under Basel I. Banks must maintain a minimum capital of 8 percent of their risk-weighted assets. However, there are two key changes relating to the capital requirement. First, two more advanced approaches for calculating credit risk are introduced. Risk sensitivity and flexibility are increased through an updated standardized approach and new internal ratings-based (IRB) approaches. Second, Basel II extended the risk calculation to include operational risk. Thus, risk-weighted assets are the sum of the assets subject to market risk, credit risk, and operational risk. Banks may use one of three different approaches — the basic indicator approach, the standardized approach and the advanced measurement approach — to measure their operational risk.

The second pillar in the Basel regulation framework is the supervisory review process, which aims not only to ensure that banks have adequate capital, but also to encourage banks to use better risk management techniques to monitor and manage their risks. Banks are expected to strengthen their risk management, apply internal limits, strengthen the level of provisions and reserves, and improve internal controls. Banks should apply forward-looking stress tests to identify possible events or changes in market conditions that may have an adverse impact. The second pillar gives a clear role to the national supervisory authorities. Supervisors are expected to evaluate how well banks are assessing their capital requirements against their risks. The supervisors are also expected to intervene in banks where appropriate. Supervisors should intervene at an early stage to prevent capital from falling below the minimum required levels and take rapid remedial action if capital is not maintained or restored.

The third pillar aims to strengthen market discipline. A set of disclosure requirements has been defined to increase the transparency of each bank's risk profile and risk policy. Disclosure requirements cover a qualitative description of the risk management objectives, policies and techniques of the bank, and quantitative details of the scope of application, capital structure (elements and instruments), capital adequacy, pillar 1 risks (credit, market, and operational risks) including equities and securitization holdings, and interest rate risk in the banking book (Docherty and Viort 2014, p. 132).

The 2007–2008 global financial crisis and the failure of many banks revealed that Basel II was not capable of covering all risks. Basel II was criticized for being a failed piece of bank regulation. However, this was a harsh criticism because Basel II was newly implemented in Europe at the time of the crisis, and the United States had not implemented Basel II when the crisis started. In addition, Basel II was imposed on commercial banks and not on investment banks. However, the crisis showed that Basel II has many potential inadequacies and that it needs reform (Crouhy et al. 2014, pp. 73–75). According to Roubini (2008), capital adequacy ratios are procyclical in Basel II and promote credit booms in good times and credit busts in bad times. There is little emphasis on liquidity risk management. Excessive reliance on internal risk management models and rating agencies are the other weaknesses of Basel II.

4.3 Basel III

While the national regulators and banks were in the process of adopting and implementing Basel II, the 2007–2008 global financial crisis began. According to the Basel Committee, the causes of the crisis were excessive leverage, weak capital bases, poor funding profiles and insufficient liquidity buffers. The Basel Committee immediately revised the market risk framework of Basel II, and the July 2009 revision is known as Basel 2.5. This revision introduced stressed value-at-risk calculations for the market risk capital calculation. Risk weights for resecuritization exposures were increased. Losses resulting from credit migration and liquidity were considered in the calculation of capital.

In 2010 the Basel Committee introduced Basel III, which contains a comprehensive set of reforms to Basel II. The three pillars of Basel II are revised and strengthened by Basel III. Basel III was a response to a global financial crisis that showed that the financial system was not sufficiently resilient. Basel III aims to increase the resilience of the banks against shocks arising from financial and economic stress. Basel III also aims to improve the supervision and risk management of the banking sector. The Basel Committee and the Financial Stability Board (FSB) have worked in collaboration, and FSB has the responsibility of coordinating and monitoring the implementation of the regulatory reforms.

Basel III extends the Basel II framework with several innovations. The quality and level of the capital base are improved by changes to the components of Tier 1 capital and Tier 2 capital. The emphasis on equity capital is increased, since equity capital is the primary shock-absorber for banks during periods of stress. Basel III gives a strict definition of what comprises "Common Equity Tier 1" capital — common shares and retained earnings. The total minimum capital requirement ratio has not changed. It is set at 8 %. However, Basel III introduces a capital conservation buffer and a countercyclical capital buffer to avoid breaches of the minimum capital requirements and to protect banks from future potential losses. The total minimum capital ratio increases by 2.5 % with the capital conservation buffer (Docherty and Viort 2014, pp. 147–149).

The aim of the Basel III capital framework is to capture all material risks. The coverage of risks is improved by considering risks related to capital market activities (trading book, securitization products, and counterparty credit risk on over-the-counter derivatives and repos). Risk weightings and the risk coverage are enhanced. In order to constrain the build-up of leverage in the banking sector, a leverage ratio that acts as a supplementary measure to the risk-based capital requirements is included in the framework. Basel II includes no measures for liquidity. However, the absence of liquidity standards damaged the banking sector in the global financial crisis. Basel III introduces internationally harmonized global liquidity standards. Excessive interconnectedness among systemically important banks transmitted shocks across the financial system in the global financial crisis, so Basel III brings in additional requirements for systemically important institutions.

Basel III is a quick response to the global financial crisis. However, the innovations of Basel III have been critized for several reasons. The Basel Committee assumed that excessive leverage, weak capital bases, poor funding profiles, and insufficient liquidity buffers were the causes of the global financial crisis. Basel III raises the quality and levels of capital required to strengthen the banking sector against the causes of the crisis. The Basel Accords focus too much on capital adequacy. Low levels of capital were a principal cause in only a few big bank failures. Although it was revealed in the global financial crisis that both internal models and the external ratings agencies for credit assessment produced unreliable

Table 1 Key aspects of Basel I, II and III

Basel I	Basel II	Basel III
– min. capital amount 8 % – covers only credit risk – risk weighted measurement of credit risk – market risk is introduced (1996 Amendment) – "one size fits all" approach	– min. capital amount 8 % – more risk-sensitive – provides incentives for better risk management – new approaches for risk measurement – operational risk is introduced – supervisory review process – market dicipline	– min. capital amount 10.5 % – enhanced risk coverage – rise in overall capital ratios – capital conservation buffer – counter-cyclical buffer – capital requirement for systemically important banks – leverage ratio – liquidity ratio

risk indicators, reliance on internal and agency assessments continues in Basel III (Docherty and Viort 2014, pp. 161–163). Another criticism is that the new regulatory framework is too costly. The Institute of International Finance (IIF) estimated the cost of Basel III implementation in the G20 countries at US$1.3 trillion in 2011. It is also suggested that Basel III is too complex and should be replaced by a simple leverage ratio (Crouhy et al. 2014, p. 113) (Table 1).

5 Literature Review on Economic Impact of Capital Requirements

The Financial Stability Board (FSB) and the BCBS established two working groups, the Macroeconomic Assessment Group (MAG) and the Long-term Economic Impact (LEI) Group, in order to measure the macroeconomic impacts of the stronger bank capital and liquidity requirements. The MAG report (BCBS, 2010a) investigates the impact of a one percentage point increase in bank capital ratios by aggregating the outputs of macroeconomic models from 15 member countries and a number of international organizations. The report employs forecasting and policy analysis models to estimate the impact on GDP. A total of 97 sets of model results and simulations were submitted to carry out these estimates. The findings reveal that the overall effect of a one percentage point capital increase would be a widening of the lending spreads by a maximum of 15.5 basis points and a reduction in the level of GDP by a maximum of 0.15 %.

The LEI report (BCBS, 2010b) assesses both the economic costs and the benefits of the stronger capital and liquidity regulations. The report uses data from a total of 6,660 banks from 13 OECD countries over the period from 1993 to 2007. The study on cost impacts concludes that a one percentage point change in the capital ratio raises loan spreads by 13 basis points. Loan spreads are estimated to rise by 14 basis points because of the cost of meeting the liquidity standards. The report also examines the impact of increases in bank capital and liquidity on the long-term level of output. Macroeconomic models find that a one percentage point increase in capital reduces long term GDP by 0.09 %. GDP reduction associated with the liquidity requirements is 0.08 %.

There are other studies that evaluate the cost of higher capital requirements on economic activity. Recent studies on the cost of capital reveal that there are opportunity costs, in terms of reduced lending and economic activity, of higher bank capital requirements. Higher capital requirements could increase lending rates, which in turn would decrease credit levels. Sutorova and Teply (2013) study the impact of Basel III on the lending rates of European Union banks. They employ a simultaneous equations model where banks choose the optimal level of capital. Using data for 594 banks in the European Union during the period 2006–2011, they find that a one percent increase in the common equity ratio would increase lending rates by 19 basis points and that full adoption of Basel III would decrease the level of loans by 2% from the current level. However they do not expect a larger drop in loans because many European banks are already complying with the Basel III capital requirements and the elasticity of demand for loans is relatively low. Fraisse et al. (2015) measure the impact of bank capital requirements on corporate borrowing and business activity. In their study they use a large sample of loans extended by French banks to French firms over the period 2008–2011. Their findings reveal that a one percentage point increase in capital requirements leads to a reduction in lending of approximately 10%. Noss and Toffano (2014) estimate the effects of capital requirements on lending using data from UK banks. Their findings support the theory that an increase in the aggregate bank capital requirements is associated with a reduction in lending. The impact on GDP growth is found to be statistically insignificant.

Despite the unfavorable effects of the capital requirements on lending and GDP growth, the costs of a higher capital ratio appear to be small when compared to the estimated benefits. Better capitalized banks are less vulnerable to shocks. The literature on the benefits of capital requirements reveals that greater bank capital reduces the probability and costs of banking crises (BCBS 2010b; de Bandt and Chahad 2015; De Ramon et al. 2012; Miles et al. 2013). The LEI report (BCBS 2010b) uses three different methods (reduced-form models, calibrated portfolio models and calibrated stress test models) in order to estimate the relationship between regulatory requirements and the probability of a crisis. Using banking data for 13 OECD countries over the period between 1980 and 2008, the report concludes that there is a significant reduction in the likelihood of a banking crisis with higher levels of capitalization and liquidity. Increasing the capital ratio from 7 % to 8 % reduces the probability of a banking crisis by one third. The findings also support the argument that higher capital and liquidity standards are likely to reduce not just the probability, but also the severity, of banking crises. The report also analyse the net benefits of the capital requirements. Net benefits are measured by the percentage change in the yearly level of output. The findings conclude that the net benefits are positive and there is considerable scope to increase capital and liquidity standards while yielding positive net benefits.

6 Conclusion

The banking sector is susceptible to risk because it carries out intermediary business. Globalization and increased financial integration have decreased the volatility of the banking sector. In addition, bank operations have become more complex and sophisticated as a result of financial innovations. The variety of risks has increased in the banking sector over time. Credit risk, market risk, operational risk, liquidity risk, reputational risk, business risk, and systemic risk are the key risks for banks, with credit risk, market risk, liquidity risk, and operational risk being the most important of these. However, systemic risk also became a crucial risk for the banking sector in the global financial crisis.

Bank capital plays an important role in protecting banks against risks. It is a buffer that absorbs unexpected losses made by banks. Banks maintain capital in order to protect themselves against financial risks and failures. Banking regulators also aim to ensure the safety and soundness of the banking system. They impose minimum capital requirements on banks in order to protect them from bankruptcy and the costs of financial distress. Banks allocate regulatory capital and economic capital to match their risks. Regulatory capital is mandatory capital that is calculated according to the rules and methodologies of the regulators, while economic capital is calculated internally by the bank itself and is the estimate that is used internally of the capital needed to run the business and manage the bank's risks. Economic capital measures are used in decision-making areas such as profitability, pricing, and portfolio optimization, and to assist with senior management decisions.

A common regulatory framework for capital allocation in the banking sector was proposed because of the growing international risks. For that purpose, the Basel Capital Accords were prepared by the Basel Committee on Banking Supervision. The Basel Accords aim to enhance the risk management functions of banks and to strengthen the stability of the international banking system. The Basel Capital Accords are international guidelines to encourage convergence toward common standards in the banking sector across the world.

The Basel I Accord, which was introduced in 1988, advised banks to maintain capital equal to at least 8 percent of their total risk-weighted assets. Basel I became successful in the banking industry by raising the amount of capital in the banking sector. Basel I has been adopted in more than 100 countries. Basel I covers only credit risk, and it is not risk-sensitive. Market risks were incorporated into the capital measurement by the 1996 Amendment. The Committee started to develop a more sophisticated regulatory framework in 1999, and Basel II was introduced in 2004. Basel II comprises three pillars — minimum capital requirements, a supervisory review process and market discipline. Risk coverage is enhanced and risk sensitivity and flexibility are increased. New approaches to risk calculation are included. However, the global financial crisis revealed that the Basel II requirements are not sufficient to cover all risks. The Committee made a comprehensive set of reforms to Basel II and introduced Basel III in 2010. The quality and level of the capital base are raised, the coverage of risks is improved, and liquidity and leverage ratios are introduced. The minimum capital requirement is increased with the capital conservation buffer.

The economic impacts of the higher capital requirements have been studied in the literature. There is an overall consensus that higher capital requirements increase lending rates and widen the loan spreads in the banking sector. There is also a small reduction in the level of loans because of the increased lending rates. On the other hand, higher bank capital reduces the probability and costs of banking crises. The costs of the higher capital ratio appear to be small when compared to the estimates of the benefits. The net result is positive.

References

Balthazar L (2006) From Basel 1 to Basel 3. Palgrave Macmillan UK, London

Basel Committee on Banking Supervision (1999) Principles for the management of credit risk. Bank for International Settlements, Basel

Basel Committee on Banking Supervision (2005) International convergence of capital measurement and capital standards. Bank for International Settlements, Basel

Basel Committee on Banking Supervision (2008) Range of practices and issues in economic capital modelling. Bank for International Settlements, Basel

Basel Committee on Banking Supervision (2009) Range of practices and issues in economic capital framework. Bank for International Settlements, Basel

Basel Committee on Banking Supervision (2010a) Assessing the macroeconomic impact of the transition to stronger capital and liquidity requirements. Bank for International Settlements, Basel

Basel Committee on Banking Supervision (2010b) An assessment of the long-term impact of stronger capital and liquidity requirements. Bank for International Settlements, Basel

Basel Committee on Banking Supervision (2015) A brief history of the Basel Committee. Bank for International Settlements, Basel

Bessis J (2015) Risk management in banking, 4th ed. John Wiley & Sons, West Sussex

Crouhy M, Galai D, Mark R (2014) The essentials of risk management, 2nd ed. McGraw-Hill, New York

de Bandt O, Chahad M (2015) A DSGE model to assess the post crisis regulation of universal banks. European Banking Authority, 4th Annual Research Workshop

De Ramon S, Iscenko Z, Osborne M, Straughan M, Andrews P (2012) Measuring the impact of prudential policy on the macroeconomy. Occasional paper series 42

Docherty A, Viort F (2014) Better banking: understanding and addressing the failures in risk management, governance and regulation. Regulation of the banking industry. John Wiley & Sons, West Sussex

Fraisse H, LÉ M, Thesmar D (2015) The real effects of bank capital requirements, HEC Paris research paper no FIN-2013-988

Jablecki J (2009) The impact of Basel I capital requirements on bank behavior and the efficacy of monetary policy. Int J Econ Sci Appl Res 2(1):16–35

Miles D, Yang J, Marcheggiano G (2013) Optimal bank capital. Econ J 123(567):1–37

Noss J, Toffano P (2014) Estimating the impact of changes in aggregate bank capital requirements during an upswing, Bank of England working paper, no 494

Roubini N (2008) Financial crises, financial stability, and reform: supervision and regulation of financial systems in a world of financial globalization. Financ Develop Rep 2008:33–46

Saita F (2007) Value at risk and bank capital management: risk adjusted performances, capital management and capital allocation decision making. Academic Press, Massachusetts

Schroeck G (2002) Risk management and value creation in financial institutions. John Wiley & Sons, New Jersey

Sutorova B, Teply P (2013) The impact of Basel III on lending rates of EU banks. Finance a uver-CJEF 63(3):226–243

Serpil Kuzucu is a banking expert and has been working for a multinational banking group's affiliate in Istanbul for more than ten years. She holds a PhD in banking from Marmara University School of Banking. She has an MA and BA degree in economics from Marmara University. Her research areas are emerging markets and banking.

Narman Kuzucu is an assistant professor of finance and accounting at Beykent University, Turkey. Earlier in his career, he worked for several multinationals as financial manager, auditor and advisor. He has more than fifteen years of experience in several industries including banking, energy and manufacturing. He holds a BA in economics, an MA and a PhD in Accounting and Finance from Marmara University. His research areas are corporate finance and banking.

Part II
Managing Risks in Capital Markets

The Calibration of Market Risk Measures During Period of Economic Downturn: Market Risks and Measures

John Weirstrass Muteba Mwamba

Abstract This study explores the calibration of market risk measures during period of economic downturn. This calibration is done in two frameworks: firstly individual profit and loss distribution is modelled using two different types of extreme value distribution namely: the generalized extreme value (GEV) distribution, and the generalized Pareto distribution (GPD). The resulting shape parameters are all positive indicating that these distributions can in fact capture the negative skewness and excess kurtosis of the profit and loss (P&L) distribution during period of economic downturn. We show that the presence of such positive shape parameters indicates the existence of large probabilities of extreme price drops in the left tail of the P&L distribution. Based on these results the second framework used in this study builds two multivariate copula distributions with GEV and GPD marginals. This procedure captures the dependence structure of stock markets during periods of financial crisis. To illustrate the computation of market risk measures; we consider one elliptical copula (student t copula) and one Archimedean copula (Gumbel copula). Using two stock market indices we compute what we refer to as EVT based mark risk measures and the copula based market risk measures for both the left and right tails of the P&L distribution. Our results suggest that copula based risk measures are more reliable in predicting the behavior of market risks during period of economic downturn.

JEL Classification G1 • G13 • G14

J.W. Muteba Mwamba (✉)
Department of Economics and Econometrics, University of Johannesburg, Auckland Park, South Africa
e-mail: johnmu@uj.ac.za

H. Dinçer, Ü. Hacioğlu (eds.), *Risk Management, Strategic Thinking and Leadership in the Financial Services Industry*, Contributions to Management Science, DOI 10.1007/978-3-319-47172-3_7

1 Introduction

After the 2007–2008 financial crisis; the practice of risk management has undergone significant changes related to market risk modelling. The Basel III a recently modified version of the late Basel II aimed at determining the minimum capital requirements that financial institutions need to keep on their balance sheet in order to promote stability and make global financial institutions more resilient to financial crises. Since then, there is a significant increase in the number of academic publications aimed at proposing new risk models that can predict large losses observed during financial crises. Furthermore the new Basel III encourages financial institutions (banks) to develop their own internal market risk models under the supervision of the national central bank authorities in order to regularly meet the minimum capital requirement. These market risk models make use of different risk factors including interest rate, currencies spread, credit spread, equity prices and their respective volatility, as well as other balance sheet items. The minimum capital requirement is calculated using the value-at-risk (VaR) and the expected shortfall (ES) measures which are essentially the quantile of the profit and loss (P&L) distribution. In many applications the P&L distribution is essentially assumed to be Gaussian (see for example Longin 1996)

This study contributes to the ongoing literature by calibrating different market risk measures using a combination of different extreme value theory (EVT) distributions, GARCH processes, and copulas; and highlighting their impact in predicting extreme losses during financial crises. The study explores the computation of two market risk measures (VaR and ES) under non-normality conditions i.e. under periods of economic downturn. To overcome the effect of extreme market conditions on the modeling of the market risk measures, two frameworks are considered in this study: -firstly we consider individual market risk factor and compute its corresponding market risk measures by making use of two extreme value distributions namely the generalized extreme value (GEV) distribution and the generalized Pareto distribution (GPD). Secondly we consider a portfolio made of a finite number of assets or risk factors and build their corresponding joint distribution using multivariate copulas. Both elliptical and Archimedean unconditional copulas are used. Although this technique is relatively known by few lucky quants and financial practitioners; the contribution of this study is in stressing on the use of the multivariate copula distributions in market risk modeling with GEV distribution as marginal rather than the usual GPD distribution (see for example Frad and Zouari 2014). The two market risk measures (VaR and ES) are computed for the lower and upper tails of empirical P&L distribution.

We illustrate the computation of copula and the EVT market risk measure with two stock indices collected from the Bloomberg database. The two indices considered are the weekly U.S. SP500, and UK FTSE100 from April, the 17th of 2000 to February, the 29th of 2016.

The computation of the copula and EVT market risk measures is done in three different steps. The first step consists in removing the effects of autocorrelation and heteroscedasticity pattern in the returns series. This is done by fitting the return series to a ARMA(1,1)—APARCH(1,1)[1] model of order one. The estimation results are reported in Table 1. All coefficients are found to be statistically significant, and lead to the conclusion that both the leverage effect and the Taylor effect[2] have significant impact on the stock market returns.

The second step involves the fitting of the standardized residuals of the ARMA-APARCH model to the GEV and GPD respectively. The estimated coefficients are reported in Table 2. The shape parameters are all found to be positive indicating that the presence of negative skewness and excess kurtosis during period of financial crisis. The presence of such excess skewness and kurtosis indicates serious deviations from the normal distribution and may suggest that the P&L empirical distribution is asymmetric and exhibit a fat-tailed behaviour. During financial crisis, a positive shape parameter implies extreme price drops with large probabilities on the left tail of the P&L distribution. Many studies (Giacomini and Hardle 2005; Hotta and Palaro 2006; Hotta et al. 2008) intended to deal with the fat-tail behavior of stock markets have failed to highlight these characteristic features of fat tailed distributions. These features have prevented many of these EVT models from being of practical use in risk management during financial crisis period as they result in unrealistic market risk measures.

Based on these characteristic features, the third step consists in modeling the dependence structure of P&L distributions during financial crisis. We do so by building two multivariate copula distributions: the first with an elliptical copula (student t distribution) and second with an Archimedean copula (Gumbel copula). Lastly the four step consists in computing the copula market risk measures for both the left and right tail of the P&L distribution. These market risk measures are reported in Tables 3, 4, and 5 for the GPD, GEV, and copula distribution respectively. We find that the GEV based risk measure (return level) is invariant of the significance level at which it is calculated. Copula based risk measures are found to be coherent since they are less than the sum of individual risks. We find that during financial crisis copula based market risk measures are larger than during period of tranquility. This can be explained by the fact that stock market tend to co-move together in downturn than in normal period. The rest the study is structured as follows. Section 10.1 will discuss in details the process fitting the data to an ARMA—GARCH process in order to remove the effect of the autocorrelation and heteroscedasticity in the data. This will be followed by the fitting of the standardized residuals to the GEV and GPD distribution; and the building of the multivariate copula distribution. Section 10.3 will present the empirical analysis, while Sect. 10.4 will conclude.

[1]ARMA(1,1)-APARCH(1,1) stands for the Autoregressive Moving Average with Asymmetric Power Autoregressive Conditional Heteroscedasticity model proposed by Ding et al. (1993).

[2]The Taylor effect: the sample correlation of absolute returns are larger than that of squared returns (Taylor 1986).

2 Methodology

The computation of the copula and EVT based market risk measures involves three steps. These steps are described in details below:

STEP 1: The filtering of the returns i.e. removing the effect of autocorrelation and heteroscedasticity in the data is done by fitting the returns series to autoregressive model of the following form:

$$r_t = a_0 + a_1 r_{t-1} + b_1 u_{t-1} + u_t \tag{1}$$

$$u_t \rightarrow N(0,\ \sigma_t)$$

$$\sigma^{\delta}{}_t = \omega + \sum\nolimits_{i=1}^{p} \alpha_i(|u_{t-i}| - \gamma_i.u_{t-i}).^{\delta} + \sum\nolimits_{j=1}^{q} \beta_j \sigma^{\delta}{}_{t-j} \tag{2}$$

where r_t, u_t, σ_t, δ, and γ_i are the returns series of a market risk factor, the error term of the model, the volatility of the return, the Taylor effect, and the leverage effect respectively. This model is estimated by making use of the maximum likelihood method.

STEP 2: the residuals of the above-mentioned model are after standardized and fitted to two extreme value theory (EVT) distributions namely the GEV and the GPD distributions. We refer to these standardized residuals as filtered returns. The process of fitting these filtered returns to EVT distributions is described below.

2.1 *The Generalised Extreme Value Distribution*

The process of fitting filtered returns of each risk factor to the GEV distribution is often referred to as the Block of Maxima method. This method collects the largest losses (profits) of each monthly, quarterly or yearly block period and fits them to the GEV distribution. Assume that $X_1, X_2, \ldots, X_n$ is a sequence of *iid* random variables representing the largest losses (profits) for the left tail (right tail) of the P&L distribution of risk factors with common density function F. The limiting distribution of the normalised largest losses (profit) $X_1,\ X_2,\ \ldots,\ X_n$ is known as the generalized extreme value distribution and is expressed as:

$$H_{(\xi,\mu,\sigma)}(x) = \exp\left\{-\left(1 + \xi\frac{x-\mu}{\sigma}\right)\right\}^{-1/\xi} \tag{3}$$

ξ represents the shape parameter of the tail distribution, μ its location, and σ its scale parameter. When $\xi = \alpha^{-1} > 0$, Eq. (3) corresponds to the Fréchet type of distributions which includes some well-known fat-tailed distributions such as the Pareto, Cauchy and Student-t distributions. When $\xi = \alpha^{-1} < 0$ Eq. (3) corresponds to the Weibull type of distributions which includes among others the Pareto type II distribution. When $\xi = 0$ Eq. (3) corresponds to the Gumbel type of distributions which include most exponential distributions.

Muteba Mwamba et al. (2016) show that the Gumbel type of distributions has zero skewness and displays symmetric behaviour in its right and left tails. Its tail index value is infinite, implying that all moments of the distribution are either finite or zero. Generally when $\xi \neq 0$, Eq. (3) imposes a truncation of the probability distribution and a distinct asymmetric behaviour in the right and left tails such that when there is high probability of the realization of an extreme event at one tail, there is also an absolute maxima (or minima) in the other tail beyond which values of ξ have zero probability (Embrechts et al. 1997). Following Gilli and Kellezi (2006), we re-parameterise the generalized extreme value distribution above in order to derive a tail risk measure which is referred to as the "return level":

$$H_{(\xi,\sigma,R^K)}(x) = \begin{cases} \exp\left\{-\left[\frac{\xi}{\sigma}\left(x - R^k\right) + \left(\log\left(1-\frac{1}{k}\right)\right)\right]^{-\xi}\right\}^{-1/\xi}; \forall \xi \neq 0 \\ \left(1-\frac{1}{k}\right)^{\exp\left(-\frac{x-R^k}{\sigma}\right)}; \quad \forall \xi = 0 \end{cases} \tag{4}$$

where R_n^k represents the *return level* that is the maximum loss expected in one out of k periods of length n computed as:

$$R_n^k = H_{\xi,\mu,\sigma}^{-1}\left(1 - \frac{1}{k}\right) \tag{5}$$

The Maximum Likelihood method is used to estimate the parameters of the re-parameterised GEV distribution. It consists in maximizing the following log-likelihood function:

$$L\left(R^k\right) = \max_{\xi,\sigma} L\left(\xi, \sigma, R^k\right) \tag{6}$$

2.2 Generalised Pareto Distribution

To fit the filtered returns of each risk factor to a GPD distribution one needs to have an optimal threshold set in consultation with an experienced risk manager or set by making use of the empirical mean excess function introduced by Davison and Smith (1990). The mean excess function plots the conditional mean of the largest losses (profits) above different thresholds using the following expression:

$$me(u) = \frac{\sum_{i=1}^{N_u} (x_i - u)}{\sum_{i=1}^{N_u} I_{u(x_i > u)}} \tag{7}$$

where $I_u = 1$ if $x_i > u$ and 0, otherwise. N_u is the number of extreme returns over the threshold u. If the empirical mean excess function has a positive gradient above a certain threshold u, it is an indication that the return series follows the GPD with a positive shape parameter ξ. In contrast, an exponentially distributed log-return series would show a horizontal mean excess function, while the short tailed log-return series would have a negatively sloped function.

The process of fitting filtered returns to a GPD distribution is often referred to as the pick over threshold approach. Let X be a vector of filtered returns representing the largest losses for the left tail (or the profits for the right tail) above a specific threshold u, and assume that the density function of X is given by F. The limiting distribution of X above this threshold is known as the GPD distribution and is given by the following expression:

$$G_{\xi,\beta(u)}(x) = \begin{cases} 1 - \left(1 + \xi \frac{x}{\beta(u)}\right)^{-\frac{1}{\xi}}; & \xi \neq 0 \\ \text{1-exp}\left(-\frac{\text{x}}{\beta(\text{u})}\right); & \xi = 0 \end{cases} \tag{8}$$

where ξ is the shape, and u is the threshold parameter, respectively. It is assumed that the random variable x is positive and that $\beta(u) > 0;\ x \geq 0$ for $\xi \geq 0$ and $0 \leq \text{x} \leq -\frac{\beta(\text{u})}{\xi};$ for $\xi < 0$.. The shape parameter ξ is independent of the threshold u. If $\xi > 0$ then $\text{G}_{\xi,\beta(\text{u})}$ is a Pareto distribution, while if $\xi = 0$ then $\text{G}_{\xi,\beta(\text{u})}$ is an exponential distribution. If $\xi < 0$, then $\text{G}_{\xi,\beta(\text{u})}$ is a Pareto type II distribution. These parameters are estimated by making use of the Maximum Likelihood method. The parameters of the GPD distribution are obtained by maximising the following log-likelihood function:

$$\text{L}(\xi, \beta) = -\text{N}_\text{u}\text{Log}(\beta) - \left(1 + \frac{1}{\xi}\right) \sum_{\text{i}=1}^{\text{N}_\text{u}} \text{Log}\left(1 + \frac{\xi \text{x}_\text{i}}{\beta}\right) \tag{9}$$

Embrechts et al. (1997) show that the tail distribution of the GPD distribution can be expressed as follows:

$$\hat{F}(x) = 1 - \frac{N_u}{n}\left(\frac{1 + \hat{\xi}(x - u)}{\hat{\beta}}\right)^{-\frac{1}{\hat{\xi}}} \tag{10}$$

Two risk measures can directly be calculated as quantiles of the GPD distribution—the VaR and the ES. Since the VaR is not a coherent risk measure and doesn't satisfy the diversification principle, it is advisable to use the ES which measures the maximum loss of a portfolio, given that the VaR is exceeded.

$$VaR(p) = u + \frac{\hat{\beta}}{\hat{\xi}}\left(\left(\frac{1-p}{N_u/n}\right)^{-\hat{\xi}} - 1\right) \tag{11}$$

$$ES(p) = E(Y/Y > VaR(p)) = VaR(p) + E(Y - VaR(p)/Y > VaR(p)) \tag{12}$$

$$ES(p) = \frac{VaR(p)}{1-\hat{\xi}} + \frac{\hat{\beta} - \hat{\xi}u}{1-\hat{\xi}} \tag{13}$$

where p is the significance level at which the VaR is computed. For example, when $p = 0.99$, Eqs. (11) and (12) produce the VaR and ES measures at the 99 % significance level. Most VaR and ES methodologies (except historical simulation method) assume that the joint P&L distribution of the risk factors is a multivariate normal distribution. The dependence structure between different risk factors is therefore defined by the correlation between those factors. Correlation is very often incorrectly used to model dependence structure (Embrechts et al. 2002). The authors argue that thought independence of the two random variables can imply that the correlation is equal to zero; generally speaking the opposite is not correct i.e. zero correlation does not imply independence. A more prevalent approach which overcomes this disadvantage is to model the dependency between risk factor with copulas.

STEP 3: consists in modelling the dependence structure between different risk factors with copulas rather than correlation. The word copula comes from the Latin for a "link" or "bond" and was coined by Sklar (1959) who first proved the theorem that a collection of marginal P&L distributions can be coupled together via a copula to form a multivariate distribution. To overcome the effects of the extreme market conditions; we will assume that the marginal P&L distribution are GEV or GPD distributions. Therefore market risk measures will be computed from the simulated data using Monte Carlo simulation methods.

2.3 *Definition of Copula Distribution*

A copula function $C : [0,1]^n \rightarrow [0,1]$ is an n-dimensional copula if it satisfies the following properties:

$$\circ\ \forall u \in [0,1],\ C(1,....,1,\ u,\ 1,....,\ 1) = u,$$

$$\circ\ \forall u_i \in [0,1],\ C(u_1, u_2, u_3, u_4....., u_n) = 0, \text{ if at least one of the } u_i's \text{ equal to zero}$$

There are two families of copulas:—Elliptical copulas and Archimedean copulas. Elliptical copulas are derived from multivariate elliptical distributions. The two most important copulas of this family are the normal (Gaussian) copula and the Student's t-copula. By construction, these two copulas are close to each other in their central parts and become closer in the tails when the number of degrees of freedom of the t-copula increases. The t-copula is an elliptical copula derived from the multivariate t distribution. The t-copula has the advantage of capturing fat-tail behavior observed in financial time series. Let $T\upsilon$ be the standard t-distribution function with υ degrees of freedom and $T_{n,\rho,\upsilon}$ be the multivariate t distribution function with υ degrees of freedom and shape matrix ρ. Then the corresponding t-copula is:

$$C_{n,\rho,\upsilon}(u_1, u_2, u_3 \ldots, u_n) = T_{n,\rho,\upsilon}\left(T_\upsilon^{-1}(u_1), ...,\ T_\upsilon^{-1}(u_n)\right) \tag{14}$$

Since the t-distribution tends to the normal distribution when υ goes to infinity, the t-copula also tends to the normal copula as $\upsilon \to +\infty$.

Archimedean copulas on the other hand allow for a great variety of different dependence structures. This family of copulas include Clayton copula, Franck copula, Joe copula, Symetric Joe copula, Gumbel etc. The dependence structure between different risk factor is embedded into one function of a single parameter called the generator $\phi(\theta)$ for Archimedean copulas. Let for example the generator function for a Gumbel copula be given by:

$$\phi(\theta) = (-\log u)^\theta \tag{15}$$

The Gumbel copula is therefore given by the following expression:

$$C_{n,\theta}(u_1, u_2, u_3 \ldots, u_n) = \exp\left\{-\left[\sum_{i=1}^{n} (-\log u_i)^\theta\right]^{1/\theta}\right\} \tag{16}$$

2.4 Estimation of Copula Parameters

There exist different methods to estimate the parameters of copulas; these include the parametric method (ML method), the inferences function margins, semiparametric and nonparametric method. Given that we have precise marginal distributions which are GEV and GPD distributions, we will make use of the ML method to estimate the parameters of the copula in Eq. (20) shown below. The ML method proceeds as follows. Let F be a multivariate distribution function with continuous marginals F_i and copula C. Then getting the first derivative of Eq. (20) we obtain the joint density function f(.):

$$f(x_1, \ldots, x_2) = c(F_1(x_1), \ldots., F_n(x_n))\prod_{i=1}^{n} f_i(x_i) \tag{17}$$

where f_i is the density function of marginal F_i and c is the density of the copula given by:

$$c(u_1, \ldots., u_n) = \frac{\partial\, C(u_1, \ldots.., u_n)}{\partial\, u_1 \ldots.\partial\, u_n} \tag{18}$$

Let $\delta = (\beta_1, \ldots.., \beta_2, \alpha)$ be the vector of all the parameters to estimate, where β_i is the vector of the parameters of marginal distribution F_i, and α is the vector of the copula parameters. The log-likelihood of the Eq. (17) can be written as:

$$l(\delta) = \sum_{t=1}^{T} \ln c\left(F_1\left(x_1^t;\ \beta_1\right), \ldots., F_n\left(x_n^t;\ \beta_n\right);\ \alpha\right) + \sum_{t=1}^{T}\sum_{i=1}^{n} \ln\left(f_i\left(x_i^t;\ \beta_i\right)\right) \tag{19}$$

2.5 Sklar's Theorem

(Sklar 1959) shows that given an n-dimensional distribution function F with continuous marginals $F_1, F_2, \ldots, F_n$ there exists an n-copula $C : [0, 1]^n \to [0, 1]$ such that:

$$F(x_1, x_2, \ldots., x_n) = C(F_1(x_1), F_2(x_2), \ldots, F_n(x_n)) \tag{20}$$

Conversely given a multivariate distribution function F with marginals $F_1, F_2, \ldots, F_n$, for any $(u_1, u_2, \ldots, u_n)$ in $[0, 1]^n$

$$C(u_1, u_2, \ldots., u_n) = C\left(F_1^{-1}(u_1), F_2^{-1}(u_2), \ldots, F_n^{-1}(u_n)\right) \tag{21}$$

An important practical application of copulas this theorem consists in simulating random variables with predefined marginals and various dependence structures C using Monte-Carlo simulations as follows:

1. Generate n random variables $u_1, \ldots.., u_n$ with uniform marginals and copula C,
2. Apply the inversion method for each u_i in order to generate each x_i:

$$x_i = F_i^{-1}(u_i) \tag{22}$$

where F_i^{-1} denotes the inverse of F_i, i.e. the quantile of F_i

3 Empirical Analysis

In this section we illustrate the application of the three steps discussed above. We consider two weekly stock market indices: the U.S SP500 and the UK FTSE100 indices. The sample period starts from April the 17th, 2000 to February the 29th, 2016; making a total of 829 weekly observations. We first start by fitting the log-return series of each index to an autoregressive model shown in Eqs. (1) and (2). The resulting estimates are reported in Table 1.

This table shows that the coefficients of the leverage effect (gamma) and the Taylor effect (delta) are all statistically significant. The leverage effect shows that bad news have more impact on these stock market volatilities than good news do. The Taylor effect shows that the sample autocorrelation of absolute log returns are larger than that of squared residuals. The rest of the coefficients reported in Table 1 are all significant except the independent terms suggesting that previous shocks and volatilities have a significant impact on current level of return.

To model the effect of the extreme market conditions on the market risk measures, we fit the filtered returns to the left and right tail of the P&L distribution using the GEV and the GPD distributions respectively (Table 2).

The estimated shape parameters for the left tail of the P&L distribution are found to be positive suggesting moderately high probability of price drops during financial crises. Positive shape parameters is an indication that the Fréchet type of distributions which includes well-known fat-tailed distributions such as the Pareto, Cauchy and Student-t distributions best fit the left tail of the P&L distribution. All EVT estimated parameters are statistically significant.

Risk measures under extreme market condition are calculated as the quantile of the GPD distribution. The GPD based VaR and the ES for both the right tail (which

Table 1 ARMA–APARCH model estimates

	SP500		FTSE100	
	Coefficient	T-stats	Coefficient	T-stats
a0	0.1094	9.0718	0.0284	1.669
ar1	−0.878	−63.52	−0.799	−12.580
ma1	0.8263	54.244	0.7575	11.023
w	0.1084	9.45	0.155	0.935
alpha	0.1102	20.4122	0.126	2.1926
Beta	0.8664	67.083	0.83171	6.7711
Gamma	1.0000	2953.93	1.0000	356.808
Delta	0.6506	4.2501	0.9307	2.742
Shape	8.1912	4.4406	9.433	4.012

Table 2 GEV and GPD distribution parameters

	SP500		FTSE100	
	Left	Right	Left	Right
GEV				
ShapeParam	0.5927***	0.2909*	0.3544**	0.4717**
Location	1.1983***	1.3899**	1.2149*	1.2598*
Scale	0.3013***	0.697*	0.4406*	0.613***
GPD				
ShapeParam	0.00129*	0.2063**	0.0013*	0.0012***
Location	0.0506	0.0509*	0.0118	0.01183*
Scale	0.6738**	0.6729*	0.6737**	0.6737**

*Statistically significant at the 5 % level; **Statistically significant at the 1 % level; ***Statistically significant at the 0.1 % level

Table 3 GPD based market risk measures

VaR	TAIL	90 %	95 %	97.50 %	99 %
SP500	Left	1.1667	1.6485	2.2021	3.0667
	Right	0.8509	1.3177	1.7849	2.4032
FTSE100	Left	1.0131	1.4979	2.0583	2.9353
	Right	1.0559	1.3517	1.7177	2.3378
ES					
SP500	Left	1.98	2.5845	3.282	4.3711
	Right	1.5249	1.9923	2.4601	3.079
FTSE100	Left	1.8348	2.4477	3.1561	4.2648
	Right	1.6085	2.0353	2.5633	3.458

represents the short position on these stock market indices) and the left tail (which represents the long position on these stock market indices) are reported in Table 3.

The right tail risk measures are relatively lower than the left tail risk measures highlighting the impact of large losses during financial crisis. For example at the 99 % significant level the left tail risk measures are as follows: 3.067 % and 2.94 % weekly maximum losses for long positions in the SP500 and FTSE100 respective when the VaR measures is used; or 4.37 % and 4.26 % weekly maximum losses for long position in the SP500 and FTSE100 respectively when ES measure is used. As one can easily observe; the ES risk measure are relatively lager than the VaR measures because the ES is equal to the VaR plus mean of all other loses greater than the VaR.

In addition to computing the GPD based weekly maximum losses of the P&L distribution using the VaR and ES; this study makes use of the GEV to compute the another risk measure referred to in the literature (see for example Gilli and Kellezi 2006) as the "return level".

This risk measure is calculated using the Eq. (4) above; the estimated return level are reported in Table 4 below.

Table 4 GEV based market risk measures: the return level

ReturnLevel	TAIL	90 %	95 %	97.50 %	99 %
SP500	Left	3.822	4.212	4.212	4.212
	Right	3.4794	3.4794	3.4794	3.4794
FTSE100	Left	3.6814	3.6814	4.0384	4.0384
	Right	3.401	3.41	3.4155	3.4155

Table 5 Copula based market risk measures

Copula	Marginal	Risk measures	Tail	90 %	95 %	97.50 %	99 %
Student t	GEV & GEV	VaR	Left	4.9975	6.96	10.7649	14.9626
			Right	0.2955	0.5509	0.7057	0.8967
		ES	Left	2.4146	2.8082	2.8912	2.755
			Right	1.2819	1.4472	1.4938	2.9377
	GPD & GPD	VaR	Left	0.7567	0.7984	0.8396	0.885
			Right	0.6757	0.6747	0.6742	0.6738
		ES	Left	1.3603	1.3694	1.43	1.4394
			Right	1.347	1.331	1.3486	1.3459
Gumbel	GEV & GEV	VaR	Left	6.681	8.666	11.094	13.572
			Right	0.4215	0.599	0.7976	0.9483
		ES	Left	2.4627	3.10743	2.6756	3.8976
			Right	1.4562	3.7067	1.5766	2.9645
	GPD & GPD	VaR	Left	0.763	0.7948	0.8275	0.8658
			Right	0.67	0.6745	0.674	0.6737
		ES	Left	1.3586	1.3685	1.4304	1.4398
			Right	1.3473	1.3329	1.3481	1.3447

Considering for example the left tails, we find that the "return level" for the SP500 and FTSE100 are 4.212 % and 4.038 % respectively. Given that we have used the maximum blocks of 22 weeks each; we would interpret these risk measures as follows: 4.212 % (3.038 %) of maximum losses is expected in one out 22 weeks at the 99 % significance level if one holds a long position in the SP500 (FTS100) respectively. Our results show that the "return level" is invariant to the significance level i.e. the return level is almost identical at different significant level.

The Copula risk measures are also computed and reported in Table 5. These risk measures represent the portfolio (of two asset: SP500 and FTSE100) VaR and ES.

These risk measures are computed as the quantile of the joint P&L distributions with dependence structure embedded in the copula. We consider one elliptical copula (Student t copula) and one Archimedean copula (Gumbel copula) to model the dependence structure between these two stock markets. We build the (joint) bivariate distribution using the Sklar's Theorem expressed in Eq. (17) above. Using a Monte Carlo simulation we are able to compute the VaR and ES measures using the simulated data. Considering the left tail for example we find that at 99 % significance level; the maximum losses expected on weekly basis computed in terms of ES are is equal to 3.90 % when a t-copula with two GEV marginal are used; and 1.44 % when a Gumbel copula with two GPD marginal are used.

The copula based ES measures are reliably coherent as they fulfil the principal of diversification. The principal of diversification states that the portfolio risk should be less than the sum of individual asset risk. ES risk measures reported in Table 5 are almost lower than individual ES risk measures reported in Table 3.

4 Conclusion

This study aimed at exploring the computation of VaR and ES measures during period of financial crisis from a dependence structure point of view. Two stock market indices namely SP500 and FTSE100 have been used to implement a market risk model able to predict the behavior of financial losses during period of financial crisis. Three steps have been implemented. The first one involving the filtering of the return series with AR—GARCH process. The second step dealt with the fitting of the filtered return to two extreme value distributions:—the GPD and the GEV distributions.

We find that the estimated shape parameters were all positive and statistically significant suggesting the existence of large probability of price drop during financial crisis. The GEV and GPD based risk measures were also computed in order to estimate individual risk that one can encounter when investing in these two markets. For that reason, we investigated the impact of these risks in the left tail for an investor with long position; and in the right tail for an investor with a short position in these indices.

A copula based approach was used to estimate the portfolio risk for an investor with simultaneous positions in these two indices. Using the Sklar's theorem, we were able to build a bivariate distribution with Student t and copula Gumbel copulas and simulate 10 thousands observations using Monte Carlo simulations. The copula based risk measures were computed as the quantiles of the bivariate copula distribution. We found that our GEV distribution based ES risk measures where incredibly coherent since they fulfilled the principal of diversification.

References

Davison AC, Smith RL (1990) Models for exceedances over high thresholds. J R Stat Soc 52 (3):393–442

Ding Z, Granger CWJ, Engle RF (1993) A long memory property of stock market returns and a new model. J Empir Finance 1:83–106

Embrechts P, Klüppelberg C, Mikosch T (1997) Modelling extremal events for insurance and finance. Springer, Berlin

Embrechts P, McNeil A, Straumann D (2002) Correlation and dependence in risk management: properties and pitfalls. Cambridge University Press, Cambridge

Frad H, Zouari E (2014) Estimation of value-at-risk measures in the Islamic stock market: approach based on extreme value theory (EVT). J World Econ Res 3(2):15–20, Published

online July 10, (2014) (http://www.sciencepublishinggroup.com/j/jwer) doi: 10.11648/j.jwer.20140302.11
Giacomini E, Hardle W (2005) Value-at-risk calculations with time varying copulae. Discussion paper. Institute of Statistics and Econometrics, Humboldt University of Berlin
Gilli M, Kellezi E (2006) An application of extreme value theory to measuring financial risk. Comput Econ 27:207–228
Hotta LK, Palaro HP (2006) Using conditional copula to estimate value at risk. J Data Sci 4 (1):93–115
Hotta LK, Lucas EC, Palaro HP (2008) Estimation of VaR using copula and extreme value theory. Multinatl Financ J 12(3/4):205–218
Longin FM (1996) The asymptotic distribution of extreme stock market returns. J Bus 69 (3):383–408
Muteba Mwamba JW, Hammoudeh S, Gupta R (2016) Financial tail risks in conventional and Islamic stock markets: a comparative analysis. Pacific-Basin Finance J (in Press)
Sklar A (1959) Fonctions de Repartition a n Dimensions et Leurs Marges, vol 8. Publications de l'Institut de Statistique de l'Universite' de Paris, pp 229–231
Taylor SJ (1986) Modelling financial time series. Wiley, New York

John Weirstrass Muteba Mwamba is an Associate Professor in Financial Economics, and Coordinator of the masters' programme in Financial Economics at the University of Johannesburg, South Africa. Dr J.W. Muteba Mwamba holds a B.Sc. Honours degree in Mathematical Statistics and Computer Programming from D.R. Congo (2002), a masters' degree in financial economics (2009), and a Ph.D. degree in Financial Economics (2012) from the University of Johannesburg. Dr J.W. Muteba Mwamba also holds a certificate in Decision Sciences from the INSEAD Paris—France. His research interests lie in the areas of Portfolio Optimization, Risk Management, Financial Statistics, and Decision Theory. He is currently lecturing courses in Statistics, Mathematics, Portfolio Theory and Risk Management at both graduate and undergraduate levels. He has been an ad hoc reviewer for international journals such as European Journal of Finance, Applied Economics, Economic Modelling, Energy Economics, British Journal of Mathematics and Computer Sciences, etc. He is a current member of the South African Economic Society, a certified member of the Institute for Practicing, and the Founder of the Analytics Research Group—a think tank in Quantitative Finance.

Computation of Operational Value at Risk Using the Severity Distribution Model Based on Bayesian Method with Gibbs Sampler

John Weirstrass Muteba Mwamba

Abstract Under Basel III the minimum capital requirement due to operational risk is computed as the 99th quantile of the annual total loss distribution. This annual loss distribution is a result of the convolution between the loss frequency and the loss severity distributions. The estimation of parameters of these two distributions i.e. frequency and severity distributions is not only essential but crucial to obtaining reliable estimates of operational risk measures. In practical applications, Poisson and lognormal distributions are used to fit these two distributions respective. The maximum likelihood method, the method of moments as well as the probability-weighted moments used to obtain the parameters of these distributions can sometimes produce nonsensical estimates due to estimation risk and sample bias. This paper proposes a different calibration of the frequency and the severity distributions based on Bayesian method with Gibbs sampler. Further to that, the paper models the severity distribution by making use of the lognormal and the generalised Pareto distribution simultaneously. Simulated results suggest that computed operational value at risk estimates based of this new method are unbiased with minimum variance.

JEL Classification G1 • G13 • G14

1 Introduction

Operational risk is the risk emanating from loss due to inadequate or failed internal processes, people, systems or external events. The tier 1 of the recent Basel III refers to the computation of the minimum capital requirements due to market, credit, and operational risk. The market risk is the risk due to fluctuations in the

J.W. Muteba Mwamba (✉)
Department of Economics and Econometrics, University of Johannesburg, Auckland Park, South Africa
e-mail: johnmu@uj.ac.za

H. Dinçer, Ü. Hacioğlu (eds.), *Risk Management, Strategic Thinking and Leadership in the Financial Services Industry*, Contributions to Management Science, DOI 10.1007/978-3-319-47172-3_8

trading books, while the credit risk is the risk that the borrowers will not be able to meet their obligations. Since losses arise from errors and ineffective operations the approach used in modelling operational risk are quite different from the one used in market and credit risk. Table 1 below highlights fundamental differences in market, credit, and operational risk modelling. Examples of operational risk include *internal fraud*: *UBS London, 2011* (*Kweku Adoboli*: *unauthorised trading*): *US $ 2 billion*; *Société Générale, 2008* (*Jérôme Kerviel*: *fictitious trades to hide big bets he took*): *Euro 4.9 billion. System failure*: *Bank of America*: *US $225 million*; *external events*: *September 11 terrorist attacks*, etc. Based on these examples one can define operational risk in terms event types and business lines. Unfortunately data related events types and business lines are not exhaustive. Furthermore implementing statistical models for operational risk model remain a challenge for both academics and practitioners.

This chapter reviews available statistical models for operational risk modelling, discusses their pitfalls and develops a new operation risk model based on Bayesian inferences. The following Table 2 summarises recent studies done in operational risk modelling. This table shows that the three commonly used operational risk methodologies are the basic indicator approach (BIA), the standardised approach (STA), and the advanced measurement approach (AMA). The main focus of this chapter is on the advanced measurement approach under the loss distribution technique. Studies have shown that the AMA methodology is more reliable than the first two. For example Teply (2012) shows that when the AMA is used in lieu of BIA or the STA; banks are likely to save between 6 % and 8 % of their capital requirement due to operational risk. Similar findings were also obtained by Lin et al. (2013). They argue that it is more appropriate to adapt the AMA in operational risk modelling since it can help banks to enjoy a much lessened capital requirement.

Table 1 Theoretical differences between market, credit, and operational risks

	Market risk	Credit risk	Operational risk
Risk factors	Interest rate	Default probabilities	Processes
	Equity	Downgrade Default and recovery distributions Correlation	People
	Currency		Systems
	Commodity Volatility Correlations etc		External events
Risk measures			Loss distributions
	Market VaR Market Shortfall	Credit VaR	Operational VaR
		Operational expected shortfall	Operational expected shortfall

Table 2 Major studies on operational risk and methodology

Studies	Methodologies	Findings/critics
Correa, R and Raju, S. (2010); Lin T. T., Chia-Chi Lee, Yu-Chuan Kuan (2013); Lin, Tt, Lee, Cc And Kuan, Yc (2013); Maike Sundmacher (2007);	Basic indicator approach (BIA); Standardized approach (STA);	Capital requirement involves simple calculations. However it is not directly linked to the loss data. The BIA and STA are often criticized for not considering individual risk profile of each business lines.
Teply, P (2012); Feng, JC, Li, JP, Gao, LJ and Hua, ZS (2012); Opdyke, John Douglas J. D, (2014); Cope, Eric W.; Mignola, Giulio; Antonini, Gianluca; at al.(2009); Jimenez Rodriguez, Enrique Jose; Feria Dominguez, Jose Manuel; Martin Marin, Jose Luis (2009)	Advanced measurement approach (AMA); *basic indicator approach*; *Standardized approach*	Most findings show that when using the AMA rather than the BIA or STIA; the banks might save approximately 6 % to 8 % of their capital requirement on operational risk. These results indicate that it is more appropriate to adopt the AMA to estimate the operational risk capital requirement; this way can help a bank enjoy a much lessened capital charge Required And Subsequently Its Available Capital Increases.

2 Basic Indicator Approach

The minimum capital requirement (MCR) related to operational risk is calculated by multiplying the three years average of gross operating income by an alpha (a fixed percentage of 15 % determined by the central bank).

$$MCR = \frac{1}{3}\sum_{i=1}^{3} GOI_i \times \alpha \quad (1)$$

3 Standardised Approach

The minimum capital requirement using the standardized approach is calculated by multiplying the three years average of the gross operation income of each business line, by a factor Beta (assigned to that business line by the *Basel Committee on banking Supervision*—BCBS). The Basel II identifies 8 business lines:

1. Corporate finance (Beta = 18)
2. Trading and sales (Beta = 18)
3. Retail banking (Beta = 12)
4. Commercial banking (Beta = 15)
5. Payment and settlement (Beta = 18)
6. Agency services (Beta = 15)
7. Asset management (Beta = 12)
8. Retail brokerage (Beta = 12)

Therefore the minimum capital requirement related to operational risk is computed using the following formula:

$$MCR = \frac{1}{3}\sum\nolimits_{i=1}^{3}\left\{\sum\nolimits_{j=1}^{8}(GOI)_{ij} \times \beta_{ij}\right\} \tag{2}$$

Table 3 below illustrates a hypothetical example of the computation of the operational risk minimum capital requirement using both the basic indicator and the standardised approaches. The left panel of Table 3 reports the annual gross incomes in \$1000's for year -1, year -2, and year -3 for all 8 business lines. The minimum capital requirement is obtained by multiplying positive annual gross income with an alpha value determined by the Basel committee or the central bank. Notice that a negative annual gross income is omitted in the calculation of the average. For this specific example the minimum capital requirement using the basic indicator approach is equal to the average of the two gross income 16,000 and 320,000 times the alpha value of 15 %. The negative annual gross income is therefore omitted.

The right panel of Table 3 reports the product of the annual gross income shown in the left panel with its corresponding beta value in percentages. For example the first row of the right panel is found by multiplying the first row of the left panel by 18 %. The minimum capital requirement corresponding to the standardised approach is found as the weighted average of the total annual gross income such that negative total annual gross income is considered as zero! For this specific example the minimum capital requirement using the standardised approach is found as the average of 2400, 48000, and 0. The minimum capital requirement corresponding to the basic indicator approach is found as the average of the bank

Table 3 An hypothetical example of the basic indicator and standardised approaches (in \$000)

Business line	Year-3	Year-2	Year-1	Beta	Beta*Year-3	Beta*Year-2	Beta*Year-1
Corporate finance	2000	3000	40,000	18 %	360	540	7200
Trading and sales	2000	3000	40,000	18 %	360	540	7200
Retail banking	2000	3000	40,000	12 %	240	360	4800
Commercial banking	2000	3000	40,000	15 %	300	450	6000
Payment and settlement	2000	−100,000	40,000	18 %	360	−18,000	7200
Agency services	2000	−100,000	40,000	15 %	300	−15000	6000
Asset management	2000	30,000	40,000	12 %	240	3600	4800
Retail brokerage	2000	30,000	40,000	12 %	240	3600	4800
Total for the bank	16,000	−128,000	320,000		2400	−23,910	48,000

total annual gross income of 16,000, and 320,000 multiplied by an alpha of 15%, that is 168,000 multiplied by 15% which equals 25,200 keeping in mind that negative total annual gross income is omitted.

4 Pitfalls of the Basic Indicator and Standardised Approaches

The critics toward the two methodologies are related to the fact that they do not consider individual risk profile corresponding to each business lines (Hull 2012). In addition the minimum capital requirement obtained with these two methodologies is not linked to the operational loss data; and that the risk profile of each event type within the same business line is not reflected in the process of the calculation of the minimum capital requirement.

To overcome these pitfalls the Basel Committee for banks Supervision (BCBS) identifies for each business line a number of event types that can impact the computation of the minimum capital requirement. These event types are classified in terms of their frequency and severity they have. Event types with low frequencies and higher severities are considered as dangerous and need particular attention during the modeling process. Low frequency, high severity event types can put the future of a financial institution at risk. These events cannot be actively managed on a day-to-day basis. In contrast the high frequency low severity event types have high expected loss but low unexpected loss. The medium frequency medium severity event types are often the main focus of operational risk capital measurement provisions of the business since they can be managed with suitable systems and processes.

Table 4 exhibits the business lines and event types as per BCBS proposal. For example internal fraud has low frequency and higher severity in corporate finance. Examples of internal fraud include for instance intentional misreporting of trading positions, employee theft, and insider trading on an employee's own account. Whereas external fraud in the corporate finance business line has a low frequency and medium severity. Example of external fraud include for instance computer hacking, robbery and forgery.

Other examples of event types can include worker compensation claims and sexual discrimination claims for *employment practices and workplace safety*. Fiduciary breaches, misuse of confidential customer information, improper trading activities on the bank's account and money laundering for *clients, products, and business practices*. Earthquakes, fires and floods for *damage to physical assets*. Hardware and software failures, telecommunication problems, and utility outages for *business disruption and system failures*. Data entry errors, collateral management failures, incomplete legal documentation, unapproved access given to clients' accounts for *execution, delivery and process management*. These seven distinct event types and sources of operational losses, need particular individual attention in the modelling of operational risk.

Table 4 Event types per business lines

Business lines	Internal fraud	External fraud	Employment practice and workplace safety	Clients, products distr. Bus. Practice	Damage to physical assets	Business disruption and system failures	Execution delivery and process management
Corporate finance	L-H	L-M	L-L	L-H	L-L	L-L	L-L
Trading and sales	L-H	L-L	L-L	M-M	L-L	L-L	H-L
Retail banking	L-M	H-L	L-L	M-M	M-L	L-L	H-L
Commercial banking	L-H	M-M	L-L	M-M	L-L	L-L	M-L
Payment and settlement	L-M	L-L	L-L	L-L	L-L	L-L	H-L
Agency services	L-M	L-L	L-L	L-M	L-L	L-L	M-L
Asset management	L-H	L-L	L-L	L-H	L-L	L-L	M-L
Retail brokerage	L-M	L-M	L-L	L-M	L-L	M-L	M-L

5 The Advanced Measurement Approach

Under the advanced measurement approach the minimum capital requirement due to operational risk is calculated with the bank's internal operational risk models based on four elements:

Internal Data: negative economic flow for which it is possible to identify the impact on the profit & loss account as consequence of an operational event.

External data: operational loss events occurred to other financial institutions and banks.

Scenario analysis: a scenario is a fictitious operational event (also inspired from an occurred external event). The goal is to evaluate the impact in case the scenario occurs in the bank.

Risk indicators: risk indicators are quantitative metrics reflecting operational risk exposure of specific processes or products for example a drop in sales or in asset prices.

As mentioned earlier, a major challenge in operational risk modelling is that data on the severity and frequency of historical losses are often not available. Internal historical data on high frequency low severity might be available within the bank. Therefore combining internal, external, and scenarios based—loss data is crucial in determining the minimum capital requirement due to operation risks.

The minimum capital requirement under the AMA method is the one obtained with in-house operational risk models. These models include:—the Internal Measurement Approach: IMA, the Loss Distribution Approach: LDA, and the Scorecard Approach.

This study makes use of the loss distribution approach. Under this approach, the operational loss data is fitted separately to two different distributions: -the loss frequency distribution, and the loss severity distribution. The loss frequency distribution is the probability of the number of loss events over a fixed interval of time. Whereas the loss severity distribution is the probability of the magnitude of the loss once it occurs. These two distributions are then combined using the convolution technique described below. The resulting distribution known as the annual loss distribution is depicted in Fig. 1.

Figure 1 illustrates graphically how operational risk measures can be derived as the quantile of the total annual loss distribution. It also shows the size of expected operational losses (EL), the unexpected operational losses, and the 99th quantile of the annual loss distribution which represents the operational risk measure.

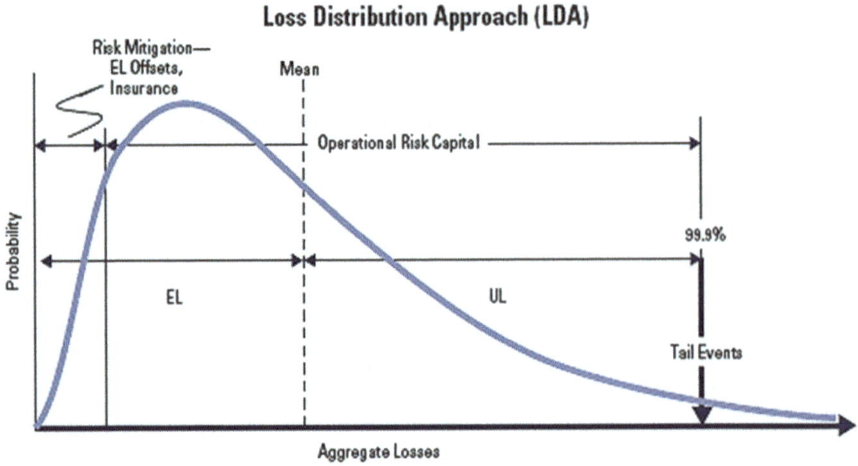

Fig. 1 Total annual loss distribution

6 Using the Convolution Technique to Build the Total Annual Loss Distribution

The total annual operational loss S is the sum of the annual operational losses s_j related to the jth business lines. The annual operational loss s_j, related to business line j, is affected by two sources of uncertainty:—the number of losses n_j in one year time horizon, and—the impact i.e. severity of each single loss x_{ij}. Therefore

$$s_j = \sum_{i=1}^{n_j} x_{ij} \tag{3}$$

$$S = \sum_{i=1}^{K} s_i, \quad i = 1,\ 2,\ \ldots,\ K; \tag{4}$$

Let $p(n_j)$ be the loss frequency distribution, and $f(x_{ij})$ the loss severity distribution of the jth business line. The total annual loss distribution corresponding to the jth business line denoted by $D(s_{ij})$ is built in the following steps:

Step 1: draw randomly the number n_j of losses per annum from the frequency distribution $p(n_j)$ for example $n_j = 3$;

Step 2: draw randomly x_{ij} severe losses from the severity distribution $f(x_{ij})$ of the jth business line; for example $x_{1j} = 578$, $x_{2j} = 883$, and $x_{3j} = 498$ given that the randomly drawn number of losses per annum $n_j = 3$

Step 3: get the sum S_{1j} of the first x_{ij} severe losses; that is for our example $578 + 883 + 498$ i.e. $S_{1j} = 1959$ which represents the first observation of the total annual loss distribution corresponding the jth business line.

Repeat step 1, step 2, and step 3 K times to get $S_{2j}, \ldots, S_{Kj}$ observations of the total annual loss distribution $D(s_{ij})$ corresponding to the jth business line.

7 Modelling Loss Frequency and Severity Distributions

7.1 Loss Frequency Distribution

A number of theoretical discrete probability distributions are used to model the loss frequency distributions. The most common ones include Poisson distribution, and the Negative Binomial distribution. A random variable x follows a Poisson probability distribution if its density is given by:

$$P(X = n_j, \lambda) = \frac{e^{-\lambda}(\lambda)^{n_j}}{n_j!}, \quad n_j = 0,\ 1,\ 2,\ \ldots \tag{5}$$

where, λ is the average number of operational losses in an interval of one year. Poisson distribution plays an extremely important role in operational risk management, since it models perfectly the occurrence of loss frequency in a bank. The average number of operational losses occurring in a year is equal to its variance i.e. $E(n_j) = Var(n_j) = \lambda$.

The second discrete probability distribution used to model the arrival of losses in operational risk management is the Negative Binomial distribution whose density is shown in Eq. (6) below:

$$f(X = n_j) = \binom{n_j - 1}{k - 1} p^k (1 - p)^{n_j - k}, \quad n_j = k,\ k + 1,\ k + 2, \ldots, \tag{6}$$

where, n_j is the number of trials, k is the kth success, and p the probability of success. The mean number of losses occurring in a year and its variance are given by:

$$E(n_j) = \frac{k(1-p)}{p} \tag{7}$$

$$Var(n_j) = \frac{k(1-p)}{p^2} \tag{8}$$

7.2 Loss Severity Distribution

A number of theoretical continuous probability distributions are used to model the severity distribution, these include the lognormal distribution, the gamma distribution, and the exponential distribution. A random variable x follows a lognormal distribution if its probability distribution is given by:

$$p(x) = \frac{1}{\sigma\sqrt{2\pi}} \frac{1}{x} \exp\left[-\frac{1}{2}\left(\frac{\ln x - m}{\sigma}\right)^2\right] \quad (9)$$

Since this is the distribution of a positive random variable whose logarithm exists and follows a Normal (Gaussian) distribution; m and σ are the mean and the standard deviation not of the variable x but of the logarithm of this variable.

The second continuous probability distribution used in the modelling of the severity distribution in operational risk management is the gamma distribution whose density is expressed as:

$$f(x) = \frac{1}{\Gamma(\alpha)\beta^\alpha} x^{\alpha-1} e^{-\frac{x}{\beta}}, \quad \mathrm{x} > 0, \beta > 0. \quad (10)$$

The mean and variance of the Gamma distribution are given by: $E(x) = \alpha\beta$, $Var(x) = \alpha\beta^2$ respectively. The exponential distribution is a special case of the Gamma distribution. It is given by the following expression:

$$f(x) = \begin{cases} \frac{1}{\theta}\exp\left(-\frac{x}{\theta}\right) & ; x > 0, \quad \theta > 0 \\ 0 & \end{cases} \quad (11)$$

NB: If a bank has more than one business lines then the total annual loss distribution corresponding to each business line needs to be calibrated. The overall loss distribution for the entire bank can be obtained by making use of copula functions.

8 Estimation of the Loss Distribution's Parameters

Traditionally the maximum likelihood method is often used to estimate the parameters of both the loss frequency and severity distributions. The maximum likelihood method consists in maximising the log-likelihood function of the sample data:

$$LogLik = Log\left[\prod_{i=1}^{n} f(x_i, \theta)\right] \quad (12)$$

where $f(x_i)$ is the probability distribution of either a loss frequency, or severity distribution expressed above. The vector of parameters θ is obtained by getting the partial derivative with respect to each entry of θ and solving the resulting system of equations:

$$\theta = \frac{\vartheta LogLik}{\vartheta\theta} = 0 \tag{13}$$

Furthermore the method of probability weighted moment can also be used to estimate the parameters of the loss frequency and severity distributions. The rth probability weighted moment is given by:

$$\omega_r = \int_0^1 f(x)x^r dx; \tag{14}$$

When $r = 1 \Rightarrow \omega_1 = E(x) = \mu$;

When $r = 2 \Rightarrow \omega_2 = E(x - \mu)^2 = \sigma^2$.

The characteristics of the loss data used in operational risk management is quite unique. This data comes from different sources:—internal loss data, external loss data, and scenario based -loss data. This mixture of loss data makes the method of maximum likelihood and the probability weighted moment inadequate due to sample bias and presence of outliers. For mixture distributions with generalised Pareto distribution Bermude and Turkman (2003) show that maximum likelihood and the probability weighted moment methods fail to obtain the shape parameter ξ when it is greater than -0.5 or less that 1 $(\xi > -0.5 \; or \; \xi \leq 1)$. To overcome this drawback; the present study recommends the use of the Bayesian method.

9 Bayesian Method

Bayesian techniques consists in estimating unknown parameters θ_k of the loss frequency and mixture severity distribution. If the $p(\theta_k)$ *represents the prior distribution* (based on operational risk manager's expert views); $p(y_i/\theta_k)$ *the likelihood distribution* (distribution assumption concerning the frequency and mixture severity distributions) we can use the Bayesian rule as follow:

$$p(\theta_k/y_i) = \frac{P(y_i/\theta_k)P(\theta_k)}{\int P(y_i/\theta_k)P(\theta_k)d\theta_k} \tag{15}$$

Bayesian technique consists in generating the unknown parameters θ_k from the posterior probability distribution obtained as the product of the prior and likelihood distribution.

$$posterior \propto Prior \times Likelihood \tag{16}$$

Our Bayesian approach to loss distribution technique consists of the following steps.

9.1 *Bayesian Estimation of the Loss Frequency: Poisson Distribution*

The number of losses occurring during a year are assumed to be Poisson distributed, that is

$$n_1,\ n_2,\ \ldots,\ n_j \rightarrow P(n_j/\theta_k).$$

We assume a sub-exponential family of prior: the Gamma distribution

$$\Gamma_{\alpha,\beta} = \frac{1}{\beta^{\alpha}\Gamma(\alpha)} x^{\alpha-1} e^{-\beta x}, \quad \alpha > 0,\ \beta > 0; \tag{17}$$
$$\Gamma(\alpha) = (\alpha - 1)!$$

Based on external loss data and expert opinions i.e. ϕ_k; we assume that the likelihood function is a gamma distribution. Therefore the Posterior distribution of J business lines is given by:

$$P\left(\frac{n_j}{\theta_k},\ \phi_k\right)\prod_{k=1}^{J}\Gamma_{\theta}\left(\frac{\theta_k}{N_j},\ \phi_k\right)\Gamma(\theta_k) \tag{18}$$

Equation (18) is a *Generalised Inverse Gamma distribution* where $\theta_k = (\alpha,\ \beta)$. The predictive distribution of future losses h-step ahead can be expressed as:

$$\hat{n} = (n_{J+1},\ n_{J+2},\ \ldots, n_{J+h}) \tag{19}$$

$$p(\hat{n}/n_j) \approx \iint p(\hat{n}\ /\ \alpha,\ \beta,\ n_j) \times p(\alpha,\ \beta/n_j)d\alpha d\beta \tag{20}$$

where $\theta_k = (\alpha_k,\ \beta_k)$

9.2 Bayesian Estimation of Loss Severity: The Body part with Lognormal Distribution

Let $y = ln(x) \rightarrow N(\mu, \quad \sigma^2)$ be the loss data constituting the body part of the severity distribution. We consider a diffuse prior for both the mean and the standard deviation of the log-normal distribution:

$$p(\mu, \sigma) = \frac{1}{\sigma^2} \tag{21}$$

The likelihood function is considered as the Fisher information:

$$l(\mu, \sigma^2) = \int_0^\infty \left(\frac{\vartheta LogLik}{\vartheta \theta} f(x, \theta) \right)^2 f(x, \theta) dx \tag{22}$$

Therefore the joint posterior of the body part of the severity distribution is expressed as:

$$p(\mu, \sigma^2 / \ lossData) = \iint \left\{ \int_0^\infty \left(\frac{\vartheta LogLik}{\vartheta \theta} f(x, \theta) \right)^2 f(x, \theta) dx \right\} \frac{1}{\sigma^2} d\mu d\sigma^2 \tag{23}$$

And the conditional distribution of mean μ:

$$\mu / \ \sigma^2, \ lossData \rightarrow N\left(\hat{\mu}, \ \frac{\sigma^2}{n} \right) \tag{24}$$

While the conditional posterior distribution of σ^2 is an inverted gamma distribution:

$$p(\sigma^2 / \ \mu, \ lossData) = \left(\frac{v\hat{\sigma}^2}{2} \right)^{\frac{1}{2}v} \left(\frac{(\sigma^2)^{-\frac{1}{2}(v+2)} exp\left[-\frac{v\sigma^2}{2\sigma^2} \right]}{\Gamma\left(\frac{v}{2}\right)} \right) \tag{25}$$

Hence the predictive distribution:

$$p(\tilde{y}/lossData) = \iint p(\tilde{y}/ \ \mu, \ \beta, \ lossData) p(\mu, \ \sigma^2 / \ lossData) d\mu d\sigma^2 \tag{26}$$

To consider the truncation at the threshold; we need to adjust the severity distribution using this formula:

$$\frac{f(y_i;\theta_k)}{P(Min \le y_i \le Thresh)} = \frac{f(y_i;\theta_k)}{F(Thresh) - F(Min)} \tag{27}$$

9.3 Bayesian Estimation of the Loss Severity: The Tail Part with the Generalised Pareto Distribution

Let x_1 , x_2, ..., x_n be a sequence of iid random variables. The distribution of x_i's over a certain threshold u is known as the generalised Pareto distribution (GPD) whose expression is:

$$G_{\xi,\,\beta}(x) = \begin{cases} 1 - \left(1 + \frac{\xi x}{\beta}\right)^{\frac{-1}{\xi}} & ;\ \xi \neq 0 \\ 1 - exp\left(-\frac{x}{\beta}\right) & ;\ \xi = 0 \end{cases} \tag{28}$$

where ξ, β represent the shape and scale parameters to be estimated given a appropriate threshold u. The log-likelihood function is given by:

$$LogL = (\xi,\ \beta,\ x) = -nLog(\beta) + \left(\frac{1}{\xi} - 1\right)\sum\nolimits_{i=1}^{n} Log\left(1 - \frac{\xi x}{\beta}\right) \tag{29}$$

Bermudez and Turkman (2003) show that the maximum likelihood estimator of ξ, *and* β exist only if $\xi \le 1$. If $\xi > 1$ the log-likelihood tends to infinity as $\frac{\beta}{\xi}$ approaches x_n. Hosting and Wallis (1987) show that PWM of ξ and β exist only when $\xi > -0.5$. Similarly Castillo and Hadi (1997) have also shown that for small sample size the maximum likelihood and the probability weighted moment methods produce biased estimates.

Given that the shape ξ and location β parameters do not exist when $\xi > 1$ (see Bermudez and Turkman, 2003; Smith 1984). Our Bayesian setting for the estimation of these two parameters is as follows. Firstly we restrict the shape parameter to be positive i.e. $\xi > 0$; thus the generalised pareto distribution becomes:

$$G_{\xi,\,\beta}(x) = p(x/\ \xi,\ \beta) = 1 - \left(1 - \frac{\xi x}{\beta}\right)^{-\frac{1}{\xi}} \quad ; \quad 0 < x < \frac{\beta}{\xi} \tag{30}$$

The joint posterior distribution of ξ *and* β can be found by making use of Bayesian theorem:

$$p(\xi,\ \beta/x)\frac{p(x/\ \xi,\ \beta)p(\xi)p(\beta)}{\iint p(x/\ \xi,\ \beta)p(\xi)p(\beta)d\xi d\beta} \tag{31}$$

where $p(\xi) \to Gamma(\alpha_0,\ \beta_0);\ \alpha_0 > 0,\ \beta_0 > 0$

$$p(\beta) \to Inverted - Gamma(\alpha_1,\ \beta_1) \tag{32}$$

Therefore predictive distribution for the h step ahead for severity loss data can be given by :

$$\widetilde{y} = \left(y_{K+1},\ y_{K+2},\ \ldots, y_{K+h}\right) \tag{33}$$

$$p(\widetilde{y}/\ y) = \iint p(\widetilde{y}/\ \xi,\ \beta,\ x)p(\xi,\ \beta/x)d\xi d\beta \tag{34}$$

9.4 Simulating the Posterior Distribution: The Gibbs Sampler

The Predictive distributions (Poisson, Lognormal and GPD) are obtained from their posterior distributions. Let $\theta_k = (\alpha,\ \beta)$ be either the parameters of the posterior of Poisson distribution in Eq. (18); or $\theta_k = (\mu,\ \sigma^2)$ the parameters of the posterior of Log-normal distribution in Eq. (23). Or $\theta_k = (\xi,\ \beta)$ the parameters of the posterior of GPD in Eq. (31). Given the posterior distribution $p(\theta_k/\ \theta_{-k},\ LossData)$; we simulate from this distribution using the Gibbs sampler as follows:

- Step 1: Draw ${\theta_1}^{(t)}$ from $p\left(\theta_1/\ \theta^{(t)}{}_2,\ LossData\right)$
- Step 2: Draw $\theta^{(t)}{}_2$ from $p\left(\theta_2/\ \theta^{(t)}{}_1,\ LossData\right)$
- Repeat step 2 until convergence

In our simulations of the posterior distribution; we fix the starting values $(\alpha_0,\ \beta_0)$ or $(\mu_0,\ \sigma^2{}_0)$ or $(\xi_0,\ \beta_0)$ and follow the abovementioned steps:

- Step 1: Draw $\alpha^{(1)} \to p(\alpha/\ \beta_0,\ LossData)$ or

$$\mu^{(1)} \to p\left(\mu/\ \sigma^2{}_0,\ LossData\right) \quad \text{or}$$

$$\xi^{(1)} \to p(\xi/\ \beta_0,\ LossData)$$

- Step 2: $\beta^{(1)} \rightarrow p\left(\beta / \alpha^{(1)}, \textit{LossData}\right)$ or

$$\sigma^{2^{(1)}} \rightarrow p\left(\sigma^2 / \mu^{(1)}, \textit{LossData}\right) \quad \text{or}$$
$$\xi^{(1)} \rightarrow p\left(\xi / \beta^{(1)}, \textit{LossData}\right),$$

- Repeat step 2 until we draw:

$$\beta^{(K)}, \alpha^{(K)} \quad \text{or} \quad \mu^{(K)}, \sigma^{2^{(K)}} \quad \text{or} \quad \xi^{(K)}, \beta^{(K)} \quad \text{or} \quad \xrightarrow{converge\ \ in\ \ Pbty\ \ to} (\alpha, \beta)$$
$$\text{or} \quad (\mu, \sigma^2) \quad \text{or} \quad (\xi, \beta)\ as\ t \rightarrow \infty$$

Once the parameters of both the loss frequency and mixtured loss severity distributions are estimated using Bayesian technique described above; the total annual loss distribution is obtained by making use of the convolution method.

10 The Overall Annual Loss Distribution Using Copula Function

Let $f(S_1), \ldots, f(S_J)$ be the individual total annual loss distribution corresponding to business line $1, 2, \ldots, J$. The overall annual loss distribution for the entire bank $f(S_1, S_2, \ldots, S_J)$ is obtained by making use of a copula function.

A function $C : [0, 1]^n \rightarrow [0, 1]$ is n-dimensional copula if it satisfies these properties:

- $\forall u \in [0, 1], \ C(1, 1, \ldots 1, u, 1, 1, \ldots, 1) = u.$

- $\forall u_i \in [0, 1], C(u_1, \ldots, u_n) = 0$; if at least one of the u's is equal to zero

We make use of the probability integral transform to transform the empirical loss distribution of each business line into a uniform distribution:

$$Y = \int_{-\infty}^{S_j} f(S_j) dS_j = F(S_j) \ni [0, 1] \tag{35}$$

10.1 Sklar (1959) Theorem

Given n-dimensional distribution function F with marginals $F_1, \ldots., F_n$ there exists an n-copula $C : [0, 1]^n \rightarrow [0, 1]$ such that:

- $F(S_1, S_2, \ldots, S_n) = C(F_1(S_1), \ldots, F_n(S_n))$ (36)

where C is the n-dimension copula. There are two families of copulas:—Elliptical copulas: Gaussian and t copulas; and Archimedean copulas (Clayton, Gumbel and Frank copula, etc). This study makes use of the Student t copula.

11 Empirical Analysis with Simulated Data

We simulate 5000 loss data for two business lines using the software R available at www.r-project.org. We use the Poisson distribution with parameter lambda = 750 for the first business line, and 751 for the second business line in order to model the loss frequency distribution. We also use the lognormal distribution with mean equal to 150 and sigma = 200 for the first business line, and 151 with sigma = 201 for the second business line respectively in order to model the body part of the loss severity distribution. The tail part of the loss severity is modelled using the generalised Pareto with shape parameter equal to 0.5 and scale of 1550 for the first business line, and 0.6 and 1551 respectively for the second business line based on a threshold of 1500.

Table 5 reports the estimated parameters of the loss frequency i.e. Poisson distribution, the mixed loss severity (lognormal and generalised Pareto) distributions using three estimation methods namely the maximum likelihood, the probability weighted moment, and the Bayesian methods. In addition to that; Table 5 also reports the value at risk, the minimum capital requirement, and its bootstrapped confidence interval for the maximum likelihood and the probability weighted methods.

We find that the estimation method has a huge impact on the operational value at risk, and the minimum capital requirement. Frequentist methods (i.e. the maximum likelihood and the probability weighted moment methods result in contracting findings: the shape parameter of the generalised Pareto distribution for instance is

Table 5 Simulated analysis

	Parameter	ML	PWM	Bayesian
Lognormal	mu $-\mu$	153.2295	154.2899*	156.2000*
	sigma $-\sigma^2$	261.5054	152.8240*	134.8000*
Poisson	lambda $-\lambda$	791.7354*	791.7350*	801.2413*
	xi $-\xi$	0.4878*	0.4534	1.6680*
GPD	beta $-\beta$	1025.8805	1049.2301*	1133.6027*
	Op VaR	250114.3000	251891.5000	264329.7000
	The MCR	200152.8000	202131.6800	214981.0000
Bootstrap 10,000	C.I of MCR: $\pm\sigma$	142859–262215.6	164875.5–242102.1	
Bootstrap 10,000	std error of MCR	21502.11	111088.49	

*Statistically significant at the 5% level

found to be statistically significant when the maximum likelihood method is used than when the probability weighted moment method is used. We argue that this has to do with the sample bias and the type mixed loss data used in the estimation process. The Bayesian method produces more reliable estimates since all estimated parameters are unbiased and statistically significant. The minimum capital requirement obtained with the Bayesian method is higher than that obtained with other methodologies. Higher operational risk capital requirement can promote confidence in the financial sector and insure stability during financial turmoil.

12 Conclusion

This chapter aimed at developing a new operational risk methodology that can generate reliable minimum capital requirement and promote financial stability in a banking sector during period of economic turmoil. To achieve this aim, the chapter started by introducing the basic methodologies in operational risk management. The basic indicator and standardised approach were discussed. Through an example of the calculation of the minimum capital requirement, we were able to show the pitfalls of these two traditional operational risk methodologies. We showed that the minimum capital requirement was not linked to the operational loss data, and that the risk profile of each business line was not taken into consideration.

We thereafter introduced the advanced measurement approach under the loss distribution methodology. Under this approach banks are required to develop their own in-house operational risk models under the guidance of the central bank authorities. This method relies heavily on the accurate estimation of the parameters of the loss frequency, and loss severity distributions.

Given the small sample size of available external and internal operational loss data, we have shown that the maximum likelihood method as well as the probability weighted moment method produce biased estimates that can misrepresent the minimum capital requirement due to operational risks.

To overcome this estimation problem, the present chapter proposes the use of the Bayesian technique to estimate the parameters of the loss frequency, and loss severity distributions. Through a simulated example, we have been able to highlight the significant differences in the minimum capital requirement calculations. Our Bayesian technique was able thanks to Monte Carlo simulations, to generate unbiased and significant parameters, and higher minimum capital requirement due to operational risks. Higher minimum capital requirement can promote stability and confidence in financial sector. Higher minimum capital requirement can also make it less likely that banks would fall back on the local government to mitigate their losses, hence discourages them from taking excessive risks. Finally higher minimum capital requirement lead to more common equity which can basically help banks to absorb severe losses.

References

Castillo E, Hadi AS (1997) Fitting the generalized Pareto distribution to data. J Am Stat Assoc 92(440):1609–1620
De Zea Bermudez P, Turkman MA (2003) Bayesian approach to parameter estimation of the generalized Pareto distribution. Test 12(1):259–277
Hosting JRM, Wallis JR (1987) Parameter and quantile estimation for the generalized pareto distribution. Technometrics 29:339–349
Hull J (2012) Risk management and financial institutions, + Web Site, vol 733. Wiley, New York
Smith RL (1984) Threshold methods for sample extremes. In: Trago de Oliveita J (ed) Statistical extremes and applications. Springer, Netherlands, pp 621–638
Teply P (2012) The application of extreme value theory in operational risk management. Ekonomicky Casopis 60(7):698–716
Lin TT, Lee C-C, Kuan Y-C (2013) The optimal operational risk capital requirement by applying the advanced measurement approach. Centr Eur J Oper Res 21(1):85–101
Sklar A (1959) Fonctions de Répartition à n Dimensions et leurs Marges, vol 8. *Publication de* L'Institut de Statistique de L'Universsité de Paris, pp 229–231

John Weirstrass Muteba Mwamba is an Associate Professor in Financial Economics, and Coordinator of the masters' programme in Financial Economics at the University of Johannesburg, South Africa. Dr J.W. Muteba Mwamba holds a B.Sc. Honours degree in Mathematical Statistics and Computer Programming from D.R Congo (2002), a masters' degree in financial economics (2009), and a Ph.D. degree in Financial Economics (2012) from the University of Johannesburg. Dr J.W. Muteba Mwamba also holds a certificate in Decision Sciences from the INSEAD Paris—France. His research interests lie in the areas of Portfolio Optimization, Risk Management, Financial Statistics, and Decision Theory. He is currently lecturing courses in Statistics, Mathematics, Portfolio Theory and Risk Management at both graduate and undergraduate levels. He has been an ad hoc reviewer for international journals such as European Journal of Finance, Applied Economics, Economic Modelling, Energy Economics, British Journal of Mathematics and Computer Sciences, etc. He is a current member of the South African Economic Society, a current certified member of the Institute for Practicing Statisticians and the Founder of the Analytics Research Group—a think tank in Quantitative Finance.

Liquidity Risk and Optimal Redemption Policies for Illiquid Investments

Cenk C. Karahan

Abstract We consider a risk-averse investor whose investable assets are held in a perfectly liquid asset (a portfolio of cash and liquid assets or a mutual fund) and another investment that has liquidity restrictions. The illiquidity could be due to restrictions on the investments (such as hedge funds) or due to nature of the asset held (such as real estate). The investor's objective is to maximize the utility he derives from his terminal wealth at a future end date of his investment horizon. Furthermore the investor wants to hold his liquid wealth above a certain subsistence level, below which he incurs hefty borrowing costs or shortfall penalty. We consider the optimal conditions under which the investor must liquidate his illiquid assets. The redemption notification problem for hedge fund investors has certain affinity with the optimal control methods used in widely studied inventory management problems. We find that the optimal policy has a monotone structure similar in nature to inventory management problems.

1 Introduction

Alternative investments such as hedge funds, private equity and real estate have come to hold a considerable weight in portfolios of most investors, both individual and institutional, over the recent decades. The market participants agree that the common feature of such investments is *illiquidity*, even though they may not agree on the exact meaning of the term, which will be addressed later. Therefore, it becomes an ever more important issue how to balance an investment portfolio among liquid and illiquid ones.

Consider a wealthy investor who divides his investable assets between a liquid portfolio such as a mutual fund and an illiquid alternative investment. The investor's main objective is to maximize the expected utility derived from total wealth at

C.C. Karahan (✉)
Department of Management, Bogazici University, Bebek 34342, Istanbul, Turkey
e-mail: cenk.karahan@boun.edu.tr

H. Dinçer, Ü. Hacioğlu (eds.), *Risk Management, Strategic Thinking and Leadership in the Financial Services Industry*, Contributions to Management Science, DOI 10.1007/978-3-319-47172-3_9

a future terminal date, at which time he liquidates his entire holdings. We are not interested in what he does with the money after the terminal date. The terminal date could be considered as the planned retirement time and the investor would be trying to maximize his retirement fund. The investor studied here has a standard risk-averse utility function.

The general problem doesn't put far-reaching restrictions on the market dynamics. The value of each investment is a Markovian process evolving over time stochastically and independently of each other. The liquid investment has an expected return that is lower relative to the illiquid investment's. We may consider it to be perfectly hedgeable, thus return the risk-free rate. The illiquid investment is not hedgeable and has a higher expected return commensurate with the risks and restrictions associated with it.

The investor needs liquidity if his liquid investments fall in value below a critical level. In this event, the investor would instantly liquidate his illiquid holding if it was possible. However, instant liquidation is not an option when part of the wealth is tied to illiquid investments. If the investor finds himself needing liquidity due to shortfall in his liquid investments, he suffers a liquidity cost as a function of deficit he faces until he can gain access to his illiquid holdings. This cost may well be considered as a heavy borrowing cost on the amount the investor has to borrow to fund the deficit.

Most financial literature defines illiquidity as a cost incurred while trading a security. The cost is paid as a transaction fee or bid/ask spread, thus reducing the return on the security. Such a definition of the illiquidity assumes one can trade the said security whenever he wants as long as he is willing pay the hefty fee associated with the transaction. The asset pricing implications of illiquidity as transaction cost has been studied extensively starting with Amihud and Mendelson (1986), Constantinides (1986) and more recently by Stambaugh (2003). Asset allocation problems similar to our study in spirit have been studied under transaction costs by the likes of Davis and Norman (1990) and Shreve and Soner (1994).

This study takes a different and more easily observable definition of illiquidity into consideration, one similar in nature to Lippman and McCall's (1976 and 1986) operational measure of liquidity. They present a precise definition of liquidity in terms of its most important characteristic—the time until an asset is exchanged for money. Thus any factor extending that time or putting restrictions on it renders the asset in question relatively illiquid. Asset pricing and portfolio implications of illiquidity in this form have been studied in theoretical papers by Longstaff (2001), Schwartz and Tebaldi (2006), Cetin and Zapatero (2015) and empirically by Aragon (2007) and others.

The illiquidity defined as such can be in many forms and be attributed to many factors. The version studied in this paper is imposed by the asset managers of an investment pool such as in the form of redemption restrictions in a hedge fund.

2 Optimal Redemption Policies for Hedge Fund Investments

We turn our attention to restrictions on liquidity imposed by investment pools such as hedge funds, private equity funds or retirement accounts. This study will use the terminology and structure of hedge funds to represent all inherently illiquid investment pools with similar redemption restrictions.

Assume a wealthy investor that holds part of his investable assets in a perfectly liquid investment such as cash, a portfolio of easily tradable securities or a mutual fund, and another part in a hedge fund. The investor wants to keep the value of his liquid portfolio above a certain value, which could be considered a subsistence level. If the liquid holdings fall below this level, the investor faces heavy borrowing costs. On the other hand, the hedge fund imposes restrictions on when and how investors can trade in and out of their holdings. These are commonly known as *redemption restriction provisions* such as lockup, advance notice, and redemption periods. *Lockup period* refers to amount of time following the initial investment investors are prohibited from withdrawing their money from the fund. Once the initial lockup period passes, investors are allowed to liquidate their investment only at specific times of the year with an *advance notice*. The period between two consecutive redemption dates is called *redemption period*. Hedge funds may also impose what is called a *gate provision*, a restriction limiting the amount of withdrawals to a certain percentage of the invested amount.

The hedge funds charge various fees. As with other investment funds, the *management fee* is calculated as a percentage of the fund's net asset value. Management fees typically range from 1 % to 4 % per annum, with 2 % being the standard figure. Hedge funds generate most of their income through *performance fee*, which is calculated as a percentage (20 % is the norm) of the fund's gains. The point of reference used in computing the gains could be *high water mark*, the highest asset value the fund has previously achieved; or a *hurdle rate*, a specific benchmark return such as LIBOR or Treasury bill yield. Hedge funds also charge a percentage of withdrawn funds as *redemption fee*. They may also charge a fraction of invested assets as *placement fee*, analogous to mutual fund sales charges. The hedge funds are typically *open-ended*, accepting new investments at certain dates. However, certain funds choose to *close* themselves to new investments. The liquid investment opportunity may have its own fee structure. However, the one considered in this study will be modeled free of such complications for simplicity. The investor's only concern is to keep his liquid holding above a certain level, below which he will incur a *liquidity cost* proportional to the deficit in funds at an onerous borrowing rate.

Under these circumstances, the investor faces the issue of how much, if any, of his hedge fund investments he should redeem at each redemption date to ensure his liquidity cost is manageable; or, if allowed, how much of his liquid investments he should channel back to potentially higher-earning hedge fund with the eventual goal of maximizing his utility at terminal date. The decision the investor faces is a stochastic control problem with state variables as the amount held in each investment fund and the remaining time until the end of the investment horizon; and the decision variable as the amount that should be transferred between the two funds. The problem in this form resembles cash management problem, an extensively studied subfield of inventory management.

Earliest studies on stochastic cash management problems are due to Girgis (1968), Eppen and Fama (1968, 1969, 1971), Neave (1970) and Heyman (1973). The problem considered in these preceding studies is as follows: A firm keeps its cash balance either in the form of cash on hand or as a bank deposit. The goal of the firm is then to choose a policy on cash transfer to minimize its cost over some period. Bensoussan et al. (2009) is a recent application of a similar idea in a financial market setting in continuous time, where an investor balances his portfolio between a bank account and a risky stock. Yan (2006) and Nascimento and Powell (2010) study the cash management problem in a context similar to ours: mutual fund cash holdings. Since the amount that can be transferred is limited by the investor's wealth, the problem considered here reflects an inventory problem with capacity restrictions. This trading limitation has been addressed as a finite production capacity within the traditional inventory management framework by Whisler (1967), Federgruen and Zipkin (1986a, b) and more recently by Özer and Wei (2004). Penttinen (1991) studies myopic and stationary solutions for stochastic cash balance problems.

Our study differs from inventory management in general and cash management problems in particular in its objective function, cost function, the fact that both investments move stochastically and limitations put on the amount that could be moved between accounts. Therefore, the problem studied here is a more realistic modeling of an actual financial problem. The eventual goal of this study is to show that the optimal policy structure in hedge fund redemption problem displays a structure similar to the ones found in the traditional inventory problems.

3 Setting and Notation

The economy under consideration is a dynamically complete financial market described by an underlying probability space $(\Omega, \mathfrak{I}, P)$ within a finite time horizon $[0, T]$. Ω represents the state space with sample paths denoted by ω, $\mathfrak{I} = \{\mathfrak{I}^S, \mathfrak{I}^H\}$ the sigma algebra generated by a two dimensional process $W = [W^S, W^H]'$ and P the probability measure. The liquid investment—a stock denoted by S—and the hedge fund holdings denoted by H are square-integrable processes adapted to the augmented filtration $\{\mathfrak{I}_t : t \in [0, T]\}$. These properties ensure that the processes and expectations are uniformly bounded in $[0, T] \times \Omega$, for every finite $T > 0$.

An investor has an investment horizon of T, at which time he will liquidate his entire holdings and retire. He has an initial sum as his investable assets. His two investment alternatives include a perfectly liquid stock, which is hedgeable, thus it returns risk-free rate under risk-neutral conditions, and a hedge fund that he can only trade in or out at certain dates $\Gamma = \{t_i : i = 0, 1, \ldots, k\}$ such that $0 = t_0 < t_1 < \ldots < t_k = T$. The possible redemption dates are assumed to be equally spaced with the exception of the first date as an extended lock-up period.

Hedge fund is assumed to offer a higher expected return than the liquid stock holdings.[1] At each of these possible dates, the investor chooses an appropriate action, the amount to be transferred between accounts to rebalance his holdings, in order to maximize his eventual expected utility at time T.

The other parameters are defined and denoted as follows:

S_i''	The amount held in stock at time t_i before fees
H_i''	The amount held in hedge fund at time t_i before fees
S_i'	The amount held in stock at time t_i before rebalancing
H_i'	The amount held in hedge fund at time t_i before rebalancing
S_i	The amount held in stock at time t_i after rebalancing
H_i	The amount held in hedge fund at time t_i after rebalancing
a_i	The amount to be transferred for rebalancing at time t_i
s	Placement fee charged by hedge fund as a percentage of invested amount
c	Redemption fee charged by hedge fund as a percentage of redeemed amount
t	Redemption period ($t = t_i - t_{i-1}$ for all i)
r	Risk-free interest rate
σ^S	Volatility of stock
μ	Expected return of hedge fund
σ^H	Volatility of hedge fund
L_i	Liquidity costs incurred since time t_{i-1} and to be paid at time t_i
P_i	Performance fees earned since time t_{i-1} to be paid at time t_i
g	Gate provision as a percentage of hedge fund holdings
$U(.)$	Investor's utility as a function of his terminal liquid wealth

The amounts invested in liquid stock and illiquid hedge fund follow the processes

$$\begin{aligned} dS &= S\left(rdt + \sigma^S dW_t^S\right) \\ dH &= H\left(\mu dt + \sigma^H dW_t^H\right) \end{aligned} \tag{1}$$

[1]The evidence of positive alpha in hedge fund returns has been well-documented in various empirical studies. See Ackermann et al. (1999), Agarwal and Naik (2004), Aragon (2007) and references therein for examples.

absent rebalancing and fees, where parameters r, σ^s, μ and σ^H are essentially bounded and adapted to their respective filtrations. The fees that the investor incurs change the level of wealth at each epoch through the following relationships.

$$\begin{aligned} S_i' &= \max\left(S_i'' - L_i, 0\right) \\ H_i' &= H_i'' - P_i \end{aligned} \tag{2}$$

Note that we put a lower limit of zero to the investor's liquid holdings as a solvency requirement. This essentially assumes the investor does not pay a liquidity cost beyond what he has in liquid holdings at his disposal at any settlement date. The assumption is not unrealistic, if we assume the liquidity cost as interest paid on borrowed funds. The investor would not owe more than he already has, as he can only use his liquid holdings as collateral when borrowing. Solvency issue does not arise in a hedge fund, because fees are paid only above a certain threshold as a fraction of the excess return.

The amount to be transferred between the two investment opportunities a_i is bounded by

$$-S_i' \leq a_i \leq gH_i' \tag{3}$$

where the upper limit is due to gate provision of the hedge fund. Let a positive action a_i denote a redemption, i.e., transfer of funds from hedge fund to the liquid stock; while a negative a_i means transferring of liquid holdings back to the hedge fund. Then the amounts held in each investment after rebalancing would be

$$\begin{aligned} S_i &= \begin{cases} S_i' + (1-c)a_i & \mathit{if}\ a_i \geq 0 \\ S_i' + a_i & \mathit{if}\ a_i < 0 \end{cases} \\ H_i &= \begin{cases} H_i' - a_i & \mathit{if}\ a_i \geq 0 \\ H_i' - (1-s)a_i & \mathit{if}\ a_i < 0 \end{cases} \end{aligned} \tag{4}$$

Note that *advance notice period* is ignored in this setup. The assumption that the funds are instantly transferred at the time of redemption simplifies the calculations and notation without taking away from the general insight of the solution. The arguments on the general structure of the optimal solution can easily be extended to a setup with a time lag between the notification and actual redemption, not unlike the lag in delivery studied in conventional inventory models. In order to keep the model general, we do not impose restrictions on the liquidity cost L_i and performance fee P_i functions for the time-being aside from being bounded and adapted to the respective filtrations.

4 Dynamic Programming Setup

The sequential decision problem investor faces is to determine at each redemption date $\Gamma = \{t_i : i = 0, 1, \ldots, k\}$ such that $0 = t_0 < t_1 < \ldots < t_k = T$ how much, if any, money to transfer between his two accounts. This is essentially a Markov decision process under aforementioned market conditions. The current state variables, the possible set of actions and future state variables are Markovian, i.e., they are conditionally independent of the past history given the current state and current action. We next turn out attention to translating this problem into mathematical language.

Let $(S_i^{'}, H_i^{'})$ be the state variables at each time t_i.. This notation clearly suppresses all other auxiliary parameters such as interest rate, returns, volatility etc. that are adapted to the appropriate filtration. These parameters are implicitly denoted via subscript i throughout the study, where the most important state variables, the amounts held in each account before rebalancing, are explicitly written. Note that $(S_i^{'}, H_i^{'}) \in [0, \infty) \times [0, \infty)$. The action taken is defined as the amounts held in each account after rebalancing (S_i, H_i), where $(S_i, H_i) \in S_i^a \times H_i^a$ and feasible sets are

$$\begin{aligned} S_i^a &= \{S_i : 0 \leq S_i \leq S_i^{'} + (1-c)gH_i^{'}\} \\ H_i^a &= \{H_i : H_i^{'} - gH_i^{'} \leq H_i \leq H_i^{'} + (1-s)S_i^{'}\} \end{aligned} \tag{5}$$

due to limited wealth and gate provisions as in Eq. (4).

Define an auxiliary process $J_i(S_i, H_i; S_i^{'}, H_i^{'})$ as the maximal expected terminal utility given the state $(S_i^{'}, H_i^{'})$ the amounts held respectively in stock and hedge fund at time t_i prior to rebalancing, and rebalancing action (S_i, H_i) taken at time t_i. Let $V_i(S_i^{'}, H_i^{'})$ be the maximal expected terminal utility given $S_i^{'}$ and $H_i^{'}$.

Assume the investor liquidates his hedge fund holdings at time T to reach total liquid wealth of W_T. Thus $a_k = H_k^{'}$, $W_T = S_k = S_k^{'} + (1-c)H_k^{'}$ and $H_k = 0$. The utility of terminal wealth is deterministic at time $T = t_k$ via

$$V_k\left(S_k^{'}, H_k^{'}\right) = U\left(S_k^{'} + (1-c)H_k^{'}\right) \tag{6}$$

For any time t_i, $0 \leq i < k$

$$\begin{aligned} J_i(S_i, H_i; S_i^{'}, H_i^{'}) &= E_i\left[V_{i+1}(S_{i+1}^{'}, H_{i+1}^{'}) | S_i, H_i; S_i^{'}, H_i^{'}\right] \\ V_i(S_i^{'}, H_i^{'}) &= \sup_{S_i} \left\{ \begin{array}{c} J_i(S_i, H_i; S_i^{'}, H_i^{'}); \\ (S_i, H_i) \in S_i^a \times H_i^a \end{array} \right\} \end{aligned} \tag{7}$$

Note that we simplify the notation from previous conditions and optimize over liquid investment holdings S_i, as it defines the hedge funds holdings through rebalancing equations. The actions implied by the change in the liquid holdings become

$$a_i = \begin{cases} \dfrac{S_i - S_i^{'}}{1-c} & \text{if } S_i \geq S_i^{'} \ (\text{or } a_i \geq 0) \\ S_i - S_i^{'} & \text{if } S_i < S_i^{'} \ (\text{or } a_i < 0) \end{cases} \tag{8}$$

The hedge fund holdings are defined through the Eqs. (5) and (8) as

$$H_i = \begin{cases} H_i^{'} - \dfrac{S_i - S_i^{'}}{1-c} & \text{if } S_i \geq S_i^{'} \\ H_i^{'} - (1-s)(S_i - S_i^{'}) & \text{if } S_i < S_i^{'} \end{cases} \tag{9}$$

The sequential decision problem is further subject to (1), the processes governing the market dynamics and (2), the fee payments on each investment opportunity. This general problem defined by Eqs. (5)–(9) yields a recursive formula on the value function V, yet it doesn't reveal any valuable information about the optimal policy. We next try to analyze the structural properties of the value function and in turn the optimal policy.

5 Structure of the Optimal Redemption Policy

The structure of the optimal policy is closely related to the concavity of the auxiliary function and the value function. In order to prove the concavity of $V_i(.)$ and $J_i(.;.)$, we make the following unrestrictive assumptions on utility function of the investor and the fees associated with maintaining investments in the two accounts described above.

Assumption 1 Utility function $U(x)$ is a *concave*, *increasing* and *continuously differentiable* function of liquid wealth $x > 0$. Risk-averse utility functions, such as constant relative risk aversion, that have become the de facto standard in the literature as well as risk-neutral utility functions carry this property.

Assumption 2 Liquidity cost L_{i+1} incurred between time t_i and t_{i+1} and to be paid at time t_{i+1} is a *convex, decreasing* and *continuously differentiable function* of the liquid stock holdings S_i at time t_i. This assumption is a very general and non-restrictive one on the borrowing costs incurred in case of liquidity need.

Assumption 3 Performance fee P_{i+1} incurred between time t_i and t_{i+1} and to be paid at time t_{i+1} is a *convex, increasing* and *continuously differentiable* function of hedge fund holdings H_i, thus a *convex* and *decreasing* function of the liquid stock holdings S_i at time t_i, due to Eq. (9).

Assumption 4 Liquidity costs L_{i+1} and performance fees P_{i+1} incurred between time t_i and t_{i+1} and to be paid at time t_{i+1} are *finite* and their respective expectations are *well-defined.* The assumption holds given the market dynamics assumed to govern the movements of investments.

What follows is a set of fairly simple technical lemmas that would help establish the concavity.

Lemma 1 *If $f(x)$ is a concave non-decreasing function and $g(x)$ is a concave one on convex set C, then $f(g(x))$ is also a concave function.*

Proof Pick any $x_1, x_2 \in C$ and $\lambda \in (0, 1)$

$$g(\lambda x_1 + (1-\lambda)x_2) \geq \lambda g(x_1) + (1-\lambda)g(x_2)$$

due to concavity of $g(x)$. Since $f(x)$ is a non-decreasing function

$$\begin{aligned} f(g(\lambda x_1 + (1-\lambda)x_2)) &\geq f(\lambda g(x_1) + (1-\lambda)g(x_2)) \\ &\geq \lambda f(g(x_1)) + (1-\lambda)f(g(x_2)) \end{aligned}$$

where the second inequality is due to concavity of $f(x)$. Hence $f(g(x))$ is also concave. ∎

Lemma 2 *If $f_t(x)$ is a concave function on convex set C and $p(t) \geq 0$ for all $t \in T$, then*

$$g(x) = \int_T p(t) f_t(x) dt$$

is a concave function on any convex subset of C, where the integral is finite.

Proof Pick any $x_1, x_2 \in C$ and $\lambda \in (0, 1)$. Then due to concavity of $f_t(x)$ and $p(t) \geq 0$ for all $t \in T$

$$p(t) f_t(\lambda x_1 + (1-\lambda)x_2) \leq \lambda p(t) f_t(x_1) + (1-\lambda) p(t) f_t(x_2)$$

Since integral is sum of these positive and finite amounts, the inequality becomes

$$g(\lambda x_1 + (1-\lambda)x_2) \leq \lambda g(x_1) + (1-\lambda)g(x_2)$$

proving concavity of $g(x)$. ∎

Lemma 3 *If $f(x, Y)$ is a concave function of $x \in C$ and Y is a random variable for which $g(x) = E[f(x, Y)]$ exists and finite for all $x \in C$, then $g(x)$ is a concave function of x.*

Proof Under certain technical conditions, the concavity of expectation function is a direct result of Lemma 2, as it is a special case of integral defined. A more general proof is beyond the scope of this study. ∎

Lemma 4 *Let X be a nonempty set with A_x a nonempty set for each $x \in X$. Let $C = \{(x, y) : x \in X,\ y \in A_x\}$ be a convex set and J a real valued and concave function on C. Then*

$$f(x) = sup\{J(x, y) : y \in A_x\} \ for\, x \in X$$

is a concave function on any convex subset of $X^* = \{x : x \in X, f(x) < \infty\}$.

The following proof is adapted from an analogous result for convex functions proven in Heyman and Sobel (1984) in a similar fashion.

Proof Pick x_1 and x_2 in X^* such that $f(x_i)$ are finite for both $i = 1$ and 2. Then for all $\gamma \geq 0$, there exist y_i with $(x_i, y_i) \in C$ such that $f(x_i) \leq J(x_i, y_i) + \gamma$ for $i = 1$ and 2. Pick $\lambda \in (0, 1)$ and let $(x, y) = \lambda(x_1, y_1) + (1 - \lambda)(x_2, y_2)$. Note that $(x, y) \in C$ due to convexity of C. Then

$$\begin{aligned} \lambda f(x_1) + (1 - \lambda)f(x_2) &\leq \lambda J(x_1, y_1) + (1 - \lambda)J(x_2, y_2) + \gamma \\ &\leq J(x, y) + \gamma \\ &\leq f(x) + \gamma \end{aligned}$$

with the second inequality due to concavity of $J(x, y)$ on C. Taking the limit $\gamma \to 0$, yields concavity of f. ∎

Theorem 1 *$V_i(S_i^{'}, H_i^{'})$ and $J_i(S_i, H_i; S_i^{'}, H_i^{'})$ are continuously differentiable and increasing in each variable if all other variables are held constant.*

Proof Monotonicity of functions in each individual variable is trivial, as investor cannot be worse off with more money in either account.

The proof of differentiability is via induction. At the penultimate redemption date

$$\begin{aligned} J_{k-1}\left(S_{k-1}, H_{k-1}; S_{k-1}^{'}, H_{k-1}^{'}\right) &= E_{k-1}\left[V_k\left(S_k^{'}, H_k^{'}\right) \middle| S_{k-1}, H_{k-1}, S_{k-1}^{'}, H_{k-1}^{'}\right] \\ &= E_{k-1}\left[U\left(S_k^{'} + (1 - c)H_k^{'}\right) \middle| S_{k-1}, H_{k-1}, S_{k-1}^{'}, H_{k-1}^{'}\right] \end{aligned}$$

due to Eq. (7). Equations (1) and (2) yield

$$\begin{aligned} S_i^{'} &= S_{i-1}e^{\left(r - \sigma_S^2/2\right)t + \sigma_S\sqrt{t}W^s} - L_i \\ H_i^{'} &= H_{i-1}e^{\left(\mu - \sigma_H^2/2\right)t + \sigma_H\sqrt{t}W^H} - P_i \end{aligned} \tag{10}$$

Assumptions 2 and 3 along with Eqs. (9) and (10) reveal that the terminal wealth is a differentiable and increasing function of S_{k-1} and H_{k-1}. Note that $U\left(S_k^{'} + (1 - c)H_k^{'}\right)$ is differentiable and increasing in liquid wealth, thus in each of $S_k^{'}$ and $H_k^{'}$ due to assumption 1. Assumption 4 and Eq. (10) would prove that $J_{k-1}\left(S_{k-1}, H_{k-1}; S_{k-1}^{'}, H_{k-1}^{'}\right)$ is also increasing and differentiable since the well-defined expectation is also continuously differentiable and increasing. Since supremum preserves monotonicity and differentiability under fairly general technical conditions, the proposition is indeed true at time t_{k-1}.

Assume it is true for t_{i+1}. By Eq. (10) and the same arguments as above, $J_i(S_i, H_i; S_i^{'}, H_i^{'})$ of Eq. (7) is increasing and continuously differentiable in each variable. Since supremum preserves monotonicity and differentiability, $V_i(S_i^{'}, H_i^{'})$ is also increasing and continuously differentiable in $S_i^{'}$ and $H_i^{'}$. Therefore, theorem 1 is true by induction. ∎

Theorem 2 *$V_i(S_i^{'}, H_i^{'})$ and $J_i(S_i, H_i; S_i^{'}, H_i^{'})$ are concave in $(S_i^{'}, H_i^{'}) \in [0, \infty) \times [0, \infty)$ and $(S_i, H_i) \in S_i^a \times H_i^a$ where feasible sets are defined as in (5).*

Proof In order to prove that the value function V_i and auxiliary function J_i are concave in their variables, we use the above lemmas and induction.

Note that the utility function $U(x)$ is concave in wealth, which all risk-averse and risk-neutral utility functions of interest are. The terminal liquid wealth is a linear function of state variables via $W_T = S_k = S_k^{'} + (1-c)H_k^{'}$. The value function at the terminal date becomes $V_i(S_i^{'}, H_i^{'}) = U(S_k^{'} + (1-c)H_k^{'})$. Therefore $V_i(S_i^{'}, H_i^{'})$ is a concave function of a linear function, which becomes concave in $(S_i^{'}, H_i^{'})$ at terminal date due to lemma 1.

Now consider

$$J_{k-1}\left(S_{k-1}, H_{k-1}; S_{k-1}^{'}, H_{k-1}^{'}\right) = E_{k-1}\left[U\left(S_k^{'} + (1-c)H_k^{'}\right) | S_{k-1}, H_{k-1}, S_{k-1}^{'}, H_{k-1}^{'}\right]$$

Due to Eq. (10),

$$\begin{aligned} & J_{k-1}(S_{k-1}, H_{k-1}; S_{k-1}^{'}, H_{k-1}^{'}) \\ & = E_{k-1}\left[U\left(S_{k-1}e^{\left(r-\sigma_S^2/2\right)t+\sigma_S\sqrt{t}W^s} - L_k + \ (1-c)H_{k-1}e^{\left(\mu-\sigma_H^2/2\right)t+\sigma_H\sqrt{t}W^H} - P_k\right)\right] \end{aligned}$$

$S_{k-1}e^{\left(r-\sigma_S^2/2\right)t+\sigma_S\sqrt{t}W^s}$ is a linear, thus concave function of S_{k-1}. Due to assumption 1, L_k is a convex function of S_{k-1}, thus $-L_k$ is a concave function. $(1-c)H_{k-1} e^{\left(\mu-\sigma_H^2/2\right)t+\sigma_H\sqrt{t}W^H}$ is a linear and concave function of H_{k-1}. $-P_k$ is also a concave function of H_{k-1} by assumption 2. Also note that H_{k-1} is a linear function of S_{k-1} , $S_{k-1}^{'}$ and $H_{k-1}^{'}$ as shown in Eq. (9). This linear relationship makes $(1-c)H_{k-1} e^{\left(\mu-\sigma_H^2/2\right)t+\sigma_H\sqrt{t}W^H}$ and $-P_k$ concave in $S_{k-1}, S_{k-1}^{'}$ and $H_{k-1}^{'}$.

The expression inside the utility function $S_{k-1}e^{\left(r-\sigma_S^2/2\right)t+\sigma_S\sqrt{t}W^s} - L_k + (1-c) H_{k-1}e^{\left(\mu-\sigma_H^2/2\right)t+\sigma_H\sqrt{t}W^H} - P_k$ is the sum of functions that are concave in variables $(S_i, H_i; S_i^{'}, H_i^{'})$. Therefore, it is a concave function of those 4 variables.

The utility function is then a concave function of a concave expression. Due to Lemma 1, $U(S_k^{'} + (1-c)H_k^{'})$ is concave in $(S_i, H_i; S_i^{'}, H_i^{'})$. Since expectation preserves that concavity by Lemma 3, J_{k-1} is concave in its parameters as well.

Note that the set the four variables belong to $\left(S_i, H_i; S_i^{'}, H_i^{'}\right) \in [0,\infty) \times [0,\infty) \times S_i^a \times H_i^a$ is a convex set, since it's a combination of affine sets. Consider

$$V_i\left(S_i^{'}, H_i^{'}\right) = \sup_{S_i}\left\{J_i\left(S_i, H_i; S_i^{'}, H_i^{'}\right); (S_i, H_i) \in S_i^a \times H_i^a\right\}$$

As a direct result of Lemma 4, $V_{k-1}\left(S_{k-1}^{'}, H_{k-1}^{'}\right)$ is also concave in $\left(S_i^{'}, H_i^{'}\right)$.

We now have established concavity J_{k-1} and V_{k-1} for the penultimate trading opportunity. Extending the result to all times is done via inductive use of the above lemmas. Assume the proposition holds at time t_{i+1}, $V_{i+1}\left(S_{i+1}^{'}, H_{i+1}^{'}\right)$ is concave in $\left(S_{i+1}^{'}, H_{i+1}^{'}\right)$. Consider

$$J_i\left(S_i, H_i; S_i^{'}, H_i^{'}\right) = E_i\left[V_{i+1}\left(S_{i+1}^{'}, H_{i+1}^{'}\right)|S_i, H_i; S_i^{'}, H_i^{'}\right]$$

Using arguments similar to above, $S_{i+1}^{'}$ and $H_{i+1}^{'}$ are each concave functions of the variable set $\left(S_i, H_i; S_i^{'}, H_i^{'}\right)$ by assumptions 2 and 3, Eqs. (9) and (10). We would like to show that $V_{i+1}\left(S_{i+1}^{'}, H_{i+1}^{'}\right)$ and by extension $J_i\left(S_i, H_i; S_i^{'}, H_i^{'}\right)$ are concave functions of $\left(S_i, H_i; S_i^{'}, H_i^{'}\right)$. For ease of notation, let $A = \left(S_i, H_i; S_i^{'}, H_i^{'}\right)$, $S_{i+1}^{'} = g(A)$ and $H_{i+1}^{'} = h(A)$ where $g(A)$ and $h(A)$ are concave functions. Pick any A_1, A_2 in the feasible set and $\lambda \in (0, 1)$

Since $g(A)$ and $h(A)$ are concave functions

$$g(\lambda A_1 + (1-\lambda)A_2) \geq \lambda g(A_1) + (1-\lambda)g(A_2)$$
$$h(\lambda A_1 + (1-\lambda)A_2) \geq \lambda h(A_1) + (1-\lambda)h(A_2)$$

Due to Theorem 1, $V_{i+1}\left(S_{i+1}^{'}, H_{i+1}^{'}\right)$ is an increasing function of $S_{i+1}^{'}$ and $H_{i+1}^{'}$.

Given above inequalities and monotonicity of $V_{i+1}\left(S_{i+1}^{'}, H_{i+1}^{'}\right)$

$$\begin{aligned}
&V_{i+1}(g(\lambda A_1 + (1-\lambda)A_2), h(\lambda A_1 + (1-\lambda)A_2)) \\
&\geq V_{i+1}(\lambda g(A_1) + (1-\lambda)g(A_2), \lambda h(A_1) + (1-\lambda)h(A_2)) \\
&= V_{i+1}(\lambda(g(A_1), h(A_1)) + (1-\lambda)(g(A_2), h(A_2))) \\
&\geq \lambda V_{i+1}(g(A_1), h(A_1) + (1-\lambda)V_{i+1}(g(A_2), h(A_2))
\end{aligned}$$

where the last inequality is due to concavity of $V_{i+1}\left(S_{i+1}^{'}, H_{i+1}^{'}\right)$. This inequality proves concavity of V_{i+1} in $A = \left(S_i, H_i; S_i^{'}, H_i^{'}\right)$.

Therefore we establish concavity of V_{i+1} in the four variables of the previous epoch. Since $J_i\left(S_i, H_i; S_i^{'}, H_i^{'}\right)$ is the expected value of $V_{i+1}\left(S_{i+1}^{'}, H_{i+1}^{'}\right)$, we can argue that J_i is also concave in $A = \left(S_i, H_i; S_i^{'}, H_i^{'}\right)$ by Lemma 3. By Lemma 4 and convexity of the feasible set, $V_i\left(S_i^{'}, H_i^{'}\right)$ is concave in $\left(S_i, H_i; S_i^{'}, H_i^{'}\right)$ as well, not unlike the first part of the proof for V_{k-1}.

By induction the concavity of $V_i(S_i', H_i')$ and $J_i(S_i, H_i)$ holds in general. ∎

Note that given the amount held in each account prior to rebalancing and only one of the values after rebalancing, the other state variable and the action taken are determined. S_i, the liquid holdings after rebalancing the portfolio, is considered the control variable in this problem. The optimal action is defined as the optimal level of liquid holdings given the amounts prior to rebalancing. H_i, the optimal holdings in the hedge fund, will be determined by the control variable S_i, and state variables S_i' and H_i' via Eq. (9).

The following two theorems are the main results on optimal hedge fund redemption policies. The main structure of the optimal policy is as follows. If the hedge funds is an open ended one, meaning the investor can invest back into the hedge fund at the same dates he can redeem his investments: the investor has two critical values; one upper bound and one lower bound. If the liquid holding of the investor is above the upper bound, he should transfer excess amount back to hedge fund to bring his liquid holdings down to that certain level; if his liquid holdings are below the lower bound, he should redeem his hedge funds holdings to bring his liquid holdings up to that critical level or as close to it as possible. For close ended hedge funds, where the hedge fund is closed to new investments, the policy is of a single critical value. If the liquid holdings are below that certain level, the investor should redeem his hedge fund holdings to bring his liquid holdings up to that critical level or as close it as possible.

Theorem 3 Consider the dynamic programming setup in Eqs. (5)–(9). If $J_i(S_i, H_i; S_i', H_i')$ is concave in $(S_i, H_i) \in S_i^a \times H_i^a$, and

$$V_i\left(S_i', H_i'\right) = \sup_{S_i} \left\{J_i\left(S_i, H_i; S_i', H_i'\right)\right\} \tag{11}$$

then for each $t_i \in \Gamma$, there are numbers $L_i \leq U_i$ such that optimal policy is of the form

$$S_i = \begin{cases} U_i & \text{if } U_i < S_i' \\ S_i' & \text{if } L_i \leq S_i' \leq U_i \\ max\left(L_i,\ S_i' + (1-c)G_i\right) & \text{if } S_i' < L_i \end{cases}$$

Proof Concavity of J_i in pair (S_i, H_i) argued in Theorem 2 implies concavity in S_i. Theorem 1 proves continuity and differentiability of the auxiliary function J_i. Therefore, the supremum is attained and there exists an optimal policy. Consider the first order condition of the optimization problem in (11) with respect to S_i. Due to concavity, S_i^* is the optimal action in (11) if, and only if,

$$\frac{dJ_i}{dS_i}(a) \geq 0 \quad \text{for} \quad \forall a \leq S_i^* \\ \frac{dJ_i}{dS_i}(a) \leq 0 \quad \text{for} \quad \forall a > S_i^* \tag{12}$$

Consider the derivative

$$\frac{dJ_i}{dS_i} = \frac{\partial J_i}{\partial S_i} + \frac{\partial J_i}{\partial H_i}\frac{dH_i}{dS_i}$$

Due to Eq. (9)

$$\frac{dJ_i}{dS_i} = \left\{ \begin{array}{l} \frac{\partial J_i}{\partial S_i} - \frac{\partial J_i}{\partial H_i}\frac{1}{(1-c)}\, if\ S_i \geq S_i^{'} \\ \frac{\partial J_i}{\partial S_i} - \frac{\partial J_i}{\partial H_i}(1-s)\ if\ S_i < S_i^{'} \end{array} \right\} \tag{13}$$

Define

$$U_i = \sup_{a \in [0,\infty)} \left\{ a;\ \frac{\partial J_i}{\partial S_i}(a) \leq \frac{\partial J_i}{\partial H_i}\ (1-s) \right\}$$

If $U_i < S_i^{'}$, then the optimality condition (12) is satisfied at U_i and the optimal liquid investment level should be $S_i^* = U_i$.

With an analogous definition

$$L_i = \sup_{a \in [0,\infty)} \left\{ a;\ \frac{\partial J_i}{\partial S_i}(a) \leq \frac{\partial J_i}{\partial H_i}\frac{1}{(1-c)} \right\}$$

and similar arguments $S_i^* = \max\left(L_i,\ S_i^{'} + (1-c)G_i\right)$ becomes optimal if $S_i^{'} < L_i$. Note that the constraint put by gate provision limits the amount the investor can redeem to increase his liquid holdings but it satisfies the optimality condition.

Due to monotone decreasing nature of the derivative $\frac{dJ_i}{dS_i}$, it's clear that $L_i \leq U_i$.

If $L_i \leq S_i^{'} \leq U_i$, we want to argue that $S_i^* = S_i^{'}$, hence no rebalancing needed. Since J_i is concave in S_i, the derivative $\frac{dJ_i}{dS_i}(a)$ is monotone decreasing. $\frac{dJ_i}{dS_i}(a) \geq \frac{dJ_i}{dS_i}\left(S_i^{'}\right) \geq 0$ for $\forall a \leq S_i^i$ and $\frac{dJ_i}{dS_i}(a) \leq \frac{dJ_i}{dS_i}\left(S_i^{'}\right) \leq 0$ for $\forall a > S_i^i$. Therefore, $S_i^{'}$ satisfies the optimality conditions in Eq. (12). ∎

The policy described by the two critical values has a natural intuition. If the liquid holdings are too high, the investor should transfer his holdings back to hedge fund as long as marginal benefit of the hedge fund exceeds that of the liquid investment. Conversely, if his liquid investment is too low, he should redeem his hedge fund holdings as long as the marginal benefit of the liquid investment is larger than that of the hedge fund. Since he has to pay a fraction of each dollar transferred as either placement or redemption fee, there is a range of values where it is optimal to abstain from any adjustments.

Theorem 4 Consider a closed-end hedge fund, where the investor cannot invest any more of his liquid funds back into the hedge fund. The dynamic programming setup in Eqs. (6) and (7) holds. Concavity of $J_i\left(S_i,H_i;S_i^{'},H_i^{'}\right)$ in $(S_i,H_i) \in S_i^a \times H_i^a$, where

$$\begin{aligned} S_i^a &= \left\{S_i : S_i^{'} \leq S_i \leq S_i^{'} + (1-c)gH_i^{'}\right\} \\ H_i^a &= \left\{H_i : H_i^{'} - gH_i^{'} \leq H_i \leq H_i^{'}\right\} \end{aligned} \tag{14}$$

is still valid. The rebalancing equations now become

$$a_i = \begin{cases} \dfrac{S_i - S_i^{'}}{1-c} & \textit{if } S_i > S_i^{'} \ (\textit{or } a_i > 0) \\ 0 & \textit{otherwise} \end{cases} \tag{15}$$

The hedge fund holdings are defined through the Eq. (15) as

$$H_i = \begin{cases} H_i^{'} - \dfrac{S_i - S_i^{'}}{1-c} & \textit{if } S_i > S_i^{'} \\ H_i^{'} & \textit{otherwise} \end{cases} \tag{16}$$

Then for each $t_i \in \Gamma$, there is a critical number L_i such that optimal policy is of the form

$$S_i = \begin{cases} \max\left(L_i,\ S_i^{'} + (1-c)G_i\right) & \textit{if } S_i^{'} < L_i \\ S_i^{'} & \textit{if } L_i \leq S_i^{'} \end{cases}$$

Proof The proof is based on a similar concavity argument made in Theorem 3 for open-ended hedge funds, where the investor can trade in our out of the hedge fund. The fact that he is now constrained to a one-way trade doesn't affect the concavity of the function J_i.

We define

$$L_i = \sup_{a \in [0,\infty)} \left\{a;\ \frac{\partial J_i}{\partial S_i}(a) \leq \frac{\partial J_i}{\partial H_i}\frac{1}{(1-c)}\right\}$$

If $S_i^{'} < L_i$, the optimality condition (12) is satisfied at L_i or as close to it as the investor's holdings allow him to get, thus $S_i^{*} = \max\left(L_i,\ S_i^{'} + (1-c)G_i\right)$ becomes optimal. If $S_i^{'} \geq L_i$, then $\frac{dJ_i}{dS_i}(a) \leq \frac{dJ_i}{dS_i}\left(S_i^{'}\right) \leq 0$ for $\forall a > S_i^{i}$, which satisfies the optimality condition. $a < S_i^i$ is not in the feasible set in this case. Therefore, $S_i^* = S_i^{'}$ is optimal when $S_i^{'} \geq L_i$. ∎

The two critical values $L_i \leq U_i$ defining the optimal policy are functions of state variables and other market dynamics such as interest rates, volatility etc. in the general form of the model. General behavior patterns of the critical values in terms of state variables are discussed next.

6 Monotonicity of the Critical Values

The critical values that define the portfolio allocation policy for the investor are in terms of the amount he has in liquid holdings. This section provides the structural properties of the critical values in terms of other state variables, particularly the hedge fund holdings and the time until investment horizon ends.

Theorem 5 Critical values L_i and U_i are increasing in hedge fund holdings prior to rebalancing $H_i^{'}$.

Proof Consider the critical values

$$U_i = \sup_{a \in [0,\infty)} \left\{ a;\ \frac{\partial J_i}{\partial S_i}(a) \leq \frac{\partial J_i}{\partial H_i}(1-s) \right\}$$

$$L_i = \sup_{a \in [0,\infty)} \left\{ a;\ \frac{\partial J_i}{\partial S_i}(a) \leq \frac{\partial J_i}{\partial H_i} \frac{1}{(1-c)} \right\}$$

Since J_i is concave in S_i and H_i, $\frac{\partial J_i}{\partial S_i}$ and $\frac{\partial J_i}{\partial H_i}$ are decreasing in S_i and H_i respectively. Therefore, it is sufficient to show that $\frac{\partial J_i}{\partial H_i}$ is also decreasing in $H_i^{'}$. By chain rule

$$\frac{\partial^2 J_i}{\partial H_i \partial H_i^{'}} = \frac{\partial^2 J_i}{\partial H_i^2} \frac{\partial H_i}{\partial H_i^{'}}$$

$\frac{\partial^2 J_i}{\partial H_i^2} \leq 0$ due to concavity of J_i. $\frac{\partial H_i}{\partial H_i^{'}} = 1$ by Eq. (16). Therefore, $\frac{\partial^2 J_i}{\partial H_i \partial H_i^{'}} \leq 0$, proving that $\frac{\partial J_i}{\partial H_i}$ is decreasing, thus L_i and U_i are increasing in $H_i^{'}$. ∎

The monotonicity of the critical values in hedge fund holdings is an intuitive result, as the investor can afford to keep more money in liquid holdings to avoid liquidity costs, if he has enough in the hedge fund that would earn him the superior returns he seeks. One interesting result in numerical tests not reported here was that the critical values were independent of hedge fund holdings if the investor is risk-neutral. Hence, if an investor's objective is maximizing the dollar value of his portfolio at the end of an investment horizon, he would try to keep his liquid holdings within a certain range, which does not depend on how much wealth he has tied to an illiquid investment.

Theorem 6 Critical values L_i and U_i are decreasing in time remaining until investment horizon, i.e., increasing in time index $\Gamma = \{t_i : i = 0, 1, \ldots, k\}$ such that $0 = t_0 < t_1 < \ldots < t_k = T$.

Proof We forgo a rigorous proof and make a heuristic argument about the monotonicity of the critical values in time. We conjecture that the expected utility would be more sensitive to changes in hedge fund holdings further away from the end of investment horizon. In mathematical terms

$$\frac{\partial J_i}{\partial H_i} \geq \frac{\partial J_{i+1}}{\partial H_{i+1}}$$

for $\Gamma = \{t_i : i = 0, 1, \ldots, k\}$ such that $0 = t_0 < t_1 < \ldots < t_k = T$. We argue that the amount held longer would have much more impact on the expected utility, which is intuitive.

Once again considering the critical values and concavity of J_i, we can argue that $U_{i+1} \leq U_i$ and $L_{i+1} \leq L_i$. ∎

The result implies that investor can afford to pay more liquidity costs upfront with the expectation that he would recover lost wealth through time with the superior earnings coming from his hedge fund holdings. As the end of investment horizon nears, the investor becomes more cautious and tries to preserve wealth by avoiding paying liquidity costs.

7 Conclusion and Future Research

Here we study a portfolio allocation of a risk-averse investor between a perfectly liquid investment and another that has trading restrictions rendering it illiquid. We consider the hedge funds as the archetypal illiquid investment with its redemption restrictions. The investor faces liquidity costs if his liquid holdings fall below a certain threshold. The asset allocation problem as defined in this study resembles cash management problems studied inventory management.

We frame the problem as a specific case of the cash management problem and search for the optimal amount to redeem or to transfer back to hedge fund. When we define the control variable as the level of liquid holdings an investor would hold at any trading opportunity, the optimal policy has a very elegant structure due to concavity of the value function. The policy requires the investor to keep his liquid investments within a range as much as his wealth restrictions allow. The two critical values defining the policy in terms of upper and lower bound of liquid holdings are increasing in the wealth held in the hedge fund. Furthermore, these two values are decreasing as the end of investor's investment horizon nears.

This study is among the few who study portfolio allocation under illiquidity. Here I take a practical view of the illiquidity imposed by trading restrictions of a hedge fund. As an extension of this study, I intend to analyze the impact of illiquidity in the former of longer expected time of sale due the innate thinness of the market for individual assets such as real estate or exotic derivatives. Optimal time and price to sell such a single illiquid asset is an area will be considered in a separate study.

As the hedge funds and investors realized during the recent financial crisis and its aftermath, liquidity is should be deliberately managed. This study proposed a simple objective in that regard to keep liquid holdings above a threshold or else pay a penalty. Although this is not far from goals of most investors, more sophisticated objectives can be considered for institutional investors with other liquidity needs.

This study provides a simple structure to the optimal redemption policies. Quantifying these policies and its superiority to ad hoc approaches to redemption would be welcome extension of this study. The structural analyses are also limited to monotonicity in time and amount held in hedge funds. One can analyze the impact of changes in risk aversion factor, interest rates or volatility in the optimal policies.

This study is admittedly simple and lacks rigorous economical foundation. In a more theoretical study, it would be a natural extension to bring in intertemporal consumption as a new control variable and add a new dimension to the problem. One can also consider the impact of correlation between liquid and illiquid holdings on the optimal policies.

The implication of this study from the hedge fund managers' point of view is that they would not be immune to market fluctuations, where the investors hold their liquid holdings. As the recent crisis have shown, even if a hedge fund has a low beta and is not correlated with the wider stock market, a plummeting stock market, where most investors hold their liquid assets, means that hedge funds would be inundated with redemption requests. Such a flood of redemption requests put irreversible strains on the hedge funds and assets they hold. A further study would approach the problem from a game theoretical point of view to optimize the redemption restrictions that hedge fund management imposes.

References

Ackermann C, McEnally R, Ravenscraft D (1999) The performance of hedge funds: risk, return, and incentives. J Financ 54(3):833–874

Agarwal V, Naik NY (2004) Risks and portfolio decisions involving hedge funds. Rev Financ Stud 17(1):63–98

Amihud Y, Mendelson H (1986) Asset pricing and the bid-ask spread. J Financ Econ 17 (2):223–249

Aragon GO (2007) Share restrictions and asset pricing: evidence from the hedge fund industry. J Financ Econ 83(1):33–58

Bensoussan A, Chutani A, Sethi SP (2009) Optimal cash management under uncertainty. Oper Res Lett 37(6):425–429
Cetin C, Zapatero F (2015) Optimal acquisition of a partially hedgeable house. Math Financ Econ 9(2):123–147
Constantinides GM (1986) Capital market equilibrium with transaction costs. J Polit Econ 94:842–862
Davis MH, Norman AR (1990) Portfolio selection with transaction costs. Math Oper Res 15 (4):676–713
Eppen GD, Fama EF (1968) Solutions for cash-balance and simple dynamic-portfolio problems. J Bus 41(1):94–112
Eppen GD, Fama EF (1969) Cash balance and simple dynamic portfolio problems with proportional costs. Int Econ Rev 10(2):119–133
Eppen GD, Fama EF (1971) Three asset cash balance and dynamic portfolio problems. Manag Sci 17(5):311–319
Federgruen A, Zipkin P (1986a) An inventory model with limited production capacity and uncertain demands I. The average-cost criterion. Math Oper Res 11(2):193–207
Federgruen A, Zipkin P (1986b) An inventory model with limited production capacity and uncertain demands II. The discounted-cost criterion. Math Oper Res 11(2):208–215
Girgis NM (1968) Optimal cash balance levels. Manag Sci 15(3):130–140
Heyman DP (1973) A model for cash balance management. Manag Sci 19(12):1407–1413
Heyman DP, Sobel MJ (1984) Stochastic models in operations research, vol II. McGraw Hill, New York
Lippman SA, McCall J (1976) The economics of job search: a survey. Econ Inq 14(2):155–189
Lippman SA, McCall JJ (1986) An operational measure of liquidity. Am Econ Rev 76(1):43–55
Longstaff FA (2001) Optimal portfolio choice and the valuation of illiquid securities. Rev Financ Stud 14(2):407–431
Nascimento J, Powell W (2010) Dynamic programming models and algorithms for the mutual fund cash balance problem. Manag Sci 56(5):801–815
Neave EH (1970) The stochastic cash balance problem with fixed costs for increases and decreases. Manag Sci 16(7):472–490
Özer Ö, Wei W (2004) Inventory control with limited capacity and advance demand information. Oper Res 52(6):988–1000
Penttinen MJ (1991) Myopic and stationary solutions for stochastic cash balance problems. Eur J Oper Res 52(2):155–166
Schwartz ES, Tebaldi C (2006) Illiquid assets and optimal portfolio choice (No. w12633). National Bureau of Economic Research
Shreve SE, Soner HM (1994) Optimal investment and consumption with transaction costs. Ann Appl Probabil: 609–692
Stambaugh RF (2003) Liquidity risk and expected stock returns. J Polit Econ 111(3)
Whisler WD (1967) A stochastic inventory model for rented equipment. Manag Sci 13(9):640–647
Yan XS (2006) The determinants and implications of mutual fund cash holdings: theory and evidence. Financ Manag 35(2):67–91

Cenk C. Karahan, PhD is an Assistant Professor of Finance at Bogazici University Department of Management in Istanbul, Turkey. Dr. Karahan has received his B.S. degree in Industrial and Systems Engineering with minor degrees in Cinema-Television and Business Administration at University of Southern California (2004). He subsequently earned his Master's degree in Engineering Management (2006) and doctoral degree in Industrial and Systems Engineering department (2011) of the same university with a research focused on financial engineering. Dr. Karahan's research and teaching interests include quantitative finance, risk management, derivatives, asset pricing and entertainment economics. He has taught portfolio management, risk management and financial derivatives at both graduate and undergraduate level.

Credit Derivatives, Their Risks and Role in Global Financial Crisis

Fatma Sezer Dural

Abstract Derivatives are financial instruments that derive its value from underlying asset such as bond, loan or credit. Credit derivatives are a subgroup of derivatives and mainly consist of credit default swaps, credit linked note, credit swap options and collateralized debt obligations. Credit derivatives market has experienced an exponential growth in recent years. From almost nothing in 1990s, approached to $60 trillion in 2008. Growth was particularly strong in credit default swaps. Force behind this fast growth is rising demand for hedging and transferring the credit risk. After the credit crisis, misuse of credit derivatives and insufficient regulations are come into light and mostly argued. Many claimed to ban these instruments whereas many other tried to find alternative solutions. The purpose of this paper is to explain the issue of credit derivatives, their mechanism and their role in financial system and global credit crisis.

1 Introduction

Credit derivatives are financial agreements that allow credit risk transfer between buyer and seller. Credit derivatives are a subgroup of derivatives market that includes futures, forward, swaps and options. Since its inception in the mid-1990s, the market for credit derivatives has grown rapidly and has gone through rapid change. More sophisticated and complex credit derivatives instruments have introduced. From $631 billion in notional amount in the first half of 2001, credit derivatives market reached to $17 trillion at the end of 2005, to $26 trillion by the mid-2006 (Tijoe 2007).

F.S. Dural (✉)
Department of Banking and Finance, Vocational School, Beykent University, Beylikdüzü Campus, Büyükçekmece, Istanbul, Turkey
e-mail: fatmasezer@beykent.edu.tr

H. Dinçer, Ü. Hacioğlu (eds.), *Risk Management, Strategic Thinking and Leadership in the Financial Services Industry*, Contributions to Management Science, DOI 10.1007/978-3-319-47172-3_10

It's very hard to give a certain time about when credit derivatives emerged firstly. But roughly it is said that it emerged around 1993. Loan trading market and collateralized loan obligations are two main driving forces behind the evolution of credit derivatives. Because these loan market has revealed some necessities and bring about new developments like credit ratings, quantitative pricing models and pricing of default risk. High trading volume in loan market yield to transfer of credit risk. But still market has problems about pricing of defaultable loans and transfer of credit risk. In order to fill the gaps in the market credit-linked notes emerged first as credit derivative (Kothari 2011).

The evolution of credit derivatives market can be analysed in four stages. In the pre-1997 stage usage of credit derivatives were mostly one-time transactions. In this stage total return swaps and equity-linked swaps were dominate the market. In the second stage between 1997–1999, there has been new developments about standardization of CDS and the need of protection from credit risk especially during the Asian, Russia and Mexican crisis. In the third stage between the years 1999–2003 credit derivatives transactions began to made by dealers, and in the same period liquidity of credit default swap has increased extremely. During this period lots of credit events have occurred like Enron, Worldcom, Argentina and National Power. In the fourth stage credit derivatives indices has introduced to the market (Kothari 2011). Credit derivatives has been seen a breakthrough in managing credit risk. Credit derivatives provide helpful tools to hedge, to reduce and to transfer credit risk. It enables to decompose risk and reallocate risk, without transferring ownership of underlying asset, to different parties who are willing to bear these risks. Even by using credit derivatives it is possible to make out a replicating portfolio. One of the most important reason behind the exponential growth of credit derivatives is the raising usage of LİBOR as an interest rate benchmark. Because it indicates the credit quality of banks and the cost of hedging. Also owing to new pricing models and quantitative approaches to credit risk, derivatives market has reached its new position (O'Kane 2001).

2 Types of Credit Derivatives

2.1 *Credit Default Swaps*

Credit default swaps are financial contracts that is used to transfer credit risk of reference entity between credit protection buyer and credit protection seller. CDS buyer, in return for transferring credit risk to CDS seller, accepts to make periodic fee payment to protection seller. Protection seller collects these fees and has to make default payment to CDS buyer in the case of credit event. CDS buyer continues to make periodic payment until the occurrence of credit event that triggers default payment. After the credit event the contract terminates. Credit default swap contract can be closed either physical delivery or cash settlement (IOSCO 2012).

As it is indicated in Fig. 1, in a credit default swap (CDS), protection seller commit to compensate the loss of protection buyer if the reference entity experiences one of a number of defined credit events. Figure 1 indicates an example for 5 year maturity CDS issued with notional value of $100 million at an annual spread of 100 basis points. XYZ corporation is the reference entity. The protection seller is paid premium, typically expressed as an annualised percentage of the notional value of the transaction in basis points and paid quarterly over the life of the transaction (Rule 2001).

Selling protection via CDS resembles to take a leveraged long position on a floating rate note of reference entity. Since both of CDS and FRN reflects the credit risk, periodic fee payment of CDS must be equal to return of FRN that is spread over Libor. From this point CDS prices should be equal to bond prices. Likewise, buying protection through CDS is similar to take a short position on underlying asset. Protection buyer can easily replicate CDS contract by shorting reference bond and investing on riskless rate (IOSCO 2012).

CDS contract Credit default contracts can be designed on a specific reference asset as well as on a portfolio of reference entities, so called index or tranche CDS. Markit as a main provider of CDS indices, developed two main index families called "CDX" and "iTraxx" by using the most liquid single-name CDS. "CDX" index family use North American and Emerging Markets reference entities whereas "iTraxx" index family use European and Asian reference entities. These index families have sub-indices varying depending on region, industry or maturity (IOSCO 2012).

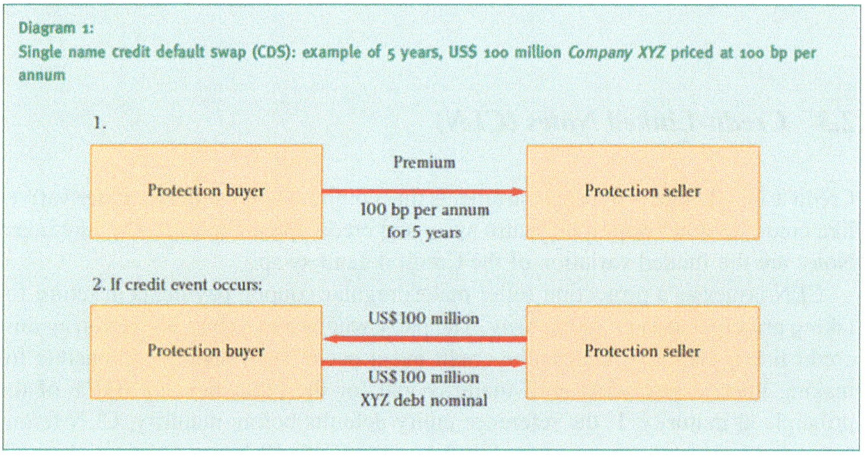

Fig. 1 Single name credit default swap

2.2 Total Return Swaps

Total Return Swaps are also bilateral agreements that enables the transfer of credit risk between total return buyer and total return receiver. Different from CDS, total return swaps transfer credit risk by exchanging total return and the credit risk of the asset for another cash flow. The receiver of the total rate of return refers to investor who get the benefits of total return without taking ownership of the security. Payments between TR receiver and TR payer changes depending on market valuation of the security (JP Morgan 1999).

Two parties of total return swap is total return receiver and total return payer. As seen from the chart, without taking the ownership of the underlying asset, TR receiver gets the total return of the reference obligation (underlying asset), in exchange for making payment of LİBOR plus a fixed spread. Total return on the reference asset is interest, fees and the changes in the market value of reference asset. In the case of increase in the market value of underlying asset, TR payer makes the payment whereas in the case of negative total return, TR receiver must compensate the loss and makes the payment to the TR payer (JP Morgan 1999).

The maturity of the underlying asset and the total return swap does not need to be the same. Total return swaps can be terminated both cash settlement or physical settlement.

Total return swap bring about some risks that counterparties have to bear in mind. The first risk is caused by a decrease in the value of the reference asset and the default of TR receiver. The second risk involves the joint default of reference asset obligator and TR receiver before making payment to the TR payer related to the decrease market value of the asset.

Total return swaps are mainly used for funding and trading purposes. In the trading based usage of TR swap, it is possible to create a new synthetic asset or to short asset without selling it. By using TR swap it is easier to leverage credit view (Choudhry 2004).

2.3 Credit-Linked Notes (CLN)

Credit-Linked Note is hybrid instruments that combine bond with credit derivatives like credit default swap, total return swap and credit spread options. Credit-Linked Notes are the funded variation of the Credit default swap.

CLN issuer as a protection seller makes regular coupon payments in return for taking principal amount at maturity. The party who wants to buy protection against credit risk issue CLN. Unless the credit event occur, the issuer is responsible for making interest payments until maturity and for the repayment of 100 % of the principle at maturity. If the reference entity defaults before maturity, CLN terminates and interest payments stop. Similar to the CDS, CLN can terminate by cash settlement or physical delivery (Bruyere et al. 2006).

In a Credit-Linked Note protection buyer doesn't take the risk of joint default of protection seller and reference entity, contrary to CDS. Because in CLN, protection buyer receives the principal amount at the beginning and repays it if credit event does not occur (Bruyere et al. 2006).

To illustrate CLN, think of a bank that invested on X bond. As an alternative way to protect itself from a potential default of X bond, bank can issue a credit-linked note. Bank B as protection seller buys $10 million CLN at par. Unless the credit event occur, cash flows between CLN issuer and investor (Bank B) continue and at maturity it terminates. In the case of default, if the market value of the bond declines 35 %, then the recovery value on 65 % will be ($10 million*65 %) $6.5 million. Bank A's gain of $3.5 million from CLN will compensate the loss of $3.5 million ($10 million*%35) due to Bond X.

Credit-linked notes were very popular in 1990s, however when credit derivatives market has developed and credit swap and credit options have used widely, the use of CLN has decreased (Finnerty 1998).

2.4 Credit Spread Options

A put option gives investor a right to sell and a call option gives a right to buy. To illustrate suppose that the strike spread is 125 bp. If an investor believes that the yield spread on bond will rise (for ex. 200 bp) above strike spread, then he must invest on credit spread put option. Because the option will be in the money. However, if the investor expects that yield spreads will decrease (for ex.100 bp) below strike spread must invest on credit spread call option. Because credit spread put option will be out of money. By using credit spread options investors can separate credit risk from market risk and other types of risk. Suppose an investor that demands a protection against a decrease in credit ratings of bond. In this situation the investor would better buy credit spread put option. Instead suppose that the investor expects an upgraded credit rating, means a decrease in spreads and increase in bond price. This time the investor realize a profit by buying credit spread call option (Finnerty 1998).

2.5 Collateralized Debt Obligations (CDOs)

Besides decomposing the credit risk, CDS can also be used to design new portfolio instruments with different risk and return characteristics. This use of CDS leads to a discovery of collateralized debt obligations. The simplest form of CDO is shown in Fig. 2 (Rule 2001).

CDOs are asset-backed securities that derives its value from the underlying collateralized asset portfolio. These asset portfolio consist of loans, mortgages, credit card receivables and even other CDOs. CDOs can be used for three different

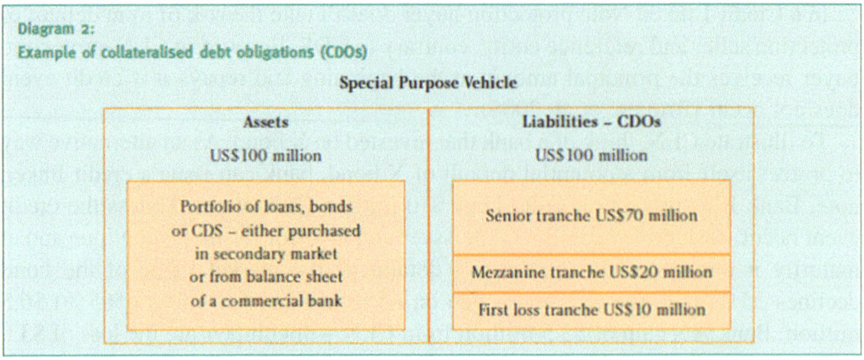

Fig. 2 Example of collateralized debt obligations

purposes. The main reason behind the issuance of CDO is to remove assets from bank's balance sheet and arbitrage.

Banks put pool of assets together and sell this package to Special Purpose Entities as collateralized debt obligations. These securities are divided into different asset tranches such as senior, mezzanine, equity and sold to investor. Between these CDOs, the senior tranches have the lowest risk and return, whereas equity tranches have the highest risk and possible return. In the case of losses senior tranch is the first to take compensation, mezzanine is the second and equity tranch comes after. Investors would select the tranch that is consistent with their risk preferences. Risk avoidance investors would tend to prefer senior tranches, high risk tolerance investor would prefer equity tranches. Collateralized debt obligations can be divided into three groups (Russell and Kyle 2012).

Cash Flow CDOs, in this most common type of CDO, cash flow of the underlying assets of the CDO are sufficient to cover all of the payments made to investors.

Arbitrage CDOs give an opportunity to make profit from the spread between the yield on underlying asset and the yield that is paid to investors in the CDO. For example, assume that the yield of underlying asset is 15 % and the yield required by CDO investor is %10. CDO issuer can make a profit of %5.

Synthetic CDOs, unlike to other types of CDOs, synthetic CDOs don't need to have an underlying asset at all. Investors enjoy the opportunity to take a share of a diversified underlying portfolio. So that the investors do not care whether CDO owns underlying asset or not, they just expect to take cash flows. Being conscious of this situation, CDO issuers look for a new way to pay these cash flows without owning underlying asset. At this point "credit default swap" and "total return swap" come into daylight. Rather than buying assets, the special purpose entity sells CDS protection, and then sells the cash flows from the CDS to investors, just like a regular CDO.

3 Size of Credit Derivatives Market

According to Chart 1, the major product of credit derivatives is credit default swaps. OCC's Quarterly Report 2013 stated that CDSs constitute 97 percent of total credit derivatives. The largest four banks hold 93% of the total notional amount of derivatives, JP Morgan, Citigroup, Bank of America and Goldman Sachs. Investment grade reference entities constitutes 49% of all credit derivatives notional, the largest part of the market. Efforts related to compression operations as well as reduced demands for structured products, resulted a decline in the amount of notional outstanding credit derivatives. According to the OCC's Quarterly Report 2015, trading volumes of credit derivatives started to decline in 2007 and this trend continued in the first half of 2015.

One of the main reason behind the rise of CDS is the regulation of International Swap and Derivatives Association that is founded in 1985 to improve operational infrastructure in derivative market. ISDA developed Master Agreement to strengthen the effect of netting and collateral and revised in 2002. ISDA defined a format and standardized documentation for CDS in terms of reference entity, credit event, CDS premium, maturity date and nominal value. An increasing demand to CDS market reveals the necessity for more standardization and transparency. In 2009, ISDA developed a new Master Confirmation Agreement (Big Bang Protocol) to strengthen the CDS contract standardization in terms of expiration date, periodic premium payments and to develop central counterparties. Single-name CDS premiums were set at 100 or 500 basis points for US contracts and at 25, 100, 500 or 1000 basis for European market (IOSCO 2012).

Credit default swap market has experienced an exponential growth since its inception. Notional amounts of outstanding CDS rose by 60% in the first half of

Chart 1 Credit derivatives composition by product type

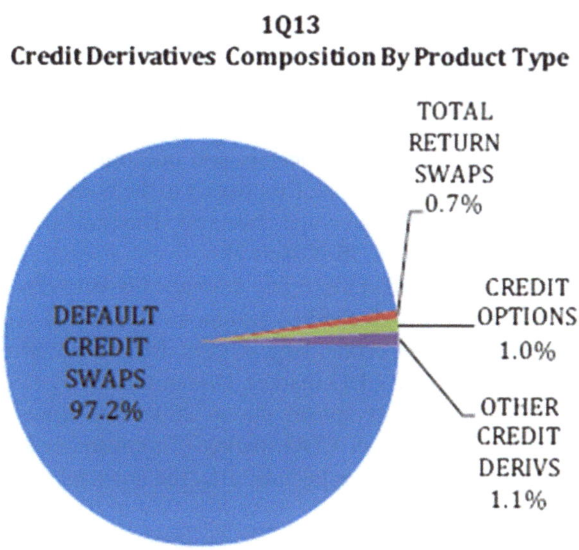

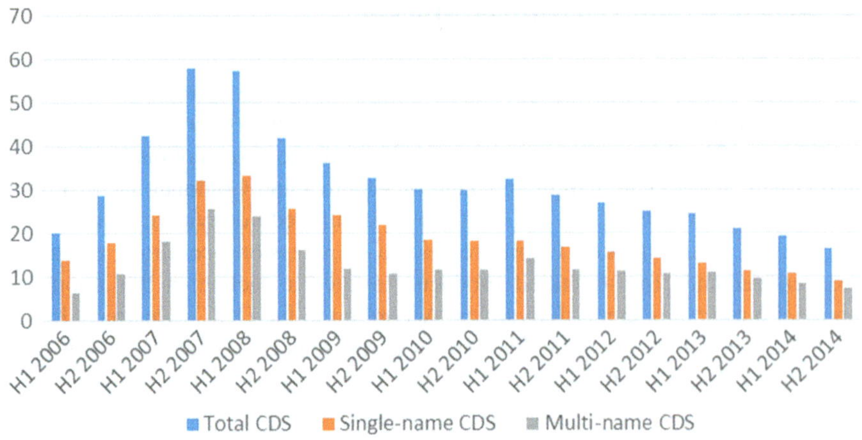

Graph 1 Notional amounts outstanding CDS (billions of US dollars)

2005 and reached 13.7 trillion dollar at the end of the year. Growth rate of single-name CDS was 40% while Multi-name CDSs' 21%. At end of 2007, the volume of outstanding CDS peaked at approximately $60 trillion. It is noteworthy that in the same period global GDP was $54 trillion. After this upward trend CDS market size declined sharply to $29 trillion at end 2011 and approximately $21 trillion at the end of 2013. Especially after the financial crisis, it is argued that CDS lost some of its appeal. Actually, the decline in volumes of outstanding CDS reflects the result of the efforts to reduce counterparty risk, and compression operations. Indeed, according to Markit, trading volumes have continued to rise and it is almost twice as high in the first nine months of 2010 as in the same period in 2007. According to BIS December 2015 Quarterly Review, downward trend continued in 2014 with 16.4 trillion dolar and declined to 14.5 trillion dollar in the first half of the 2015 (Graph 1).

Trading activities in CDSs is mostly occur in interbank market. BIS Derivatives Report 2006 indicates that two thirds of the total notional amounts outstanding transactions is done by dealers and one third of remaining is done by financial institutions. Furthermore, Comparing to the bond market CDS market has low trade frequency but large average trade size. The trade frequency of index CDS is higher than single-name CDS (Graph 2).

The CDO market also grew dramatically between 1996 and 2007. The issuance reached a new high of $312 billion, an increase of 102 % on 2005. In 2006 CDOs represented the second largest asset backed securities. The year 2006 brought innovation to the CDO market. Driven mostly by US housing market, high grade structured products spread out in 2006 and represent nearly two-thirds of the structured product of CDO market (Thompson et al. 2007). The market reached the peak by 2008 and especially after the financial crisis the market declined and got abreast of year 2000.

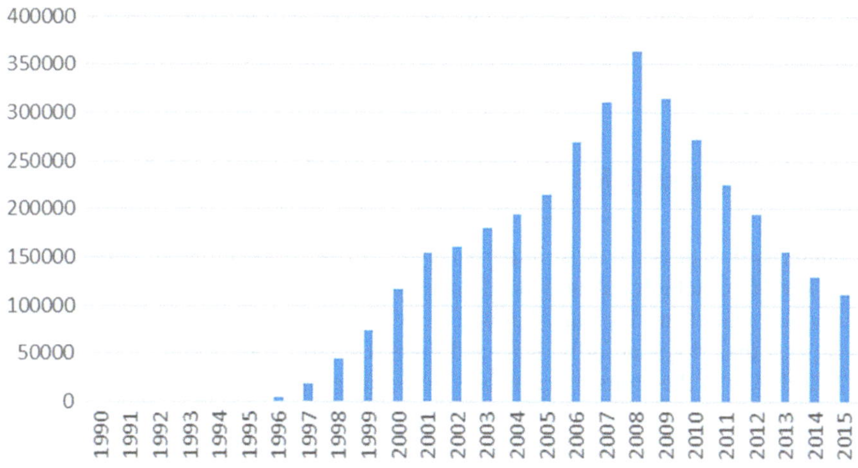

Graph 2 Outstanding global CDO (million $)

4 Risks Associated With Credit Derivatives

Credit derivatives can be used either to bear risk or to avoid risk. A market participant holds a bond, credit or a loan and thereby exposed to credit risk can hedge its position by buying protection from credit derivatives market, even without transferring the ownership of the underlying asset. Similarly, a market participant who is willing to bear more risk in return for realizing a profit can sell protection via credit derivatives (Bomfim 2001).

Risk has always existed when a new product enters the financial market due to a lack of infrastructure. And the lack of infrastructure may have costly consequences as it has had in credit derivatives market. For that reason credit derivatives pose some additional risks to financial markets, beside allocating and hedging risk (Tijoe 2007).

4.1 Credit Risk

Credit risk refers to the default of the reference credit. Credit derivatives shift it around rather than eliminating. As a result, when default rise in credit cycle someone will lose money. Credit derivatives transfer credit risk in a way that isn't very easy to understand and to follow. Most of the market participants even are not aware of the amount of exposures they have had. Financial institutions lost billions of dollars on investment in credit derivatives, Especially, in the 2001–2002 credit cycle CDO investors suffered losses (Gibson 2007).

Credit is the main risk of protection seller. Depending on contract terms, in the case of default protection seller has to make either a payment to compensate the fall in value of the reference asset or buy the asset at the notional contract amount (Scott-Quinn and Walmsley 1998).

4.2 *Counterparty Risk*

Counterparty risk is the most important type of risk to the financial markets. It is also known as default risk and mostly caused by asymmetric information. Because individuals and firms typically know more about their own financial condition and prospects than do other individuals and firms (Bullard et al. 2009).

The buyer of the protection can face with counterparty exposure that is opposing party of the contract can fail in meeting its payment obligations. As a result protection buyer remains unprotected and lose money. Counterparty risk is found depending on the mark-to-market value of credit derivative and potential future credit exposure. In order to eliminate counterparty risk, protection buyer can require collateral post (Scott-Quinn and Walmsley 1998).

Collapse of Lehman is a good example to illustrate. The notional amount of protection bought on Lehman was unclear at the time of the bankruptcy. Estimates for the total notional amount of credit default swaps written on Lehman ranged from $72 billion to $400 billion. When Lehman failed, it had close to one million derivatives contracts on its books with hundreds of financial firms. But Lehman failed to fulfill its payment obligations.for that reason the biggest protection is generally the use of collateral, and usually the amount of collateral insuring a counterparty's performance on a contract changes with the value of the contract (Stulz 2009).

4.3 *Systemic Risk*

Systemic risk is the imparing effects of a triggering event, such as the failure of a large financial firm, on financial markets and it harms the broader economy. Complex mortgage-backed securities and insufficient transparency, high leverage, and inadequate risk management created systemic risk in global credit crisis. That trade of large commercial and investment banks with each other through deposit markets and the transactions in OTC derivatives increased interconnectedness and cause systemic risk. Also highly leveraged positions enable banks and hedge funds to invest heavily in mortgage-related securities and to finance their holdings by borrowing heavily in debt markets (Bullard et al. 2009). Lehman Brothers, AIG, and other organizations were the major writers of credit default swaps. When coupled with high leverage, CDS protection sellers became highly vulnerable to mortgage defaults (Harrington 2009). In this context the failure of Bear Stearns, Lehman Brothers and AIG contributed to systemic risk. Because of interconnections risk and losses transfersred across financial institutions quickly (Fouque and Langsam 2013).

Properly designed and implemented capital regulation can reduce systemic risk (Allen and Gale 2006). In order to mitigate systemic risk the users of derivative contracts must hold more collateral or margin must be posted to CCPs to cover potential losses. Because central counterparties reduces systemic risk (Singh 2010).

4.4 Transaction Risk

Transaction risk may occur unless the allocation of credit risk is done under the ISDA documentation. Because parties may be in contradiction about the credit event that trigger the default payment, or about the deliverable asset. So relying on standardized documentation and agreement terms enables a clear understanding of transaction (Scott-Quinn and Walmsley 1998).

4.5 Liquidity Risk

For hedging purposes, thereby for protection buyer liquidity risk is relatively unimportant. In contrast for issuers of credit derivatives and for investors who plan to close out their positions liquidity risk is crucial (Scott-Quinn and Walmsley 1998).

OTC market permits greater customization and this customization means that it is difficult to liquidate an OTC position. An investor with an illiquid product will have a very difficult time unloading the risk or minimizing the loss. Therefore, holding illiquid products on the balance sheet may negatively and significantly affect a party's cash flow. As a result, during the credit crisis financial institutions and governments have suffered from illiquidity (Tijoe 2007).

5 Credit Derivatives and Their Role in Global Financial Crisis

Credit derivatives have stayed on the focal point of arguments during and after the financial crisis. Many have argued that credit derivatives (CDS) must be banned and on the contrary many other claimed that credit derivatives can not be totally excluded, only the misuse of these instruments must be prevented and new regulations must be done (Al-shakrchy and Almsafir 2014). Difference of opinion can be seen also between Warren Buffet who defined derivatives as"weapons of mass destruction" and the former Chairman of the Federal Reserve System, Alan

Greenspan, who claimed that CDS is an efficient vehicle of credit risk transfer (Augustin et al. 2015).

According to Stulz (2009), credit default swap market remained liquid especially during the first year of credit crisis, between July 2007 and July 2008 and market processed the defaults successfully as it was in the default of Lehman. However, it is true that credit default swap market has some problems. Although the collateral arrangements became widespread in 2007, consisting of %63 of derivatives contract, still they were not universal and may cause large losses. Furthermore, it is difficult to measure the size of gross exposures of dealers. However, even the net amount of risk is zero and mark-to-market and collateral mechanism is running properly, still dealers can pose some risks to financial system as a result of limited transparency and counterparty risk. Even so, these problems does not require to ban CDS.

CDS are highly leveraged and unfunded credit derivatives so that financial institutions enter into large positions without restrictions and without having underlying asset. This feasible use of CDS has brought about the misusage and decreased transparency (Al-shakrchy and Almsafir 2014).

Especially concurrently with the bancruptcy of Bear Stearns, Lehman Brothers and AIG credit derivatives are blamed. According to Al-Shakrchy and Almsafir (2014) in the case of Bear Stearns, Lehman Brothers and AIG, opaqueness of derivatives market prohibited market participants from knowing accurate amount of exposures of counterparties. Incorporation of this opaqueness and willingness to bear more risk and more profit, has caused bankruptcies and spilled over global financial markets.

AIG bankruptcy is mostly argued in this context. Actually the reason behind the AIG bankruptcy is its subsidiary company called AIG Financial Product Corporation that heavily issued and traded CDS on mortgage-backed securities. AIG FP sold protection to make money especially on "super senior risk tranches of diversified pools of loans and debt securities." AIG had an AAA credit rating of AIG convince investors to pay higher premium for protection in respect of AIG's quarantee for all present and future payment obligations of AIG FP transactions. Because according to investor, default possibility of AIG was very low and even counterparties didn't require to post collateral. As of December 31, 2007, AIG had total assets of $1.06 trillion, shareholders' equity of $95.8 billion, and a market capitalization of $150.7 billion. AIG has $61.4 billion of CDSs on multi-sector CDOs with subprime mortgage loan exposure. AIG collapsed because collateral obligations embedded in the CDSs it wrote triggered a chain reaction. When AIG's share market value drop sharply, financial distress began and forced it to put up $14.5 billion in collateral. AIG had to raise funds or quickly sell off some of its trillion dollars in assets to satisfy the collateral demand (Sjostrom 2009). As in the case of AIG, many failures experienced during the credit crisis were caused by counterparty risk. Because most of CDS contracts were bilateral and depending on directly negotiated terms, even without any collateral (Calistru 2012). Furthermore highly leveraged CDS positions that enables large selling positions and misleading risk models (ERM) that prevent the accurate measure of credit exposures and default probabilities are other reasons that cause financial crisis, except CDS (Skeel and Partnoy 2007; Wacek 2008).

As a result of all these agreements, in September 2009, G-20 Leaders agreed that "*All standardized OTC derivative contract should be traded on exchange or electronic trading platforms, where appropriate, and cleared through central counterparties by end-2012 at the latest. OTC derivative contracts should be reported to trade repositories. Non centrally cleared contracts should be subject to higher capital requirements.*" By providing full knowledge about derivative transactions and introducing central counterparties and standardization, regulatory policies aimed to increase transparency and to provide proper evaluation of risk. Through central counterparties (CCPs), insolvency of one of the parties is going to be absorbed and contagion effect is going to be prevented. As a result CCPs play an active role in risk mitigation (Calistru 2012).

6 Conclusion

Credit derivatives emerged as an alternative solution to managing credit risk. They enables market participants to transfer or to hedge credit risk. Major types of credit derivatives are; CDSs that transfer credit risk of reference entity in terms of periodic payments, CDOs that derives its value from the underlying collateralized asset portfolio, CLN that are the funded variation of the credit default swap and total return swap that transfer credit risk by exchanging total return and the credit risk of the asset for another cash flow.

Credit derivatives are the most innovative financial instruments and the fastest growing segment of the OTC derivatives. Rising demand of banks and financial institutions to hedge and transfer credit risk fostered the growth of credit derivatives. Credit derivatives has played an important role in global credit market by allowing risk transfer with lowest cost. Credit derivatives market reached $60 trillion in 2008 while world GDP was $54 trillion.

Such an exponential growth of derivatives market and global credit crisis bring about some arguments. Many claimed that these credit derivatives are not innocent as it is seemed to be and claimed to ban these instruments. It is true that while hedging and transfering credit risk to other counterparties also credit derivatives pose some other risks to financial markets. Insufficient regulations enables market participants to make highly leveraged transactions and to sell protections even without holding of underlying asset. Furthermore the opaqueness of market prevent the accurate measure of credit exposure of counterparties, so does computation of default probabilities. Collateral arrangements before and during crisis is insufficient and risk models used did not serve risk management effectively. These factors summarizes the bankruptcy of large institutions like Lehman Brothers and AIG. Especially after the credit crisis policy makers issued new regulations in respect to standardization, infrastructure, CCPs, collateral post and transparency. However, it would be helpful to bear in mind that not only these factors but also immoral and irresponsible trade of market participants, especially major large banks, and their ambitions to use gaps in regulations against the market has caused financial distress. Expectations and actions of some CDS investors who does not hold the underlying bond but anticipating any bankruptcy that can trigger payment, is another unethical business action.

Every financial innovation bring about some problems and risks together. Thing that should be done is to achive effective risk management via credit derivatives is to complement the clearing requirements of central counterparties, settlement infrastructure, collateral arrangements and to increase transparency.

References

Allen F, Gale D (2006) Systemic risk and regulation. In: Carey M, Stulz RM (eds) The risks of financial institutions. University of Chicago Press, Chicago, p 341

Al-shakrchy E, Almsafir MK (2014) Credit derivatives: did they exacerbate the 2007 global financial crisis? AIG: case study. Proc Soc Behav Sci 109:1026–1034

Augustin P, Subrahmanyam MG, Tang DY, Wang SQ (2015) Credit default swaps: past, present, and future. Present and Future (October 14, 2015)

BIS (2006) Statistics retrieved from http://www.bis.org/statistics/

Bomfim AN (2001) Understanding credit derivatives and their potential to synthesize riskless assets. Board of Governors of the Federal Reserve System, Washington, DC, p 50

Bruyere R, Copinot R, Fery L, Jaeck C, Spitz T (2006) Credit derivatives and structured credit: a guide for investors. John Wiley & Sons, New York

Bullard J, Neely CJ, Wheelock DC (2009) Systemic risk and the financial crisis: a primer. Fed Reserve Bank St Louis Rev 91(5):403–418

Calistru RA (2012) The credit derivatives market—a threat to financial stability? Proc Soc Behav Sci 58:552–559

Choudhry M (2004) Total return swaps: credit derivatives and synthetic funding instruments. Consultado en Yield. com

Finnerty JD (1998) The Pricewaterhousecoopers credit derivatives primer. Pricewaterhousecoopers LLP, New York

Fouque JP, Langsam JA (eds) (2013) Handbook on systemic risk. Cambridge University Press, Cambridge

Gibson MS (2007) Credit derivatives and risk management

Harrington SE (2009) The financial crisis, systemic risk, and the future of insurance regulation. J Risk Insur 76(4):785–819

IOSCO (2012) Report of the International Organization of Securities Commissions. Retrieved from https://www.iosco.org/library/pubdocs/pdf/IOSCOPD385.pdf

JP Morgan guide to credit derivatives. Risk Publications, 1999

Kothari V (2011) Credit derivatives and structured credit trading, vol 749. John Wiley & Sons, New York

O'kane D (2001) Credit derivatives explained. Lehman Brothers

Office of the Comptroller of the Currency (2013) Quarterly report on bank trading and derivatives activities

Office of the Comptroller of the Currency (2015) Quarterly report on bank trading and derivatives activities

Rule D (2001) The credit derivatives market: its development and possible implications for financial stability. Financ Stabil Rev 10:117–140

Russell A, Kyle G (2012) Understanding collateralized debt obligations. Retrieved from https://www.batesresearch.com/BR_Publications/CDOExplained/CDO%20Explained.pdf
Scott-Quinn B, Walmsley J (1998) The impact of credit derivatives on securities markets. International Securities Market Association
Singh MM (2010) Collateral, netting and systemic risk in the OTC derivatives market (No 10-99). International Monetary Fund
Sjostrom WK Jr (2009) AIG bailout. The Wash Lee L Rev 66:943
Skeel DA, Partnoy F (2007) The promise and perils of credit derivatives. Univ Cinci Law Rev 75:1019
Stulz RM (2009) Credit default swaps and the credit crisis (No w15384). National Bureau of Economic Research
Thompson A, Callahan E, O'Toole C, Rajendra G (2007) Global CDO market: overview and outlook. Deutsche Bank Global Securitisation and Structured Finance
Tijoe L (2007) Credit derivatives: regulatory challenges in an exploding ındustry. Ann Rev Bank Fin L 26:387
Wacek M (2008) Derivatives, AIG and the future of enterprise risk management. Risk management: the current financial crisis, lessons learned and future implications

Fatma Sezer Dural is a Lecturer at Beykent University Vocational School, Department of Banking and Insurance, Istanbul, Turkey. She received her BS in Business Administration from Eskişehir Anadolu University in 2006. During 2003–2004 academic year, she attended Mateja Bela University in Slovakia as an Erasmus Student. In 2006, she won a Graduate scholarship from Tübitak and earned an MBA degree from Marmara University in Financial Markets and Investment Management (2008). Since 2010, she is continuing her Phd study at Istanbul University in Finance Department. Her studies focus mainly on financial markets and derivatives. She is teaching financial management, financial statement analysis and general accounting courses at Beykent University.

An Approach to Measure Financial Risk Relative Indices: A Case Study of Indonesian Insurance Companies

Heri Kuswanto

Abstract The number of insurance companies in Indonesia has been increasing over the years. This is a good indicator of the society's awareness ofthe importance of insurance. In order to ensure the sustainability of acompany as well as its customers' safety, the insurance companies have to maintain the quality of their performance. To deal with this, the Financial Service Authority (OJK) of Indonesia needs to monitor the risk level of each insurance company. For the company, financial risk analysis is required to formulate strategies for reducing its risk. Financial risk analysis is also important for prospective investors or creditors as one of the considerations to formulate a business plan with the company. This chapter introduces an approach to measure financial risk through financial performance data as reported in the company's annual report. In this case, the risk variables in the balance sheet are available only on a yearly basis, and hence, a time series based approach for measuring risk, such as Value at Risk (VaR), cannot be applied. The limited number of series will explode the variance estimate of the parameter distribution used to calculate VaR. As an alternative, the risk can be measured by an index showing the financial risk of a company relative to the others. The fact that financial risk is a latent variable, which can be measured only through its indicators, leads to the idea of calculating the index by using the concept of the Confirmatory Factor Analysis (CFA). This chapter applies that idea to calculate the financial risk relative indices of life insurance companies in Indonesia. This approach offers another benefit, the ability to investigate variables which significantly contributes to increase the risk. The analysis shows that a company is said to have a high financial risk relative to the others if the index is below 0.29.

H. Kuswanto (✉)
Department of Statistics, Institut Teknologi Sepuluh Nopember (ITS), Kampus ITS, Sukolilo 60111, Surabaya, Indonesia
e-mail: heri_k@statistika.its.ac.id

H. Dinçer, Ü. Hacioğlu (eds.), *Risk Management, Strategic Thinking and Leadership in the Financial Services Industry*, Contributions to Management Science, DOI 10.1007/978-3-319-47172-3_11

1 Introduction

Indonesia has been ranked as the fourth most populated country in the world. However, this high number is not linearly correlated with the number of citizens equipped with health services and facilities, as indicated by the low percentage of citizens covered by health insurance. The latest data shows that only 10 % of Indonesians have been fully covered by health insurance. Moreover, only 5 % are covered by life insurance as reported by Indonesian Life Insurance Association (AAJI) in 2014. Nevertheless, it has been predicted that the number of Indonesians covered by life insurance will increase over the years; this is supported also by the increasing growth in the number of insurance companies in Indonesia. The large Indonesian population should be able to make insurance a promising financial industry in Indonesia.

One of the reasons which contribute to the low participation rate in Indonesia is the little trust society places in the insurance business, such as its complicated claim procedure, unclear terms and conditions in advance, as well as its trust in the sustainability of the insurance companies, this last referring to the "health" factor of the company. One of the health indicators is financial risk. Dealing with this, the approach which is commonly applied to measure risk is Value at Risk (VaR), first introduced by Markowitz (1959), which has been proven to be a valid way to measure a company's health. Several works have discussed the application of VaR to risk management, e.g., Basak and Shapiro (2001), Culp et al. (1998), among others. Ufer (1996) specifically discussed the concept of VaR for an insurance company. Majumdar (2008), at the 10th Global Conference of Actuaries, described a simple model to measure insurance risk through VaR. Moreover, Kaye (2005) discussed in detail measuring risk in insurance companies using VaR as well as other approaches.

It is well known that a risk calculation using VaR is applied to time series data. Furthermore, this method performs well if we have sufficiently long time series data in order to obtain unbiased parameters for the distribution. However, the availability of a long series of data usually becomes a major challenge, which means that in some cases we are required to estimate the company's risk but we do not have enough data available. Consequently, we need an alternative approach to measure the risk, which does not require long time series data, such as using cross-sectional data.

An anual financial report is an example of cross-sectional data, consisting of information required to assess the company's financial condition, and hence, it can be used to measure the financial risk. Blach (2010) discussed assessing financial risk based on the information available in the balance sheet, and described in detail three components to identify financial risk: capital structure risk, liquidity risk, and insolvency risk. In statistics, financial risk is a latent variable, which can be measured only from those three risk components. Ho et al. (1998) discussed also the required information in a balance sheet which can be used to measure risk using VaR. However, the data used in the research consist of a long (multiple) period of annual balance sheet reports, and hence it is still feasible to apply VaR.

The challenge of evaluating financial risk using cross-sectional data as reported in balance sheets (financial reports) can be solved by using the concept of latent variable, which is usually known as a unidimensionality test, e.g., using the Confirmatory Factor Analysis (CFA) developed by Jöreskog (1969). From the CFA, we obtain weights used to calculate the company's financial risk index. A similar approach has been applied to develop indices in various fields. Long and Perkins (2003) used CFA to develop the Sense of Community Index. Meanwhile, Fernando et al. (2012) used factor analysis to develop a composite index of urbanization in Sri Lanka. Unlike those two indices, the procedure of developing financial risk indices has to be carried out by pre-processing the raw data presented in the financial report. The CFA approach employs a data-driven concept, which means that the weight will be directly estimated from the available data, instead of using weights assigned by external sources, such as an Analytical Hierarchical Process (AHP). The benefit of using CFA is its ability to detect indicators which are significantly valid to measure the risk. Furthermore, the index can be used as a tool to assess the annual performance of the company's health based on financial risk. This chapter applies this approach to calculate indices of life insurance companies in Indonesia as a case study. As the weights are calculated by isomg records from all the companies, the resulting indices are interpreted as relative risk indices.

2 Data and Methodology

The CFA approach proposed in this study is applied to calculate risk relative indices of life insurance companies in Indonesia based on the dataset reported in the *Statistic of Indonesian Insurance 2013* published by OJK Indonesia. The risk indices are calculated based on the variables which are available in the report. The report covers the financial performance of 23 national life insurance companies and 18 joint venture life insurance companies. In the analysis, the two types of companies will not be distinguished, and therefore, the total size of the sample (insurance companies) to be analyzed is 41 companies. Several companies are excluded from the analysis due to incomplete information in the balance sheet. Table 1 lists the names of the insurance companies.

The data available in the annual balance sheet report that will be used as the financial risk indicators are Assets (including Fixed Assets and Current Assets) and Capital (Equity Capital and Debt Capital/liability). Several risk components used to calculate risk indices are based on the research carried out by Blach (2010):

1. Capital Structure Risk measured from a Debt Ratio Analysis consisting of the following indicators:
   - Debt/Equity Ratio (D/E),
   - Debt/Asset Ratio (D/A),
   - Equity/Asset Ratio (E/A)

Table 1 List of life insurance companies in Indonesia

No	National life Insurance company	No	Joint venture life insurance company
1	PT Asuransi Jiwa Adisarana Wanaartha	1	PT AIA Financial (d/h PT AIG Life)
2	PT BNI Life Insurance	2	PT Asuransi Allianz Life Indonesia
3	PT Asuransi Jiwa Bringin Jiwa sejahtera	3	PT Asuransi Aviva Indonesia (d/h PT Winterthur Life Indonesia)
4	PT Asuransi Jiwa Central Asia Raya	4	PT Avrist Assurance (d/h PT Asuransi AIA Indonesia)
5	PT Equity Life Indonesia	5	PT Axa Financial Indonesia
6	PT Heksa Eka Life Insurance	6	PT Axa Life Indonesia
7	PT Indolife Pensiontama	7	PT Axa Mandiri Financial Services
8	PT Asuransi Jiwa InHealth Indonesia	8	PT Asuransi CIGNA
9	PT Asuransi Jiwasraya (Persero)	9	PT CIMB Sun Life (d/h PT Commerce International)
10	PT Asuransi Kresna Life (d/h PT A.J. Mira Life)	10	PT Commonwealth Life (d/h PT Astra CMG Life)
11	PT Asuransi Jiwa Mega Life	11	PT Asuransi Jiwa Generali Indonesia (d/h PT A.J. Arta Mandiri Prima)
12	PT MNC Life Assurance (d/h PT UOB Life Sun Assurance)	12	PT Great Eastern Life Indonesia
13	PT Multicor Life Insurance	13	PT Tokio Marine Life (d/h PT MAA Life Assurance)
14	PT Panin Life (d/h PT Panin Anugrah Life)	14	PT Asuransi Jiwa Manulife Indonesia
15	PT Pasaraya Life Insurance	15	PT Prudential Life Assurance
16	PT Asuransi Jiwa Recapital	16	PT Asuransi Jiwa Sinar Mas MSIG
17	PT Asuransi Jiwa Sequis Financial	17	PT Sun Life Financial Indonesia
18	PT Asuransi Jiwa Sequis Life	18	PT Zurich Topas Life (d/h PT Mayapada Life)
19	PT Asuransi Jiwa Tugu Mandiri		
20	PT Asuransi Jiwa Mega Indonesia		
21	PT Asuransi Jiwa Reliance		
22	PT Central Asia Financial		
23	PT ACE Life Assurance (d/h PT A.J. Bhumi Artha Reksatama)		

2. Liquidity Risk measured from a Liquidity Ratio Analysis consisting of the following indicators:

   – Current Ratio = Current Asset/Liability (CuR)
   – Cash Ratio = Cash/Liability (CaR)

3. Insolvency Risk measured from a Financial Balance Analysis consisting of the following indicators:

   – Equity/Fixed Asset (E/F)
   – Capital / Fixed Asset (C/F)

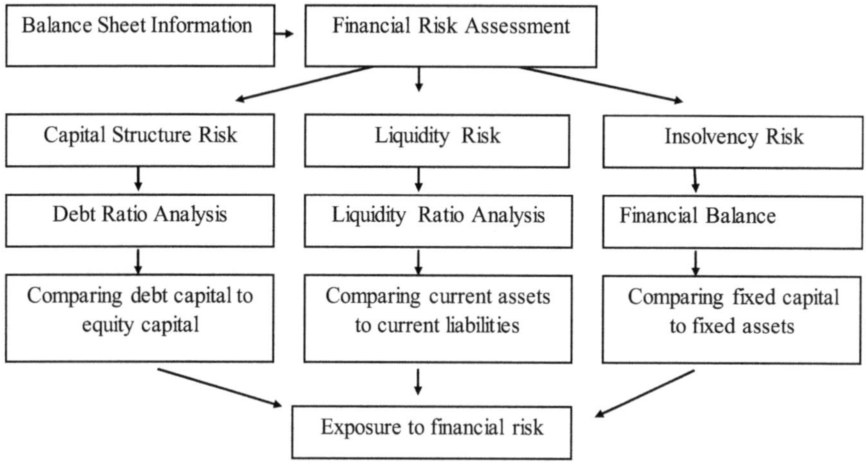

Fig. 1 Theoretical framework to measure financial risk [adopted from Blach (2010)]

In this case, the Capital Structure Risk, Liquidity Risk and Insolvency Risk are latent variables from which will be constructed the financial risk. The theoretical framework as the basis of using those variables refers to the following scheme (Fig. 1):

The steps of the data analysis can be summarized as follows:

1. Preprocessing the data: The raw data will be transformed using simple linear scoring to obtain a new dataset with values within the range of 0 to 1, to make it interpretable and comparable with others. Meanwhile, the data which are available in the balance sheet are on the raw currency rate (Rupiah). Moreover, the preprocessing step will transform the raw data in the same direction (positive and negative indicators), which means that an index should have the same definition for all risk indicators. Indices of 1 and 0 represent the lowest risk and highest risk.
2. CFA stage 1: Estimation of weights connecting indicators to risk components
   The estimation of the weights is conducted by applying two stages of the CFA approach to the indicators, with the path structure shown in Fig. 2. The parameters are estimated by the maximum likelihood method.
   The weights will be used to calculate the performance index of each risk component by the following formula

$$\text{Index}\left(X1_j\right) = \sum_{i,j=1}^{i=n,j=k} w_i{*}\text{Index}\left(X_{ij}\right)$$

   where i indicates the number of the indicator and j is the number of the insurance company. The X1 indicates the risk performance at stage 1 measured by the risk indicators and e_i represents the measurement error of the ith indicator.
3. CFA step II: Estimate the weights connecting risk components to financial risk

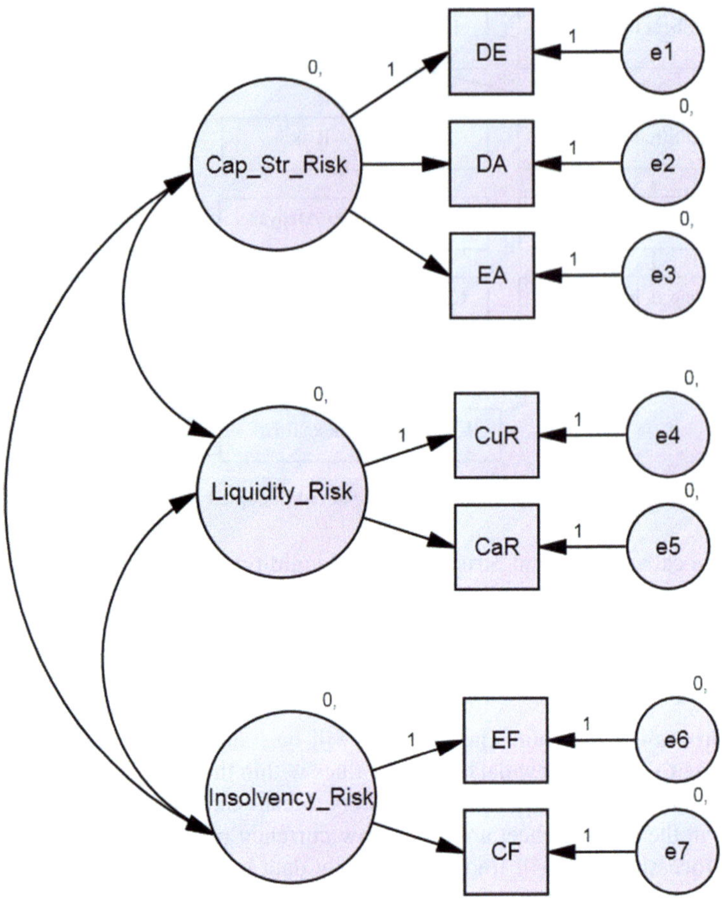

Fig. 2 CFA structure to estimate weight of indicators

This step is conducted by a similar procedure as estimating the weights of the indicators. The CFA structure can be composed as Fig. 3 below:
Calculate the financial risk relative indices as follow

$$\text{Index}\left(X2_j\right) = \sum_{i=1}^{3} w_p{*}\text{Index}\left(X_j\right)$$

where p indicates number of risk components and $X2_j$ denotes the risk performance for each company.

4. Mapping the result of financial risk relative indices

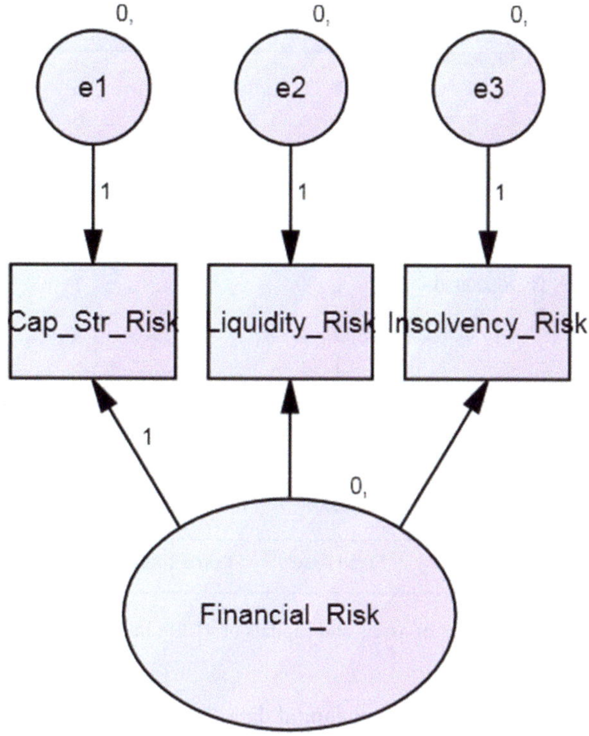

Fig. 3 Structure of CFA to estimate the weights of risk component

3 Descriptive Statistic and Calculation of Relative Risk Indices by CFA

We begin this section by summarizing the descriptive statistics of the variables used to calculate the relative risk indices. Figure 4 shows boxplots of total assets and capital (raw data) of 41 Indonesian life insurance companies in 2013.

From the figure, we see that there are five companies with extremely high amounts of assets and capital. These companies are PT. Asuransi Jiwa Manulife Indonesia, PT. Prudential Life Assurance, PT. Asuransi Allianz Life Indonesia, PT. AIA Financial, and PT. Asuransi Jiwa Sraya (Persero). Four of them are joint venture life insurance companies and another one (Persero) is managed by the government. In fact, those five companies are big insurance companies and hold the biggest market shares in Indonesia compared to other companies. Do those companies have the lowest financial risk? The answer is not as simple as just looking directly at how much assets and capital they have, because financial risk is a latent variable. Moreover, financial risk is a result of interaction among several financial indicators with their complexity. This means that a company with a large amount of assets does not always have a low risk, while a company with little assets does not always have a high risk.

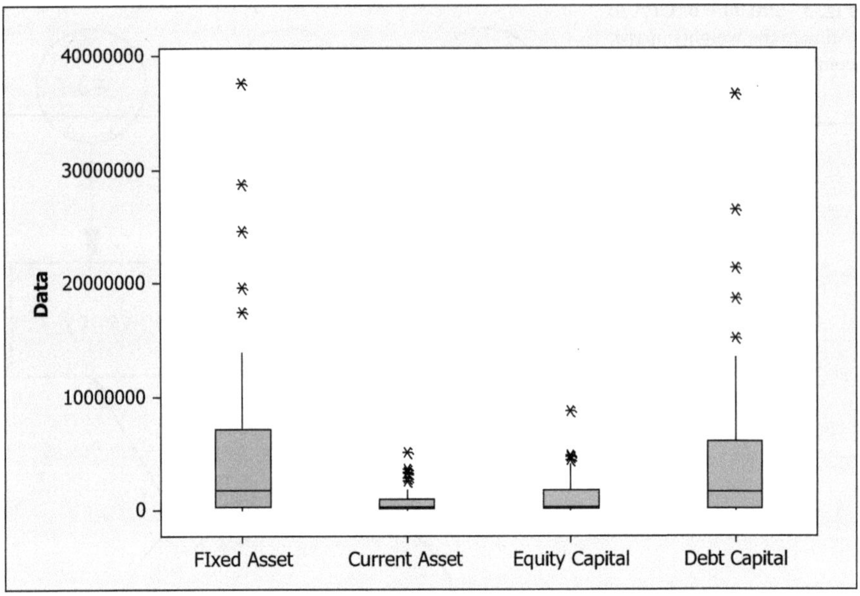

Fig. 4 Boxplot of assets and capitals of 41 life insurance companies in Indonesia

From the asset and capital data, we can derive several indicators to calculate the companies' performance on the risk components. Table 2 lists several statistics of transformed indicators with the range of values between 0 and 1, where 0 represents the highest risk, while 1 indicates the lowest risk.

The values in the Table 2 are indices of indicators showing the performance of the companies in general. From these seven indicators, the average Current Ratio (CuR) and Cash Ratio (CaR) are very low, which indicates that on average the liquidity risk of the companies is very high. However, the indices for capital risk structure, in particular, the Debt to Equity Ratio (D/E), are high, which indicates that on average the companies in Indonesia are able to generate enough cash to satisfy their debt obligations. The performance of companies in terms of insolvency risk is shown by the indicators E/F and C/F, which tend to be average, especially for C/F, while E/F shows relatively high risk.

From the standardized indicators data, the Confirmatory Factor Analysis (CFA) will estimate the weights connecting the indicators to the risk components. The weights in this case can be interpreted as the contribution of the indicator to the exposure to the corresponding risk component. The structure of the CFA path is shown in Fig. 5.

The estimated values that result from the CFA path in Fig. 5 are listed in Table 3.

Table 3 summarizes all estimated parameters of a CFA model which can be used to determine whether the indicators are valid indicator for the underlying risk component. The P-values of all indicators are below the 5 % significance level, meaning that the D/E, D/A and E/A are valid indicators of Capital Structure Risk;

Table 2 Descriptive statistics of standardized risk indicators

Risk indicators	Mean	Standard deviation	Q1	Q3
D/E	0.7802	0.2368	0.6339	0.9563
D/A	0.4056	0.2719	0.1700	0.5900
E/A	0.3383	0.2482	0.1200	0.4600
CuR	0.0964	0.1724	0.0329	0.1029
CaR	0.0967	0.1698	0.0368	0.1054
E/F	0.2544	0.2135	0.1731	0.3880
C/F	0.5931	0.1338	0.5379	0.6062

the Current Ratio and Cash Ratio are valid indicators of Liquidity Ratio; while E/F and C/F are valid indicators for Insolvency Risk. The CFA requires a setting of an indicator (within a risk component) which is assumed to be significantly valid, i.e., the one with an estimated value of 1.

The estimated values in Table 4 show how big is the contribution of each indicator to generating the corresponding risk component. For the Capital Structure, the D/A and E/A have relatively the same contribution, i.e., about 0.9, while D/E has a relatively smaller contribution than those two. For the Liquidity risk component, the Current Ratio and Cash Ratio have almost the same contribution. A very significantly different contribution is obtained for the Insolvency risk indicators. The E/F has a very high contribution to the insolvency risk, while the Capital/Fixed Asset has a very low contribution. The estimated values are standardized to obtain weights, and we can see the weights in the last column of Table 4.

The fact that the among-risk components are related each other is confirmed by the statistical evidence listed in Table 5 showing the linear relationships between the variables.

In Table 5, the P-values are lower than the significance level of 5 %, meaning that the among-risk components are significantly related although the correlation is low. The value 0.028 connecting liquidity risk with insolvency risk means that increasing the liquidity risk will be followed by increasing the insolvency risk, and vice versa. The other values can be interpreted similarly.

Another important part of this analysis is to study the contribution of each risk component to exposure to financial risk simultaneously. The results of the CFA can be seen in Fig. 6, Tables 6 and 7. Based on the P-values in Table 6, the Capital Structure Risk, Liquidity Risk and Insolvency Risk are the three components which are significantly valid indicators of financial risk.

Based on the weights listed in Table 7, the weight of Insolvency Risk is 0.4304, much higher than the weights of Capital Structure Risk and Liquidity Risk with values of 0.275 and 0.293, respectively. This shows that the financial risk of the insurance companies is mostly determined by the Insolvency Risk.

Furthermore, the risk index of each company can be seen from Fig. 7, where the blue box represents the Capital Structure Risk index, red shows Liquidity Risk, and green represents Insolvency Risk. The company's performance with respect to these three risk components shows a high degree of variation. There are some

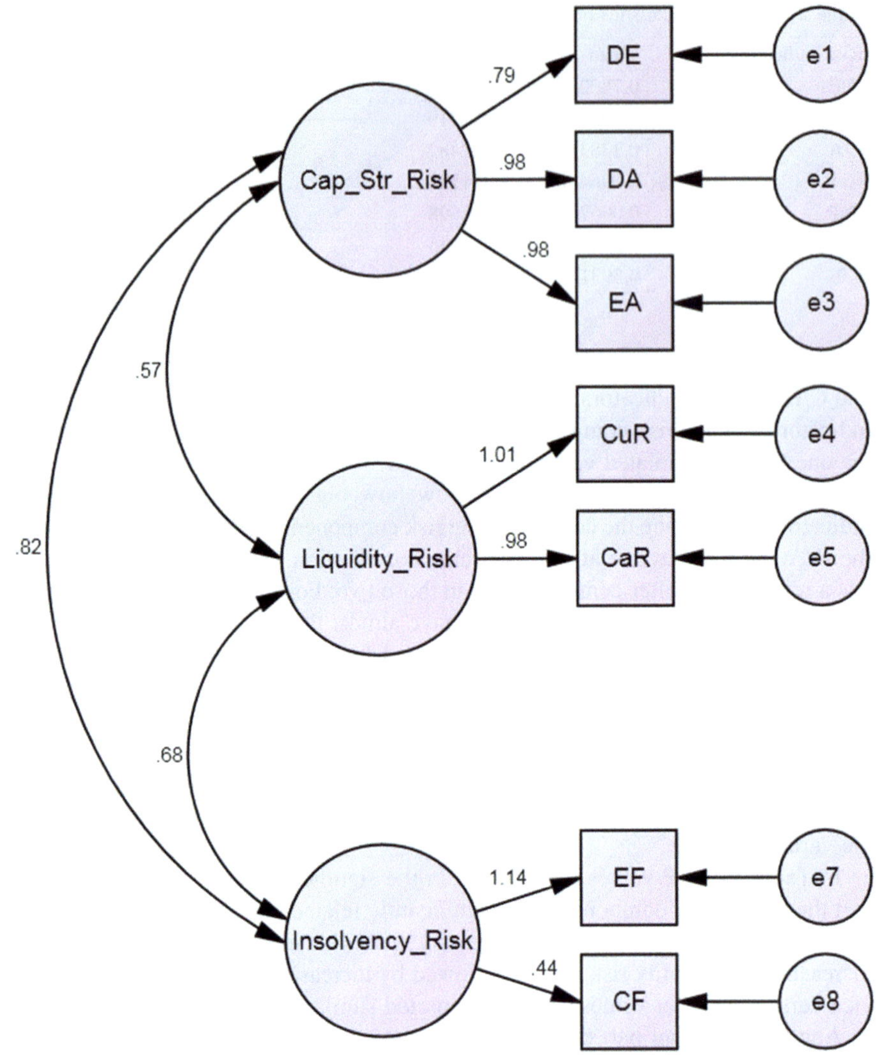

Fig. 5 Structure of CFA to estimate the weight of indicator

companies with a very low degree of Liquidity Risk, but high Capital Risk Structure. Meanwhile, several companies have low Capital Risk but high Liquidity Risk, etc. These combinations lead to complications in measuring the actual financial risk, and hence, an index representing the financial risk as an aggregate definition needs to be calculated. Figure 8 shows the financial risk relative indices of the life insurance companies in Indonesia calculated by a CFA. The indices have been sorted from the lowest index (highest risk) to the largest index (lowest risk). A summary of the indices for all companies can be seen in Fig. 9.

Table 3 Parameter estimation by CFA for risk indicator

			Estimate	S.E.	C.R.	P
D/E	<—	Cap_Str_Risk	1.000			
D/A	<—	Cap_Str_Risk	1.435	0.186	7.732	<0.05
E/A	<—	Cap_Str_Risk	1.304	0.170	7.677	<0.05
CuR	<—	Liquidity_Risk	1.000			
CaR	<—	Liquidity_Risk	0.962	0.021	45.018	<0.05
E/F	<—	Insolvency_Risk	1.000			
C/F	<—	Insolvency_Risk	0.240	0.089	2.710	0.007

Table 4 Estimate and standardized weight

			Estimate	Weight
D/E	<—	Cap_Str_Risk	0.785	0.2860
D/A	<—	Cap_Str_Risk	0.982	0.3578
E/A	<—	Cap_Str_Risk	0.977	0.3560
CuR	<—	Liquidity_Risk	1.008	0.5057
CaR	<—	Liquidity_Risk	0.985	0.4942
E/F	<—	Insolvency_Risk	1.142	0.7227
C/F	<—	Insolvency_Risk	0.438	0.2772

Table 5 Testing the relationship among financial risk components

			Estimate	S.E.	C.R.	P
Cap_Str_Risk	<—>	Liquidity_Risk	0.018	0.006	2.932	0.003
Liquidity_Risk	<—>	Insolvency_Risk	0.028	0.007	3.902	<0.005
Cap_Str_Risk	<—>	Insolvency_Risk	0.036	0.010	3.797	<0.005

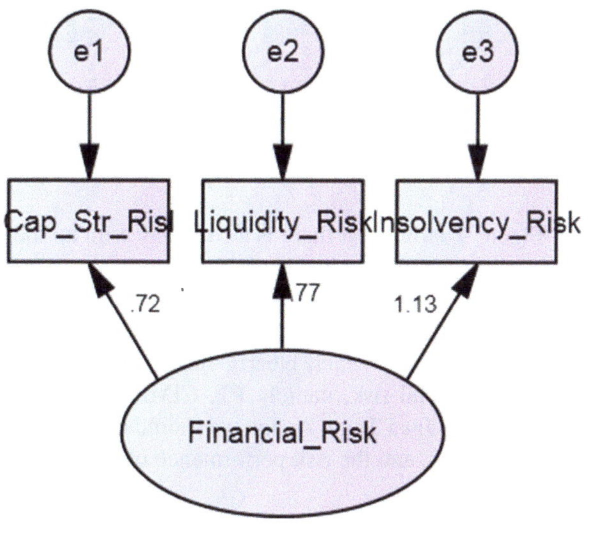

Fig. 6 Structure of CFA to estimate weight of risk components

Table 6 Parameters of CFA for financial risk components

			Estimate	S.E.	C.R.	P
Cap_Str_Risk	<—	Financial_Risk	1.000			
Liquidity_Risk	<—	Financial_Risk	0.758	0.135	5.605	<0.05
Insolvency_Risk	<—	Financial_Risk	1.144	0.198	5.779	<0.05

Table 7 Weight of standardized risk components

			Estimate	Weight
Cap_Str_Risl	<—	Financial_Risk	0.722	0.2759
Liquidity_Risk	<—	Financial_Risk	0.768	0.2935
Insolvency_Risk	<—	Financial_Risk	1.126	0.4304

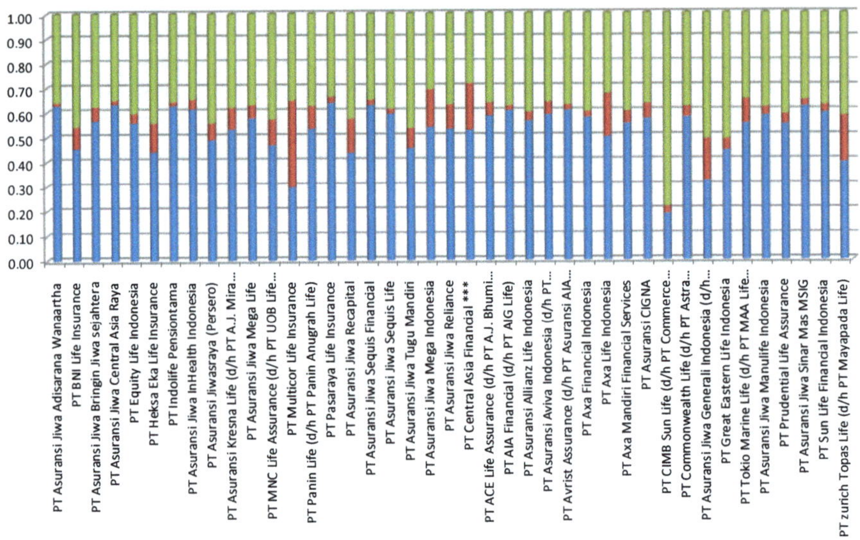

Fig. 7 Performance of financial risk components index for life insurance companies in Indonesia 2013

Figure 9 shows that there is a company with an index of 0.96, namely, Multicar Life Insurance. This shows that this company has very low financial risk relative to the others. Meanwhile, the first quartile means that 25 % of the companies have risk index lower that 0.175, which is high risk. The detailed names of the companies can be seen in Fig. 8, which clearly shows that there are three companies with the highest financial risk, namely PT. CIMB Sun Life, PT. Great Eastern Life and PT. Asuransi Jiwa Tugu. Again, we should note that the measured relative risk is an aggregate risk, and the risk performance of each indicator can be seen from Fig. 8.

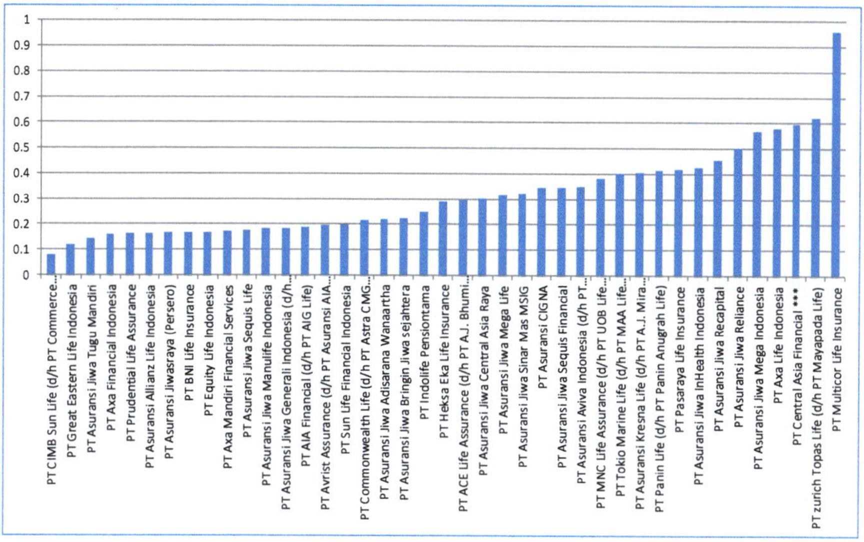

Fig. 8 Performance of financial risk relative index for life insurance companies in Indonesia 2013

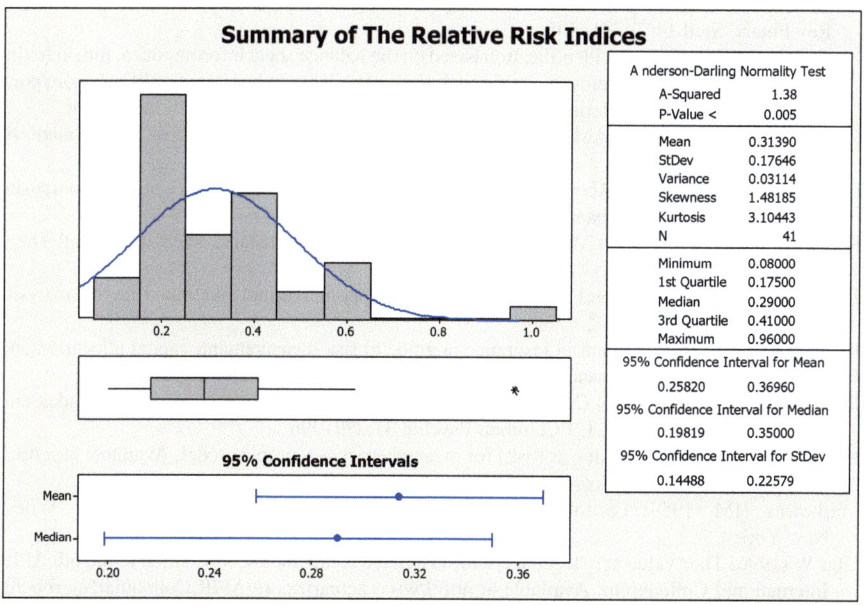

Fig. 9 Summary of the financial risk relative indices of life insurance companies in Indonesia 2013

4 Conclusion

This chapter proposed the use of a simple statistical approach, namely, Confirmatory Factor Analysis, which has received less attention in the insurance field, in particular for measuring risk, but has been used in many other fields. From the analysis, we know that a relative risk index can be developed or calculated by using information which is publicly available. This research confirms the established theoretical framework that Insolvency Risk, Capital Structure Risk and Liquidity Risk are valid indicators of the financial risk of the companies. For Indonesian life insurance companies in 2013, Insolvency Risk is the highest exposure to financial risk. Information about the evaluation of each company in terms of these three risk components can be used as guidance to reducing the risk by focusing on one or two indicators with a high index. The median value. 0.29, can be used as a threshold to justify whether a company has a lower or higher financial risk than the others.

References

Basak S, Shapiro A (2001) Value at risk based risk management: optimal policies and asset prices. Rev Financ Stud 14(2):371–405

Blach J (2010). Financial risk Identification based on the balance sheet information. 5. mezinárodní konference Řízení a modelování finanč ních rizik. Available at http://www.ekf.vsb.cz/export/sites/ekf/rmfr/.content/galeriedokumentu/2014/plne-zneni-prispevku/Blach.Joanna.pdf

Culp CL, Miller MH, Neves AMP (1998) Value at risk: uses and abuses. J Appl Corpor Financ 10 (4):26–38

Fernando MACS, Samita S, Abeynayake R (2012) Modified factor analysis to construct composite indices: illustration on urbanization index. Trop Agric Res 23(4):327–337

Ho T, Abrahamson A, Abbott M (1998) Value at risk of a bank's balance sheet. Int J Appl Theor Finance 2(1)

Jöreskog KG (1969) A general approach to confirmatory maximum likelihood factor analysis. Psychometrika 34:183–202

Kaye (2005) Risk measurement in insurance, a guide to risk measurement, capital allocation and related decision support issues. Casualty Actuarial Society discussion paper program

Long DA, Perkins DD (2003) Confirmatory factor analysis of the sense of community index and development of a brief SCI. J Commun Psychol 31:279–296

Majumdar C (2008) VaR (Value at Risk) for insurance risk—a simple model. Available at: http://www.actuariesindia.org/downloads/2008-actuariesindia.org

Markowitz HM (1959) Portfolio selection: efficient diversification of investments. Wiley, New York

Ufer W (1996) The "value at risk" concept for insurance companies. Contribution to the 6th AFIR International Colloquium. Available at http://www.actuaries.org/AFIR/Colloquia/Nuernberg/Ufer.pdf

Heri Kuswanto is a lecturer and researcher at the Department of Statistics, Institut Teknologi Sepuluh Nopember (ITS) Indonesia. He is a member of the Laboratory for Economic Statistics, Financial and Actuarial Science in the department. Dr. Kuswanto has Bachelor and Master Degree in Statistics from ITS Indonesia. In 2006, he started to work as PhD fellow at the Institute of Statistics, School of Economics and Management, Leibniz Hannover University Germany. He was awarded with PhD in Economics in 2009. In 2010, Dr. Kuswanto worked as a Postdoctoral Fellow at Laval University Canada. His research interests lie in the methodological development for time series forecasting and econometrics which are applied mainly to financial cases. He is now working also in the field of extreme events. He has been intensively works in the field of risk estimation, and did projects dealing with the risk modelling in some financial institutions. Dr. Kuswanto is now the Head of Postgraduate Program at the Department of Statistics-ITS.

Part III
Volatility, Hedging and Strategy in Risky Environment

Extreme Value Theory in Finance: A Way to Forecast Unexpected Circumstances

B. Esra Aslanertik, Sabri Erdem, and Gülüzar Kurt Gümüş

Abstract EVT works on extreme affairs and those affairs are generally classified as outliers. Although in some analyses it is preferred to exclude extreme events, oppositely EVT directly focuses on extreme events and analyze them. Financial data also contain outliers due to crashes, breaks and peaks. Since extremal events are more commonly seen in financial data than many other data types and excluding of those results in under or overestimation, academicians and financial institutions utilize EVT especially in risk management as a contributing function to Value-at-Risk. Additionally, distribution characteristics of financial data which do not fit normal distribution are other major points to use EVT. The finance literature on EVT indicates the EVT does the best especially in fat-tail modeling and extremal event analysis.

1 Introduction

During the last decades, the globalization in financial markets and financial product innovations have shown a significant increase. Therefore, fundamental changes required in financial environment due to:

- Advances in technology,
- Rapid innovation in financial instruments,
- Changes in the structure of the banking systems,
- Growing interest on stock markets,

B.E. Aslanertik • S. Erdem
Faculty of Business, Department of Business Administration, Dokuz Eylül University, Tınaztepe Campus, Buca 35390, İzmir, Turkey
e-mail: esra.aslanertik@deu.edu.tr; sabri.erdem@deu.edu.tr

G. Kurt Gümüş (✉)
Faculty of Business, Department of International Business and Trade, Dokuz Eylül University, Tınaztepe Campus, Buca 35390, İzmir, Turkey
e-mail: guluzar.kurt@deu.edu.tr

H. Dinçer, Ü. Hacioğlu (eds.), *Risk Management, Strategic Thinking and Leadership in the Financial Services Industry*, Contributions to Management Science, DOI 10.1007/978-3-319-47172-3_12

- Diverse investor base and their various behaviour patterns.

These factors has led to the entrance of uncertainty and risk to the economy but with a different structure. Basel II accord has emphasized the different aspects of financial risk. These aspects can be defined as (Brodin and Klüppelberg 2008):

- Market Risk: the risk that the value of an investment will decrease due to the movements in market factors.
- Credit Risk: the risk of loss due to a debtor's non-payment of a loan (principal or interest).
- Operational Risk: the risk of losses resulting from inadequate or failed internal processes, people and systems, or external events.

The most important and distinguished one is the market risk because it reflects the effects of different factors of potential economic loss caused by the decreases in the market values. Within a long time period, the stock prices will fluctuate but the expected variations in these fluctuations can be relatively small and assumed to be normally distributed. When these variations become more significant and unforeseen, huge losses or market crashes will occur. Several market crashes have affected financial markets within the last two decades such as Black Monday on October 1987, Asian financial crisis in 1997–1998, hedge fund crisis in 1998, mortgage and credit crisis in 2007–2008. The most powerful result of these crashes is the fact that forecasting risk is a major issue for financial institutions and for market regulators. In order to handle this forecasting and risk management problem, the first task is to quantify and measure risk and the second task is to distinguish between extreme and non-extreme events. According to Rocco (2014), the best and most informative risk measure is the return of the financial activity measured by the whole tail of distribution and this distribution in general is either unknown (only time series of returns are known) or difficult to deal with (richness of data). As a solution to deal with too much information, several risk measures have been used; Volatility of a portfolio selection (Markowitz 1952), Value-at-Risk (VAR) developed by J.P. Morgan in 1994 and Expected Shortfall (ES) as a coherent risk measure (Artzner et al. 1999). Although very significant studies have been made in risk modelling, there is no consensus on which methodology can make the best estimation of the distribution. VAR and ES concentrates on extreme quantiles of distribution rather than the distribution itself (Rocco 2014) but it is crucial to model the distribution tails properly in order to predict the frequency and magnitude of extreme stock price returns (Furió and Climent 2013).

Extreme Value Theory (EVT) is a well-developed tool that provides more appropriate estimations of distributions for extreme events. Some EVT techniques can be used to solve very high quantiles in predicting crashes and extreme loss situations (Bensalah 2000). EVT uses two different modelling approaches (Bensalah 2000; Gilli and Kellezi 2006):

1. The asymptotic distribution of a series of maxima (minima) within a time-series. These selected observations constitute the extreme events called block maxima. This method is generally used to analyze data with seasonality.

2. The distribution of excess over a given threshold in terms of modelling the behaviour of the excess loss once a high threshold is reached, also called as Peaks-Over-Threshold (POT). This approach uses data more efficiently and that makes it more preferable in recent studies.

This chapter aims to discuss foundations of EVT and its applications in finance supported by an extended theoretical framework and comparison of methods in terms of risk management. Section 2 introduces a mathematical and statistical background for EVT. Section 3 concentrates on use of EVT in finance. The chapter concludes with an evaluation of risk management and EVT by giving important remarks on the usage of EVT in finance.

2 Theoretical Background of EVT

EVT is a special research field in Statistics Science that tries to model the tail loss of well-known distributions through model fitting approximations, iterative techniques (e.g. Maximum Likelihood) and simulations (e.g. Markov Chain Monte Carlo). Thus Extreme Value (EV) distributions are used to model maximum and minimum values of a set of normal distributed random variables. Extreme value distributions are asymptotic distributions and can be regarded as family of distributions. EVs are widely used in modeling peak and/or deep flows of data streams come from any kind of events in daily. It is not a new research area because of initial studies emerged in early 1900s (Kotz and Nadarajah 2000).

Gumbel (1954, 1958), who is the pioneer of extreme value theory, opened a new field of research for statisticians and engineers. It was just as trials of experiments before his researches. In the first half of 1900s, Gumbel initially used meteorological data for preliminary models in those researches. There are many other contributors to this new field of science during these years and it is shaped around several classifications of methods as block maxima, peak over threshold, *r*th largest order models (see Fig. 1); it was also studied as univariate, bivariate and multivariate models; from another view of classification, methods are ordered by means of their parameter estimation techniques like approximation methods by calculus, iterative techniques through maximum likelihood method and Markov Chain Monte Carlo Method as simulation based techniques.

2.1 Generalized Extreme Value (GEV) Distribution

Generalized Extreme Value (GEV) Distribution is used to model the block maxima type of extreme value distributions. GEV is family of distributions in which Gumbel (Type 1) and Frechet (Type 2) distribution where the parent distribution is unbounded against extreme values and for minimum values, Weibull (Type 3) is

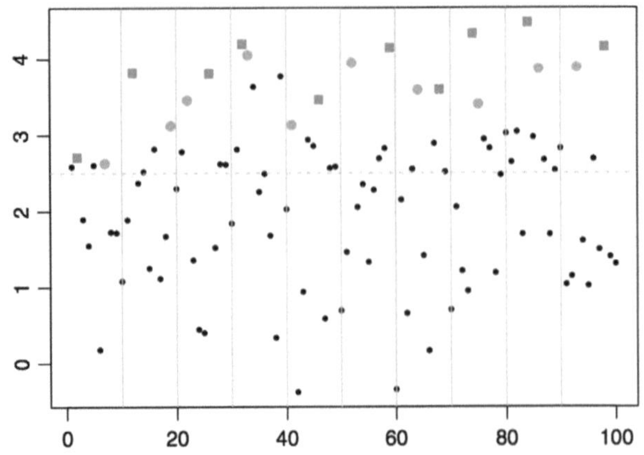

Fig. 1 Block maxima, rth largest orders and peaks-over-threshold. Source: Pfaff (2012)

the parent distribution that has an upper bound (see Fig. 2). It can be presented in (1) through (3) below. The reason for having three different type of tail modeling distribution is to obtain best estimator parameters of the original distributions' loss tail on the right and left side, which depends on the characteristics of the research.

$$\text{Type 1 Gumble}: \; P(X \leq x) = e^{-e^{\frac{x-\mu}{\sigma}}} \tag{1}$$

$$\text{Type 2 Frechet}: \; P(X \leq x) = \begin{cases} 0, & x < \mu \\ e^{-\left(\frac{x-\mu}{\sigma}\right)^{-\xi}}, & x \geq \mu \end{cases} \tag{2}$$

$$\text{Type 3 Weibull}: P(X \leq x) = \begin{cases} e^{-\left(\frac{x-\mu}{\sigma}\right)^{\xi}}, & x \leq \mu \\ 0, & x > \mu \end{cases} \tag{3}$$

Where μ, $(\sigma > 0)$ and $(\xi < 0)$ are parameters.

In Table 1 forms of limiting distributions for maxima and minima is summarized for most widely used continuous distributions.

Here the distributions (2) and (3) can be transformed to Gumbel (Type 1) family of distributions by the simple transformations respectively as:

$$Z = \log(X - \mu) \quad Z = -\log(\mu - X) \tag{4}$$

In (1) least values of limiting distributions can be obtained by replacing X by (-X). In fact, all these models can be generalized in a simplified form such that:

$$P(X \leq x) = \left[1 + \xi\left(\frac{x - \mu}{\sigma}\right)\right]^{-\frac{1}{\xi}} \tag{5}$$

Fig. 2 GEV family of distributions. Source: Shukla et al. (2012)

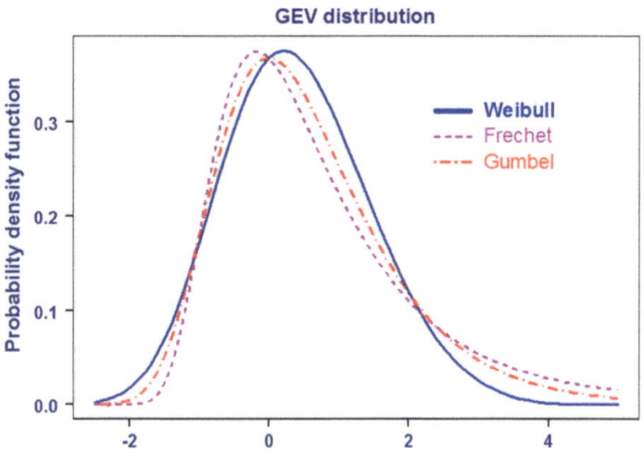

Table 1 Initial and limiting EV distributions

	Limiting distribution for extremes	
Initial distribution	Maxima	Minima
1. Exponential	Type 1	Type 3
2. Gamma	Type 1	Type 3
3. Normal	Type 1	Type 1
4. Log-Normal	Type 1	Type 1
5. Uniform	Type 3	Type 3
6. Pareto	Type 2	Type 3
7. Cauchy	Type 2	Type 2

Type 1: Gumbel, Type 2: Frechet, Type 3: Weibull
Source: Kotz and Nadarajah (2000)

Where

$$1 + \xi\left(\frac{x-\mu}{\sigma}\right) > 0$$

and $-\infty < \xi < +\infty, \quad \sigma > 0.$

Here,

If $\xi \to -\infty$ or $\xi \to +\infty$ then the distribution is Gumbel (Type 1)
If $\xi > 0$ then the distribution is Frechet (Type 2)
If $\xi < 0$ then the distribution is Weibull (Type 3)

For this reason Equation (2) is known as the *generalized extreme value distribution. It* is also called as the *von Mises* or the *von Mises–Jenkinson type distribution.*

Here specifically, Gumbel Distribution's parameters can be derived using (1) moment functions:

$$\alpha = \sigma 1.283 \quad \text{where } \sigma = \text{standard deviation} \tag{6}$$

$$\hat{\beta} = \overline{X} \pm 0.45\sigma \quad \text{where } \overline{X} = \text{mean}, \quad '' - '' \text{ for max } \; '' + '' \text{ for min}) \tag{7}$$

Mean or expected value:

$$E[X] = \beta \pm 0.5772\alpha \;\; \text{where } '' - '' \text{ form in and } '' + '' \text{ for } max \tag{8}$$

Variance:

$$Var(X) = 1.645\alpha^2 \tag{9}$$

Skewness Coefficient:

$$\gamma = 1.1296 \;\; \text{which is constant value} \tag{10}$$

There were many studies in early years of emerging of EV different research areas such as human lifetimes, radioactive emissions, strength of materials, flood analysis, seismic analysis and rainfall analysis, quality assurance systems, describing yearly maximum of rain falls, river flows, wind pressures and so on (Kotz and Nadarajah 2000).

2.2 Block Maxima Method

EVT seeks for a distribution that best fits the maximums or minimums of i.i.d. random variables in a time horizon n starting from X_1 through X_n. Time horizon can be expressed as half-months, months, quarters and even years in that data is observed daily.

Data for block maxima models can simply be presented as in (11)

$$M_n = \max\{X_1, \ldots, X_n\} \tag{11}$$

Where $X1, \ldots, Xn$: sequence of i.i.d random variable on a time basis of n periods.

In Fig. 1, there are ten blocks and maximum of each block is considered to create a model. Assuming the distribution function for the Xi is known, the distribution of Mn can be derived as:

$$\begin{aligned} P\{M_n \le x\} &= P\{X_1 \le x, \ldots X_n \le x\} \\ &= P\{X_1 \le x\} \times \ldots \times P\{X_n \le x\} \\ &= \{F(x)\}^n \end{aligned} \tag{12}$$

Here the problem is to find a family of distributions F^n that approximates to any type of F. In case of $n \to \infty$, M_n transformed into M_n^* so that the distributions are approximated by GEV:

$$M_n^* = (M_n - b_n)/a_n \tag{13}$$

where

an > 0 and *bn* are sequences of constants.

Finally if *an* and *bn* exist, the probability expression can be expressed as:

$$P\left\{M_n^* = \frac{M_n - b_n}{a_n} \le x\right\} \to G(x) \quad \text{for} \quad n \to \infty \tag{14}$$

Where G(x) is one of the following family of GEV distributions in (1) through (3).

2.3 rth Largest Order Models

One of the basic problems with block maxima for EVT in real world applications is lack of data on a sequence of time periods. It causes a uncertainty and the error in modeling since variance of parameter estimation is reduced. On the other hand there may be a problem due to biased sample because of newcomers are not really extreme losses. *r*th largest order models considers up to the *r*th data in each block to characterizing the GEV distributions. The data pattern to the block maxima and the *r* largest order model is presented in Fig. 1 where 10 blocks are constructed, maximum losses are depicted in dark grey squares and second largest data in each block is shown by solid light grey circles and a dashed horizontal line is sketched at the ordinate of 2.5 as a threshold.

2.4 The Peaks-Over-Threshold Method

In the last decades, Peaks-over-threshold (POT) models are getting popular because of controlling the number of extreme values by a certain threshold value that set by researcher. Therefore POT is more applicable in case of small amount of data on extreme values (McNeil 1999).

Since the lack of data (especially data regarding in financial markets), unknown distribution parameters and not exactly real maximum values in the block maxima, the POT method is more preferable when financial risks are of interest. In POT method, instead of the block maxima data points or the *r*th largest values within a block are considered as extreme observations, all observations above a certain threshold value are evaluated.

The probability of any observation has a higher value than the threshold *u* is expressed as below:

$$P\{X > u+y|X > u\} = \frac{1 - F(u+y)}{1 - F(u)}, \quad y > 0 \tag{15}$$

The exceedances $(X - u)$ are distributed according to the generalized Pareto distribution (GPD),

$$H(y) = 1 - \left(\frac{1 + \xi y}{\widetilde{\sigma}}\right)^{-\frac{1}{\xi}} \tag{16}$$

Where $y{:}y > 0$ and $\widetilde{\sigma} = \sigma + \xi(u - \mu)$

It means that if the threshold value u is sufficiently large enough and GEV can approximate sample for block maxima, then observations above threshold can be approximated by GPD.

A threshold is set by graphically using a mean residual life (MRL) value. In the most cases GPD characteristics are estimated by maximum likelihood method but other methods are taken into account as well in some applications (Pfaff 2012).

As specific to financial data, the VaR and ES risk measures can be inferred directly from the GPD as follows:

$$VaR_\alpha = q_\alpha(F) = u + \frac{\widetilde{\sigma}}{\xi}\left(\left(\frac{1 - \alpha}{\overline{F}(u)}\right)^{-\xi} - 1\right) \tag{17}$$

$$ES_\alpha = \frac{VaR_\alpha}{1 - \xi} + \frac{\widetilde{\sigma} - \xi u}{1 - \xi} \tag{18}$$

3 EVT in Finance

Modern portfolio theory is based on the normally distributed financial returns assumption. As a result of normal distribution, variance and correlation are accepted as risk measure and dependence measure respectively. Mandelbrot (1963) demonstrated the poor fitting of normal distribution for financial data. Deviation from normal distribution is also found for exchange rates (Patton 2006).

Measuring risk is a popular topic in finance and there has been an increasing interest in risk management due to financial market crashes. Risk managers specifically focus on the risk of low-probability and extreme-loss generating occasions, which are interpreted by the profit and loss' tail distribution. Hence the risk measurement methods are evolving continuously in order to find the best method. Value-at-Risk and expected shortfall are the most widely used measures of risk. VaR is described as the extreme quantile of the marginal loss distribution. It estimates the size that the loss of a portfolio may exceed with a specific small probability within a specific time period. Although it was first developed by RiskMetrics, the commonly use of VaR as a market risk measure has been started after the inclusion of market risk in regulatory capital calculation besides credit risk (Basel I). Misestimation of the market risk causes holding improper amount of capital and rise in insolvency risk (in case of underestimation) or inefficient allocation of cash resources (in case of overestimation). The ways of risk measurement in VaR estimation are historical simulation, GARCH models (assumption of conditional normality instead of normality) and EVT (calculation of extreme events' probabilities).

Usefulness of EVT in VaR estimation is shown by some studies in finance literature (Ergen 2010; Gencay and Selcuk 2004; McNeil and Frey 2000).

Since VaR does not give information about the size of the possible loss and is not a coherent risk measure, another risk measure "expected shortfall" is introduced. Expected shortfall, namely conditional VaR provides an estimate of the size of loss under the worst scenarios which are quantified by VaR. It does not fix a specific confidence level, it averages Var for all levels.

Employing EVT in VaR for risk measurement is one of evolving steps in finance literature, because estimation of extreme quantiles in the presence of pre-mentioned stylized facts such as fat tails, skewness, high dependence and volatility clustering is of natural interest. EVT emerged as a beneficial method in order to model extremal financial data both for univariate and multivariate conditions. Commonly referenced point for EVT use in risk measurement is fat distribution tails problem.

The main goal of investors and risk managers is to generate cash flows under both extreme and non-extreme market conditions. EVT concentrates on modelling of extreme events through asymptotic models of distribution and it finds an important area of research in finance. There has been various studies of EVT in finance literature that presents a comprehensive background and its applications in order to emphasize the role of EVT especially in financial markets (Embrechts et al. 1999; McNeil 1999; Bensalah 2000; Gilli and Kellezi 2006; Brodin and Klüppelberg 2008; Rocco 2014).

McNeil (1999) provided an overview of the role of EVT in risk management and concentrated on POT approach by emphasizing the generality of it. The paper includes a structure about how the POT approach can be integrated in a stochastic volatility framework to achieve best estimates of VaR and ES for market risks. In addition, McNeil discusses multivariate extremes, models for stress losses and software for EVT. Diebold et al. (2000) emphasized the importance of using EVT but also argued that caution is needed because estimation of aspects of very low frequency events from short historical samples is fraught with pitfalls. Longin (2000) claimed that in financial markets, extreme prices subject to market corrections in ordinary and extraordinary periods (e.g. crisis, crashes) and extreme value approach offers a wide range of application of VaR from the usual environment to stress testing. Longin also stated that univariate extreme value theory is used to compute the VaR of a fully aggregated position while multivariate extreme value theory is used to compute the VaR of a position decomposed on risk factors.

Ho et al. (2000) made an empirical research on VaR measures by modelling the tails of the return distributions of six Asian financial markets during the financial turmoil. They found that the maxima and minima of the return series were satisfactorily modelled by an extreme value framework and the VaR measures generated under this structure were different than those generated by traditional approaches such as variance-covariance or historical methods, especially for markets with high degrees of leptokurtosis like Malaysia and Indonesia. Bensalah (2000) provided a complete example of EVT techniques applied to a series of daily exchange rates of Canadian/U.S. dollars over a 5 year period between 1995 and 2000. It was argued that EVT techniques enable to concentrate on the different behaviour patterns of extreme observations that allow us to make the best estimations over a very large threshold.

Gencay and Selcuk (2004) investigated the relative performance of VaR models with the daily stock market returns of nine different emerging markets. They have generated VaR estimates and provided the tail forecasts of daily returns with 95 % confidence intervals for stress testing purposes. Their results indicated that EVT based VaR estimates are more accurate at higher quantiles.

Chan and Gray (2006) applied an EVT based model to estimate the tails of the return distribution for daily electricity spot prices and determined that compared to a number of other parametric models EVT performed well in forecasting out of sample VaR. The statistical tests showed that the EVT based proposed model offers the most appropriate interval coverage in both unconditional and conditional events in electricity markets.

Ozun et al. (2010) structured eight filtered EVT models created with conditional quantile to estimate value-at-risk (VaR) for the Istanbul Stock Exchange. The performances of the filtered EVT models are compared to those of generalized autoregressive conditional heteroskedasticity (GARCH), GARCH with student-t distribution. Their results indicated that filtered EVT performs better in terms of capturing fat-tails in stock returns than parametric VaR models. An increase in the conditional quantile decreases h-step ahead number of exceptions and this shows that filtered EVT with higher conditional quantile such as 40 days should be used for forward looking forecasting.

Furió and Climent (2013) combined GARCH type models with the extreme value theory to estimate the tails of S&P 500, FTSE 100 and NIKKEI 225 index returns. The results indicated that EVT based estimates are more accurate than those from traditional GARCH models for both in-sample and out-of sample estimations.

Dutta and Biswas (2015) conducted nonparametric and EVT based estimation of extreme quantiles for varying size and probability conditions. In this method, tails speak for themselves and the largest negative log-returns for extreme quantile estimation is used merely. Quantiles for the values of $1\text{-}p$ close to 1 is estimated according to the theorem of Pickands-Balkema-de Haan. This theorem fits the Generalized Pareto Distribution to the k largest observations in the sample, so the conditional loss distribution's tail is approximated and it indicates that the loss exceeds the threshold value. EVT outperformed under large sample size and very low probabilities conditions for time series with heavy (fat) tailed marginal distributions. The sample quantile provided by Monte Carlo simulation with EVT and nonparametric approaches is used to estimate VaR and shortfall of stock market index.

3.1 *Financial Stress Tests with Copula*

Copula function provides describing the dependence behavior of financial returns in a more realistic way than correlation by using subjective judgments of marginal distributions. Copula method divides the joint distribution of financial returns in two parts as the marginal densities and the dependence structure. The modeling is twofold: specifying marginal distributions and determining best characterizing copula function of return dependence. Copula approach can be used for univariate models which is beneficial specifically for the analysis of dependence between foreign exchange rates and be extended to multi-variable models which is useful especially for risk management and portfolio analysis (Wang 2007).

In one of the latest studies combining EVT with copula, Koliai (2016) employed a semi-parametric copula-GARCH risk model for financial return series (equity indices, exchange rates, and commodity prices) in order to conduct financial stress tests. EVT is used to specify marginal distributions of the returns by especially emphasizing the extreme returns. The findings support a better static and dynamic properties of the model in comparison to most commonly used approaches

3.2 *Utilizing EVT for Crisis/Stress Event Classification*

EVT has recently been also utilized in extreme stress events' identification in the financial markets. EVT, as explained before, works on asymptotic behaviors of extremal observations of the variables. This special kind of probability theory offers methods for modeling the events with extremely low probabilities by considering the special characteristic of the financial data, non-normal pattern. Another reason of using EVT approach is that it does not require any a priori assumption for distributional properties of data series. Studies of Guru (2016), Lestano and Jacobs (2007), and Pozo and Dorantes (2003) are some of the distinctive papers which indicates that EVT use is better for identifying and characterizing crisis/stress events. One of the latest studies in this field (Guru 2016) uses EVT to identify extreme stress events in the Indian financial system using the Financial Sector Stress Index (a combination of crises indices for currency, banking and stock markets in India over the period April, 2001 to December, 2012). The application mainly focuses on the fact that extreme stress events are very rare and have a very small probability of occurrence. Hence, definition of stress events entails pre-specification of the above-mentioned small probability. Probability of a crisis event is pre-specified as p and stress situation is indicated as exceedance of a value of the index series to $100(1-p)$th percentile. At the same time, this percentile builds a threshold value for crisis events' identification. In other words, when the value of an index is higher than the threshold, it will be the indicator of financial stress. If the probability of the crisis is determined as 0.01, the 99th percentile on the distribution of the Financial Sector Stress Index series are used as thresholds for stress event identification. Though the quantiles are located in the tail regions of the distribution, tail pattern of the distribution should be known as a requirement for stress event identification. Peaks-Over-Threshold approach of EVT is used in the study in order to parametrically estimate tail quantiles of the distribution.

4 Conclusion

EVT is a science field that can be used to model tail loss of well known distributions since early 1900s. GEV and GPD are basic modeling approaches, that considers block maxima of data periods and an appropriate threshold, used for best model fitting with respect to data available. There are many potential application areas such as meteorology, engineering and finance. Utilizing EVT in finance mainly focus on tail modeling due to stylized facts of financial data such as fat tails, skewness and volatility clustering. Distinctive performance of EVT in tail modeling makes it a useful tool especially in risk related topics. Hence EVT is employed in risk management as a new method under VaR. Additionally EVT is used for describing crisis events and for stress tests as well.

References

Artzner P, Delbaen F, Eben JM, Heath D (1999) Coherent measures of risk. Math Financ 9:203–228

Bensalah Y (2000) Steps in applying extreme value theory to finance: a review. Bank of Canada

Brodin E, Klüppelberg C (2008) Extreme value theory in finance. Encyclopedia of quantitative risk analysis and assessment

Chan KF, Gray P (2006) Using extreme value theory to measure value-at-risk for daily electricity spot prices. Int J Forecast 22(2):283–300

Diebold FX, Schuermann T, Stroughair JD (2000) Pitfalls and opportunities in the use of extreme value theory in risk management. J Risk Finance 1(2):30–35

Dutta S, Biswas S (2015) Extreme quantile estimation based on financial time series. Commun Stat Simul Comput. doi: 10.1080/03610918.2015.1112908

Embrechts P, Resnick SI, Samorodnitsky G (1999) Extreme value theory as a risk management tool. North Am Actuar J 3(2):30–41

Ergen İ (2010) Essays in financial risk management. PhD Thesis, Rice University

Furió D, Climent FJ (2013) Extreme value theory versus traditional GARCH approaches applied to financial data: a comparative evaluation. Quant Financ 13(1):45–63

Gencay R, Selcuk F (2004) Extreme value theory and value-at-risk: relative performance in emerging markets. Int J Forecast 20(2):287–303
Gilli M, Kellezi E, Hysi H (2006) A data-driven optimization heuristic for downside risk minimization. Swiss Finance Institute Research Paper, 06-2
Gumbel EJ (1954) The maxima of the mean largest value and of the range. Ann Math Stat 25:76–84
Gumbel EJ (1958) Statistics of extremes. Columbia University Press, New York
Guru A (2016) Early warning system of finance stress for India. Int Rev Appl Econ 30(3):273–300
Ho LC, Burridge P, Cadle J, Theobald M (2000) Value-at-risk: applying the extreme value approach to Asian markets in the recent financial turmoil. Pac Basin Finance J 8(2):249–275
Koliai L (2016) Extreme risk modelling: an EVT–pair-copulas approach for financial stress tests. J Bank Finance. doi:10.1016/j.jbankfin.2016.02.004
Kotz S, Nadarajah S (2000) Extreme value distributions: theory and applications. World Scientific
Lestano JP, Jacobs AM (2007) Dating currency crises with ad-hoc and extreme value based thresholds: East Asia 1970-2002 [dating currency crises]. Int J Finance Econ 12:371–388
Longin FM (2000) From value at risk to stress testing: the extreme value approach. J Bank Finance 24(7):1097–1130
Mandelbrot B (1963) The variation of certain speculative prices. J Bus 36(4):394–419
Markowitz H (1952) Portfolio selection. J Financ 7:77–91
McNeil AJ (1999) Extreme value theory for risk managers. Departement Mathematik ETH Zentrum
McNeil AJ, Frey R (2000) Estimation of tail related risk measures for heteroscedastic financial time series. J Empir Finance 7:271–300
Ozun A, Cifter A, Yilmazer S (2010) Filtered extreme-value theory for value-at-risk estimation: evidence from Turkey. J Risk Finance 11(2):164–179
Patton AJ (2006) Modeling asymmetric exchange rate dependence. Int Econ Rev 47(2):527–556
Pfaff B (2012) Extreme value theory. Financial risk modelling and portfolio optimization with R, pp 84–111
Pozo S, Dorantes CA (2003) Statistical distributions and the identification of currency crises. J Int Money Finance 22(4):591–609
Rocco M (2014) Extreme value theory in finance: a survey. J Econ Surv 28(1):82–108
Shukla RK, Trivedi M, Kumar M (2012) On the proficient use of GEV distribution: a case study of subtropical monsoon region in India. arXiv preprint arXiv:1203.0642.
Wang X (2007) Essays on financial analysis: capital structure, dynamic dependence and extreme loss modeling. PhD thesis, Rice University

Esra Aslanertik is a Professor of Accounting at Dokuz Eylul University Department of Business Administration, Izmir-Turkey. Dr. Aslanertik has a master of International Business from Dokuz Eylul University (1999) and a PhD in Business from Dokuz Eylul University (2002). Her research interests lie in financial accounting, cost and managerial accounting, and international accounting standards. She has taught Financial Accounting, Cost Accounting, Financial Statement Analysis, and Managerial Accounting courses, among others, at both graduate and undergraduate levels.

Sabri Erdem is associate professor at Dokuz Eylül University, Faculty of Business, Business Administration Department, Chair of Quantitative Methods Division and member of Faculty Board. He is Industrial Engineer since 1996 and holds two MSc degrees both in Computer Engineering and Business Administration. He received PhD in Computer Engineering in 2007. He who received Associated Professor title by April 2011, published many articles in national and international journals and has many proceedings at national and international symposium and congress and partner of three patents about automated medical dispensing machines. He is member of Chamber of Turkey Mechanical Engineers (Industrial Engineers Branch), Information Association of Turkey, Turkish Operations Research Association, vice chair of DEU Entrepreneurship,

Business and Economics Applied Research Center, board member of DEU Biomedical Calibration and Metrology Applied and Research Center, advisory board member of Dokuz Eylül University Information Technology Research Center. Main interest areas are optimization algorithms, nature inspired algorithms, intelligent systems, data mining, healthcare information technologies, healthcare materials management, data envelopment analysis and structural equation modeling. He is also co-founder and board member of CENOS AS at Health Technopark in DEPARK.

Gülüzar Kurt Gümüş is an Associate Professor of Finance at Dokuz Eylul University Department of International Business, Izmir-Turkey. Dr. Kurt Gumus has an MBA from Dokuz Eylul University (2004) and a PhD in Business from Dokuz Eylul University (2007). Her research interests lie in responsible investment, corporate finance, sustainability in finance, capital markets and investment, and international finance. She has taught Responsible Investment, International Financial Management, Corporate Finance courses, among others, at both graduate and undergraduate levels.

Value at Risk Performance of Emerging Market Equity Portfolios During the Fed's Tapering

Mehmet Baha Karan, Ertuğrul Umut Uysal, and Mustafa Kaya

Abstract This paper investigates the issue of market risk quantification for twelve emerging market equity portfolios during the FED tapering period. The performance of most popular VaR methods, namely Variance-Covariance, Classical and Weighted Historical Simulation Methods are compared. The results indicate that Classical and Weighted Historical Simulation outperform Variance-Covariance VaR. Kupiec back testing is supporting this argument. In the second stage of analysis, VaR performance of equally weighted equity index and US Government Bond portfolios are analysed. We obtain lower VaR values than equity portfolios. Russia, Turkey and Brazil are the worst performers out of 12 countries. The performance of portfolios are measured by Sharpe ratio and VaR adjusted Sharpe Ratios and found parallel rankings.

1 Introduction

Quantitative Easing (QE) policy of Federal Reserve (FED) has increased capital flows to Emerging Market Economies (EMEs) and put upward pressure on asset prices and exchange rates after 2008 financial crisis. Meanwhile, most of the portfolio managers were using Value at Risk (VaR) tools to manage their risk, and they were exploiting the favourable conditions of QE program. The first signal about the end of purchases under the Fed's QE program which is called tapering is given in May 22, 2013. Just after the first announcement that has been expected for a while by the market players, foreign investors started to withdraw their investment in EMEs, leading to capital outflows, a drop in EME currencies and stock

M.B. Karan (✉) • M. Kaya
Department of Business Administration, Hacettepe University, Beytepe Kampusu, Ankara, Turkey
e-mail: mbkaran@hacettepe.edu.tr

E.U. Uysal
T.C. Ziraat Bankası Genel Mudurlugu, Atatürk Bulvari. No:8, Altındag, Ankara, Turkey

H. Dinçer, Ü. Hacioğlu (eds.), *Risk Management, Strategic Thinking and Leadership in the Financial Services Industry*, Contributions to Management Science, DOI 10.1007/978-3-319-47172-3_13

markets, and a rise in bond yields (Rai and Suchanek 2014). Thus, the new volatile market conditions became significant tests to evaluate risk management tools of emerging market fund managers.

The main research question of this study is that to test the performance of VaR models and how the fund managers of emerging markets could have managed their market risk during the extreme market conditions. Most of the risk models that worked perfectly during the resilient periods slogged to estimate real picture in volatile market conditions. Nevertheless, Value at Risk (VaR) that is recommended by the Basel II directives, has been widely employed by fund managers to manage market risk of their portfolios in last decades. VaR assesses possible losses in a portfolio over a target horizon at a certain confidence level. Although this model is simple and popular, there are no widely recognized methods to arrive at the VaR of a particular portfolio (Dimitrakopoulos et al. 2010). The most popular of VaR estimation methods are Variance Covariance VaR and Historical VaR. Both of them has significant drawbacks. Variance Covariance VaR is a parametric model and assumes that returns of risk factors are normally distributed. Hence, it underestimates extreme outcomes that occur in volatile periods. On the other hand, Historical Simulation has no normal distribution assumption and estimates the Value at Risk by simulating or constructing the cumulative distribution function (CDF) of assets returns over time. Classic (Equally weighted) and Weighted Methods are two important versions of Historically Simulation. However, it has deficiencies during the crisis period when the returns are very volatile and explosive. To solve the limitations of VaR methods, researchers have formulated different versions of VaR to develop a systematic way to segregate extreme events and mitigate problems associated with the original measure, like Expected Shortfall and Extreme Value Theory methodologies. However, the new models are not only impractical for business professionals but also but have significant limitations (Embrechts 2000). The complex nature of emerging markets is continuously creating new risks to portfolio managers. It imposes them to draw lessons from market movements and construct their portfolios and risk model accordingly. Therefore, performances of risk models on equity investments are low at the beginning of crisis periods in emerging markets, and it improves during the post-crises periods due to the inclusion of extreme events in the estimation sample (Dimitrakopoulos et al. 2010).

The success of VaR models doesn't only depend on conditions of the market, but also, the types of assets in the portfolio. Particularly risky portfolios such as equity and derivatives are severely affected by volatile market conditions. As previous studies indicate that the VaR models on equity portfolios are more successful in developed economies that are more liquid and stable, whereas less in emerging countries that have more volatile and fragile conditions (Andjeli et al. 2010).

Most of the previous studies have analysed the performance of VaR models from the viewpoint of international investors and calculated US dollar or Euro denominated risk and return. However, this paper investigated the performance of VaR models of local investors who made an investment with local currencies. It should be noted that when the currency of an emerging economy is expected to depreciate, locals may invest in US dollar currency and attempt to maximize their income in terms of local currency. It may give them great opportunities in equity, real estate and other markets, whose values have low or negative correlation with US currency.

In sum, in the first part of the study, we analysed performance of equity indices funds using three popular VaR approach during the Fed's Tapering period, namely April 1, 2013–September 30, 2015 and compared the results of 12 emerging countries. In the second part of the paper we propose to local fund managers to diversify their equity portfolios with US dollar denominated less risky securities. It would not only decrease volatility but also to make the portfolio more manageable with VaR models. We think that US government bonds are a noteworthy choice for local investors. These bonds are safe but and available with a wide range of maturity dates. Moreover, dollar-denominated US bonds will hedge local investors to currency risks. Expecting negative or low correlation between emerging market equity performances and the exchange rate of US dollar with local currencies, makes US Dollar denominated security a considerable investment option for local fund managers, particularly approaching ends of sunny days. Then we investigated VaR of equally weighted equity-US bond portfolios for 12 emerging countries during April 1, 2013–September 30, 2015.

Lastly, our paper has three purposes. First one is to test the performances of Variance Covariance Classic and Weighted Historical Simulation VaR approaches in twelve emerging markets equity portfolios during the Fed's tapering. Second one is to improve the VaR performances of portfolios by diversifying with US government bonds. Finally to present the risk adjusted performance of equity and equally weighted equity-US bond portfolios for twelve EME countries.

The rest of the paper is organized as follows. Section 2 explains the impact of Fed's tapering announcements on EMEs, Sects. 3 and 4 summarizes previous studies and methodology. Data and Empirical results on equity indices and equally weighted equity-US bond portfolios are given in Sects. 5 and 6. Discussion exists in Sect. 7 and the paper concludes in Sect. 8.

2 The Impact of Fed's Tapering Announcements on Emerging Market Economies

The Quantitative Easing (QE) program of FED, which is employed just after the financial crisis of 2008, expanded its balance sheet dramatically by purchasing debt instruments from financial institutions. Hence, it raised the prices of those financial assets and lowered their interest while simultaneously increased the money supply. This policy has created a great opportunity for portfolio managers to generate a considerable return on their equity investments. It had been implemented in different phases from 2008 to 2013 and has raised capital flows to emerging market countries and put upward pressure on asset prices and exchange rates. The general effect of QE on these countries was positive because of the beneficial trade and confidence stemming from stronger economic activity (Lavigne et al. 2014). Although it was clear that this policy was inevitably unsustainable in the long run, emerging markets *have been addicted to the liquidity* of FED and have greedily exploited the positive market conditions. After all, US long term bonds yields have started to increase in late 2012. Then, IMF and other financial authorities frequently warned the risk of QE for emerging economies in early 2013 (IMF 2013). They expressed that when advanced economies begin to normalize monetary policy, a certain amount of capital-flow reversal and higher borrowing costs are likely in some EMEs (Lavigne et al. 2014). Finally, the signal of FED tapering that is the gradual decreasing of central bank interventions used to improve the conditions for economic growth had given in May 22, 2013 when Bernanke, the president of FED testified the intention of FED in US Congress. Consequently, an anxiety begun over the global markets and currencies and stock markets in emerging markets have fallen dramatically. The successive FED announcements during 2013–2015 period caused an increase in U.S. government bond yields and emerging market bonds. Besides, capital flows to EMEs slowed and markets became more volatile with fall in stock market indices, and depreciated currencies (Fig. 1). Particularly the announcements in 2013[1] had more impact on EMEs and reaction of the market decreased over time. The new market conditions for emerging economies hardened the performance of portfolio managers with incompetent risk management tools and enforced them to be more selective in their investments. The market pressures became more concentrated on particular economies with important financial or macroeconomic vulnerabilities (Rai and Suchanek 2014). Interestingly the Emerging Market Economies experienced a significantly stronger depreciation in nominal exchange rates during the taper-talk period than during the actual taper period (Diez 2014).

The reports of IMF points out five emerging countries; Brazil, India, Indonesia, Turkey, and South Africa, which have larger external financing needs and macroeconomic imbalances. The countries which diminish their macroeconomic imbalances since May 2013 have shown more resilience (Mishra et al. 2014).

3 Literature Review

Previous studies indicate that application of risk management models in emerging markets has structural difficulties. Insufficient liquidity, the small scale of trading, the asymmetrical and low number of trading days with certain securities (Andjeli et al. 2010). Moreover, weak legal infrastructure and high political risks make the tasks of fund managers too complicated. Particularly during the periods of financial turmoil, the accuracy of the models dramatically decreases. Stoyanov et al. (2010)

[1]Important FED announcement days in 2013 are May 22, June 19 and September 18.

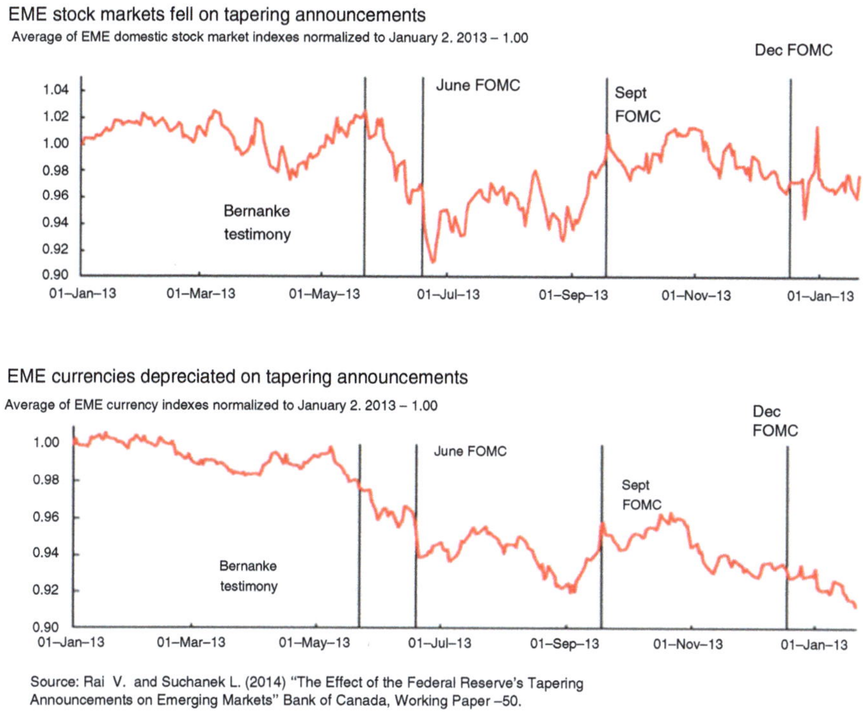

Fig. 1 Fed's tapering announcements and emerging market economies. (**a**) **EME stock markets fell on tapering announcements.** Average of EME domestic stock market indexes normalized to January 2, 2013—1.00. (**b**) **EME currencies depreciated on tapering announcements**. Average of EME currency indexes normalized to January 1, 2013—1.00. Source: Rai V. and Suchanek L. (2014) "The Effect of the Federal Reserve's Tapering Announcements on Emerging Markets" Bank of Canada, Working Paper -50

underlined the difficulties of risk estimation in volatile markets. They claimed that the risk model has to be capable of describing well the marginal distribution phenomena of the returns series such as fat-tails, skewness, and clustering of volatility. Also, the model has to capture the dependence structure, and the risk model has to incorporate an appropriate measure.

Many of the papers indicates that estimation power of the VaR models is poor for emerging markets. For example, Silva and Mendes (2003) and Bao et al. (2006) found that the estimation performance of the EVT was poor for Asian stock market indexes. Žiković and Aktan (2009) arrived the similar result by analysing the daily returns of Turkish (XU100) and Croatian (CROBEX) stock index models during the 2008 crisis with VaR models. They revealed that all tested VaR model except EVT and HHS models seriously underpredict the true level of risk in the crisis period. Andjeli et al. (2010) tested the performance of historical simulation and Variance Covariance VaR methods in four central and east European emerging markets and claimed that these methods are not working in emerging markets. The study of Dimitrakopoulos et al. (2010) backed up the previous results and found that VaR estimation during periods of financial turmoil is not possible for emerging markets. However, the performance of the parametric (non-parametric) VaR models improves (deteriorates) during post-crises periods due to the inclusion of extreme events in the estimation sample.

In the recent study of Köksal and Orhon (2013), the performance of VaR as a risk measure across a large sample of developed and emerging countries are investigated. They underlined three main conclusions. First one is the performance of VaR as a risk measure was worse for developed countries than for emerging ones during the global financial crisis. Secondly they found evidence about the decoupling of emerging and developed countries regarding market risk during the global financial crisis. They lastly they suggested alternative measures of risk, used together with VaR, and the performance of these risk measures should be regularly evaluated to improve the assessment of risks in a market.

Recent studies employed more complicated methodologies to increase the estimation power of risk models. Mendes et al. (2000) investigated the robustness of EVT to estimate the VaR in South American stock markets. He showed that the EVT performed more precise risk estimates than the traditional estimation procedures. Seymour and Polakow (2003) revealed that established methods such as historical simulation are prone to underestimating value-at-risk in such developing market, and the combined GARCH-type time-series approach and extreme value theory model is found to provide significantly better results than both straightforward historical simulation as well as the extreme value model. Gencay and Selcuk (2004) searched the relative performance of Value-at-Risk (VaR) models with the daily stock market returns of nine different emerging markets, and their results indicated that EVT-based VaR estimates are more accurate at higher quantiles.

Snoussi and El-Aroui (2012) claimed that the adjustment of VaR in emerging market is far more reliable than that of other method used in the developed market. Cifter (2011) showed that the wavelet-based extreme value theory increases predictive performance of financial forecasting according to number of violations and tail-loss tests by analysing the Istanbul Stock Exchange (ISE) and the Budapest Stock Exchange (BUX).

These studies indicate that the success of two basic VaR method, historical simulation and Variance Covariance have a very limited success in volatile emerging economies. Moreover, estimation power the advanced risk methods are also questionable. In spite of these results, most of the financial institutions and investment funds are employing these techniques, because of the simplicity and practicality of them.

Measurement of portfolio performance is an important component of the portfolio management process. It refers to the determination of how a particular investment portfolio has performed relative to some comparison benchmark. Sharpe ratio is the most popular tool amongst the others. However Sharpe Ratio is subject to estimation errors including data limitations, negative skewness and positive excess kurtosis of returns. In addition, the ex-post Sharpe ratio implicitly assumes that the returns of the asset under consideration are independent and identically distributed normal random variables. However, these assumptions are violated by real world financial data (Deng, et al. 2013). Thus, we also measured the risk adjusted performance of the portfolios using the calculated VaR values (Grau-Carles et al. 2009).

VaR adjusted Sharpe Ratio (VaRSR) has some advantages over Sharpe Ratios. It covers the uncertainty involved in estimating the Sharpe ratio, and include the effects of higher order moments of the return distribution. VaRSR is particularly adjusted to assets with non-normal return distributions like our data. Furthermore, Sharpe Ratio and VaRSR may not give us same rankings under non-normality assumptions (Alexander and Baptista 2003).

VaRSR is, similar to the Sharpe ratio but with the risk measured using the different VaR measures in the denominator, namely (Grau-Carles et al. 2009);

$$VaRSR = \frac{(R_i - R_f)}{VaR(R_i)}$$

$(Ri - Rf)$ = The average portfolio return in excess of the risk-free rate of return
$VaR(R_i)$ = Value at Risk of portfolio

4 Methodology

Three popular methods of VaR estimating are used to estimate emerging market portfolios in this study: Variance-Covariance VaR, Classic Historical VaR, and Weighted Historical VaR and. These methods have significant superiors but also drawbacks. In the all above three methods for calculating the yields, the natural log is usually preferred because small changes in the natural log are equivalent to percentage changes.

$$Yield(r_t) = \ln\left({}^{f_t}/_{f_{t-1}}\right)$$

The results of VaR methods are tested using Kupiec back testing, then risk adjusted ratios are used to rank the portfolio performances.

4.1 *Variance Covariance VaR*

Variance-Covariance VaR is a parametric method based on statistical parameters such as variance and covariance of the risk factor distributed. Using these parameters and the Variance-Covariance of the position, VaR is determined directly from the risk factor distribution. Shortly, the Variance-Covariance of the position serves as an estimation for the transition from the risk factor distribution to profit-loss distribution (Ammann and Reich 2001). The Variance-Covariance VaR depends on two main assumptions: (1) the distribution of potential portfolio returns is normally distributed, (2) the portfolio value changes in a linear manner with changes in the underlying prices. Although it is simple and analytical, the most important shortcoming is normality assumption of risk factors. The normality assumption does not mostly hold and linearity hypothesis is not validated for nonlinear assets such as fixed income securities and options (Lleo 2010).

Calculation of volatility is the most important step of VaR methods. EWMA (Exponentially Weighted Moving Average) which is introduced with Risk Metric from JP Morgan is used in this paper. It assumes returns on financial assets have serial correlations and give more weight to the latest returns than the old ones. Moreover, it is an extension of the standard weighting scheme of weighted historical simulation that assigns equal weight to every point in time for the calculation of the volatility, by assigning (usually) more weight to the most recent observations using an exponential scheme. λ is the decay factor in the formula and a high λ, puts less weight, and low λ provides more weights on the most recent estimate.

The volatility of the investment becomes the volatility of a linear function of random variables. Moving from volatility to VaR implies an assumption about the normal distribution of the changes of value. The confidence level of the model is 99 % in this paper. The following formulas of Variance Covariance methods are used to estimate VaR in this paper;

$$\text{var}iance = \sigma_t^2 = \lambda\sigma_{t-1}^2 + (1-\lambda)r_{t-1}^2$$

$$volatility = \sigma_t = \sqrt{\sigma_t^2}$$

$$\text{cov}ariance = \sigma_{xy_{t+1}} = \lambda\sigma_{xy_t} + (1-\lambda)X_tY_t$$

$$VaR = \sqrt{WCVCW^T} * (zvalue)$$

W is the present value matrix of the portfolio, W^t is the transpose of the present value matrix of the portfolio, C is the correlation matrix, V is the volatility matrix, z value is determined for 99 % confidence level.

4.2 *Historical Simulations*

Historical simulation is the most practical way of estimating the Value at Risk for portfolios. Pérignon and Smith (2010) revealed that 73 % of banks among 60 US, Canadian and large international banks over 1996–2005 applied VaR methodology with historical simulation. Historical Simulation uses a sample of historical observations for the risk factors. For every historical data, the portfolio return is found out according to a non-linear pattern. The positions are re-priced under each scenario. The VaR is computed as a percentile of the historical data of portfolio returns. This approach does not require a normal distribution. Although the other models can include skewed and heavy-tailed risk factor returns, they must still fit a parametric form for modelling the multivariate risk factors. So, the main advantage of historical simulation is that it makes no assumptions about risk factor changes being from a particular distribution. It only employs the empirical distribution of historical data to generate realistic future scenarios. The dynamic behaviour of risk factors is included in the model in a natural and realistic manner. On the other hand, the major shortcoming of the method is that it does not consider the future changes in the market. Mostly economic problems may alter the volatility of the market and past data does not reflect the further developments in the economy.

We used both classic and weighted historical simulation methods in this paper. In the classical historical simulation method, the weights assigned to past changes, in other terms scenarios are equal but in the weighted historical simulation the weights are not equal. In the weighted historical simulation weights (w_t) are assigned using an exponentially declining function.

$$weight_t = (1 - \lambda)*(\lambda^t)/\left(1 - (\lambda)^{251}\right)$$

The parameter λ, referred to as the "decay factor," determines the smoothing constant on past observations. λ is as usual, between 0 and 1. We assigned the probability weight 1–λ to the most recent observation on the return, the weight λ(1–λ) to the preceding that, and then weights of $(\lambda)^2$ (1–λ), $(\lambda)^3$ (1-λ), $(\lambda)^4$ (1–λ) ... as the observations move progressively further in the past. The λ is 0,98 in our calculations. Therefore, as we approach the recent data the label of the data increases from 1 to 251.

Using this approach one-year time series of risk factors are determined and transferred to logarithmic values that are yields. Then these values are applied to the current risk factor values to mimic the historical changes starting from today's values of the risk factor. A daily variation of the value of the investment is obtained for each daily variation (the daily profit or loss) of risk factor values. Afterwards, the distribution of daily profit and loss is constructed, and VaR is calculated in a determined confidence level. In our calculations, the confidence level is 99 %.

4.3 *Back Testing*

The result of the VaR models is evaluated by back testing. These tests are techniques for assessing the validity of a VaR method by counting the number of times when the losses exceed the estimated VaR in a historical or simulated sample (Levy and Post 2005). The Kupiec's test is a statistical test and a standard way of back testing different models used to forecast VaR. If the model used produces significantly more or significantly fewer losses exceeding VaR, the Kupiec's test will reject the model. Kupiec test assumes that the losses follow a binominal distribution. For adopting this approach, the likelihood ratio form is used and assumed to be $\chi 2$ distributed which is a test-statistic with one degree of freedom. This makes it possible to compute the p-value of the Kupiec's test that can easily be interpreted. In our paper, the level of the confidence level is 99 %.

$$LR = -2\ln[(q) \times (1-q)n - x/[(1-(\mathrm{x/n}))(\mathrm{n}-\mathrm{x})(\mathrm{x/n})\mathrm{x}] \sim \chi^2$$
$$LR = -2\ln[(0,01) \times (0,99)n - x/[(1-(\mathrm{p}))(\mathrm{n}-\mathrm{x})(\mathrm{p})\mathrm{x}] \sim \chi^2$$

x = the number of exceedances
n = the number of observations
p = x/n = the probability of exceedances
$q=1-\alpha$ where α is the level of confidence

5 Data of the Equity Portfolios and Results

We analysed the VaR performance of 12 emerging economies during April 1, 2013, to September 30, 2015, which covers starting the period of FED tapering. During this period, the currencies of emerging economies depreciated and their equity indexes are substantially decreased. Briefly, this is one of the most striking periods in last five years for portfolio managers.

The descriptive statistics are given in Table 1. The most interesting result of the table is that half of the countries has negative mean. Turkey and Russia are the worst performers of the period. Skewness and kurtosis values for the yields of equity indices exceed the rule of thumb criteria of 1.0. This indicates that almost all yield of indices may have no normal distribution. Then, we evaluated our values with Kolmogorov-Smirnov and Shapiro-Wilk tests. The both of the tests reveals that except Brazil, values are not normally distributed. Inevitabley, these results decrease the reliability of Variance-Covariance VaR methodology that assumes a normal distribution of the data.

The Result of the VaR models and their Kupiec tests are presented in Table 2. The critical Chi-Square value for 99 % confidence level is 6,63. The Kupiec back testing statistics indicates that the most unsuccessful method is Variance-Covariance. Half of the countries failed to pass critical values. On the other hand test, each of other two historical simulation approaches failed only one. The Classic Simulation failed in India and Weighted Historical Simulation failed in Poland once. Number of exceedances of Poland is the highest; the number is two digits for every method. Most interestingly, maximum exceedances in Russia and Turkey are remarkable. This value is nearly 9 for Russia and 8 for Turkey. The results indicate that the Kupiec tests of the both countries are successful and the Fed's tampering announcements negatively affected these countries.

Table 1 Descriptive statistics of equity index yields

	Mean	Std. error	Median	Std. deviation	Skewness	Kurtosis
Brazil	−.00035895	.014693513	−.00097500	.014693513	.080	.323
Turkey	−.00023375	.015867534	.00020700	.015867534	−.599	4.942
India	.00050813	.010245530	.00073800	.010245530	−.507	2.843
S. Africa	.00036544	.009529770	.00063300	.009529770	−.296	1.596
Russia	.00021156	.013158963	.00017000	.013158963	−.823	9.258
Chile	−.00029625	.008249260	−.00046200	.008249260	.115	1.358
Taiwan	.00005288	.008271327	.00042800	.008271327	−.540	3.643
Poland	.00015823	.009375206	.00046000	.009375206	−.884	5.108
Hungary	.00025329	.011205338	.00018200	.011205338	−.200	2.721
S. Korea	−.00003443	.007471502	.00025100	.007471502	.004	1.249
Malaysia	−.00004965	.006025080	.00018400	.006025080	−.070	3.349
Colombia	−.00061511	.009471184	−.00033500	.009471184	−.122	2.759

6 Data of Equally Weighted Emerging Equity-US Bond Portfolios and Results

In the second stage, we constructed equally weighted equity indices and dollar-denominated US Bond portfolios as a robustness test of our approach. Five-year US government bond yields are used for the period of April 1–September 30. There was rationality behind this approach for a domestic portfolio manager. The general expectation in the market is that the forthcoming announcements in the spring of 2013 may start a reversal in the QE program of Fed. These decisions of Fed inevitably would have negative impact on EMEs' equity markets and local currencies. At early spring of 2013, the reports of international companies have already underlined the risk of emerging market equities pointing out forthcoming Fed announcements. Therefore the portfolio managers of EMEs should consider a new strategy that decrease equity and currency risk of the portfolio. Moreover, the previous studies, has showed that there was not only a low correlation between emerging and developed markets but also a negative correlation between developed and emerging market currencies during the crisis period (Bénétrix et al. 2015). Certainly there were many options for domestic investors to hedge their risk at the end of QE program. But investing in the portfolio of equally weighted equity indices and dollar-denominated US Bond is one of the easiest strategies. In this way, the fund managers expect to obtain low and more manageable VaR and increase the performance of the portfolios.

Descriptive statistics of new equally weighted portfolios for 12 countries are given in Table 3. The first important difference of new portfolio is that daily means of all portfolios are positive. However, skewness and kurtosis values for the yields of equity indices exceed the rule of thumb criteria of 1.0. This picture indicates that almost all yield of indices may have no normal distribution. Since the probability associated with the Kolmogorov-Smirnov (KS) test of normality is < 0.01 is less

Table 2 VaR values and tests of Kupiec for local stock exchange index

Countries	Methods	Average VaR	Exceed	Min. Exceed	Aver. Exceed.	Max. Exceed.	Stat.
Brazil	Weighted His. Sim.	3.31 %	10	0.12 %	0.69 %	2.16 %	1.96
	Classical His. Sim.	3.50 %	10	0.01 %	0.62 %	2.08 %	1.96
	Var-Cova	3.30 %	9	0.01 %	0.56 %	1.70 %	1.1
Turkey	Weighted His. Sim.	4.75 %	8	0.07 %	1.65 %	7.30 %	0.45
	Classical His. Sim.	4.53 %	6	0.42 %	2.34 %	7.60 %	0.01
	Var-Cova	3.58 %	13	0.05 %	1.35 %	8.13 %	5.62
India	Weighted His. Sim.	2.65 % %	9	0.09 %	0.94 %	3.69 %	1.14
	Classical His. Sim.	2.63 %	14	0.10 %	0.80 %	3.62 %	**7.36**
	Var-Cova	2.27 %	14	0.05 %	0.73 %	4.02 %	**7.36**
South	Weighted His. Sim.	2.39 %	8	0.21 %	0.74 %	1.32 %	0.46
Africa	Classical His. Sim.	2.48 %	11	0.12 %	0.60 %	1.35 %	2.99
	Var-Cova	2.05 %	15	0.02 %	0.57 %	1.08 %	**8.92**
Russia	Weighted His. Sim.	3.69 %	6	0.19 %	2.07 %	8.90 %	0.01
	Classical His. Sim.	2.91 %	6	0.13 %	1.93 %	8.85 %	0.01
	Var-Cova	2.97 %	5	0.29 %	2.32 %	8.90 %	0.28
Chile	Weighted His. Sim.	1.96 %	9	0.04 %	0.60 %	1.26 %	1.1
	Classical His. Sim.	2.00 %	8	0.08 %	0.63 %	1.31 %	0.47
	Var-Cova	1.82 %	11	0.01 %	0.48 %	1.33 %	3.02
Taiwan	Weighted His. Sim.	2.23 %	13	0.11 %	0.64 %	1.93 %	5.82
	Classical His. Sim.	2.18 %	9	0.12 %	0.58 %	2.05 %	1.16
	Var-Cova	1.75 %	17	0.15 %	0.76 %	2.63 %	**13.03**
Poland	Weighted His. Sim.	2.77 %	15	0.05 %	0.80 %	3.40 %	**8.97**
	Classical His. Sim.	2.72 %	10	0.08 %	1.14 %	3.56 %	1.96
	Var-Cova	2.07 %	18	0.01 %	0.81 %	3.82 %	**14.92**
Hungary	Weighted His. Sim.	2.93 %	9	0.02 %	1.17 %	4.03 %	1.13
	Classical His. Sim.	2.66 %	8	0.12 %	1.19 %	3.77 %	0.49
	Var-Cova	2.53 %	8	0.06 %	1.24 %	3.93 %	0.49

(continued)

Table 2 (continued)

Countries	Methods	Average VaR	Exceed	Min. Exceed	Aver. Exceed.	Max. Exceed.	Stat.
South Korea	Weighted His. Sim.	1.76 %	12	0.02 %	0.24 %	0.73 %	4.4
	Classical His. Sim.	1.83 %	8	0.01 %	0.37 %	0.85 %	0.11
	Var-Cova	1.64 %	13	0.05 %	0.30 %	0.92 %	5.84
Malaysia	Weighted His. Sim.	1.61 %	9	0.01 %	0.52 %	1.14 %	1.14
	Classical His. Sim.	1.67 %	7	0.01 %	0.42 %	1.01 %	0.5
	Var-Cova	1.27 %	16	0.03 %	0.41 %	1.27 %	**10.96**
Colombia	Weighted His. Sim.	2.59 %	9	0.35 %	0.84 %	1.51 %	1.21
	Classical His. Sim.	2.57 %	8	0.07 %	0.65 %	2.07 %	0.54
	Var-Cova	2.05 %	17	0.07 %	0.78 %	1.62 %	**13.25**

The critical Chi-Square value for 99 % confidence level is 6.63

than or equal to the level of significance (0.01), the results indicate that the half of the countries have normal distribution. However, Shapiro-Wilk test does not fully support the findings of KS and present only one normally distributed country portfolio, which is South Kore. According to the literature, these models have different assumptions and there is no concensus about the power of tests (Razali and Wah 2011). Asserting that the new portfolios relatively more close to normal distribution shape than the equity portfolios, will not be a mistake. So, we can employ the Variance -Covariance VaR methodology to the data of some country portfolios.

Results of VaR tests and Kupiec back testing are given in Table 4. The performance of all VaR tests is more successful than the equity portfolios that are presented at the first stage of our paper. There are only a few unsuccessful results, for example, Taiwan failed in Weighted Historical Simulation and Variance-Covariance VaR, Colombia is failed only in Variance-Covariance VaR and rest of the countries are successful. Another significant result of the test is the fall in exceedance levels of the countries. Not only is the average level of exceedances in the new portfolio lower than the equity portfolio performances, but also the maximum exceedances. Still Turkey and Russia have maximum hits, but not more than 5.02.

Table 3 Descriptive statistics of portfolio of local stock exchange and US bond index

	Mean	Std. error	Median	Std. deviation	Skewness	Kurtosis
Brazil	.00043788	.007300624	.00061000	.007300624	−.240	1.970
Turkey	.00030754	.007138048	.00050000	.007138048	−.945	8.760
India	.00038236	.005373770	.00066000	.005373770	−.452	2.905
S. Africa	.00048035	.006308015	.00082000	.006308015	−.228	1.422
Russia	.00071188	.010292500	.00066000	.010292500	.381	11.433
Chile	.00016385	.004694002	.00002000	.004694002	.134	.647
Taiwan	.00008391	.004446973	.00029000	.004446973	−.216	1.724
Poland	.00017705	.005479638	.00018000	.005479638	−.603	3.585
Hungary	.00023385	.006315546	.00040000	.006315546	−.780	6.625
S. Korea	.00001258	.004293592	.00005000	.004293592	−.095	.353
Malaysia	.00025176	.003520506	.00039000	.003520506	−.062	.711
Colombia	.00022229	.005375756	.00024000	.005375756	.000	1.555

7 Discussion

Turkey, Russia and Brazil are the most volatile countries with respect to their VaR values. We also find that the impact of May 22, 2013 declaration is relatively low, with the help of the diversification. Except Russia, VaR volatility level of the market is considerable low. Russia is committed to a series of international sanctions which caused heavy problems in her economy due to invasion and annexation of Crimea after 2014. The result is similar for the Classic and Weighted Historical Simulation models.

At the second step of our comparison. We measured the risk adjusted performance of equity and equally weighted equity- US Bond portfolios. The results reveals that Sharpe and VaRSR indexes are giving parallel rankings and risk adjusted performances of equally weighted equity- US Bond portfolios outperform equity portfolios in every country. The highest performing countries in equity indexes are India, S. Africa and Hungary. The lowest preforming ones are Brazil Chile and Colombia. The ranking is remarkably changed in equally weighted equity- US Bond portfolios, but interestingly South Africa keeps again a high ranking. The best performers are S. Africa, Malaysia and Russia. Turkey, Taiwan and S. Africa are placed in bottom lines (Table 5).

Emerging markets experienced a stressful period during the Fed's tapering period, after the QE program that makes currency more abundant.

8 Conclusion

Emerging markets were waiting a stressful period after the revocation sign of the QE program that makes currency more abundant. This policy change was expected to reverse the capital flows directed to the EME. In accordance with the estimations,

Table 4 VaR values and tests of Kupiec for portfolio of local stock exchange and US bond index

Countries	Methods	Average VaR	Exceed	Min. Exceed	Aver. Exceed.	Max. Exceed.	Stat.
Brazil	Weighted His. Sim.	1.71 %	10	0.04 %	0.52 %	1.96 %	1.96
	Classical His. Sim.	1.73 %	11	0.01 %	0.45 %	1.88 %	3.02
	Var-Cova	1.60 %	9	0.06 %	0.59 %	1.96 %	1.10
Turkey	Weighted His. Sim.	2.04 %	7	0.05 %	0.85 %	3.79 %	0.09
	Classical His. Sim.	1.97 %	5	0.11 %	1.46 %	3.99 %	0.27
	Var-Cova	1.59 %	9	0.06 %	0.85 %	4.27 %	1.08
India	Weighted His. Sim.	1.35 %	10	0.05 %	0.46 %	1.55 %	2.01
	Classical His. Sim.	1.27 %	11	0.02 %	0.46 %	1.56 %	3.08
	Var-Cova	1.19 %	11	0.07 %	0.49 %	1.89 %	3.08
South	Weighted His. Sim.	1.63 %	10	0.01 %	0.36 %	1.52 %	1.94
Africa	Classical His. Sim.	1.75 %	9	0.02 %	0.50 %	1.90 %	1.08
	Var-Cova	1.42 %	12	0.06 %	0.31 %	1.39 %	4.23
Russia	Weighted His. Sim.	2.40 %	11	0.01 %	0.90 %	3.77 %	2.94
	Classical His. Sim.	2.13 %	11	0.02 %	1.17 %	5.02 %	2.94
	Var-Cova	2.05 %	8	0.01 %	1.10 %	3.50 %	0.44
Chile	Weighted His. Sim.	1.09 %	11	0.01 %	0.17 %	0.51 %	3.02
	Classical His. Sim.	1.08 %	11	0.01 %	0.14 %	0.31 %	3.02
	Var-Cova	1.06 %	11	0.01 %	0.18 %	0.28 %	3.02
Taiwan	Weighted His. Sim.	1.08 %	15	0.02 %	0.21 %	0.94 %	**9.15**
	Classical His. Sim.	1.03 %	10	0.01 %	0.27 %	1.07 %	2.03
	Var-Cova	0.96 %	15	0.01 %	0.27 %	1.18 %	**9.15**
Poland	Weighted His. Sim.	1.46 %	10	0.01 %	0.55 %	2.34 %	1.96
	Classical His. Sim.	1.38 %	8	0.21 %	0.70 %	2.43 %	0.47
	Var-Cova	1.23 %	12	0.01 %	0.51 %	2.44 %	4.27
Hungary	Weighted His. Sim.	1.64 %	5	0.23 %	1.08 %	3.33 %	0.25
	Classical His. Sim.	1.50 %	9	0.03 %	0.69 %	3.27 %	1.13
	Var-Cova	1.38 %	10	0.01 %	0.62 %	3.65 %	2.00

(continued)

Table 4 (continued)

Countries	Methods	Average VaR	Exceed	Min. Exceed	Aver. Exceed.	Max. Exceed.	Stat.
South	Weighted His. Sim.	1.04 %	9	0.06 %	0.20 %	0.48 %	1.17
Korea	Classical His. Sim.	1.08 %	9	0.01 %	0.14 %	0.36 %	1.17
	Var-Cova	0.96 %	11	0.01 %	0.19 %	0.49 %	3.13
Malaysia	Weighted His. Sim.	0.85 %	9	0.03 %	0.20 %	0.60 %	1.14
	Classical His. Sim.	0.87 %	10	0.01 %	0.12 %	0.42 %	2.01
	Var-Cova	0.78 %	10	0.01 %	0.16 %	0.71 %	2.01
Colombia	Weighted His. Sim.	1.31 %	6	0.01 %	0.45 %	0.93 %	0.00
	Classical His. Sim.	1.33 %	7	0.01 %	0.32 %	0.70 %	0.13
	Var-Cova	1.17 %	15	0.01 %	0.23 %	0.83 %	**9.32**

The critical Chi-Square value for 99 % confidence level is 6.63

the currencies of emerging markets substantially depreciated and market indices dramatically declined during the taper talk period. Particularly the economically fragile EMEs are affected the most. The fund managers of the EMEs were using various risk management tools to decrease risk and increase return of their portfolios. VaR is the most popular one and the suggested risk management tools of the Basel directives.

The performance of VaR models in the volatile periods of emerging markets is questionable, due to inherited assumptions of the models. Normality assumption of the Covariance-Variance method, and using the past returns assumption of the Historical Simulation method decrease the reliability of the estimations. Fed's announcements after 2013 had a significant impact on to emerging market equity portfolios and started a volatile environment. We firstly tested the relative performance of three most popular VaR models for 12 emerging market equity portfolio during the Fed's tapering period. Classic and Weighted Historical VaR methods became more successful in Kupiec back testing than the Covariance-Variance method. We note that performance of the models is evaluated from the viewpoint of local investors. In the second stage of the study, we employed the same approach for equally weighted equity indices and US government bonds as a robustness test. We were expecting to decrease VaR of the portfolios and increase their performances. The findings supported our expectations. Average and Maximum exceedances in VaR of equally weighted portfolios were lower than the equity portfolios. Russia, Turkey and Brazil were the most volatile countries during the Fed's tapering, and their performances improved like other countries by diversification. Lastly performances of these two portfolios are measured using Sharpe and VaRSR indexes. Although the Sharpe ratio is the most common tool to evaluate

Table 5 Risk adjusted performance of portfolios and country rankings

Panel A-equity index portfolios				
Countries	Sharpe	Weighted His. VaRSR	Class. His. VaRSR	Covar-Var VaRSR
India	0.0275	0.0106	0.0107	0.0124
S. Africa	0.0201	0.0080	0.0077	0.0093
Hungary	0.0167	0.0064	0.0070	0.0074
Poland	0.0074	0.0025	0.0026	0.0034
Taiwan	0.0011	0.0004	0.0004	0.0005
Russia	−0.0019	−0.0007	−0.0009	−0.0008
S. Korea	−0.0130	−0.0055	−0.0053	−0.0059
Malaysia	−0.0225	−0.0084	−0.0081	−0.0107
Turkey	−0.0299	−0.0100	−0.0105	−0.0133
Brazil	−0.0461	−0.0205	−0.0194	−0.0205
Chile	−0.0476	−0.0200	−0.0196	−0.0216
Colombia	−0.0775	−0.0283	−0.0285	−0.0358
Panel B-equally weighted equity-US bond portfolios				
Countries	Sharpe	W.His. VaRSR	C. His. VaRSR	V-C VaRSR
S. Africa	0.0485	0.0188	0.0175	0.0215
Malaysia	0.0471	0.0195	0.0191	0.0212
Russia	0.0462	0.0198	0.0223	0.0232
India	0.0291	0.0116	0.0123	0.0131
Hungary	0.0265	0.0102	0.0112	0.0121
Colombia	0.0193	0.0079	0.0078	0.0089
Brazil	0.0163	0.0070	0.0069	0.0074
Poland	0.0162	0.0061	0.0064	0.0072
Chile	0.0144	0.0062	0.0063	0.0064
Turkey	0.0093	0.0033	0.0034	0.0042
Taiwan	0.0091	0.0037	0.0039	0.0042
S. Korea	−0.0116	−0.0048	−0.0046	−0.0052

portfolio performance, VaRSR is particularly adjusted to assets with non-normal return distributions. However, the results of the both indexes gave similar rankings. The equally weighted portfolios achieved higher index values and outperform than the equity ones.

In brief, this study has two important findings; the first one is that Classic and Weighted Historical VaR methods are appropriate methods to evaluate portfolio performance of EME after the QE period. Lastly, during the tapering period, equally weighted equity- US Bond portfolios outperform the equity portfolios, according to Sharpe and VaRSR portfolio performance indexes.

References

Alexander G j, Baptista AM (2003) Portfolio performance evaluation using value-at-risk. J Portf Manag 29:93–102
Ammann M, Reich C (2001) VaR for nonlinear instruments—linear approximation or full Monte Carlo? Financ Mark Portf Manag 15(3):363–378
Andjeli G, Djakovi V, Radišic S (2010) Application of VaR in emerging markets: a case of selected Central and Eastern European Countries. Afr J Bus Manag 4(17):3666–3680
Bao Y, Lee T, Saltoglu B (2006) Evaluating predictive performance of value-at-risk models in emerging markets: a reality check. J Forecast 25(2):101–128
Bénétrix AS, Lane PR, Shambaugh JC (2015) International currency exposures, valuation effects and the global financial crisis. J Int Econ 96(S1):S98–S109
Cifter A (2011) Value-at-risk estimation with wavelet-based extreme value theory: evidence from emerging markets. Phys A 390:2356–2367
Deng G, Dulaney T, McCann CJ, Wang O (2013) Robust portfolio optimization with value-at-risk adjusted Sharpe ratio. J Asset Manag 14(5):293–305
Diez FJ (2014) The emerging market economies in times of taper-talk and actual tapering. Curr Policy Persp. Federal Reserve Bank of Boston. http://www.bostonfed.org/economic/current-policy-perspectives/index.htm
Dimitrakopoulos DN, Kavussanos MG, Spyrou SI (2010) Value at risk models for volatile emerging markets equity portfolios. Q Rev Econ Finance 50:515–526
Embrechts P (2000) Extreme value theory: potential and limitations as an integrated risk management tool. Deriv Use Trad Regul 6:449–456
Gencay R, Selcuk F (2004) Extreme value theory and value-at-risk: relative performance in emerging markets. Int J Forecast 20(2004):287–303
Grau-Carles P, Sainz J, Otamendi J, Doncel LM (2009) Different risk-adjusted fund performance measures: a comparison. Economics discussion papers, no 2009-54. Kiel Institute for the World Economy. http://www.economics-ejournal.org/economics/discussionpapers/2009-54
IMF (2013) Annual report. https://www.imf.org/external/pubs/ft/ar/2013/eng/pdf/ar13_eng.pdf
Köksal B, Orhon M (2013) Market risk of developed and emerging countries during the global financial crisis. Emerg Mark Finance Trade 49(3):20–34
Lavigne R, Sarker S, Vasishtha G (2014) Spillover effects of quantitative easing on emerging-market economies. Bank Canada Rev 2014(Autumn 2014): 23–33
Levy H, Post T (2005) Investments. FT/Prentice Hall, Harlow
Lleo S (2010) Risk management: a review. The research foundation of CFA institute literature review. http://www.cfapubs.org/doi/pdf/10.2470/rflr.v4.n1.1
Mendes BVM, Ferreira RR, Duarte AM Jr (2000) Extreme market events in Latin American stock markets. J Emerg Mark 5(1):21–48
Mishra P, Moriyama K, N'Diaye P, Nguyen L (2014) Impact of fed tapering announcements on emerging markets, IMF working paper
Pérignon C, Smith DR (2010) The level and quality of value-at-risk disclosure by commercial banks. J Bank Finance 34:362–377
Rai V, Suchanek L (2014) The effect of the federal reserve's tapering announcements on emerging markets. Bank of Canada, working paper-50
Razali N, Wah YB (2011) Power comparisons of Shapiro–Wilk, Kolmogorov–Smirnov, Lilliefors and Anderson–Darling tests. J Stat Model Anal 2(1):21–33
Seymour AJ, Polakow DA (2003) Coupling of extreme-value theory and volatility updating with value-at-risk estimation in emerging markets: a South African test. Multinatl Finance J 7(1/2): 3–23
Silva A, Mendes B (2003) Value-at-risk and extreme returns in Asian stock markets. Int J Bus 8: 17–40
Snoussi W, El-Aroui MA (2012) Value-at-risk adjusted to the specificities of emerging markets: an analysis for the Tunisian market. Int J Emerg Mark 7(1):86–100

Stoyanov SV, Racheva-Iotova B, Rachev ST, Fabozzi FJ (2010) Stochastic models for risk estimation in volatile markets: a survey. Ann Oper Res 176:293–309
Žiković S, Aktan B (2009) Global financial crisis and VaR performance in emerging markets: a case of EU candidate states—Turkey and Croatia. Zb rad Ekon fak Rij 27(1):149–170

Prof. Dr. Mehmet Baha Karan has been with Hacettepe University (Turkey), Department of Business Administration, since 1995. He organized numerous national and international seminars and conferences focusing on finance and business management. He has served as chair of the Finance Society, Turkey, president of the Multinational Finance Society, vice president of the Center for Energy and Value, Amsterdam, member of the advisory board of Central Asia Productivity and Research Center, Chicago. He was the co-director of the Turkish Regional Chapter, PRMIA (Professional Risk Managers' International Association) during period of 2011–2014. Currently he is the independent board member of important publicly traded companies of Turkey. His current research areas of interest are finance and energy markets, risk management, portfolio management and market efficiency. Karan's accomplishments include three finance textbooks, three Springer book editorship and more than 60 articles published in national and international journals such as Corporate Governance: An International Review, Multinational Finance Journal (MFJ), Journal of Business Economics & Management and Emerging Markets Finance & Trade.

Dr. Ertuğrul Umut Uysal worked at the Treasury Management and Risk Management Departments for 4 and 13 years respectively and has been working at the Enterprise Architecture Department for 2 years at Ziraat Bank. He holds FRM charter and has publications on risk management. He has a title of PHD from Business Administration of Hacettepe University and has a master's degree in Economy Politics of Gazi University and bachelor degree of Middle East Technical University.

Mustafa Kaya has been with Hacettepe University (Turkey), Department of Business Administration, since 1997. His current research areas of interest are risk management, market efficiency, data mining and business process management. Kaya's accomplishments include one public finance textbooks, some articles published in national and international journals.

Jumps and Earnings Announcement: Empirical Evidence from An Emerging Market Using High Frequency Data

Shabir A.A. Saleem and Abdullah Yalaman

Abstract This chapter aims to measure the company-level informational shocks based on the jump dynamics of stock price around earnings announcement in emerging economy using high frequency data. Besides, it intends to show the profitability of earnings announcement strategy that uses jumps as trading signal. For this, the chapter divides earnings announcements as "Good" and "Bad" news and tests how jump behavior changes in accordance to "Good" or "Bad" earnings news. In another words, the chapter tests the presence of the post earnings announcement drift anomaly in Turkish Stock Market through characterizing the jumps and cumulative abnormal returns of individual stocks around the announcement days. The results show that there is a discrete jump in the stock price around both "Good" and "Bad" earnings announcement in emerging economy. The cumulative abnormal returns response significantly to "Bad" earnings news for the event window which support the validation of post earnings announcement drift anomaly in Turkish Stock Market. It can be conclude that investor can take short position in Bad earnings news to make a profit.

S.A.A. Saleem
School of Business Administration, Eskisehir Osmangazi Universitesi, IIBF Isletme Bolumu, B Blok Kat 2, 26480 Eskisehir, Turkey
e-mail: shabirmeer@gmail.com

A. Yalaman (✉)
Research Associate, Bogazici University, Center for Economics and Econometrics, Istanbul, Turkey

School of Business Administration, Eskisehir Osmangazi Universitesi, IIBF Isletme Bolumu, B Blok Kat 2, 26480 Eskisehir, Turkey
e-mail: abdullah.yalama@gmail.com

H. Dinçer, Ü. Hacioğlu (eds.), *Risk Management, Strategic Thinking and Leadership in the Financial Services Industry*, Contributions to Management Science, DOI 10.1007/978-3-319-47172-3_14

1 Introduction

It took scholars many years to analyze the jumps in asset prices and detect their causes. Merton (1976) explains the jump as the unexpected release of new information to the market. The jumps in stock prices are straightly connected to the information in the market (Ross 1989). There are two types of news that affect the asset price, usual news and unusual news. The first type is assumed to slowly evolve changes in the asset price whereas the second type causes infrequently large movements. A potential source of abnormal news can be a significant macroeconomic event or firm-specific event such as earnings announcement and anticipation of cash flows. News events with more information content bring more jumps to the asset price than the news events with less information content (Andersen 1996).

In finance literature, scholars use different measurements to capture news surprises through jumps. The price of an asset is described by a semimartingale process where logarithmic price process is decomposed into continuities (Brownian motion which is consists of locally bounded sample paths, càdlàg stochastic volatility) and discontinuities (Jump) components (Barndorff-Nielsen and Shephard 2006; Aït-Sahalia and Jacod 2010). To find out whether an asset prices experienced jumps for a particular time interval, many research papers suggest non-parametric statistical tests to detect whether an asset price movement contains any jump during a particular period. Of these tests are Barndorff-Nielsen and Shephard (2004), Jiang and Oomen (2005), Ait-Sahalia and Jacod (2007), Lee and Mykland (2008). In this study we use Barndorff-Nielsen and Shephard (2004) nonparametric statistical tests. The aim of this chapter is to measure the company-level informational shocks based on the discontinues dynamics (jump) of stock price around earnings announcement and tests the profitability of earnings announcement strategy using jumps as trading signal. Our jump based strategy is motivated by growing literature supporting the importance of accounting for the jump component in options pricing, hedging, bond premium forecasting, systematic risk management and credit risk management (Aït-Sahalia and Jacod 2010; Zhou and Zhu 2012; Patton and Verardo 2012). Post earnings announcement drift is one of the most robust anomalies challenging the efficient market hypothesis. While the researches to date has not entirely explained the reasons of post earnings announcement anomaly, the anomaly has generated interesting implications for portfolio management and trading strategies.

The purpose of this chapter is to measure the company-level informational shocks based on the jump dynamics of stock price around earnings announcement in emerging economy using high frequency data. Moreover, it intends to show the profitability of earnings announcement strategy that uses jumps as trading signal. For this, the chapter divides earnings news as "Good" and "Bad" news and tests how jump behavior change in accordance to "Good" or "Bad" news. In another words the chapter tests the validation of the post earnings announcement drift anomaly in Turkish Stock Market using the jumps and cumulative average abnormal returns (CAAR) of individual stocks around the announcement days. The results show that there is a discrete jump in the stock price around both "Good" and "Bad" earnings announcement in emerging economy. The cumulative abnormal returns response statistically significant only to "Bad" earnings news for the event window. As it can be seen in Table 2, average abnormal returns are negative for "Bad" earnings news and positive for "Good" earnings news. The results are only statistically significant for "Bad" earnings news. It can be conclude that investors can make profit by taking short position in "Bad" earnings news. Moreover the jump signals attempt to remove information about stocks future payoffs from unusual price change around earning announcement. Our results suggest that the discrete jump path of price process around earnings announcements may express exclusive information about subsequent earnings momentum which is consistent with the literature (Zhou and Zhu 2012) supporting the validation of post earnings announcement drift anomaly in Turkish Stock Market.

This chapter additionally characterize the descriptive statistics of realized volatility, returns, jump, and trade volume of individual stocks around the announcement days for supporting the validation of the post earnings announcement drift anomaly in Turkish Stock Market, however, not all the results are statistically significant except for the jumps and volume.

The chapter is designed as followings: in Sect. 2, we discuss the summary of literature. In Sect. 3 we present the methodology which includes data, jump detection procedure and the estimation of abnormal return. Sect. 4 offers and discusses our empirical findings. Sect. 5 presents the conclusion.

2 Summary of Literature

To our knowledge there is no previous study in the literature investigates the jump behavior of individual stocks around the earnings announcement date using high frequency data in the emerging economies however, there is only few ones that used high frequency data to detect the relationship between jumps and earnings announcement in developed economies (Lee and Mykland 2008; Patton and Verardo 2012). For example Lee and Mykland (2008) used high frequency data to detect the association of stocks jumps with pre-scheduled earnings announcement and Patton and Verardo (2012) studied the behavior of systematic risk (beta) around the quarterly earnings announcements period.

Many studies in the literature use daily data to test the post-earnings announcement drift anomaly using jumps in the stock prices (Zhou and Zhu 2012) or have followed Event Studies Methodology to detect the impact of earnings announcement on stocks prices through measuring the abnormal returns. Many empirical studies report that stock prices respond positively to good news and negatively to bad news for the U.S. firms (see Ball and Brown 1968; Griffin 1976; Chambers and Penman 1984; Chari et al. 1988; Landsman and Maydew 2002).

There are alot of other studies investigate the effect of earnings announcement in developed markets using event study methodology, of which are Frost and Pownall

(1994) and Mohammed and Yadav (2002) in UK, Chan et al. (2005) in Australia, Wael (2004) in France, van Huffel et al. (1996) and Laurent (2000) in Belgium, Sponholtz (2005) in Denmark, Kallunki (1996) and Vieru (2002) in Finland, Cotter (1997) in Ireland, Jermakowicz and Tomaszewski (1998) in Poland, Pellicer and Rees (1999) in Spain. Some papers emphasized that there is a rapid reaction to earnings announcement in price volatility and returns notably around the event window (Vieru 2002; Pellicer and Rees 1999; Mohammed and Yadav 2002; Cotter 1997; van Huffel et al. 1996; Chan et al. 2005), while Sponholtz (2005), Berezovskis et al. (2010) reported slow reaction of stock prices volatility and returns to earnings announcement. Some studies in the literature investigating the behavior of asset prices and volatility around the macro-economic announcement (Ball and Kothari 1991; Andersen et al. 2003, 2007; Dungey et al. 2007).

Studies from emerging markets that analyze the reaction of stocks to earnings announcement using Event Study Methodology reported that stocks prices do react to earnings announcements and the financial reports do affect the price volatility (Haw et al. 2000; Kong and Taghavi 2006; Das et al. 2008; Altiok-Yilmaz and Akben-Selcuk 2010).

Lee and Mykland (2008) investigate the relationship between jumps and company-specific news using high frequency data through developing an advanced statistical nonparametric test to detect jumps. They conclude that there is an association between jumps in stock returns and pre-scheduled earnings announcement. Following the same methodology, Zhou and Zhu (2012) support the presence of the post-earnings announcement drift anomaly in US stock market.

Previous studies in the literature show the existence of jumps in the asset prices. By following them, many other papers investigate the impacts of jumps on portfolio management, risk management, options, bond pricing and hedging (Merton 1976; Piazzesi 2005). Recently Barndorff-Nielsen and Shephard (2004) developed statistical models to measure the stochastic features of jumps. Lee and Mykland (2008) developed nonparametric test which distinguishes the actual jumps from the spurious ones using more robust detection rate.

The sign, the size, the arrival times, the intensity and the distribution of jumps are important for hedging strategies and asset pricing models. For example, Zhou and Zhu (2012) stated that a hedge portfolio could achieve an annualized abnormal return of 15.3 % by taking long position in positive-jumps stocks and short position in negative-jumps stocks. Moreover, Piazzesi (2005) improve bond pricing models by incorporating jumps related to market information.

Our study differs from previous studies in aspects of the followings:

1. No previous study in Emerging economies investigates the jump behavior of individual stocks around the earning announcement days.
2. Most of the previous studies from developed economies use daily data to detect the association of stocks jumps with pre-scheduled earnings announcement while we use high frequency data. Our study benefit individuals who are interested or are engaged in portfolio management, risk management, options and bond pricing and hedging in emerging markets.

3 Methodology

3.1 Data

Our data sample is consisting of 30 firms listed on the BIST30 index along with their quarterly earnings announcement released to public for the period of 3.1.2005 to 31.12.2013. The data is received from Borsa Istanbul in form of raw format and then it is filtered and arranged into 15-min intervals. The daily routine seans at Borsa Istanbul starts from 9:15 to 17:40 with a lunch break at 12:30–2:00. Data cleaning process was performed based on the existence literature, specifically the deleting entries related to weekends and public holidays and when the market does not trade full days (Hansen and Lunde 2006; Barndorff-Nielsen et al. 2009). The earnings announcement dates are obtained from Borsa Istanbul website. Our study covers a total number of 1,973,190 observations (30×65773).

3.2 Jump Detection Procedure

We measure significant jumps using Barndorff-Neilsen and Shephard (2004) non-parametric test. In order to detect the jumps in asset price, lets first define an asset price S(t) as:

$$dlogS(t) = \mu(t)dt + \sigma(t)dW(t) + Y(t)dJ(t) \tag{1}$$

where W(t) is the standard Brownian motion and μ(t) is the drift and σ(t) is the spot volatility, dJ(t) is a counting process independent of W(t). Y(t) is the jump size.

Following their method, the return based on intraday data are calculated by the follows formula:

$$r_{jt} = \log p(t-1+(j/J)) - \log p(t-1+((j-1)/J)) \tag{2}$$

Barndorff-Neilsen and Shephard (2004) suggest the following test statistics for jumps at the interval t_{i-1} to t_i:

$$Z_{Jt,i} \equiv \frac{\ln(RV_t - BV_t)}{\sqrt{(vbb - vqq)\frac{1}{\frac{T}{\Delta_n}\max\left(1, \frac{TP_t}{BV_t}\right)}} \rightarrow N(0,1),} \tag{3}$$

where $vbb = \left(\frac{\pi}{2}\right)^2 + \pi - 5; \text{vqq} = 2;$

$$RV_t = \sum_{i=1}^{T/\Delta_n} \left|\Delta_i^n X_i\right|^2 \tag{4}$$

$$BV_t = \left(\frac{\pi}{2}\right)\left(\frac{\frac{T}{\Delta_n}}{\frac{T}{\Delta_n} - 1}\right)\sum_{i=1}^{T/\Delta_n} |\Delta_i^n X_i||\Delta_i^n X_{i-1}| \quad (5)$$

$$TP_t = \left(\frac{T}{\Delta_n}\right)\mu_{\frac{4}{3}}^{-3}\left(\frac{\frac{T}{\Delta_n}}{\frac{T}{\Delta_n} - 2}\right)\sum_{i=1}^{T/\Delta_n} |\Delta_i^n X_{i-2}|^{4/3}|\Delta_i^n X_{i-1}|^{4/3}|\Delta_i^n X_i|^{4/3} \quad (6)$$

where $\mu_{4/3}$=0.8309.

3.3 Estimation of Abnormal Returns

We estimate the abnormal returns using the following Market Model (Fama et al. 1969; Malkiel and Fama 1970):

$$R_{it} = \alpha_i + \beta_i R_{mt} + \varepsilon \quad (5)$$

with $\mathrm{E}(\varepsilon) = 0 \, and \, Var\,(\varepsilon_{it}) = \sigma_{\varepsilon i}^2$

where R_{it} is the required rate of return of ith stocks at t time period, β_i is the beta coefficient of ith stocks, R_{mt} is market rate of return and α_i is the intercept of the model. The abnormal return is calculated as the differences between stock return and market return (the market model's residual):

$$AR_{it} = R_{it} - (\alpha + \beta_i R_{mt}) \quad (6)$$

Then we average them to obtain the average Abnormal Return (AAR_{it})

$$AAR_{it} = 1/N \sum AR_{it} \quad (7)$$

where AAR_{it} is the Average Abnormal Return, AR_{it} is Abnormal Return of individual stocks and N is the total number of stocks.

The cumulative average abnormal return ($CAAR$) is express as bellow. The event window for this calculation is [−5,+5]:

$$CAAR = \sum AAR_t \quad (8)$$

We perform t-test at the 5 % level of significance to assess the significance of AAR_{it} and $CAAR$.

$$t - test = AAR / \left(\frac{S(AAR)}{\sqrt{N}}\right) \quad (9)$$

$$t - test = CARR / \left(\frac{S(CAAR)}{\sqrt{N}} \right) \tag{10}$$

Where *S(AAR)* is the standard deviation of average abnormal return calculated over estimation period, *S(CAAR)* is the standard deviation of cumulative average abnormal return calculated over estimation period.

4 Empirical Findings

The purpose of this chapter is to measure the company-level informational shocks based on the jump dynamics of stock price around earnings announcement in emerging economy using high frequency data. Furthermore, it intends to show the profitability of earnings announcement strategy that uses jumps as trading signal. For this, the chapter divides earnings announcements as "Good" or "Bad" news and tests how jump behavior changes in accordance to "Good" or "Bad" earnings news. Moreover we test whether the jumps are caused by "Good" or "Bad" earnings news? Good earnings announcement means positive surprise whereas Bad earnings announcement means negative surprises. Following Igbal and Farooqi (2011) "Good" and "Bad" news are defined as bellow:

Good news: Actual Earning $>$ 10 % of Median Earnings
Bad news: Actual Earnings $<$ 10 % of Median Earnings

where the median is calculated for the period from 2005 to 2013 using quarterly earnings of individual firms.

We detect significant jumps of 30 individual stocks list on BIST30 index applying Barndorff-Neilsen and Shephard (2004) jump test using 15-minute interval data and then to investigate the relationship between jumps and Good/Bad earnings announcements we estimate the following model using panel logistic regression method.

$$\begin{aligned} Jumps_{it} = \beta_0 + \beta_1 D_{it-5} + \beta_2 D_{it-4} + \beta_3 D_{it-3} + \beta_4 D_{it-2} + \beta_5 D_{it-1} + \beta_6 D_{it} \\ + \beta_7 D_{it+1} + \beta_8 D_{it+2} + \beta_9 D_{it+3} + \beta_{10} D_{it+4} + \beta_{11} D_{it+5} + \varepsilon_{it} \end{aligned}$$

Where D_{it} is a dummy variables which takes the value of 1 during the announcement day and 0 otherwise. Table 1 show that there are significant jumps in stock price during Good and Bad earnings announcement window frame as [−1,0], [−2,0], and [−4,0]. Moreover we also captures some significant jumps during the event window frame as [0,1], [0,4], and [0,5]. Table 1 show that there is a discrete jump in the stock price around both "Good" and "Bad" earnings announcement in emerging economy.

To test the validation of the presence of the post earnings announcement drift anomaly in Turkish Stock Market, we further characterize cumulative abnormal

Table 1 Logistic regression for all announcement dates

	All news		Good news		Bad news	
Variables	Logit coeff	Odds ratio	Logit coeff	Odds ratio	Logit coeff	Odds ratio
RV_t	0.00171***	1.002***	0.00168***	1.002***	0.00163***	1.002***
	(0.000194)	(0.000194)	(0.000195)	(0.000195)	(0.000211)	(0.000211)
Volume	0.00520**	1.000**	5.88e-07***	1.000***	7.20e-07***	1.000***
	(0.002)	(0.002)	(2.24e-07)	(2.24e-07)	(2.34e-07)	(2.34e-07)
D_{t-5}	0.157	1.170	0.132	1.141	−0.835*	0.434*
	(0.104)	(0.122)	(0.111)	(0.127)	(0.463)	(0.201)
D_{t-4}	0.269***	1.309***	0.285***	1.330***	0.237	1.267
	(0.100)	(0.131)	(0.106)	(0.141)	(0.305)	(0.386)
D_{t-3}	0.0602	1.062	0.0733	1.076	−0.174	0.840
	(0.108)	(0.115)	(0.114)	(0.122)	(0.355)	(0.299)
D_{t-2}	0.227**	1.255**	0.205*	1.228*	−0.0548	0.947
	(0.102)	(0.128)	(0.109)	(0.133)	(0.340)	(0.321)
D_{t-1}	0.264***	1.302***	0.220**	1.246**	0.258	1.294
	(0.101)	(0.131)	(0.108)	(0.135)	(0.305)	(0.395)
D_t	0.342***	1.407***	0.362***	1.437***	0.341***	1.406***
	(0.0982)	(0.138)	(0.103)	(0.148)	(0.0982)	(0.138)
D_{t+1}	0.225**	1.252**	0.266**	1.305**	−0.172	0.842
	(0.102)	(0.127)	(0.106)	(0.139)	(0.355)	(0.299)
D_{t+2}	−0.0344	0.966	0.00825	1.008	0.164	1.178
	(0.111)	(0.108)	(0.116)	(0.117)	(0.315)	(0.371)
D_{t+3}	0.0978	1.103	0.115	1.122	−0.0488	0.952
	(0.106)	(0.117)	(0.112)	(0.125)	(0.340)	(0.323)
D_{t+4}	0.271***	1.311***	0.262**	1.300**	−0.452	0.636
	(0.100)	(0.132)	(0.106)	(0.138)	(0.397)	(0.252)
D_{t+5}	0.216**	1.241**	0.244**	1.277**	0.0618	1.064
	(0.102)	(0.127)	(0.107)	(0.137)	(0.326)	(0.347)
Constant	−1.878***	0.153***	−1.878***	0.153***	−1.880***	0.153***
	(0.0134)	(0.00205)	(0.0134)	(0.00205)	(0.0136)	(0.00207)
Obs.	68.040	68.040	67.204	67.204	60.982	60.982

Standard errors in parentheses
*** $p < 0.01$, ** $p < 0.05$, * $p < 0.1$

returns of individual stocks around the announcement days. Table 2 show that cumulative average abnormal returns (CAAR) response statistically significant to "Bad" earnings news for the event window. As can be seen in Table 2, CAAR are negative for "Bad" earnings news and positive for "Good" earnings news. The results are only statistically significant for "Bad" earnings news. It can be conclude that investor can take short position in "Bad" earnings news. Moreover the jump signals attempt to remove information about stocks future payoffs from unusual price change around earning announcement which supports the validation of post

Table 2 Cumulative Average Abnormal Returns (CAAR)

	Good news	Bad news	All news
D_{t-5}	0.100	0.276	0.003
D_{t-4}	0.036	0.456	0.073
D_{t-3}	0.000	−0.390	−0.067
D_{t-2}	0.224	−0.006	0.093
D_{t-1}	0.006	−0.255	−0.103
D_t	0.007	−0.191	−0.200
D_{t+1}	−0.046	−0.509	−0.078
D_{t+2}	0.047	−0.424	0.067
D_{t+3}	−0.062	−0.717	−0.154
D_{t+4}	−0.029	0.085	0.090
D_{t+5}	−0.273	−0.105	−0.256
CAAR	0.010	−1.780	−0.531
t-value	0.275	−16.891***	−14.327***

Standard errors in parentheses
*** $p < 0.01$, ** $p < 0.05$, * $p < 0.1$

earnings announcement drift anomaly in Turkish Stock Market consistent with the existing literature (Zhou and Zhu 2012).

In order to get more evidence to support this anomaly, the chapter additionally calculate the t-test value to characterize the descriptive statistics of realized volatility, returns, jump, and trade volume of individual stocks around the announcement days. Table 3 show that only volume and discrete jumps are statistically differ from announcement to non-announcement.

5 Conclusion

Previous studies show several different trading strategies that support post earnings anomalies drift, different from common literature this chapter focus on testing the occurrence of price discontinuities around earning announcement. The sudden and often extreme realization of the jump path of asset price around the earnings announcement may capture unique information about future asset payoff and thus predict the subsequent return drift.

This chapter investigates the jump behavior of individual stocks in emerging economy around the earnings announcement days using high frequency data. We applied the jump detection method of Barndorff-Nielsen and Shephard (2004) to identify firm-specific informational shocks. Additionally we divide earnings announcements into two part as "Good" and "Bad" earnings news. We explain whether the "Good" or "Bad" news cause jumps? The results show that there is a discrete jump in the stock price around both "Good" and "Bad" earnings announcement in emerging economy. Both "Good" and "Bad" create volatility in the stock prices. Moreover, it can be said that the effects of earnings news seem appearing

Table 3 t-statistics for post earning anomaly drift

	Dates	All news				Good news				Bad news			
		N.	Average	Std. D.	p-value	N.	Average	Std. D.	p-value	N.	Average	Std. D.	p-value
Realized volatility	Ann. day	706	11.941	35.657	0.574	630	11.833	37.554	0.564	76	12.837	11.096	0.956
	Before ann. day	3530	13.200	57.326		3530	13.200	57.326		3530	13.200	57.326	
	Ann. day	706	11.941	35.657	0.138	630	11.833	37.554	0.262	76	12.837	11.0965	0.80
	After ann. day	3530	14.342	53.834		3530	14.342	53.834		3530	14.342	53.834	
	Ann. day	706	11.941	35.657	0.361	630	11.833	37.554	0.422	76	12.8373	11.09650	0.635
	Non-ann. day	67334	10.389	44.984		67334	10.389	44.984		67334	10.3892	44.98376	
Return	Ann. day	706	−0.112	2.552	0.409	630	−0.072	2.569	0.655	76	−0.443	2.340	0.182
	Before ann. day	3530	−0.019	2.743		3530	−0.019	2.743		3530	−0.019	2.743	
	Ann. day	706	−0.112	2.552	0.344	630	−0.072	2.569	0.275	76	−0.443	2.397	0.526
	After ann. day	3530	−0.215	3.115		3530	−0.215	3.115		3530	−0.215	3.116	
	Ann. day	706	−0.112	2.552	0.164	630	−0.072	2.569	0.358	76	−0.4430	2.39689	−0.466
	Non-ann. day	67334	0.023	2.463		67334	0.023	2.463		67334	0.0228	2.46259	
Jumps	Ann. day	706	0.183	0.387	0.204	630	0.186	0.389	0.167	76	0.158	0.367	0.912
	Before ann. day	3530	0.163	0.369		3530	0.163	0.370		3530	0.163	0.369	
	Ann. day	706	0.183	0.387	0.115	630	0.186	0.389	0.094	76	0.158	0.367	0.998
	After ann. day	3530	0.158	0.365		3530	0.158	0.365		3530	0.158	0.365	
	Ann. day	706	0.183	0.387	**0.003****	630	0.186	0.390	**0.003****	76	0.1579	.36707	0.635
	Non-ann. day	67334	0.139	0.346		67334	0.14	0.346		67334	0.1390	0.34597	
Volume	Ann. day	706	28718	36130	0.504	630	630	0.013	0.823	76	36264	43183	**0.048****
	Before ann. day	3530	27700	37137		3530	0.034	2.190		3530	27700	37137	
	Ann. day	706	28718	36130	0.788	630	27808	35115	0.420	76	36264	43183	0.115
	After ann. day	3530	29144	38865		3530	29144	38865		3530	29144	38865	
	Ann. day	706	28718	36130	**0.061***	630	27808	35115	0.112	76	36264	43183	**0.011***
	Non-ann. day	67334	25632	43596		67329	25448	37133		67329	25448	37133	

** $p < 0.05$, * $p < 0.1$

4 days before the earnings news releases and last for until the fourth day after the news releases.

To test the validation of the presence of the post earnings announcement drift anomaly in Turkish Stock Market, we characterize cumulative abnormal returns of individual stocks around the announcement days. The results emphasize that cumulative average abnormal returns (CAAR) response statistically significant to "Bad" earnings news for the event window which supports the validation of post earnings announcement drift anomaly in Turkish Stock Market. This is consistent with the existing literature (Zhou and Zhu 2012).

The chapter additionally tests the presence of the post earnings announcement drift anomaly in Turkish Stock Market through using t-test for realized volatility, returns, jump, and trade volume of individual stocks around the announcement days. The results show that only discrete jumps and trade volume are statistically differed from the announcement to non-announcement period which support post earnings announcement drift anomaly in Turkish Stock Market. Moreover, our statistical tests support the profitability of earnings announcement strategy that used jumps as trading signal.

The empirical results of our chapter contributes to the existing literature on post earnings announcement drift anomalies in following ways. First, to our knowledge, no previous study in Emerging economies investigates the jump behavior of individual stocks around the earning announcement days using high frequency data. Second, our findings suggest that jumps surrounding the earnings announcement days are created by both "Good" and "Bad" news. Investor can use this anomaly to make profit by taking short position on "Bad" earnings announcements. For future studies, we suggest that an intensive study should be conducted on the relationship between systematic risk and earnings announcement in emerging economies.

References

Aït-Sahalia Y, Jacod J (2007) Volatility estimators for discretely sampled Lévy processes. Ann Stat 35(1):355–392

Aït-Sahalia Y, Jacod J (2010) Analyzing the spectrum of asset returns: jump and volatility components in high frequency data. National Bureau of Economic Research, No. w15808

Altiok-Yilmaz A, Akben-Selcuk E (2010) Information content of dividends: evidence from Istanbul stock exchange. Int Bus Res 3(3):126

Andersen TG (1996) Return volatility and trading volume: an information flow interpretation of stochastic volatility. J Financ 51(1):169–204

Andersen TG, Bollerslev T, Diebold FX, Labys P (2003) Modeling and forecasting realized volatility. Econometrica 71(2):579–625

Andersen TG, Bollerslev T, Diebold FX (2007) Roughing it up: including jump components in the measurement, modeling, and forecasting of return volatility. Rev Econ Stat 89(4):701–720

Ball R, Brown P (1968) An empirical evaluation of accounting income numbers. J Acc Res 6 (2):159–178

Ball R, Kothari SP (1991) Security returns around earnings announcements. Acc Rev 66:718–738

Barndorff-Nielsen OE, Shephard N (2004) Power and bipower variation with stochastic volatility and jumps. J Financ Econ 2(1):1–37
Barndorff-Nielsen OE, Shephard N (2006) Econometrics of testing for jumps in financial economics using bipower variation. J Financ Econ 4(1):1–30
Barndorff-Nielsen OE, Hansen PR, Lunde A, Shephard N (2009) Realized kernels in practice: trades and quotes. Econ J 12(3):C1–C32
Berezovskis P, Visnapuu V, Högholm K (2010) Post-earnings announcement drifts on the baltic stock exchanges. Working paper, Stockholm School of Economic
Chambers AE, Penman SH (1984) Timeliness of reporting and the stock price reaction to earnings announcements. J Account Res 22(1):21–47
Chan H, Faff R, Ramsay A (2005) Firm size and the information content of annual earnings announcements: Australian evidence. J Bus Financ Acc 32(1–2):211–253
Chari VV, Jagannathan R, Ofer AR (1988) Seasonalities in security returns: the case of earnings announcements. J Financ Econ 21(1):101–121
Cotter J (1997) Irish event studies: earnings announcements, turn of the year and size effects. Ir J Manag 18:34
Das S, Pattanayak JK, Pathak P (2008) The effect of quarterly earnings announcements on Sensex: a case with clustering of events. IUP J Acc Res Audit Pract 7(4):64–78
Dungey M, McKenzie MD, Smith LV (2007) News, no-news and jumps in the US Treasury Market. Working Paper
Fama EF, Fisher L, Jensen MC, Roll R (1969) The adjustment of stock prices to new information. Int Econ Rev 10(1):1–21
Frost CA, Pownall G (1994) Accounting disclosure practices in the United States and the United Kingdom. J Acc Res 32(1):75–102
Griffin PA (1976) Competitive information in the stock market: an empirical study of earnings, dividends and analysts' forecasts. J Financ 31(2):631–650
Hansen PR, Lunde A (2006) Realized variance and market microstructure noise. J Bus Econ Stat 24(2):127–161
Haw IM, Qi D, Wu W (2000) Timeliness of annual report releases and market reaction to earnings announcements in an emerging capital market: the case of China. J Int Fin Manag Acc 11 (2):108–131
Iqbal J, Farooqi FA (2011) Stock price reaction to earnings announcement: the case of an emerging market. Munich Personal Repec Archive. http://mpra.ub.uni-muenchen.de/30865/MPRA
Jermakowicz EK, Gornik-Tomaszewski S (1998) Information content of earnings in the emerging capital market: evidence from the Warsaw stock exchange. Multinatl Financ J 2(4):245–267
Jiang G, Oomen R (2005) A new test for jumps in asset prices. Preprint
Kallunki JP (1996) Stock returns and earnings announcements in Finland. Eur Acc Rev 5 (2):199–216
Kong S, Taghavi M (2006) The effect of annual earnings announcements on the Chinese stock markets. Int Adv Econ Res 12(3):318–326
Landsman WR, Maydew EL (2002) Has the information content of quarterly earnings announcements declined in the past three decades? J Acc Res 40(3):797–808
Laurent M (2000) The effect of earnings release for Belgian listed companies. Working Paper WP-CEB 03
Lee SS, Mykland PA (2008) Jumps in financial markets: a new nonparametric test and jump dynamics. Rev Financ Stud 21(6):2535–2563
Malkiel BG, Fama EF (1970) Efficient capital markets: a review of theory and empirical work. J Financ 25(2):383–417
Merton RC (1976) Option pricing when underlying stock returns are discontinuous. J Financ Econ 3(1-2):125–144
Mohammed SR, Yadav PK (2002) Quality of information and volatility around earnings announcements. In: Paper presented in EFA 2002 Berlin Meetings, Feb 2002

Patton AJ, Verardo M (2012) Does beta move with news? Firm-specific information flows and learning about profitability. Rev Financ Stud 25(9):2789–2839
Pellicer MJA, Rees WP (1999) Regularities in the equity price response to earnings announcements in Spain. Eur Acc Rev 8(4):585–607
Piazzesi M (2005) Bond yields and the Federal Reserve. J Polit Econ 113(2):311–344
Ross SA (1989) Information and volatility: the no-arbitrage martingale approach to timing and resolution irrelevancy. J Financ 44(1):1–17
Sponholtz C (2005) Separating the stock market's reaction to simultaneous dividend and earnings announcements. In: EFA 2006 Zurich meetings, Nov 2005
van Huffel G, Joos P, Ooghe H (1996) Semi-annual earnings announcements and market reaction: some recent findings for a small capital market. Eur Acc Rev 5(4):693–713
Vieru M (2002) The impact of interim earnings announcements on the permanent price effects of trades on the Helsinki stock exchange. J Multinatl Financ Manag 12(1):41–59
Wael L (2004) Market reaction to annual earnings announcements: the case of Euronext Paris. EFMA 2004 Basel Meetings Paper
Zhou H, Zhu JQ (2012) Jump on the post-earnings announcement drift (corrected). Financ Anal J 68(3):63–80

Shabir Saleem is a finance PhD student at Eskisehir Osmangazi University Department of Business and Administration, Eskisehir-Turkey. Mr. Saleem has a BBA in Business Administration from Al Azhar University, Cairo, Egypt (2005) and an MBA from Prince of Songkla University, Phuket, Thailand (2009). His research interests lie in high-frequency data analysis and financial econometrics.

Abdullah Yalaman is a Professor of Finance at Eskisehir Osmangazi University Department of Business and Administration, Eskisehir-Turkey and research associate at Bogazici University of Center for Economics and Econometrics. Dr. Yalaman has a BS in Business Administration from Eskisehir Osmangazi University (2003), an MBA from Anadolu University (2005) and a PhD in Finance from Anadolu University (2004). He has been as a visiting scholar at UTAS, Australia and University of Cambridge, UK. His research interests lie in high-frequency data analysis, volatility spillover, contagion, financial econometrics. He has taught financial management, international finance, financial econometrics, investment and portfolio analysis, among others, at both graduate and undergraduate levels. He is the finance editor of Eskisehir Osmangazi University Journal of Economics and Administrative Sciences and has been an ad hoc reviewer for journals such as Economic System, Resources Policy, Borsa Istanbul Review, Emerging Markets Finance and Trade, Journal of Asian Economics, Economic Modelling, Review of Middle East Economics and Finance, Journal of Stock & Forex Trading, Eastern European Economics, International Journal of Learning and Intellectual Capital and Bogazici Journal. He is a member of the Society for Financial Econometrics (SoFiE) and Econometric Society.

Hedging Scenarios Under Competition: Exploring the Impact of Competitors' Hedging Practices

Genco Fas and Kerem Senel

Abstract Hedging without giving regard to what competitors are doing may actually increase the variance of profits as opposed to decreasing it. In this study, a market maker and an individual firm are taken as the players of a simultaneous game. We explore the impact of competitors' hedging practices on the optimal hedging policy of an individual firm by explicitly considering the other factors such as the level of pass-through of cost shocks and the level of profitability in the industry. Computational results are based on the simulations of an analytical model which incorporates a Nash equilibrium strategy.

1 Introduction

Hedging practices in an industrial corporation aim to minimize the variance of profits due to the volatility of market prices of inputs, interest rates, and exchange rates. However, trying to hedge these types of risks without giving regard to what competitors are doing may lead to unintended consequences. If competitors are not hedging a certain type of risk, hedging that particular type of risk may actually increase the variance of profits as opposed to decreasing it. Empirical evidence documented by Nain (2004) and Adam and Nain (2013), conclude that a firm should conform to the majority in terms of hedging in order to minimize the variability of its cash flows.

G. Fas (✉)
Department of Business, Istanbul Bilgi University, Santral Campus, 34060 Istanbul, Eyup, Turkey
e-mail: genco.fas@bilgi.edu.tr

K. Senel
Graduate School of Finance, Istanbul Commerce University, Sutluce Campus, 34445 Istanbul, Beyoglu, Turkey
e-mail: keremsenel@gmail.com

H. Dinçer, Ü. Hacioğlu (eds.), *Risk Management, Strategic Thinking and Leadership in the Financial Services Industry*, Contributions to Management Science, DOI 10.1007/978-3-319-47172-3_15

However, the hedging practices of competitors is not the single determinant for the hedging decision of an individual firm. If firms can increase their output prices in response to an increase in input prices, this reduces the need to hedge. Previous research focuses on the factors that may have an impact on the firms' ability and propensity to reflect such price increases. For instance, Allayannis and Ihrig (2001) observe that it is easier (more difficult) for firms in less (more) competitive [or high (low) markup] industries to respond to exchange rate movements by increasing their prices. On the other hand, Nain (2004) shows that product prices are less responsive to foreign exchange rates in industries where currency hedging is more common.

It is also plausible that the minimization of variance of profits may not be the sole purpose for an individual firm. Adam et al. (2007) and Mello and Ruckes (2005) attribute deliberate deviation from competitors in terms of hedging practices to strategic considerations. An individual firm may choose to act differently in order to benefit from cash inflows when their competitors experience cash outflows due to their hedging activities.

The main objective of this paper is to explore the impact of competitors' hedging practices on the optimal hedging policy of an individual firm by explicitly considering the other factors such as the level of pass-through of cost shocks and the level of profitability in the industry (which is negatively correlated with the degree of competition in the industry).

In a game theoretical setting, a market maker and an individual firm are taken as the players of a simultaneous game. Firms make their order decisions for replenishment with respect to the estimated effective demand. They have to decide on their order quantities simultaneously in this competitive environment as they try to maximize their expected cash flows. Different from previous studies exploring the impact of competitors' hedging practices, the hedging ratios, the level of pass-through of cost shocks, and the level of profitability are treated as exogeneous variables. This enables us to analyze the impact of each factor separately.

Treating the hedging ratio as an exogeneous variable is also consistent with the notion of selective hedging. Brown et al. (2006) observe that firms tend to decrease hedging as prices move against them—behavior contrary to that predicted by risk management theory. These results suggest that firms attempt to time market prices, so-called selective hedging. Hence, from the viewpoint of the individual firm, it is possible to decide on the optimal hedging ratio that minimizes the variance of its cash flows given the hedging ratio of the market maker, the level of pass-through of cost shocks, and the level of profitability. If the individual firm is negligible compared to the market maker in terms of size and market impact, treating these factors as exogeneous variables is a reasonable assumption.

Our experiment setup also enables us to pinpoint the optimal hedging ratio that maximizes the risk-adjusted mean cash flow as well as the optimal hedging ratio that minimizes the cash flow variance. Comparison of these different hedging ratios sheds light on the tradeoff between risk and return in the context of hedging.

The rest of the paper is organized as follows. The literature review consists of two parts. First, we review previous studies focusing on hedging, in general, and the impact of competitors' hedging practices, in particular. In the second part, we present the fundamentals of dynamic games in a single period. The next section develops the analytical model and proves the existence and uniqueness of the Nash equilibrium by using the first and second order conditions, and the contraction mapping argument in a single period setting. Then, we discuss the simulation results. Finally, we present our conclusions.

2 Literature Review

2.1 Hedging and Risk Management

The most important question regarding hedging is whether it has an impact on valuation. Carter et al. (2006) summarize the ways hedging and risk management can increase corporate market values:

- By reducing corporate income taxes.
- By reducing the probability and expected costs of financial distress.
- By preserving management's ability and incentives to carry out all positive-NPV projects (incentives that can otherwise be distorted by the pressure for near-term cash flow faced by financially troubled firms).
- By reducing the cost of capital, asymmetric information, and managerial incentives.

They perform a study of the fuel price hedging of 28 airlines over the period of 1992–2003. Those airlines that hedge their fuel costs have been found to have Tobin's Q ratios that are 5–10 % higher than those of airlines that choose not to hedge. Their results also suggest that the main source of value added by hedging is its role in preserving the firm's ability to take advantage of investment opportunities that arise when fuel prices are high and airline operating cash flows and values are down.

Non-financial firms are not advised to engage in speculation. As documented by Allayannis and Ofek (2001), most of such firms refrain from outright speculation and use derivatives for hedging. However, it is not uncommon to observe such firms engage in some sort of market timing endeavour. Brown et al. (2006) analyze the corporate risk management policies of 44 companies in the gold mining industry. Firms tend to decrease hedging as prices move against them—behavior contrary to that predicted by risk management theory. These results, along with new survey evidence, suggest that firms attempt to time market prices, so-called selective hedging.

Industry characteristics play an important role in the hedging practices of industrial corporations. For instance, Géczy et al. (1997) observe that there is more heterogeneity in hedging practices as the number of firms in an industry increases.

Another important factor is the degree of competition in the industry. Using an industry's markup of price over marginal cost to proxy for industry structure, Allayannis and Ihrig (2001) find that in industries with less competition (high markup industries), firms can respond to exchange rate movements by changing their prices, which results in a lower exchange rate risk. In contrast, in industries with a more competitive structure (low markup industries), price is set close to marginal costs and the effects of exchange rate movements on a firm's returns can be large.

Hence, it should not be surprising to see that hedging is more prevalent in more competitive industries. Allayannis and Weston (1999) find that firms that operate in more competitive (low markup) industries are more likely to use currency derivatives than firms that operate in industries with high markups.

On the other hand, there are also some conflicting studies as well. Adam and Nain (2013) find that the prevalence of derivatives usage in an industry is negatively correlated with competition. This effect is due to smaller firms, which are less likely to use derivatives in more competitive industries. In contrast, larger firms are more likely to use derivatives in more competitive industries. These results are consistent with some firms, that is, smaller firms, strategically choosing not to hedge an exposure in order to gain a competitive advantage when the market moves against hedged firms as proposed by Adam et al. (2007) and Mello and Ruckes (2005).

Adam et al. (2007) analyze the hedging decisions of firms, within an equilibrium setting that allows to examine how a firm's hedging choice depends on the hedging choices of its competitors. Within this equilibrium some firms hedge while others do not, even though all firms are ex ante identical. The fraction of firms that hedge depends on industry characteristics, such as the number of firms in the industry, the elasticity of demand, and the convexity of production costs.

Mello and Ruckes (2005), on the other hand, study the optimal hedging and production strategies of financially constrained firms in imperfectly competitive markets. A hedging policy that minimizes the volatility of earnings reduces a firm's financial constraints most effectively on average, but makes it impossible for the firm to gain a significant financial advantage over its competitors. Because a financial advantage allows a firm to appropriate future market share, firms do not always hedge their entire risk exposure even in the absence of transaction costs. Oligopolistic firms hedge the least when they face intense competition and firms' financial condition is similar.

As the degree of competition affects the level of pass-through of cost shocks and the level of pass-through of cost shocks affects the prevalence of hedging in an industry, the opposite is also true; i.e., the prevalence of hedging in an industry affects the level of pass-through of cost shocks. Nain (2004) demonstrates that the extent of foreign currency hedging in an industry affects the pass-through of cost shocks to product prices. Using domestic producer price index data, she shows that product prices are less responsive to foreign exchange rates in industries where currency hedging is more common.

She concludes that an individual firm's foreign exchange exposure depends on the hedging decisions of its competitors. Specifically, the exposure of an unhedged firm increases with the level of hedging in its industry while that of a hedged firm decreases. Thus, a firm faces lower exposure to foreign exchange rates when it conforms to the majority.

These results are in line with the more recent findings of Adam and Nain (2013). They also find evidence suggesting an interdependence of risk management strategies across firms. They observe that the (ex-post) net FX exposure of a firm is not only a function of its own hedging decision, but also of the hedging decisions of its competitors. In particular, as more firms hedge in an industry, the exposure of derivatives users declines, while the exposure of derivatives non-users increases. Thus, firms' net exposures are lowest if their hedging decisions conform to the hedging decisions of the majority, and are highest if they deviate from the hedging decisions of the majority.

Finally, failure to conform to the hedging decisions of the majority is shown to be penalized by the market. Nain (2004) finds that if a firm chooses to remain unhedged while many of its competitors are hedging currency risk, it appears to suffer a value discount. This effect is particularly strong in less competitive industries where firms' output decisions are more likely to influence industry prices. These strategic incentives for hedging are robust and appear to be more important for currency hedging than many of the firm-specific factors highlighted by existing theory.

2.2 Game Theoretic Dynamic Models

McGillivray and Silver (1978) first studied a substitutable product inventory problem by using the Economic Order Quantity (EOQ) context. Later, Parlar and Goyal (1984) gave single period formulations for an inventory system with two substitutable products independent of each other.

Also Khouja et al. (1996) formulated a two-item newsboy problem with substitution, but they identified the optimality with a Monte Carlo simulation without an analytical solution.

Parlar (1985) proposed a Markov Decision Process model to find the optimal ordering policies for perishable and substitutable products from the point of view of a single retailer. Parlar (1988) also studied a game theoretic analysis of inventory control under substitutable demand. He modeled a two-product single period problem as a two-person nonzero-sum game and showed that there exists a unique Nash equilibrium. He proved that the expected profit function is concave to find optimal stocking levels for the two products in a single period with different revenue levels.

Netessine and Rudi (2003) considered centralized and competitive inventory models with demand substitution. They used deterministic proportions for unsatisfied demand and showed that the total profit is decreasing in demand correlation when demand is multivariate normal.

Papadimitriou and Roughgarden (2008) initiated a systematic study of algorithmic issues involved in finding Nash and correlated equilibria in games with a large number of players. They presented a polynomial-time algorithm for finding a Nash equilibrium in symmetric games without an algebraic approach.

Avsar and Baykal-Gürsoy (2002) showed that competition between retailers for a substitutable demand leads to a Nash equilibrium characterized by a pair of stationary base stock strategies which are expressed by constant order-up-to-levels for the infinite horizon problem.

Nagarajan and Rajagopalan (2009) examined the nature of optimal inventory policies in a system where a retailer manages substitutable products. They showed that a basestock policy is optimal in a multi-period problem for deterministic demand. After that, they also showed in their later work that retailers can ignore the substitution effect altogether and implement monopolistic strategies (independent order-up-to-policies) as the unique equilibrium when the total ordering units are above a threshold. They made a finite period analysis and showed the uniqueness of the Nash equilibrium with a lower bound on total ordering units.

Finally, Fas and Bilgiç (2013) extend the results coming from the work of Nagarajan and Rajagopalan (2009). They gave a threshold in a two-period game which has a total deteministic demand lower than the proposed level in Nagarajan and Rajagopalan (2009).

3 Definitions and the Model

3.1 The Parameters and Actions

D: Known total demand in a single period
i: Index denoting the individual firm
m: Index denoting the market maker
h_k: Hedging proportion where $0 \leq h_k \leq 1, k = i, m$
x_k: Amount of input (raw material), $k = i, m$
y_k: Order-up-to level, $k = i, m$
Λ_k: Effective demand, $k = i, m$
λ_k: Effective demand per unit demand, $k = i, m$
β: The proportion that customers of the individual firm switches to the market maker, given that the product sold by the individual firm is sold out
γ: The proportion that customers of the market maker switches to the individual firm, given that the product sold by the market maker is sold out
k_1: Input (raw material) cost/total cost
k_2: Proportion of the change in input (raw material) price that can be reflected in the output price

k_3: Amount of output per unit amount of input (raw material)
p: A random variable denoting the proportion of total demand going to the market maker where $p \in [0, 1]$
P_r: A random variable denoting the market price of input (raw material)
P_{r_0}: P_r at $t=0$, which is also assumed to be equal to the hedging price of input (raw material)
P_m: Market price of output which is assumed to be linked to the market price of input (raw material) via the following equation:

$$P_m = cP_r^{k_2k_1(1-h_m)}, \tag{1}$$

where c is a constant.

3.2 The Single Period Model

Total demand D is deterministic and known. For any demand D, p and $1-p$ are the proportions of demand that belong to the market maker and the individual firm, respectively. There is no penalty cost charged to the firms. Firms make their order decisions for replenishment with respect to the estimated effective demand and bring their positions to y_m and y_i. Then, the demand is realized. Costs are accrued and profit or losses are collected for the single period. Firms have to decide on their order quantities simultaneously in this competitive environment as they try to maximize their expected cash flows.

Single period cash flows for the market maker and the indivual firm are as follows:

$$\Pi_m(y_m, y_i) = P_m min(y_m, \Lambda_m) - k_3P_r(1-h_m)y_m - k_3P_{r_0}h_my_m, \tag{2}$$

and

$$\Pi_i(y_m, y_i) = P_m min(y_i, \Lambda_i) - k_3P_r(1-h_i)y_i - k_3P_{r_0}h_iy_i, \tag{3}$$

where Λ_m and Λ_i are the effective demands of the market maker and the individual firm, and they are equal to $pD + \beta[(1-p)D - y_i]^+$ and $(1-p)D + \gamma[pD - y_m]^+$, respectively, where $[x]^+$ denotes $max(0, x)$. In the above equations, the first term is the revenue from sales, the second and the third terms are the costs coming from the unhedged and hedged parts of the input, respectively. Since the cash flow functions include the random variable p, we take expectations on p. We also derive the cash flow functions per unit demand to simplify the equations and express the effective demand and inventory levels in the interval $[0, 1]$. Cash flow functions per unit demand are:

$$\pi_m(y_m, y_i) = P_m min\left(\frac{y_m}{D}, \lambda_m\right) - k_3 P_r(1-h_m)\frac{y_m}{D} - k_3 P_{r_0} h_m \frac{y_m}{D}, \tag{4}$$

and

$$\pi_i(y_m, y_i) = P_m min\left(\frac{y_i}{D}, \lambda_i\right) - k_3 P_r(1-h_i)\frac{y_i}{D} - k_3 P_{r_0} h_i \frac{y_i}{D}, \tag{5}$$

where $\lambda_m = p + \beta\left[(1-p) - \frac{y_i}{D}\right]^+$ and $\lambda_i = 1 - p + \gamma\left[p - \frac{y_m}{D}\right]^+$.

The nonnegative random variable p has a continuous density function f with finite expectation. The corresponding cumulative distribution function is denoted by F, and let $F(0) = 0$ and $F(1) = 1$, since $p \in [0, 1]$. We, first, consider concavity of the single period expected cash flow function. First order conditions give us the optimal ordering decision. Concavity also yields the existence of unique response for a firm to maximize the cash flow function for all possible strategies of the other firm. The explicit expressions for the single period formulation of the expected cash flow function per unit demand of the market maker and the individual firm are:

$$\begin{aligned} E[\pi_m(y_m, y_i)] = P_m &\left[\int_0^{\alpha_m} \left(p + \beta\left[(1-p) - \frac{y_i}{D}\right]\right) f(p)dp + \int_{\alpha_m}^1 \frac{y_m}{D} f(p)dp\right] \\ &- k_3 P_r(1-h_m)\frac{y_m}{D} - k_3 P_{r_0} h_m \frac{y_m}{D}, \end{aligned} \tag{6}$$

$$\begin{aligned} E[\pi_i(y_m, y_i)] = P_m &\left[\int_{\alpha_i}^1 \left(1 - p + \gamma\left[p - \frac{y_m}{D}\right]\right) f(p)dp + \int_0^{\alpha_i} \frac{y_i}{D} f(p)dp\right] \\ &- k_3 P_r(1-h_i)\frac{y_i}{D} - k_3 P_{r_0} h_i \frac{y_i}{D}, \end{aligned} \tag{7}$$

where $\alpha_m = \frac{\frac{y_m}{D} - \beta\left(1 - \frac{y_i}{D}\right)}{1-\beta}$ and $\alpha_i = \frac{1 - \frac{y_i}{D} - \gamma\frac{y_m}{D}}{1-\gamma}$.

Proposition 3.1 Best responses of the market maker and the individual firm are unique for the single period two-player game and they are:

$$R\left(y_m^*, y_i^*\right) = \left(\beta D + D(1-\beta)F^{-1}(A_m) - \beta y_i, D - \gamma y_m - (1-\gamma)DF^{-1}(A_i)\right), \tag{8}$$

where $A_m = 1 - \frac{k_3\left[P_r(1-h_m) + P_{r_0} h_m\right]}{P_m}$ *and* $A_i = \frac{k_3\left[P_r(1-h_i) + P_{r_0} h_i\right]}{P_m}$.

Proof Best responses of the market maker and the individual firm are found by the first order conditions of the expected cash flow functions. First order conditions are:

$$\begin{aligned}\frac{\partial E[\pi_m]}{\partial y_m} &= \frac{1}{D(1-\beta)} P_m \left(\alpha_m + \beta\left(1 - \alpha_m - \frac{y_i}{D}\right) - \frac{y_m}{D} \right) f(\alpha_m) \\ &+ P_m \int_{\alpha_m}^{1} \frac{f(p)}{D} dp - k_3 P_r (1 - h_m) \frac{1}{D} - k_3 P_{r_0} h_m \frac{1}{D} = 0\end{aligned} \tag{9}$$

and

$$\begin{aligned}\frac{\partial E[\pi_i]}{\partial y_i} &= \frac{1}{D(1-\gamma)} P_m \left(1 - \alpha_i + \gamma\left(\alpha_i - \frac{y_m}{D}\right) - \frac{y_i}{D} \right) f(\alpha_i) \\ &+ P_m \int_{0}^{\alpha_i} \frac{f(p)}{D} dp - k_3 P_r (1 - h_i) \frac{1}{D} - k_3 P_{r_0} h_i \frac{1}{D} = 0.\end{aligned} \tag{10}$$

Since $\alpha_m = \frac{\frac{y_m}{D} - \beta\left(1 - \frac{y_i}{D}\right)}{1-\beta}$ and $\alpha_i = \frac{1 - \frac{y_i}{D} - \gamma \frac{y_m}{D}}{1-\gamma}$, the first terms in the above two equations are cancelled out and the result follows as in 8. Concavity of the expected cash flow functions is shown in order to give the uniqueness of the best responses by using the second order conditions.

$$\frac{\partial^2 E[\pi_m]}{\partial y_m^2} = -P_m f(\alpha_m) \frac{1}{D^2(1-\beta)} < 0 \tag{11}$$

$$\frac{\partial^2 E[\pi_i]}{\partial y_i^2} = -P_m f(\alpha_i) \frac{1}{D^2(1-\gamma)} < 0 \tag{12}$$

∎

Finally, we show uniqueness of the Nash equilibrium as follows.

Proposition 3.2 There exists a unique Nash equilibrium for the single period two-player non-zero sum game.

Proof The proof is completed by the Implicit Function Theorem in Cachon and Netessine (2004). The property 'diagonal dominance' has to be satisfied on response functions for the uniqueness of the Nash equilibrium:

$$\sum_{i, i \neq m} \left| \frac{\partial^2 E[\pi_k]}{\partial y_m \partial y_i} \right| \leq \left| \frac{\partial^2 E[\pi_k]}{\partial y_k^2} \right|, \quad \forall k, k = i, m. \tag{13}$$

Equation 13 is used for the cross partial derivative of the single period formulations. The cross partial derivative is:

$$\frac{\partial^2 E[\pi_m]}{\partial y_m \partial y_i} = -P_m f(\alpha_m) \frac{\beta}{1-\beta} \frac{1}{D^2}. \tag{14}$$

By taking the absolute values of both sides of Eq. 14:

$$\left|\frac{\partial^2 E[\pi_m]}{\partial y_m \partial y_i}\right| = P_m f(\alpha_m)\frac{\beta}{1-\beta}\frac{1}{D^2}. \tag{15}$$

Since $\beta < 1$, comparing the absolute value of the right hand side of Eq. 11 with the right hand side of Eq. 15, we satisfy the diagonal dominance condition:

$$\left|\frac{\partial^2 E[\pi_m]}{\partial y_m \partial y_i}\right| < \left|\frac{\partial^2 E[\pi_m]}{\partial y_m^2}\right|. \tag{16}$$

Since the game is symmetric, the same is true for the individual firm. Then, there exists a unique Nash equilibrium in the single period game.

4 Simulations

4.1 Experiment Setup

For each point on a grid of 101 × 101 (h_m, h_i) couples ($h_m, h_i \in \{0, 0.01, \ldots, 1\}$), 1000 simulations have been carried out to simulate the input price, corresponding output price and proportions of demand that go to the market maker and the individual firm. For each point on the grid, these simulations have been used to find the (y_m, y_i) couple that maximizes the expected cash flows for the market maker and the individual firm. Hence, the Cournot model has been solved. Then, the simulated cash flow distributions for the optimal y_m and y_is have been used to calculate variances and risk-adjusted means (mean/standard deviation) for the cash flow of the individual firm. The parameter set is as follows:

$D = 100$,
$\beta = 50\%$,
$\gamma = 50\%$,
$k_1 = 30\%$,
$k_2 = 50\%$ (for the base case) (sensitivity analysis for $k_2 = 0, 25\%, 75\%, 100\%$),
$k_3 = 1$,
p is assumed to be normally distributed with mean 0.95 and standard deviation 0.01,
P_r is assumed to be lognormally distributed with mean 10 % and standard deviation 30 %,
$P_{r_0} = 100$,

P_m is assumed to be linked to P_r via Eq. 1 which includes a constant c. c is normalized such that P_m is 700 when P_r is 100 and h_m is 50 % (for the base case) (sensitivity analysis for $P_m = 400, 1000$).

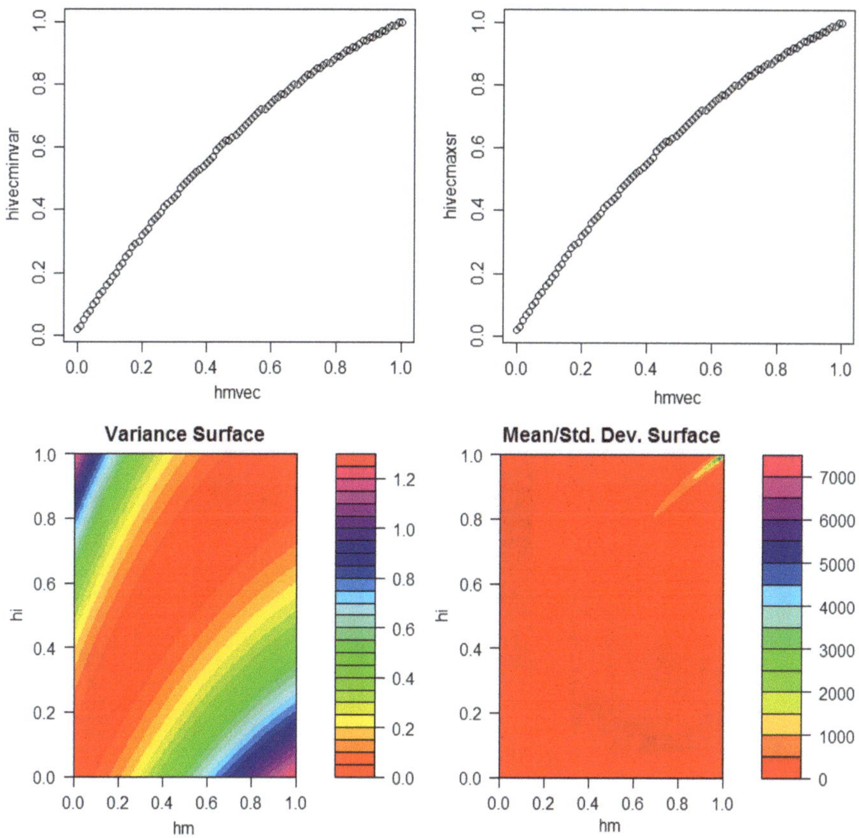

Fig. 1 Base case: 50 % pass-through of cost shocks, medium profitability

4.2 Simulation Results

The simulation results are summarized in Figs. 1, 2, 3, 4, 5, 6, and 7. Each figure consists of four separate graphs. The first graph gives the hedge ratio which minimizes the variance of cash flow. The second graph, on the other hand, gives the hedge ratio that maximizes the risk adjusted mean cash flow. The third and fourth graphs depict the corresponding variance and risk adjusted mean surfaces, respectively.

Figure 1 shows the simulation results for the base case scenario in which the pass-through level of cost shocks is set at 50 % with medium profitability. The results ratify the notion that a firm should conform to the majority in terms of hedging in order to minimize the variability of its cash flow.

Figures 2, 3, 4, and 5 deal with the sensitivity analysis with respect to the level of pass-through of cost shocks. Figure 2 shows the simulation results for the scenario in which the pass-through level is reduced to 25 %. As the level of pass-through

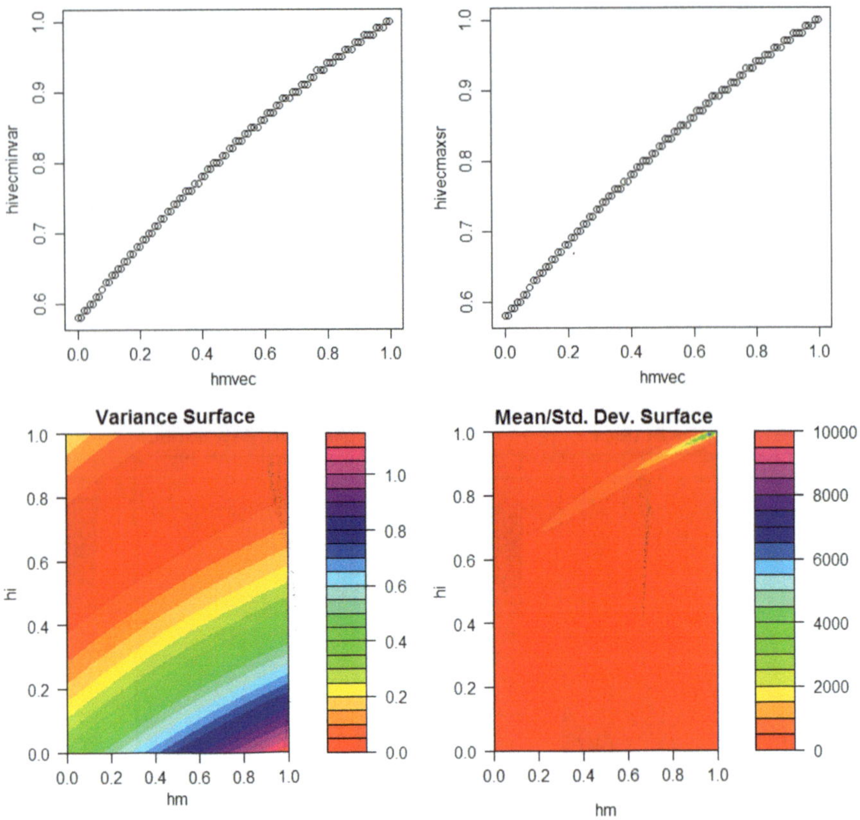

Fig. 2 25 % pass-through of cost shocks, medium profitability

decreases, the hedging ratio that minimizes the variance of cash flow increases. At the extreme level of 0 %, the optimal hedging ratio turns out to be 100 %, irrespective of the hedging ratio of the market maker. On the other hand, it turns out that as the level of pass-through increases, the hedging ratio that minimizes the variance of cash flow decreases.

Figures 6 and 7 describe the sensitivity analysis with respect to the level of profitability. Figures 6 and 7 shows the simulation results for the scenario in which the pass-through level is set at 50 % with lower (higher) profitability. As the profitability decreases (increases), the hedging ratio that minimizes the variance of cash flow increases (decreases).

In addition to the above observations, the similarity of the first and second graphs in all figures shows that the optimal hedging ratio that maximizes the risk-adjusted mean cash flow is almost the same as the optimal hedging ratio that minimizes the cash flow variance.

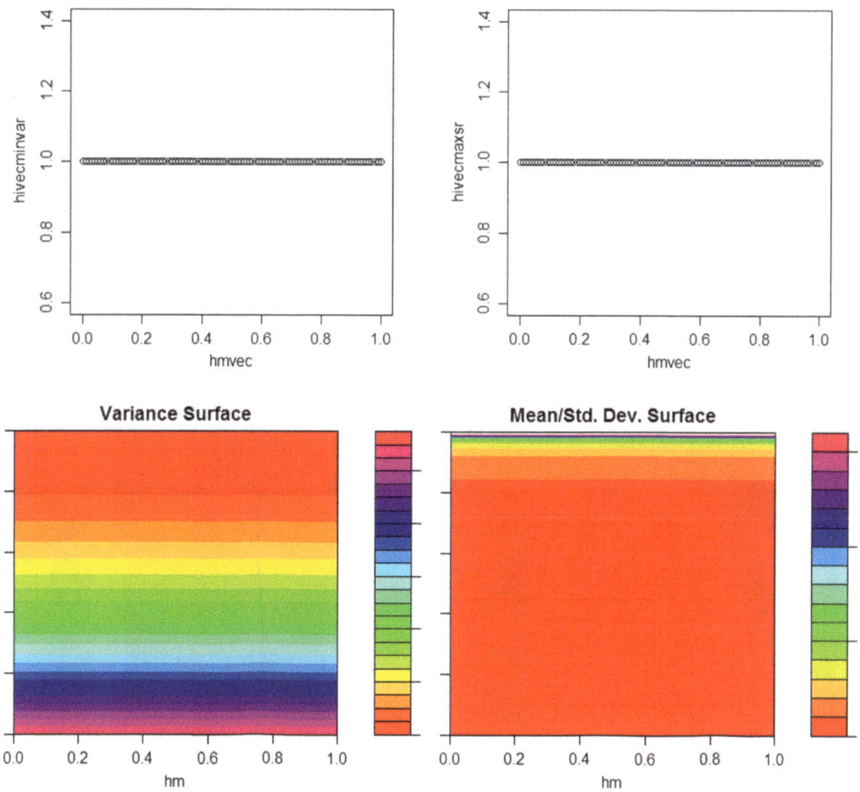

Fig. 3 0 % pass-through of cost shocks, medium profitability

4.3 Interpretation of Simulation Results

Our results confirm the hypothesis that a firm should conform to the majority in terms of hedging in order to minimize the variability of its cash flows. This result is also in line with the findings of Nain (2004) and Adam and Nain (2013). On the other hand, the results do not present a simple one-to-one correspondence of hedging ratios, but, rather, a tendency which might be drastically affected by a number of factors such as the level of pass-through of cost shocks to output prices and the degree of competition in the industry (which is negatively correlated with the level of profitability in the industry).

If firms can increase their output prices in response to an increase in input prices, this reduces the need to hedge. Previous research focuses on the factors that may have an impact on the firms' ability and propensity to reflect such price increases. For instance, Allayannis and Ihrig (2001) observe that it is easier (more difficult) for firms in less (more) competitive [or high (low) markup] industries to respond to exchange rate movements by increasing their prices. On the other hand, Nain

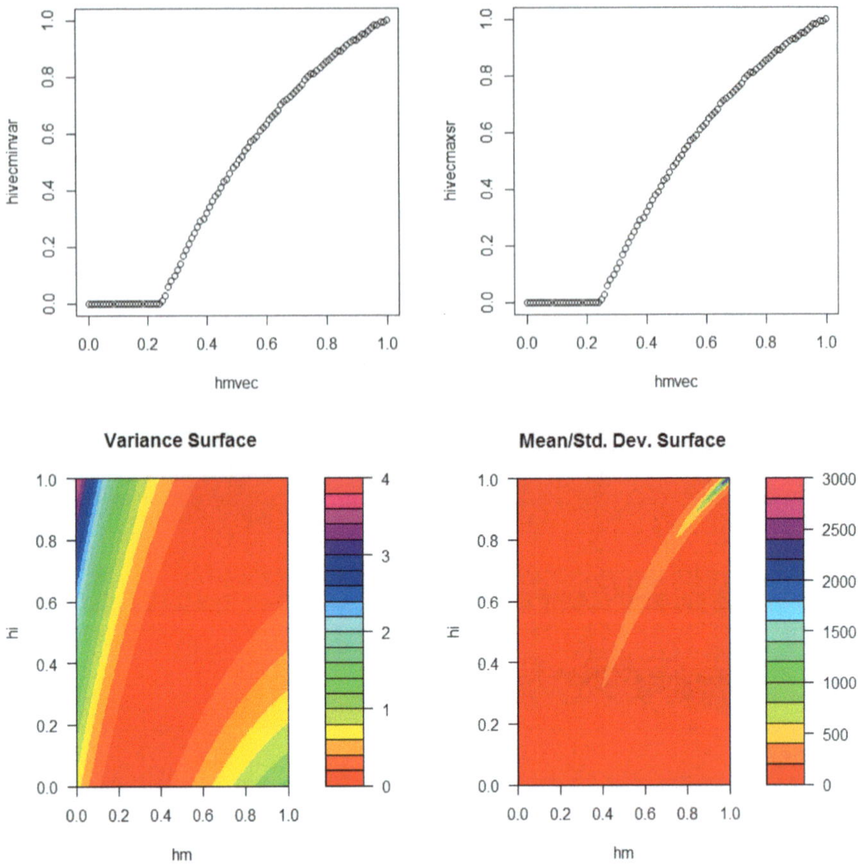

Fig. 4 75 % pass-through of cost shocks, medium profitability

(2004) shows that product prices are less responsive to foreign exchange rates in industries where currency hedging is more common.

Our model incorporates a separate parameter that enables us to observe the impact of pass-through of cost shocks regardless of the reason. Our results indicate that, as the level of pass-through decreases, the optimal hedging decision for the individual firm to minimize the variability of cash flows leans toward more hedging. This result is in line with Allayannis and Weston (1999) who find that firms that operate in more competitive (low markup) industries are more likely to use currency derivatives than firms that operate in industries with high markups (through the reasoning that the level of pass-through is lower in more competitive industries).

Our results show that, depending on the level of pass-through, the optimal hedging ratio for the individual firm may turn out to be significantly higher or lower than that of the market maker. In the extreme case when there is no pass-

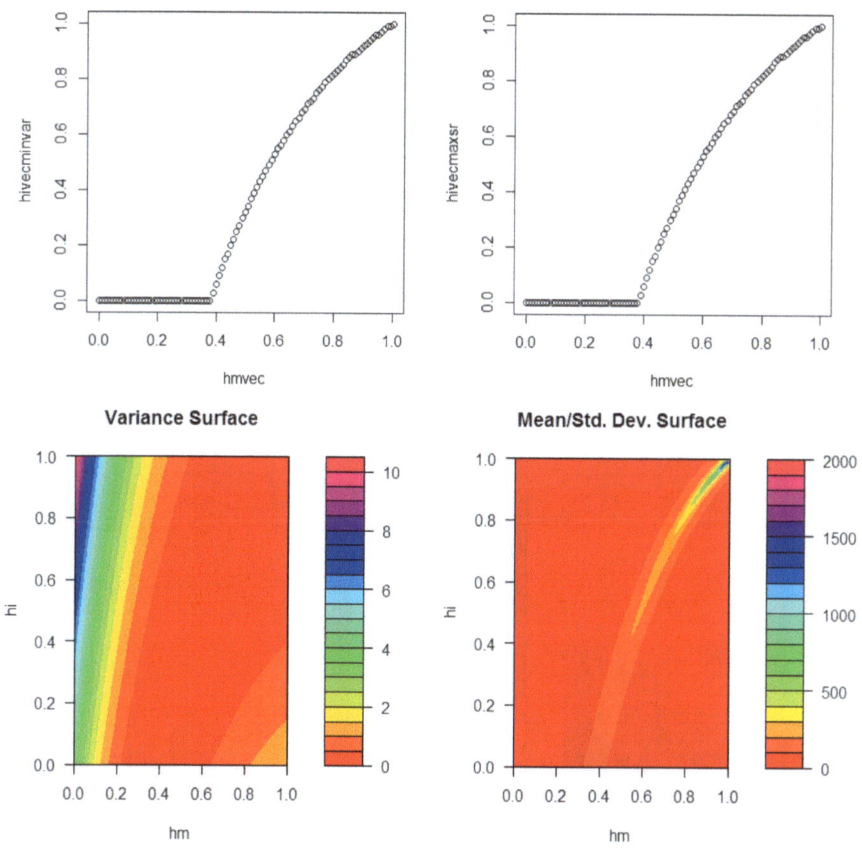

Fig. 5 100 % pass-through of cost shocks, medium profitability

through, the optimal hedging decision for the individual firm calls for hedging 100 % of the exposure, regardless of the hedging decision of the market maker.

Adam et al. (2007) and Mello and Ruckes (2005) attribute deliberate deviation from competitors in terms of hedging practices to strategic considerations. They indicate that such type of behavior should be more accentuated and lead to more heterogeneity as the level of competition increases. Allayannis and Weston (1999) find that firms that operate in more competitive (low markup) industries are more likely to use currency derivatives than firms that operate in industries with high markups.

Adam and Nain (2013) observe that smaller firms are less likely to use derivatives in more competitive industries. In contrast, larger firms are more likely to use derivatives in more competitive industries. Our results indicate that with lower levels of profitability (which is a proxy for higher level of competition), the optimal hedging decision for the individual firm leans toward more hedging. Similar to the case of pass-through, depending on the degree of competition, the optimal hedging

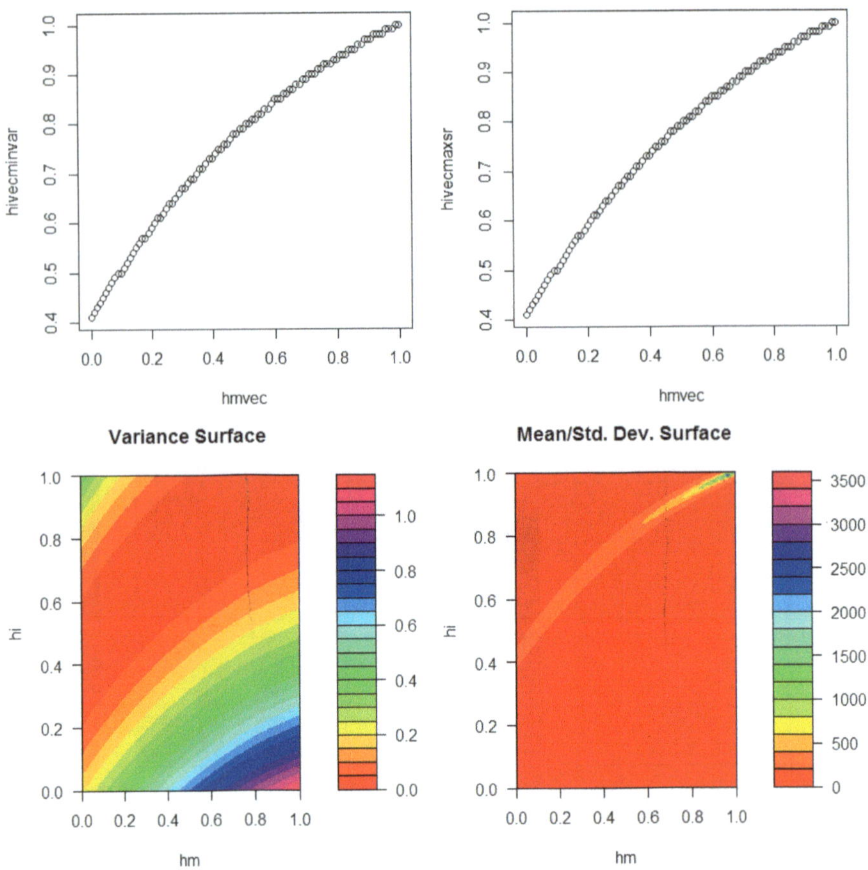

Fig. 6 50 % pass-through of cost shocks, lower profitability

ratio for the individual firm may turn out to be higher or lower than that of the market maker.

As a result, the notion that your hedging decision should conform to the majority in order to minimize the variability of cash flows is generally, but not specifically, valid. It should be a nuanced decision taking into factors such as the level of pass-through of cost shocks and the degree of competition as indicated by the level of profitability in the industry. It is worthwhile to stress that the nuances of this decision does not even take into account the strategic considerations as documented by Adam et al. (2007) and Mello and Ruckes (2005) who argue that in competitive environments some firms may strategically reduce their hedge positions, or not hedge at all, in order to benefit from cash inflows when their competitors experience cash outflows due to their hedging activities.

Our experiment setup enables us to pinpoint the optimal hedging ratio that maximizes the risk-adjusted mean cash flow as well as the optimal hedging ratio that minimizes the cash flow variance. Our simulation results show that these two

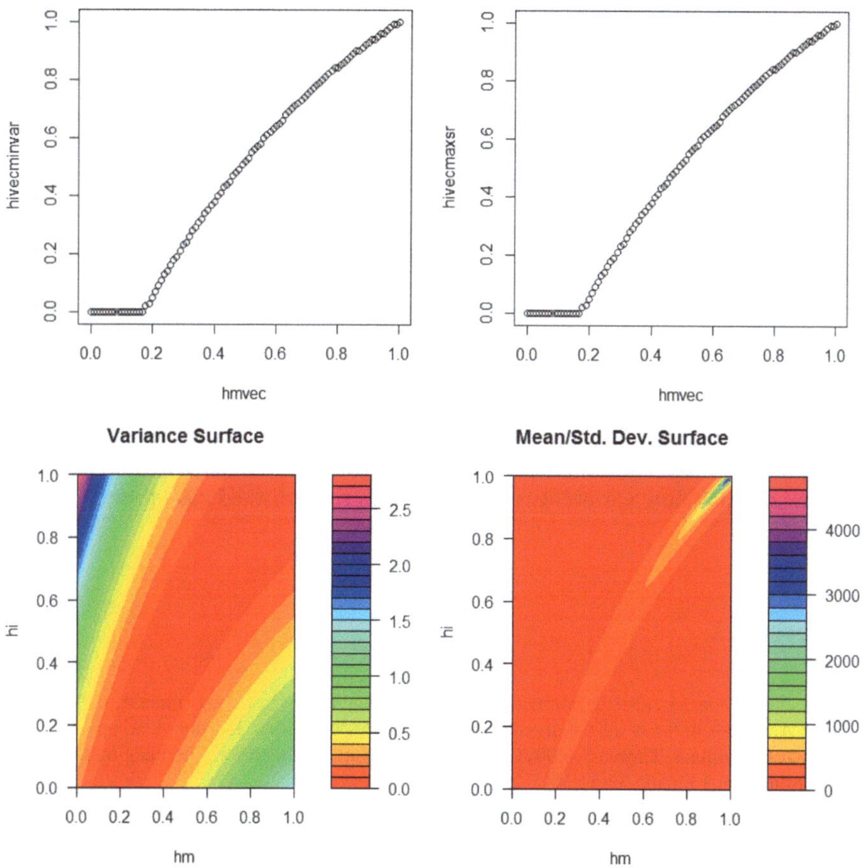

Fig. 7 50 % pass-through of cost shocks, higher profitability

optimal hedging ratios behave very similarly under all the different conditions that we have tested. This result intuitively makes sense as the impact of the hedging ratio on mean cash flow should be negligible when compared to its impact on cash flow variance. Hence, we can tentatively conclude that the optimal hedging ratio that minimizes cash flow variability also maximizes risk-adjusted mean cash flows.

5 Conclusion

Our results confirm the hypothesis that a firm should conform to the majority in terms of hedging in order to minimize the variability of its cash flows. On the other hand, the results do not present a simple one-to-one correspondence of hedging ratios, but, rather, a tendency which might be drastically affected by a number of factors such as the pass-through of cost shocks to output prices and the degree of competition in the industry.

Our results indicate that, as the level of pass-through decreases, the optimal hedging decision for the individual firm to minimize the variability of cash flows leans toward more hedging. Depending on the level of pass-through, the optimal hedging ratio for the individual firm may turn out to be significantly higher or lower than that of the market maker.

Our results indicate that with lower levels of profitability (which is a proxy for higher level competition), the optimal hedging decision for the individual firm leans toward more hedging. Similar to the case of pass-through, depending on the degree of competition, the optimal hedging ratio for the individual firm may turn out to be higher or lower than that of the market maker.

As a result, the notion that your hedging decision should conform to the majority in order to minimize the variability of cash flows is generally, but not specifically, valid. Finally, we can tentatively conclude that the optimal hedging ratio that minimizes cash flow variability also maximizes risk-adjusted cash flows.

References

Adam TR, Nain A (2013) Strategic risk management and product market competition. In: Advances in financial risk management. Palgrave Macmillan, London, UK, pp 3–29

Adam T, Dasgupta S, Titman S (2007) Financial constraints, competition, and hedging in industry equilibrium. J Financ 62(5):2445–2473

Allayannis G, Ihrig J (2001) Exposure and markups. Rev Financ Stud 14(3):805–835

Allayannis G, Ofek E (2001) Exchange rate exposure, hedging, and the use of foreign currency derivatives. J Int Money Financ 20(2):273–296

Allayannis G, Weston JP (1999) The use of foreign currency derivatives and industry structure. In: Brown G, Chew D (eds) Corporate risk: strategies and management. Risk Books

Avsar ZM, Baykal-Gürsoy M (2002) Inventory control under substitutable demand: a stochastic game application. Nav Res Logist 49(4):359–375

Brown GW, Crabb PR, Haushalter D (2006) Are firms successful at selective hedging? J Bus 79 (6):2925–2949

Cachon GP, Netessine S (2004) Game theory in supply chain analysis. Handbook of quantitative supply chain analysis. Springer, Berlin, pp 13–65

Carter DA, Rogers DA, Simkins BJ (2006) Hedging and value in the US airline industry. J Appl Corp Finance 18(4):21–33

Fas G, Bilgiç T (2013) A two-period dynamic game for a substitutable product inventory control problem. Int J Invent Res 2(1–2):108–126

Géczy C, Minton BA, Schrand C (1997) Why firms use currency derivatives. J Financ 52 (4):1323–1354

Khouja M, Mehrez A, Rabinowitz G (1996) A two-item newsboy problem with substitutability. Int J Prod Econ 44(3):267–275

McGillivray AR, Silver EA (1978) Some concepts for inventory control under substitutable demand. Infor 16(1):47–63

Mello AS, Ruckes ME (2005) Financial hedging and product market rivalry. Available at SSRN 687140

Nagarajan M, Rajagopalan S (2009) Technical note-a multiperiod model of inventory competition. Oper Res 57(3):785–790

Nain A (2004) The strategic motives for corporate risk management. In: AFA 2005 Philadelphia Meetings, March

Netessine S, Rudi N (2003) Centralized and competitive inventory models with demand substitution. Oper Res 51(2):329–335

Papadimitriou CH, Roughgarden T (2008) Computing correlated equilibria in multi-player games. J ACM 55(3):14

Parlar M (1985) Optimal ordering policies for a perishable and substitutable product: a Markov decision model. Infor 23(2):182–195

Parlar M (1988) Game theoretic analysis of the substitutable product inventory problem with random demands. Nav Res Logist 35(3):397–409

Parlar M, Goyal SK (1984) Optimal ordering decisions for two substitutable products with stochastic demands. Opsearch 21(1):1–15

Genco Fas received his BS degree in Mathematics from Bogazici University (1999), MS degree in Mathematics from Yeditepe University (2005) and PhD degree in Industrial Engineering from Bogazici University (2012). Dr. Fas is a faculty member of Department of Management, Bilgi University, Istanbul, Turkey, where currently he is an Assistant Professor of Operations Research. He provides consultancing for the banks and nonbank financial institutions. His research interests include stochastic models, inventory theory, and game-theoretic applications.

Kerem Senel is currently a part-time Professor of Finance at Istanbul Commerce University and Bogazici University, Istanbul, Turkey. Prof. Senel has a BS in Electrical & Electronics Engineering from Bilkent University (1992), an MSIA from Carnegie Mellon University (1994), and a PhD in Management from Istanbul University (2001). His research interests include asset allocation in pension funds and financial risk management. He is a member of GARP (Global Association of Risk Professionals) and a certified Financial Risk Manager (FRM) since 2004.

Option Strategies and Exotic Options: Tools for Hedging or Source of Financial Instability?

Sıtkı Sönmezer

Abstract Development of options markets has been rapid and constant development has led to innovations in the financial sector in recent decades. Despite the fact that innovations are far from complete, this chapter aims to address the prominent options strategies and exotic options. The way they are priced is questioned and behavioral approaches are addressed. Speculative nature of exotic options and financial instability relationship is discussed.

1 Introduction

Options markets has fostered in recent decades not only because they provide leverage for their users or they help to overcome restrictions, but they also help to reach market completeness. There is a steady development in these markets as the need of investors vary and subject to change in time therefore, options markets are structurally open to innovation and as a result of the changing conditions, numerous new generation options and strategies are being formed. Even though, option markets are not fully developed in emerging markets, exotic options with currencies are getting more popular and their volumes are increasing as well as number of their investors. In order to increase the number of investors in these markets, the mechanism of these contracts need to be well explained and this chapter aims to partly fulfill this mission. The main constraint here is lack of space. Only a few of the strategies and exotic options are discussed but the aim is to attract attention to this promising market.

The first part of this chapter briefly explains the option contracts to remind the readers the concept and to help them to be able to follow further strategies and options. This part is concluded with option pricing where the binomial and Black Scholes methods are discussed.

Options strategies are mainly a combination of an underlying asset and options on the particular underlying assets or are just a combination of options contracts.

S. Sönmezer (✉)
Beykent University, Istanbul, Turkey
e-mail: sitkisonmezer@beykent.edu.tr

H. Dinçer, Ü. Hacioğlu (eds.), *Risk Management, Strategic Thinking and Leadership in the Financial Services Industry*, Contributions to Management Science, DOI 10.1007/978-3-319-47172-3_16

Investors aim to reap profits by trading with the market sentiment they have via implementing these strategies. These strategies help investors to make profit regardless of the market trend. When market trend is downwards, they implement bearish strategies; When market trend is upwards, they implement bullish strategies; or even when investors think market may not be trendy for a period of time, they may find ways to extract profit from their particular market sentiment. These strategies are classified in terms of market trend. This paper aims to clarify the prominent strategies in general, how to use them and to present the maximum and minimum loss for these strategies.

Exotic options are relatively new for the literature and the prominent ones are discussed in the last part of this chapter. The advantages of these options to investors and the risks involved are presented briefly and a hindsight for their pricing is provided.

2 Option Contracts

Option Contracts are contracts that two parties agree to come to terms in the future on the followings; there has to be ***an underlying asset***, upon which pricing of the option contract is determined. ***A maturity date*** has to be predetermined; the contract is settled only at the maturity date for the *European options* contracts whereas, these contracts can be exercised any time within maturity for *American options*. ***A predetermined exercise price or strike price*** which gives the option holder the right to exercise the option at this price. ***A premium*** is paid by the holder (buyer) of the options contract to the writer (seller) of the contract for the risks undertaken. The premium amount enables investors to take a long or short position in an underlying asset in full. Thus, leverage in these contracts is another rationale for its investors.

There are also Asian Options which are so-called exotic. the payoffs for these options are determined by the average underlying price over some pre-set period of time and as they are path dependent, they are very difficult to price (Abrahamyan and Maddah 2015).

2.1 Option Types

There are two types of option contracts; namely, call and put options. The buyers of these contracts have right to walk away if conditions are disadvantageous for them but the sellers of these contracts have to honor their obligations.

2.1.1 Call Options

Call options gives the buyer of the contract the right to *buy* the underlying asset at a **predetermined price**, for a **predetermined maturity**. The writer of the call option receives a premium from the buyer and has to honor his obligation in return.

2.1.2 Put Options

Put options gives the buyer of the contract the right to *sell* the underlying asset at a predetermined price, for a predetermined maturity. The writer of the put option receives a premium from the buyer and similarly, has to honor his obligation in return.

2.1.3 Maximum Profit and Loss for the Parties in Option Contracts

Premiums are given at the beginning of the contract and is irrevocable. Theoretically, buyers of call options can have an infinite profit whereas, buyers of put options can earn the difference between the strike price and the spot price at the exercise date. It must be noted that premium amount is the highest profit the writer can achieve in return for a huge potential loss inherent in these contracts therefore, they are carefully priced by market professionals who are aware of the possible losses.

2.2 Option Pricing Models

There are two main models used to derive option prices; Binomial model and the Black Scholes model. Both models aim to calculate the intrinsic value of the underlying options.

2.2.1 Binomial Model

The binomial option model is a discrete time model introduced by Cox and Ross (1976). The model is based on the assumption that the price of the underlying asset will increase or decrease at a predetermined date and at a predetermined rate. Options are than assessed depending on the possible closing values of the underlying assets. The model is widely used in pricing European or American options and it is also referred as Cox, Ross & Rubinstein Formula. The model has few assumptions:

- Markets are perfect. Taxes and commissions are ignored. No short selling limit and assets are infinitely divisible.
- Single interest rate for borrowing and lending.
- İnterest rate for the period, stock return rate are known.
- There is at least one risky asset and one riskless asset.
- No dividends for the underlying asset.

To illustrate the model, assume a stock with a spot price(S), exercise price (X) and recall that this model assumes a down or up market in the coming period. So, when the spot price (S) of a stock increases, in an up market (U), it rises to a new price (US) or in a down market (D), it decreases to a lower price (DS). Similarly the call prices will be Cu and Cd, depending on the movement of the market. In that case, value of the call options would be;

$$\mathrm{Cu} = \mathrm{Max}\,[0,\ \mathrm{US} - \mathrm{X}]$$
$$\mathrm{Cd} = \mathrm{Max}\,[0,\ \mathrm{DS} - \mathrm{X}]$$

Value of a call option can be derived from the formula here below:

$$C = \frac{S_0(1 + r)(Cu - C_d) - (S_d{*}Cu) + (Su{*}C_d)}{(Su - S_d)(1 + r)}$$

Where,

r is the risk free rate and S_0 is the spot rate. Cu is the value of the call option in an up market and similarly Cd is the value of the call option in a down market.

2.2.2 Black-Scholes Model

Black Scholes model is a continuous time approach. Black Sholes model is also used to price European options and it also has assumptions regarding with the market and conditions. Some are as follows;

- Markets are close to perfect markets
- Single interest rate
- No dividends or interest payments
- Returns are normally distributed
- Short selling is possible

Merton's model helps us to take dividend income into account, otherwise, it is same as the Black-Scholes formula, which are both using standard normal cumulative distributive function to derive the call option price and then put-call parity may be used to find the price of the put option(Kolb and Overdahl, 2009).

$$c(S,t) = SN(d_1) - Ke^{-r\tau}N(d_2), \quad \tau = T - t,$$

$$d_1 = \frac{\ln\frac{S^*}{K} + \frac{1}{2}\sigma^2\tau}{\sigma\sqrt{\tau}} = \frac{\ln\frac{S}{K} + \left(r + \frac{1}{2}\sigma^2\right)\tau}{\sigma\sqrt{\tau}},$$

$$d_2 = \frac{\ln\frac{S^*}{K} + \frac{1}{2}\sigma^2\tau}{\sigma\sqrt{\tau}} = \frac{\ln\frac{S^*}{K} + \left(r - \frac{1}{2}\sigma^2\right)\tau}{\sigma\sqrt{\tau}}.$$

d2 can be simplified to: d2 = d1-s√t

where,

T − t represents time left until maturity; SN(d1) represents the gain of having the stock which is spot price (S) times the change in call value with respect to a change in the price of the underlying asset, K is the strike price; r denotes for the interest rate and σ denotes for the volatility.

2.3 Greeks

There are certain measures that may help investors to hedge or evaluate risks involved with option contracts. Some of them are discussed here below:

2.3.1 Delta

Delta is a measure that states the change in the price of the option contract with respect to change in the underlying asset. As underlying asset's prices increase the call price will increase from 0 to 1; similarly the put option's delta will range from −1 to 0. When delta of a call option on an underlying asset is 0.70, it means that the option price will increase by 70 % of the increase in the price of the underlying asset.

Delta neutral hedging enables investors to hedge their portfolios by combining a long position in an underlying asset and short calls. How many option to short is calculated by dividing number of shares to be hedges by the delta of the asset.

2.3.2 Theta

Theta measures the rate of the change of the value of the portfolio as time passes. As time passes, the option contract is closer to expiration and the option value diminishes. That's why, theta is always negative (Hull 1989).

2.3.3 Gamma

Gamma is the derivative of delta. It measures the change in delta when the price of the underlying asset changes. Gamma is largest when the option is at the money and can be negative or positive.

2.3.4 Rho

Rho is an option's sensitivity to changes in the risk-free rate. There is a direct relationship between a put or call option's value and a risk-free rate increase; However, call Rhos start from zero and may increase whereas a put Rho is negative. Small changes in risk free rates do not affect option prices much especially when the expiration date is close.

2.3.5 Vega

Vega is the sensitivity of the value of the portfolio to the volatility of the underlying asset. When Vega of an underlying asset is low, it means that the prices of the underlying asset may not be much affected by changes in volatility. Vice versa is valid. Measures derived from Vega are namely, Vanna and Vega and are used in option pricing. Volga is the sensitivity of the Vega with respect to a change of the implied volatility and Vanna is the sensitivity of the Vega with respect to a change in the spot FX rate.

3 Option Strategies

There are combinations and spreads of option contracts that can form a strategy to reap profits once the direction of the prices are foreseen correctly. There are numerous combinations such as; straddle, strangle, collar, fence, covered call, married put and risk reversal. Similarly, many spreads are present such as, butterfly, bull, bear, box calendar, diagonal, vertical, inter market and ratio. Due to lack of space, this chapter exemplifies a few of them by classifying them due to their usefulness in trendy and untrendy markets.

3.1 Strategies with Ownership of Underlying Securities

These strategies aim to benefit from the investors market sentiment and mitigate the potential loss of the portfolio. Options can be sold without possessing the underlying security which is called *naked*; Options can also be sold having the underlying security in the portfolio which is called *covered* in the literature.

3.1.1 Covered Call

In a covered call, An investor sells a call option and to mitigate the possible risks, the investor purchases the underlying security. The rationale of a covered call is earn premium income from the call option at the expense of a limited upside potential (Chance 2003).

3.1.2 Protective Put

In a protective put, investor possesses the underlying security and fears from a decrease in underlying asset's price and purchases a put option. Put option serves as an insurance but decreases the profits by the put premium amount. Protective puts are like car insurances.

3.2 Bullish Strategies

Bullish strategies pay when the market trend is upward sloping. Buy and hold strategy almost always has a higher payoff relative to these strategies. Despite this fact, Investors prefer these strategies over a buy and hold strategy because they believe the price increase is not expected to be a certain threshold level and they would like to sell the upside potential over that threshold level. In other words, investors don't want to buy an unnecessary bet and by selling an option contract they reduce their costs.

3.2.1 Bull Call Spread

The buyer of Bull Call Spread, purchases one call option with a lower exercise price and partially compensates the premium expense by selling a call option at a higher exercise price. The investor expects a rise in prices but believes that the rise may be a moderate one therefore, the rise beyond the higher exercise price is foregone in return for a premium.

3.3 Bearish Strategies

A downward market trend is needed to profit from bearish strategies.

3.3.1 Bear Call Spread

The buyer of Bull Call Spread, purchases one call option with a higher exercise price and partially compensates the premium expense by selling a call option at a lower exercise price. The investor aims to benefit from decreasing prices and to preserve the premium obtained by selling the option, the long call position is again works as an insurance for this strategy.

3.4 Strategies in Untrendy Markets

3.4.1 Butterfly Spreads

To exemplify a long butterfly spread, the buyer of the spread purchases an in the money call option with a lower exercise price and an out of the money call option with a higher exercise price; simultaneously, sells two call options close to the spot price to compensate the premiums paid for the purchased options. The buyer foresees that the price will end up near spot price in which case the option with the lowest exercise price will only pay off. The rest of the options will expire worthless or cost negligible amounts. In short, this strategy pays when prices don't deviate much from the spot price whereas, maximum risk that the investor faces is the net premiums paid.

3.5 Strategies in Trendy Markets

There are strategies derived from options that will lead to profits when prices move beyond break-even prices. It has to be kept in mind by writing these strategies investors may bet on untrendy markets as well. Some are introduced here below:

3.5.1 Straddle

In a long straddle strategy, the buyer of the strategy purchases a call and a put option with a same exercise price and a maturity date. Maximum risk of the investors are limited to the amount paid for the premiums. The investor expects a major price change but doesn't want to guess the direction of the price movement. İn a straddle strategy, investor will earn money when the prices move beyond the break even points.

3.5.2 Strangle

This strategy is close to straddle; almost the same strategy but in strangle, investors aim to reduce premium cost by purchasing one call and one put option that are not at the money but close to money. Break even prices will be wider and return potential is less than straddle but the cost is also relatively lower.

4 Exotic Options

Exotic options are more complex than regular options that are traded on exchanges because their pay-offs may depend on more than one triggers or the underlying asset may be extra ordinary. Examples of exotic options are namely; Asian, Barrier, Basket, Binary, Chooser, Cliquet, Commodore, Compound, Forward start, Interest rate, Look back, Mountain range, Rainbow, and Swaption. A few of them are addressed here below;

4.1 Look Back Options

Look back call options with floating exercise prices, give the holder the right to buy the underlying asset at maturity for the lowest exchange rate over the period involved whereas, Look back put options holders can enjoy the highest exchange rates over the period. Look back options can either have floating or fixed exercise prices.

A European fixed strike currency look back call option gives the holder the right to demand the difference between the highest value of the underlying asset over the period and the strike price. Whereas, a European fixed strike currency look back put option pays the difference between the strike price and the minimum value over the period.

Regarding with the pricing of these options; under continuous time assumptions of Black-Scholes, Conze and Viswanathan (1991) have improved the analytical pricing formulas offered by Goldman et al. (1979) for these contracts and Babbs (1992) has introduced his continuous time based model with Brownian motions for floating strike look back options and Cheuk and Vorst (1997) have offered a one-step variable binomial model for look back options.

4.2 Barrier Options

In Barrier options there is a strike level and a barrier level, when barrier level is crossed, a rebate may be paid. A barrier may be set above the spot price, an up barrier, or below the spot price, a down barrier. A European knock in option pays off when the option has a value at the expiration and a certain barrier is crossed over the life of the option contract. If the stock never passes over the barrier it becomes worthless and when it does, it becomes a regular option. A knock out option pays off only when the option is in the money and barrier is not crossed. Once the barrier is passed, the option is knocked out. In short, barrier options can have four forms; up-and-out, up-and-in, down-and-out, and down-and-in.

Barrier option premiums are generally cheaper than standard options with same features. An investor may elect to purchase a barrier option rather than a call or put option in order to reduce premium expenses. With barrier options, investors sell off the scenarios that they believe unlikely to happen.

Regarding with the pricing of these contracts, it is easy to notice that they are more complicated than standard option contracts; A call option's premium is almost always positively affected by a price increase in the underlying asset whereas, in an up-and-out barrier option, there will be double, opposing effects on the value of the option. On one hand, If the value increases near to barrier level, the likelihood that the option will be worthless will increase. On the other hand, the call feature embedded in the up-and-out option necessitates a price increase to finish in-the-money. When the price is too close to the barrier, referred as barrier too close problem, pricing is even harder. Lattice approaches are used to price barrier options and they are favored due to their flexibility and the other approach is the analytical approach which is favored for their efficiency (Tse et al. 2001).

Tools for Hedging or Source of Financial Instability?
Derivative Markets are a good vehicle for investors that aim to better hedge their financial positions as they decrease the premium costs substantially. Despite this benefit, the risk involved with these contracts are not apparent in financial statements and the unrealized gains and losses from these contracts have to be well assessed to determine the financial strength of institutions. 2008 financial crises has underlined the importance of closely monitoring the financial institutions and their derivatives positions.

Option strategies and exotic options are widely in use in developed countries and they are increasing their presence in developing countries day by day. A mechanism may be needed in place for the future to determine the possible losses accurately and timely in these arrangement. In order to determine the loss, methods that estimate the option prices shall be accurate, However, many studies show that rational option pricing models are insufficient to value these contracts (Bondarenko 2003; Constantinides et al. 2009) and market sentiment of investors shall be taken into account to have more realistic results.(Han 2008). An asset price may form a bubble and supervisory bodies may have increasing concerns regarding with the burst of the bubble for any reason. Regarding with risk, option prices move even faster than the underlying prices which may lead to price instability and financial stress when the loss is substantial. The case may be more dramatic for exotic options as look-back option prices are more sensitive to bubbles (Heston et al. 2007).

Financial Instability Hypothesis (FIH) asserts that profits are driven by aggregate demand and instead of hedge financing, speculative finance dominates the markets than the likelihood that the economy deviates from the equilibrium prices increases (Minsky 1992). By intuition, the fact that futures markets are not fully developed in emerging markets may be an evidence of unawareness of hedging techniques or distrust in these markets despite the existence of a clearing house. Investors that are refraining from hedging their positions in futures market, are hardly use exotic options to hedge. In that case, this chapter argues that especially in emerging markets, the usage of exotic options are heavily speculative than hedging. When exotic options markets mature in emerging markets, based on FIH, increasing usage of these contracts will eventually distort equilibrium in the economy unless close supervision and adequate regulations are in place.

Regarding with bank profits, exotic option trades are mostly off-balance sheet activities and they are almost always the counter party of the trades for investors in emerging markets. Once the volume in these instruments reach to a non-negligible point, the risk in the banking sector may also threaten the financial stability of economies of these markets.

5 Conclusion

Option markets have gained importance in hedging or converting speculations into money. These innovative products are being introduced to emerging markets where investors are mostly unaware of the mechanisms of these appealing products. It obvious that not only this chapter or any other current study will enable investors to learn how these options work fully as the pricing of these instruments are still far from being perfect and complicated. Even if small investors invest time to learn the pricing mechanisms of these strategies and exotic options, a new exotic may be formed in the meantime upon a new demand from investors. It is clear that regulating these transactions and protecting small investors are difficult. In Turkey, currently banks can offer these instruments to their customers as long as they sign a declaration that they understand the riskiness of these transactions. This chapter tries to shed light to the fact that when small investors sign the document mentioned above, it does not necessarily mean that they understand the risks involved in these contracts in full. These contracts shall only be offered to customers who can document a prior experience in options market.

By intuition, these markets will attract more investors as they learn about them. The difference between betting and investing in these contracts has to be well explained to investors who are in need of hedging their positions and who are not willing to pay unnecessary premiums for unlikely conditions when they purchase standard options. Breadth and depth of these markets are not sufficient in emerging markets to easily find a counterparty therefore, financial institutions, mainly banks, fulfill this mission. Financial literacy shall be encouraged for these markets to prosper but the question regarding with the risk these contracts introduce to emerging markets remains still.

Despite additional hedging advantages, these contracts may lead to banking crises unless they are monitored well. As these contracts are speculative in nature; when price instability hypothesis holds, the risk arisen from these contracts may not be determined by conventional methods such as Black Scholes Method as they do not incorporate behavioral issues into consideration and risks that are hard to quantify may be a threat to economies. Since the volume in these contracts are relatively small in emerging markets, the so-called risks may seem negligible but proactive measures may be necessary before these contracts become center of attention in emerging markets. Limits of the positions taken in these contracts and disclosure requirements may be dynamically monitored to avoid financial instability.

References

Abrahamyan H, Maddah B (2015) Pricing asian options via compound gamma and orthogonal polynomials. Appl Math Comput 264:21–43

Babbs S (1992) Binomial valuation of lookback options. Working paper. Midland Global Markets, London

Bondarenko O (2003) Why are put options so expensive? Q J Financ 4(3)

Cheuk THF, Vorst TCF (1997) Currency lookback options and observation frequency: a binomial approach. J Int Money Financ 16(2):173–187

Constantinides GM, Jackwerth JC, Perrakis S (2009) Mispricing of S&P 500 index options. Rev Financ Stud 22(3):1247–1277

Conze A, Viswanathan (1991) Path dependent options, the case of lookback options. J Financ 46:1893–1907

Cox JC, Ross SA (1976) The valuation of options for alternative stochastic processes. J Financ Econ 3:145–166

Chance D (2003) Risk management applications of options strategies. In: Analysis of derivatives for the CFA program, Ch 7. CFA Institute

Goldman MB, Sossin HB, Gatto MA (1979) Path dependent options: buy at the low, sell at the high. J Financ 34:1111–1127

Han B (2008) Investor sentiment and option prices. Rev Financ Stud 21(1):387–414

Heston SL, Loewenstein M, Willard GA (2007) Options and bubbles. Rev Financ Stud 20 (2):359–390

Hull J (1989) Option futures and other derivative securities. Prentice Hall, Upper Saddle River, NJ, pp 194–195

Kolb RW, Overdahl JA (2009) Financial derivatives: pricing and risk management, Ch 26. Wiley, New York, pp 371–387

Minsky HP (1992) The financial instability hypothesis. The Jerome Levy Economics Institute Working Paper No. 74
Tse WM, Li LK, Ng KW (2001) Pricing discrete barrier and hindsight options with the tridiagonal probability algorithm. Manag Sci 47:383–393

Sıtkı Sönmezer is an Assistant Professor of Finance at Beykent University Department of Business Administration, Istanbul-Turkey. Dr. Sönmezer has a BS in Sociology from Boğazici University (1999), an MBA from Bilgi University (2002) and a PhD in Accounting and Finance from Marmara University (2010). His research interests are mainly finance, volatility and return Analysis of financial Instruments, Announcement effects, Derivative markets and Behavioral Finance. He has taught Quantitative Methods in Finance, Risk Management, International Finance, Corporate Financeand Money and Banking at both graduate and undergraduate levels. He is a member of AIMR.

Part IV
Risk-Based Audit and the Structured Finance

Risk Based Internal Audit

Ali Görener

Abstract The audit has become an integral part of many activities in various fields related to business life from the past to present. Fundamental changes have been experienced in the concept of audit due to several reasons such as accounting scandals, changes in management mentality, technological developments and legal regulations experienced especially in recent years. Along with these changes, risk-based audit approach focusing on uncovering the risks of business and how to manage these risks has developed beyond the issue of benefiting from the previous period data envisaged by the traditional audit approach.

The risk-based audit is a process containing important stages such as identification, classification, and measurement of risks and determination of their weights. At the end of this process, it is possible to have considerable knowledge to what extent stress should be laid on which risks by ranging the risks identified for business according to their probability of realization.

1 Introduction

The audit is the process of collecting objective evidence with the purpose of investigating the compliance degree of transactions with financial nature of the economic activities and events related to a particular economic unit with predetermined certain criteria and informing the relevant sectors with the results obtained, and the process of the evaluation of this evidence (Durmuş and Taş 2008) Information users who are in the position of taking economic decisions need various financial and non-financial information about businesses they are concerned about. Whether this information is accurate and reliable can be revealed just by auditing.

A. Görener (✉)
Department of Business Administration, Istanbul Commerce University Sutluce Mahallesi, Imrahor-Caddesi, No: 90, Beyoglu 34445, Istanbul, Turkey
e-mail: agorener@ticaret.edu.tr

H. Dinçer, Ü. Hacioğlu (eds.), *Risk Management, Strategic Thinking and Leadership in the Financial Services Industry*, Contributions to Management Science, DOI 10.1007/978-3-319-47172-3_17

Nowadays, audit function performs the studies required for the examination of records and documents used during the creation of financial statements which are substantially prepared by an accounting system and for the determination of the accuracy of the transactions by investigating their compliance with the accounting principles and rules. Moreover, it carries out the task of presenting information and findings obtained to those concerned by preparing a report as a result of these studies (Durmuş and Taş 2008). The features of audit can be listed as follows:

- The audit includes the information of a particular economic unit and a period.
- The audit is a process.
- Audit deals with the accuracy of the information or how much reliable it is.
- The audit is an act of comparison.
- The audit is an act of evidence collection and assessment.
- The audit is performed by an expert and independent person.
- A report is issued as a result of audit works.

Above listed properties show that audit is a systematic process, and there is a series of stages in this process.

2 Audit Types

2.1 Audit Types by Purpose

2.1.1 Audit of Financial Statements

Audit of financial statements is the most widespread type of audit. The purpose of this type of audit is to investigate whether financial statements are prepared in accordance with predetermined criteria.

The information presented in financial statements contains the claims of the management of an enterprise on the financial situation and results of operation of the enterprise. The correctness of these claims is especially important for external information users. However, not only the personal needs of external information users but also the needs of all interest groups are taken into consideration while performing this type of audit.

2.1.2 Compliance Audit

In this type of audit, whether the rules determined by high authorities inside or outside the enterprise are complied with is investigated. The audit carried out on whether the rules inside the enterprise are fulfilled is performed by internal auditors. The audit on whether the laws and legislations determined by high authorities outside the enterprise are complied with is performed by persons outside the enterprise, such as government auditors.

2.1.3 Operational Audit

This type of audit is also called efficiency audit. The efficiency of the operations of the enterprise is assessed by reviewing the policies of the enterprise. The recommendations given for improving the results obtained and operations are reported to the enterprise management.

The investigations conducted in operation audit may not be limited only to accounting information. Many functions such as marketing, production, logistics and management may also be examined in this context. It is generally performed by internal auditors in practice, and whether the operation results achieve predetermined targets or standards can be measured.

2.2 Audit Types by Scope

2.2.1 Mandatory Audit

It is the type of audit that must be performed in line with legal provisions. For example, enterprises that are subject to CMB audit and banks that are subject to BRSA audit are obliged to perform the independent external audit.

2.2.2 Arbitrary Audit

It is the type of audit that enterprises carry out in line with their own wishes although there are no legal obligations.

2.2.3 Permanent Audit

The auditing of the year-end financial statements of public companies, other companies that are subject to CMB supervision, banks, and insurance companies in accordance with generally accepted audit standards.

2.2.4 Limited Audit

It is the type of audit conducted by audit companies performing annual audits in the form of auditing the interim financial statements of certain companies in interim periods.

2.2.5 Special Audit

This is the type of audit performed when enterprises go through such situations as liquidation, merger, transfer and splitting or when they become public for the first time.

2.3 Types of Audit by Status

2.3.1 External Audit

The type of audit performed by people or institutions that have no relation to the enterprise, which are outside the enterprise. The subject of external audit consists of accounting data. Whether the information recorded reflect the financial and commercial processes that occur in the relevant accounting period is assessed within the framework of generally accepted accounting principles.

2.3.2 Internal Audit

The type of audit performed by people that permanently work in the enterprise or institution and named as internal auditors. In this type of audit, the operations of the enterprise are examined in all aspects and reported to the senior management.

2.3.3 Public Audit

It is the audit performed in the name and benefit of public by people that receive their duties and authorities from law. In these audits, they audit the level of compliance of institutions and organizations with legislation, the economy policy of the state and public interest.

3 Internal Audit Concept

Internal audit is an independent and objective activity that aims to develop the activities of an institution and contribute to these activities. Internal audit helps the institution to achieve its targets by bringing a systematic and disciplined approach for the purpose of assessing and developing the effectiveness of the risk management, control and governance processes of the institution (Institute of Internal Auditors Research Foundation 2009).

As a result of internal audit, the management of the institution obtains guarantee and counselling about whether the resources are used effectively, economically and efficiently in accordance with the objectives and targets of the institution, compliance of the activities with the relevant legislation, whether the assets are protected, to which extent the current internal controls in the institution are sufficient, and the reliability of the information produced by the institution.

That internal auditing became a modern profession started with the establishment of the Institute of Internal Auditors in the US in 1948. Different definitions were made for the internal audit that fulfills the function of objective information provision that is the reason for its emergence with the establishment of the Institution of Internal Auditors, and the focal point constantly changed and developed. The effects of the institutionalization of the Institute of Internal Auditors, its becoming an institution that is taken into consideration more by increasing the number of its members, and the publication of the standards and the codes of conduct on internal audit practices may also not be disregarded in the development of internal audit (Pehlivanlı 2010).

Another institution that is important in terms of internal audit practices is the "Committee of Sponsoring Organizations of the Treadway Commission-COSO". COSO is an internationally accepted organization that is established with the support of the International Institute of Internal Auditors, US Institute of Certified Public Accountants, US Association of Accountants, the Institute of Management Accountants and Financial Executives Association. The publication of the "Internal Control Framework" by COSO in 1992 and "Corporate Risk Management Framework" in 2006 helped to overcome the obstacles to the development of the profession of internal auditing and the crisis in front of the profession (Pehlivanlı 2010).

3.1 *Types of Internal Audit*

In practice, internal audit includes 5 main areas of activity. These are (Alptürk 2008);

Financial Audit:	The assessment of whether the data in financial reports and assets and liabilities of the audited unit are compliant with their real value, sources of financing, the management of the assets and the budget allowances allocated.
Compliance Audit:	The investigation of whether the financial processes and other activities of an organization are compliant with the determined methods, rules, and legislation.
Performance Audit:	The assessment of the affordability, effectiveness and efficiency levels of the physical, financial and human sources used by the institution or organization while performing their duties.

System Audit:	The assessment of whether the audited unit is effective in terms of determining and eliminating the financial management principle deficiencies.
Information Technologies Audit:	The assessment of whether the information systems of the audited unit are safe.

3.2 Benefits of Internal Audit

The most basic benefits of modern internal audit can be listed as follows (Pehlivanlı 2010);

- The need for safe information provision is fulfilled. The effectiveness of internal audit is directly related to the effectiveness of the internal control system in a certain sense. If there is an effective internal control environment in the enterprise, the effectiveness will also be high in internal audit. Consequently, this will facilitate the access of the parties that want to obtain information on the enterprise to safe information.
- The need for the protection of the enterprise's assets and records is fulfilled. In case there is an effective internal audit system, the assets and records of the enterprise are protected at a high level.
- The need for increasing efficiency is fulfilled. The scope of internal audit also includes the effectiveness of the activities. In this context, inefficient activities can be eliminated in case internal audit works effectively.
- Adaptation to the policies determined by the senior management is ensured.

4 Risk and Risk Management

4.1 Uncertainty and Risk

It is possible to encounter many risk definitions in different fields of science. Generally speaking, risk can be expressed as any kind of incident that prevents the organization from achieving its targets. The risk is a threat that negatively affects the organization from reaching its objectives and fulfilling its strategies successfully. Accordingly, the key characteristics related to risk can be listed as follows (Griffiths 2012):

- The risk is a changing threat.
- This threat is related to an incident.
- The occurrence of the incident prevents the organization from achieving its targets.

The risk can be mentioned if the occurrence possibility of decision's possible results can be determined, and uncertainty can be mentioned when there is the

Table 1 Differences between risk and uncertainty

Risk	Uncertainty
Can be measured	Cannot be measured
Statistical assessment	Subjective possibility
Reasonable data	Personal opinions

(Tony Merna, Faisal F. Al-Thani, Corporate Risk Management (England: John Willey & Sons Ltd, 2005))

possibility that more than one result of a decision can occur, and the occurrence probabilities of these possibilities are not known at all (Merna and Al-Thani 2005):

Risk consists of two components being uncertainty and effect. While uncertainty may not have any effect in certain situations; the effect is the most important result of risk. Furthermore, while the possibility of the incident that will occur in uncertain situations is not known, possibilities may be known when risk is in question. For these reasons, it is incorrect to perceive the concepts of uncertainty and risk in the same way (Pehlivanlı 2010) (Table 1).

The institutions operating for a particular purpose maintain their activities in a particular risk environment. While they cannot eliminate the risks completely when maintaining these activities, they can keep them at a reasonable level. The most effective ways of keeping risks at an acceptable level are control and audit. The control and audits to be carried out during the activities can both reduce risks to acceptable levels and contribute to the institution's achieving its objective.

4.2 *Types of Risk*

Although risks are subject to different variations, some of the risks that institutions may encounter can be listed as follows in general:

- Market Risk: It results from the changes in market prices. Interest rate risk, currency risk, risk of commodity price change, energy price risk,
- Credit Risk: The risk that results from the possibility that the debt owners fail to pay for their debts.
- Operational Risk: In addition to the risks that are based on errors, faults and abuses in the fulfillment of an operation, any kind of risk that may occur within the framework of organization, workflow, technology and human power, will cause the institution material or fiduciary loss, which remains outside the credit and market risk, and statistical measurement of which can be made based on the past data (Kishali and Pehlivanlı 2010).
- Reputation Risk: Risks that may occur in case the enterprise loses its reputation.
- Legal Risks: The risks that result from the acts of the enterprise that do not comply with the law.
- Macroeconomic Risks: The risks that may occur due to macroeconomic changes.
- Strategic Risks: The risks that may occur due to incorrect strategic decisions.

- Country Risk: The risks that result from unexpected economic and political changes in other countries.

4.3 Corporate Risk Management

Risk management is an important concept that was born and developed in the first half of the 1970s and affects the evolution of market economies. Risk management can be defined as a process that ensures defining, assessing and managing the risks (Merna and Al-Thani 2005). In this process, the enterprises should assess and manage the risks that may emerge in the best way in order to fulfill their aims and ensure continuity.

Globalization has rapidly increased the volume of financial transactions, and an environment where financial risks vary has emerged. Serious problems occurred both in terms of banks and financial systems, and the crises that occurred from time to time led to serious economic and social costs in parallel to these developments (Bolgün and Akçay 2009).

With these crises, the interest in corporate risk management has increased, and COSO published a detailed guide called Corporate Risk Management Framework in 2006. With this framework, a guide that can be applied as standard at international scale emerged. The framework in question is a model that can be shaped in accordance with different needs and properties of enterprises and adapted to enterprises (Pehlivanlı 2010).

Corporate risk management is a process that defines potential incidents that can affect institution's achieving its targets, provides reasonable guarantee in terms of achieving the targets of the directors and institution within the limits of the will to take risks, is structured all through the institution and affected by the management of the institution and other employees. According to this definition, the main elements that emerge can be listed as follows (COSO 2010):

- It is a continuing and flowing process
- It is affected by the employees in all parts of the institution
- It is applied within the framework of the strategy
- It is applied at all levels and sections of the institution
- It is not necessary to eliminate risks completely
- Corporate risk management provides a reasonable level of guarantee in terms of helping the institution reach its targets.

It is important that the system works effectively in terms of achieving the expected benefit from corporate risk management process. The assessment of the system effectiveness and taking the necessary precautions play a big role in the monitoring of the process.

5 Risk Based Internal Audit

5.1 Definition and Scope of Risk-Based Internal Audit

That the audit is carried out based on risk provides opportunities for better management of the institution in the future rather than carrying out the audit activity as a limited process or based on individuals (Kaya 2010). The risk-based audit approach was first adopted by OCC in the US in 1995. There are three main developments that led to this. These are (Özsoy 2004, Eşkazan 2005);

- The developments in the field of technology expanded the type and scope of the activities of institutions alongside with financial theories and practices.
- The spread of derived products and other complex financial products and the creativity in derived products, the increase in commercial activities and securities based on assets, as well as the developments in secondary markets, have considerably changed the financial system.
- Consolidation experienced in the US banking system in the 1990s led to the emergence of an increased number of big and complex banks.

The use of risk-based audit practices in the banking system has become more widespread over time, and it started to be used in other sectors in different forms in the following periods.

The risk-based internal audit is the type of audit based on the presumptions that audit sources are not limited, the activities of the units to be audited face different risks and the activities of the unit to be audited have different levels of importance. The auditor makes risk-based plans that determine the priorities of internal audit activities in the light of these presumptions and in accordance with the objectives of the institution and implements them. Accordingly, the scope of risk-based internal audit can be listed as follows (Pehlivanlı 2010):

- The examination and assessment of the sufficiency and effectiveness of the internal control system,
- The examination of the implementation and effectiveness of risk management methods and risk assessment methodologies,
- The revision of management and financial information systems including the electronic information system and electronic services,
- The examination of the correctness and reliability of accountancy records and financial statements,
- The examination of the system of assessing the enterprise's own capital in line with risk estimations,
- Auditing of the operation of both the processes and a particular internal control system,
- The examination of the compliance with the conditions, ethical rules, policy and methods of the legal and regulatory authorities,
- Control of the accuracy, reliability and timeliness of regulatory reporting

The changes that result from risk perception in the risk-based internal audit include all areas of audit. In this context, first, the risk profile is revealed in risk-based internal audit, and then, subjects such as the scope, content and timing of the audit procedure, and the allocation of sources are shaped according to the risk profile. A typical risk-based audit must also include the stages of risk definition and risk assessment in order to reveal the profile. These two stages are very important in terms of risk-based audit and should be performed extensively (Kishali and Pehlivanlı 2006).

5.2 Comparison of Traditional Internal Audit and Risk-Based Internal Audit

With the risk-based internal audit, the retrospective point-of-view in audit changed and it started to focus on future. Now, the internal auditor takes into consideration all details that may prevent the institutions from achieving their targets by focusing on incidents that may happen in the future rather than past events in the audit to be performed.

While in the traditional audit understanding, the auditor focuses on past activities and tries to reveal the incorrect activities that have taken place, the occurrence of faulty activities is tried to be prevented in the risk-based internal audit. Traditional and risk-based internal audit are comparatively addressed in the table below (Table 2):

In the risk-based internal audit, the auditor will focus on the subject that current and future risks are determined rather than being constantly busy with internal control. While there are risk factors in both types of audit, the traditional audit understanding focuses on natural risk, control risk and finding risks, whereas, in the risk-based internal audit, the institutions' own risks are also addressed in addition to these risks.

While in the traditional internal audit, the auditor spends most of his working time with the details related to planning, technical and internal control system, in risk-based internal audit, the working period is spent on understanding the business processes of the institution and business risks and the management of these risks.

In the traditional internal audit, the auditor gives advice on whether the internal control system works effectively and benefit-cost effectiveness is ensured as he constantly focuses on the internal control system. Subjects such as risk variation, risk avoidance, risk transfer are emphasized in the risk-based internal audit. The internal auditor is in the position of an independent auditor in the audited institution in terms of examining accountancy data, assessing the internal control system and dealing with the surveillance of the activities in the traditional internal audit. Whereas in risk-based internal audit, the auditor is partly on the same side with the institution as he regularly examines the systems developed for measuring the

Table 2 Comparison of traditional internal audit and risk-based internal audit

Properties	Traditional internal audit	Risk-based internal audit
Focal point in internal audit	Internal control	Risk
Internal audit	Activates after reactive events, intermittent surveillance	Proactive, real-time, continuous surveillance
Risk assessment	Risk factors	Scenario planning
Internal audit tests	Control-based	Risk-based
Internal audit methods	It is important that the details in control tests are complete	It is important that the framework of works risks is determined widely
Internal audit advice	Meticulous benefit-cost efficiency should be ensured for internal control	Risk variation, risk avoidance, risk share and risk transfer for risk management
Role of internal audit in organization	In independent audit position	Integrated with risk management and senior management

(Yunus Kishalı, Davut Pehlivanlı, Risk Odaklı İç Denetim ve İMKB Uygulaması [Risk-Based Internal Audit and ISE Implementation] (Kocaeli University))

risks that the institution may face and gives the necessary recommendations to the management.

5.3 *Risk Assessment and Recording of the Risks*

Risk-based internal audit process consists of closely related stages. As this process takes place as a whole, each stage contributes to the shaping of the next stage.

Risk assessment, which is also a component of the internal control framework published by COSO, is also a work that is recommended at the stage of audit planning in internal audit standards. Risk assessment consists of the stages of measuring and ordering previously defined and classified risks that will prevent the institution from achieving its targets. As a result of risk assessment, the auditor can apply tests in the audit program to important control points. The methods that are used in risk assessment are determined in accordance with the structure of the organization and business processes. The risks are measured in terms of the possibilities and their effects with the help of one of the qualitative or quantitative methods to be used in the assessment or their mix. Then the risks that are measured are ordered with the help of a risk matrix (Pehlivanlı 2010).

5.3.1 Qualitative Analysis

Qualitative assessment techniques are used under conditions when potential probability and effect are low or numerical data and a quantitative assessment expert are not present. With these techniques, it is possible to express the potential effect levels and their possibility of emergence is also possible with the personal judgments of the person conducting the analysis.

Main qualitative assessment techniques can be listed as follows (Merna and Al-Thani 2005):

- Brainstorming
- Presumption Analysis
- Delphi Analysis
- Interview Technique
- Checklists
- Risk Recording
- Risk Mapping
- Possibility-Effect Tables

The selection of these risk assessment techniques varies depending on the structure of the institution. If the institution is not willing for risks, i.e. if its risk appetite is low, a result aimed at avoiding risky activities will be achieved with this assessment. If the institution has such a structure that is open to risks and tries to turn these into an opportunity, a contrary result will be achieved.

5.3.2 Quantitative Analysis

In this analysis, effect and possibility estimations are expressed in numerical values using data sources. The quality of analysis results depends on the accuracy and integrity of the data used and the validity of the model used (Arslan 2008).

Potential effects can be found by modeling the results of a particular event or series of events, as well as statistically from past studies or events. The effect can be revealed in the form of money, technique, damage that can happen to a person or another damage criterion. In certain cases, it may be necessary to use more than one numerical value in order to determine the risk level of the same incident (Arslan 2008).

Quantitative assessment techniques are generally computer-based techniques. The main ones among these techniques are as follows (Merna and Al-Thani 2005):

- Decision Tree Technique
- Monte Carlo Simulation Program
- Sensitivity Analyses
- Possibility-Effect Analyses

There is a consensus that the data obtained using the qualitative assessment techniques in the literature are more practical than the data obtained using the quantitative assessment techniques, and qualitative evaluation methods should be preferred especially at the beginning stage (Pehlivanlı 2010).

5.3.3 Possibility-Effect Analysis

Risks are generally analyzed by their possibility of occurrence and the extent to which they affect the institution where they emerge. Risk ranking is made according to the result of the combination of the risks' possibilities and effects.

The theoretical model that emerges in risk-based audit processes and the result obtained from this model can be formulated as follows.

Risk = *f* (Possibility, Effect)
If we are to formulate the effect and occurrence possibility of the risk;
t = r-c
t: threat, r: risk, c: control

The possibility is generally related to time and indicates the occurrence frequency of events. While risk possibilities are classified as low, middle and high in the simplest sense, the risk effect may also be similarly classified as small, middle or heavy. That scale rating limits are objective and may vary among individuals may lead to distrust against the assessment activity and consequently the risk matrix. A five-item scale is generally preferred to prevent this.

The five-item scale that is used in order to assess the effect dimension of risks can range as not important, small, important, serious and destructive, the five-item scale used in possibility evaluation can range as very low, low, middle, high and very high. While certain risks have a high effect, their possibility of occurrence is low. While some of them have a low effect, their possibility of occurrence is high. The more careful these subjects are determined while performing risk assessment, the better the risk attitude of the organization can be determined. The information sources to be used in the process of determining the effects and possibilities of risks can be listed as past records, experiences related to practices, relevant published sources, market research, voting results, economical, technical or other models and expert opinions (Pehlivanlı 2010).

5.3.4 Risk Matrix

The possibility and effect results of the risks that are assessed with the dimension of possibility and effect using qualitative and quantitative assessment techniques are shown with the risk matrix. Risk matrices can be formed in different ways. A simple matrix where the possibility and effect are shown separately can be presented as follows (Table 3).

The process of combining the possibilities and effects of risks is performed using simple average or weighted average methods. The sum of the possibility and effect results are divided into two in simple average. Thinking that the effect factor is more important has brought weighted average into the agenda.

Table 3 Risk matrix

6 High effect/Low possibility	8 High effect/Intermediate possibility	9 High effect/High possibility
3 Intermediate effect/Low possibility	5 Intermediate effect/Intermediate possibility	7 Intermediate effect/High possibility
1 Low effect/Low possibility	2 Low effect/Intermediate possibility	4 Low effect/High possibility

(Davut Pehlivanlı, Modern İç Denetim [Modern Internal Audit] (İstanbul: Beta Yayınları, 2010))

The risk matrix is made according to the voting results performed during the process of risk workshop. Nowadays, risk workshops are generally performed with the help of computer software and are often specially prepared in the framework of the institution's needs. Risk recording is preparing a list of risks that emerge as a result of risk assessment and prevent the institution from achieving its targets. Since risk management and control are the duties of the administration, they should directly be included in the processes of recording the risks that are determined and removing the risks with no probability of occurrence from the records (Griffiths 2006, Pickett 2006).

6 Conclusion

Risk management and internal audit have become the most important subjects that institutions should address while performing their activities. It is necessary that risk management processes and internal audit activities should be seriously addressed, and the relevant tools should be used effectively in order for institutions to achieve their targets.

Nowadays, integrated risk management systems which concern the institutions and in which all risks are gathered under a single roof have started to become widespread, and the degree of importance of the calculations of the risk occurrence possibility and the extent to which they will affect the institution in case they occur has gradually increased. The use of various tools in order to increase the importance of risk management processes and ensure the effectiveness of these processes is among important reasons for the development of the risk-based internal audit approach. Internal auditors suggest improving measures with the reports presented and contribute significantly to administrators by making assessments on the sufficiency and effectiveness of the risk management processes implemented by institutions.

The gradual spread of risk-based internal audit activities revealed the necessity for auditors to improve their professional knowledge and skills in these areas and that internal auditors adopt methods that require them to use information technologies and creativity more by leaving aside traditional audit methods have gained more importance.

References

Alptürk E (2008) Finans, muhasebe ve vergi boyutlarında iç denetim rehberi. Maliye ve Hukuk Yayınları, Ankara

Arslan I (2008) Kurumsal Risk Yönetimi. Maliye Bakanlığı Strateji Geliştirme BaşkanlığıYayınlanmamış Uzmanlık Tezi, Ankara

Bolgün E, Akçay MB (2009) Risk Yönetimi. Scala Yayıncılık, Istanbul

Durmuş CN, Taş O (2008) Denetim. Alfa Yayınları, Istanbul

COSO (2010) Enterprise Risk Management Integrated-Framework, Committee of Sponsoring Organizations of the Treadway Commission. 21 Oct 2015. http://www.coso.org/documents/COSO_ERM_ExecutiveSummary.pdf

Eşkazan AR (2005) Risk Odaklı İç Denetim Planlaması. İç Denetim Dergisi, Bahar, pp 32–33

Griffiths DM (2006) Risk based internal auditing: an introduction [online]. Dostupno na: 21 Feb 2015. http://www.internalaudit.biz/files/introduction.Internalauditv2_0_3.pdf

Griffiths MP (2012) Risk-based auditing. Gower, London

Institute of Internal Auditors Research Foundation (2009) International Professional Practices Framework (IPPF). Institute of Internal Auditors Research Foundation. 11 Apr 2015. http://www.theiia.org/guidance/standards-and-guidance/ippf/definition-of-internal-auditing/

Kaya HA (2010) İç denetim. Editörler: Selami Sezgin Sevinç Yaraşır Fatih Deyneli Elvan Teke, 20. Türkiye Maliye Sempozyumu Bildiriler Kitabı, pp 97–106

Kishali Y, Pehlivanlı D (2006) Risk Odaklı İç Denetim ve İMKB Uygulaması. Muhasebe ve Finansman Dergisi 30:75–87

Merna T, Al-Thani FF (2005) Corporate risk management. Wiley, Hoboken, NJ

Özsoy MT (2004) Risk Odaklı Denetim ABD Uygulaması ve Türkiye Açısından Değerlendirilmesi. Active, Mart–Nisan

Pehlivanlı D (2010) Modern iç denetim uygulamalari. Beta Yayınları, İstanbul

Pickett KS (2006) Audit planning: a risk-based approach. Wiley, Hoboken, NJ

Ali Görener is an associate professor of production and operations management. He received a BSc degree in Mechanical Engineering from Kocaeli University, Turkey in 2004. He received MSc degree in Industrial Engineering from Istanbul Commerce University (2006) and second MSc degree in Manufacturing from Yıldız Technical University (2007). In December 2011, he completed his PhD studies in Production Management at Istanbul University. Ali Görener is currently associate professor in the Department of Business Administration at Istanbul Commerce University. His research interests include supply chain management, quality management, multi criteria decision-making, lean production, logistics and maintenance.

Recent Financial Crisis and the Structured Finance: Accounting Perspective for Future

Soner Gokten and Pınar Okan Gokten

Abstract Structured finance techniques, especially synthetic structuring, were applied intensively to ensure sustainable growth of credit mechanism via developing high rated hybrid instruments before recent global shock. The system created a loop that caused systematic risk maximization derived from undesirable default correlation between collaterals. Therefore structured products were seen as the reason for financial crisis and their popularity has begun to fall. On the other side, discussions have started to take place within accounting dimension in recent years. The fundamental point of this perspective was constructed on the efficiency of accounting techniques to provide signals on future hitches and to make market participants properly informed about the values of collaterals. In this study, the tradeoff for applying fair value versus historical cost accounting is discussed in the frame of the connection between recent global shock and structured finance.

1 Introduction: Overview of Structuring

Structured finance is a system that contains tools and highly complex financial transactions created by financial engineering activities. Structured systems are developed to find solutions in order to meet unique financial needs of companies or investors that could not be fulfilled by traditional financial products. In this sense, structuring is the way of creating hybrid financial securities by developing a system that makes credit risk transfer possible via securitization and using of derivatives for optimum financing or investing.

S. Gokten (✉)
Faculty of Economics and Administrative Sciences, Department of Management, Baskent University, Baglica Campus, 06810 Baglica, Ankara, Turkey
e-mail: sgokten@baskent.edu.tr

P. Okan Gokten
Faculty of Economics and Administrative Sciences, Department of International Trade, Gazi University, 06500 Besevler, Ankara, Turkey
e-mail: pinar.okan@gazi.edu.tr

H. Dinçer, Ü. Hacioğlu (eds.), *Risk Management, Strategic Thinking and Leadership in the Financial Services Industry*, Contributions to Management Science, DOI 10.1007/978-3-319-47172-3_18

Securitization is the fundamental technique to develop structured products. A pool of selected assets are packaged and pass-through securities are formed which create liquidity for originator (owner of the assets) and return for investors based on cash flow from assets. In traditional view, this system contains two main building stones called ‘off-balance sheet structuring’ and ‘collateralized obligation’. According to the concept of ‘off-balance sheet structuring’, assets are transferred to standalone ad-hoc vehicle with a finite life called ‘special purpose vehicle or entity-SPV’ by true sale. Thus issuing of asset based securities via SPV makes obligations (liabilities) collateralized by means of retaining selected assets and prior rights on their cash flows as guarantee for possible defaults.

In the simplest term, the fundamental off-balance sheet securitization creates ‘bankruptcy remoteness’ for originator via traditional credit risk transfer (true sale) and provides an opportunity to minimize capital adequacy for banks. In this sense, the aims to apply securitization for banks could be summarized in three directions: Liquidity (financing), equity management and risk management. One forward step in order to increase efficiency of these aims is to integrate credit enhancement techniques into off-balance sheet securitization.

Sorting of collateralized obligations according to priorities of investors’ rights composes the mainframe of credit enhancement. This is a technique, called ‘subordination’ to redesign the economic structure of balance sheet by prioritizing the rights of investors on future cash flows generated by assets. Determined cash flow order, titled as ‘cash waterfall’ in the literature, specify default risk of each ‘tranche’ and the more rank in priority means increase in credit score by means of decrease in cumulative default risk of tranche statistically. Collateralized obligations with top priority for rights on future cash flows form senior tranche which has credit quality in highest degree. The others, mezzanine and junior tranches follow senior ones with lower credit quality in terms of cumulative default probability. Residual is the equity trance as workhorse for assets with highest default risk (see Fig. 1). Mind you that residual is the undermost in the cash flow order.

Cash flow collateralized debt obligations (Cash CDOs) are securities issued based on tranches that formed via subordination in the frame of off-balance sheet securitization. It is important to note that, while asset backed securities are based on complete set of assets pool, cash CDOs are based on identified tranches. This critical differentiation plays an important role on rating. In traditional

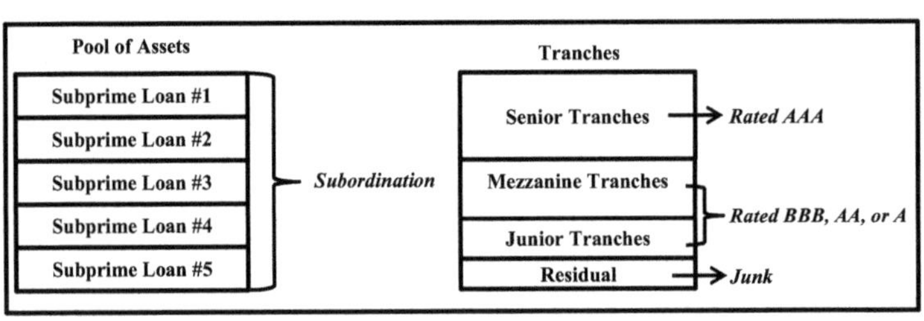

Fig. 1 Credit enhancement by subordination

securitization, in other words securitization without subordination, the default probability of whole asset pool is evaluated. However in securitization with credit enhancement, the default probability of each tranche is taking into account that means the rating of cash CDOs becomes more complex relative to asset backed securities (the traditional rating such as bonds) in terms of identification of diversification.

Making risk transfer via credit derivatives means synthetic structuring. This kind of risk transfer provides some advantages such as increase in speed of transactions, decrease in costs, increase in kinds of assets subject to packaging, and eliminate the need for collateralizing for senior tranche. Synthetic collateralized debt obligations (Synthetic CDOs) derived via credit derivatives based risk transfer varies according to way of credit protection; funded or unfunded. In fully funded mechanism existence of credit protection is provided via 'credit-linked notes' by forming portfolio consisting of securities with high credit quality as collateral for possible exposure to a specified credit event on reference tranche or asset. In unfunded synthetic structuring credit production is provided only by using 'credit default swaps' means no need for prepayment and so lack of additional collateral pool. Generally 'basket credit default swaps' are preferred for unfunded structures due to their convenience on subordination. The structure becomes partially funded when both 'credit linked notes' and 'credit default swaps' are used. Figure 2 shows the classification of products in the frame of their position to cash markets or credit derivatives.

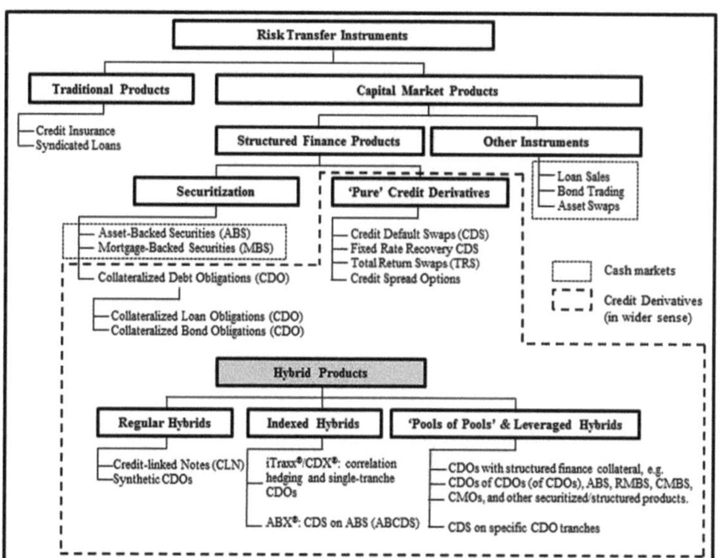

Fig. 2 Overview of credit risk transfer instruments. Source: Jobst, A.A. (2007) 'A Primer on Structured Finance' Journal of Derivatives and Hedge Funds, 13 (3), p. 5

2 Triggers of Financial Shock

Blundell-Wignall and Atkinson (2009) defined the reasons of global financial shock in the frame of by global macro liquidity policies and by a very poor framework for incentives of financial sector agents, conditioned by bad regulations, tax systems and governance standards. They identified financial crisis as follows: "The liquidity policies were like a dam overfilled with flooding water. Global liquidity distortions, including interest rates at 1 % in the United States and 0 % in Japan, China's fixed exchange rate and recycling of its international reserves, and the Sovereign Wealth Funds (SWF) investments, all helped to fill the dam to overflowing. That is how the asset bubbles and excess leverage got under way."

Expansionary monetary policy was applied in US to activate the wheels of economy again following dotcom crash and 9/11 attack realized in 2000 and 2001 respectively. Interest rates became a record low of 1 % in June 2003, after remained at that level for a year showed upside fluctuation and reached 5.25 % in June 2006. Simultaneously, increased in money supply caused a sharp and continuous increase in consumer borrowings (see Fig. 3). This situation brought up need for banks on providing liquidity and in the beginning banks used overnight repos in financing that made their value double. Later on, sustainable lending could be provided by using structured finance techniques more. Augmentation of subprime mortgages played critical role on generation of this frame, where the face value of mortgages outstanding reached $2.75 trillion in 2007, of which $1.25 trillion were subprime mortgages, $1 million Alt A debt and $500 billion jumbo ARMs (Zandi 2008, p 44).

Decrease in target rates and increase in credits create a loop which produced sufficient profit for financial market players, that means 'giving more credits and making more money' without consider diversification in the frame of minimizing default risk. Growing of the housing bubble reached the pick in 2004 with an average price increase nearly 120 % for a typical US house, and the asset values taken into account as collateral played a fictive role for credit protection. Based on

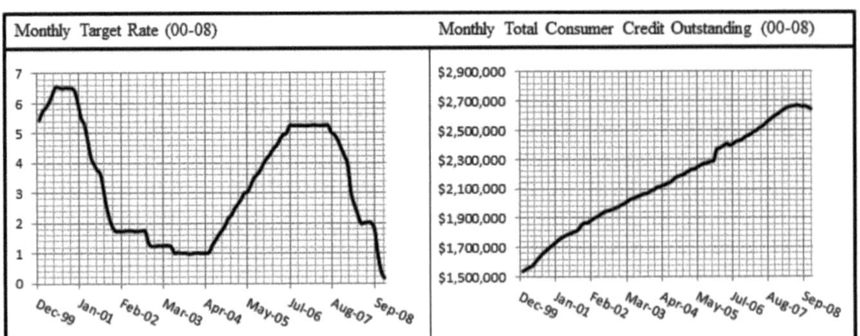

Fig. 3 Outlook of US economic indicators (00-08). Source: Federal Reserve System

high weight of subprime loans in total outstanding amount, the system gave error after sharp declined in housing prices by means of finding adequate assets in value or source to cover the loss of structured products' investors. The fundamental reason of the error is systematic risk maximization derived from undesirable default correlation between assets.

3 The Rationale of Default Correlation and Systematic Risk

Improvement on credit quality of tranche is closely related with default correlation. Allen et al. (2012) state that crisis that started in 2007 have highlighted the importance of another type of systemic risk related to usage of credit default swaps based financial products. In other words, structured finance practices realized by all financial organizations in the market simultaneously caused indiscernible systematic risk formation. Because, in such a case, diversification aims do not work in the meaning of cumulative default risk minimization. This frame shows the reality of 2007 financial crisis. In this sense, the fundamental reason of the shock could be denoted as increased in default correlation between assets.

Sensitivity of tranches to systematic risk is more than of traditional bonds. Because, traditional bonds are related with only one reference entity while tranches contain a large of variety assets. Therefore, default correlation could not be managed properly in structured finance transactions especially for synthetic ones. In other words, whereas total risk can be minimized by diversification theoretically, during pre-term of global shock default correlations positively increase in practice because of mass and similar structuring applications. This increase caused a systematic risk for packaged assets.

Default correlation between reference assets directly affects integrated default probability. In that the relations between reference assets are randomness if there is no default correlation; means integrated default probability equals to multiplying of reference assets' default probabilities in simple terms. This desirable situation could provide significant decrease in integrated default probability. Since reference assets (entities) have to be different in all aspects to ensure such a case, it is not realistic. In this sense, the main aim occurs within the scope of selecting assets with negative or poor default correlations. However, existence of mass structuring transactions especially associated with subprime ones applied by in a large number of financial institutions made diversification impracticable during pre-crisis term.

Another point as a reason of systematic risk formation is the increase in asymmetric information. Especially, synthetic structuring abolished the financial statements' transparencies of financial institutions in terms of risk assessment and valuation of collaterals. In other words during pre-crisis term there were 'visible' and 'invisible' situations. According to visible picture, the values of collaterals were adequate. On the other side, the real values of collaterals as invisible ones were not same as the values that could be seen in financial statements. In other words, accounting techniques on valuation could not be sufficient for market to obtain signal about the reality of financial market. Thus, increased asymmetry made market uninformed on increased default correlation.

4 Accounting Perspective: M2M or Historical Cost?

The Global Shock showed the weaknesses of structured finance accounting. The insufficiency in the disclosures of structured products and the valuation methods used are defended as the factors increasing the severity of financial crisis. The explanations in financial statements related with the structured finance products have to be sufficient. So, financial statement users can understand the necessary issues without having a problem and decisions taken will be much more accurate. The factor, related with the valuation of structured finance products, affects the severity of the financial crisis is the valuation of these with fair value. Before the crisis, the standard setters support the fair value accounting. As a result of this, financial crisis formed an important debate related with fair value accounting.

In many sources the expression of mark to market (M2M) accounting is used instead of fair value accounting. The definition of fair value in IFRS 13 is as: "The price that would be received to sell an asset or paid to transfer a liability in an orderly transaction between market participants at the measurement date". Fair value accounting bases on the current values of the future cash flows of assets and liabilities and reports these (Meder et al. 2011). Basically, fair value is a market-based measurement not entity-specific value.

As mentioned in IFRS 13, there are three levels in defining the fair value. These are:

- Level 1—inputs are quoted prices in active markets for identical assets or liabilities that the entity can access at the measurement date.
- Level 2—inputs are inputs other than quoted market prices included within Level 1 that are observable for the asset or liability, either directly or indirectly.
- Level 3—inputs are unobservable inputs for the asset or liability.

As the fair value relies on the efficient market hypothesis, in reporting the price in the market is grounded on. For this reason, fair value accounting presents a valuation measure that can be applied in active markets.

There are lots of studies related with the relation between fair value accounting and financial crisis (Allen and Carletti 2008; Badertscher et al. 2011; Barth and Landsman 2010; Heaton et al. 2010; Laux and Leuz 2009a, b; Plantin et al. 2008). Some of these studies support that fair value accounting has an effect on the financial crisis, some relies on that fair value accounting does not have an effect or has a little effect on the financial crisis. Actually, the expression that fair value accounting caused the financial crisis is not so accurate. Instead of this, supporting that fair value accounting increases the severity of financial crisis will be a right judgement.

During the financial crisis, there were sharp decreases in the prices of fixed assets and financial assets. As the companies having these assets applied fair value in valuation, they lost a great amount of money and as a result capital losses happened. In crisis period, since companies sold their assets in fire sales in other words at prices below the fundamental values and as they used fair values as a valuation measure, there was a decrease in the asset valuation in the market. So this situation caused capital losses, companies lost money and even failures occurred. Therefore because of the knock-on effect in other companies applying fair value accounting, the market became much worse. As fair value accounting takes market prices in consideration, a decrease in similar prices affected other companies' financial statements.

Standard setters are also blamed for the severity of financial crisis. Standards were not efficient enough in crisis period and also restrictions and rules were so strict are found among these accusations. There is an advantage in providing flexibility in the application of standards in abnormal periods as financial crisis. Especially banks were canalized in the application of fair value while reporting their financial assets. It should not be forgotten that there is also a political pressure that directs standard setters.

After the financial crisis, IASB performed some relaxations related with the fair value accounting. These amendments are reclassification of some financial instruments and issuing guidance on measurement when markets become inactive and very thin (Amel-Zadeh and Meeks 2013). In some situations, organizations are allowed to depart from fair value accounting (they may prefer historical cost).

Standards issued by IASB and related with structured finance are as follows:

- IFRS 7 Financial Instruments: Disclosures and IFRS 12—Disclosure of Interests in Other Entities: The importance of this standard is that the insufficiency in disclosures of structured finance products is one of the main reasons that have an impact on financial crisis.
- IFRS 9—Financial Instruments: This standard will supplant the IAS 39. IFRS 9 was issued in 2014 and will come into effect in 2018.
- IFRS 10—Consolidated Financial Statements: In this standard in whose financial statements Special Purpose Entities may be reported and also how they may be shown is informed.
- IFRS 13—Fair Value Measurement
- IAS 39—Financial Instruments: Recognition and Measurement

All these debates have brought to mind a new question: Instead of fair value which valuation measure will bring to a successful condition? Frequently, historical cost is the answer of this question. It is important to remember that in valuation while historical cost accounting uses book values, fair value accounting depends on market values. In other words, historical cost is the monetary amount paid in the transaction. Fair value is the current market value. In this sense, generally historical cost equals to the fair value at the time assets are subject to transaction.

5 Conclusion

Fair value accounting is procyclical. For this reason, during boom periods assets write ups and especially banks' leverage ratios increase, means high return on equity (ROE) appears. During crisis as a result of sharp decreases in market prices, company losses will appear. This situation causes a much more weak financial system and a sharper financial crisis. On the contrary, during boom periods historical cost accounting prevents asset write ups and provides lower leverage ratios (Laux and Leuz 2009a).

The proponents of fair value accounting defend that as a result of the application of this method, financial statements will be accurate and as they will reflect the current values in the market timely. So the transparency will increase. What we say may be the most important benefits of fair value accounting that cannot be ignored. There are also proponents of historical cost accounting and they oppose to the application of fair value accounting. They thought that fair value accounting leads to an artificial volatility and so in some cases, boom values may be seen. For these reasons historical cost accounting is much more useful according to them (Allen and Carletti 2008).

Each valuation method has its own positive and negative sides. In this tradeoff the main question must have the following: Is the accounting numbers well reflection of the market important for us? Or is the determination of the accounting numbers prudently against the negation that can be seen in market values in the future important for us? The global shock rekindles the debate that depends on these two questions. Currently, there is still no agreed upon answer.

References

Allen F, Carletti E (2008) Mark-to-market accounting and liquidity pricing. J Account Econ 45 (2):358–378

Allen F, Babus A, Carletti E (2012) Asset commonality, debt maturity and systemic risk. J Financ Econ 104(3):519–534

Amel-Zadeh A, Meeks G (2013) Bank failure, mark-to-market and the financial crisis. Abacus 49 (3):308–339

Badertscher BA, Burks JJ, Easton PD (2011) A convenient scapegoat: fair value accounting by commercial banks during the financial crisis. Account Rev 87(1):59–90

Barth ME, Landsman WR (2010) How did financial reporting contribute to the financial crisis? Eur Account Rev 19(3):399–423

Blundell-Wignall A, Atkinson P (2009) Origins of the financial crisis and requirements for reform. J Asian Econ 20(5):536–548

Heaton JC, Lucas D, McDonald RL (2010) Is mark-to-market accounting destabilizing? Analysis and implications for policy. J Monet Econ 57(1):64–75

Laux C, Leuz C (2009a) The crisis of fair-value accounting: making sense of the recent debate. Acc Organ Soc 34(6):826–834

Laux C, Leuz C (2009b) Did fair-value accounting contribute to the financial crisis? National Bureau of Economic Research, No. w15515

Meder A, Schwartz ST, Spires EE, Young RA (2011) Structured finance and mark-to-model accounting: a few simple illustrations. Account Horiz 25(3):559–576
Plantin G, Sapra H, Shin HS (2008) Marking-to-market: Panacea or pandora's box? J Account Res 46(2):435–460
Zandi M (2008) Financial shock: a 360o look at the subprime mortgage implosion, and how to avoid the next financial crisis. FT Press, New Jersey

Dr. Soner Gokten is an Assistant Professor at Department of Management, Faculty of Economics and Administrative Sciences, Baskent University, Ankara, Turkey. Dr. Gokten received a B.S. in Business Administration from the Baskent University, master's degree and Ph.D. in finance from the Gazi University, Ankara, Turkey. He specializes in structured finance, energy financial management, risk management and financial analysis. He has authored and co-authored many academic papers, books, research notes and columns. Dr. Gokten participated in national and international research projects as researcher, coordinator and manager.

Dr. Pinar Okan Gokten is a Research Assistant at Department of International Trade, Faculty of Economics and Administrative Sciences, Gazi University, Ankara, Turkey. Dr. Gokten received a B.S. in Business Administration from the Baskent University, master's degree and Ph.D. in accounting from the Gazi University, Ankara, Turkey. She specializes in financial accounting, cost accounting and positive accounting theories. She has authored and co-authored many academic papers and research notes.

Compliance and Reporting Trends: Essential Strategies

Semen Son-Turan

Abstract The digital age, with decreasing barriers to entry, paving the way for low-cost competition, saw an influx of new financial products and services globally. Soon the increasingly technology-driven financial landscape transformed itself with the democratization of finance diffusing to all levels of society. The standing rules and regulations of financial markets were confronted with an epitome of complexities marked by higher transparency, increased efficiencies, a wide range of substitutes, abundant information, a huge number of stakeholders and a bulk of aspiring entrepreneurs. However, a new game necessitates new rules, and a considerable disruption in old ways of doing is sure to witness unorthodox problems that need to be dealt with, and preferably foreseen, through a different lens. Sooner or later, these new digitally enhanced financial markets are destined to break down, dragging down everyone who once had faith in them, if not supported by proper compliance and corporate social performance and reporting standards. This chapter explores newly emerging trends in compliance and reporting standards for financial institutions.

1 Introduction

There is no doubt that stable financial institutions are indispensible for economic growth and job creation. However, the financial services industry has increasingly been challenged by the decline in trust of customers thanks to consecutive crises, frauds, regulatory pressures and disruptive innovations by non-traditional financial services providers. Also regulators are imposing more stringent control measures over businesses' operations to avoid a recurrence of the recent financial history that is marked by trouble and tragedy. Consequently, the presence of effective corporate

S. Son-Turan (✉)
Department of Business Administration, MEF University, Ayazaga Cad. No. 4, Maslak Sariyer, Istanbul, Turkey
e-mail: semen.son@mef.edu.tr

H. Dinçer, Ü. Hacioğlu (eds.), *Risk Management, Strategic Thinking and Leadership in the Financial Services Industry*, Contributions to Management Science, DOI 10.1007/978-3-319-47172-3_19

compliance structures and corporate social responsibility reporting standards have become sought-after elements by consumers and financial market participants as well.

The financial services industry, by its nature, is one of the most complex and dynamic industries with millions of customers and investors. Thus, it is also subject to more stringent control, compliance and reporting standards. Clearly, regulators have learned their lessons the hard way, especially from the recent financial crises. One of the most recent of such lessons was the 2008 sub-prime mortgage crisis (also called the 2008 financial crisis) leaving thousands of people jobless and homeless. Financial failures draw attention to previously unrecognized or neglected risks. Surely, governments and regulators are trying to foresee potential problem and mitigate possible risks. In such effort, the USA PATRIOT Act was passed in 2001. This Act serves multiple aims and includes a number of changes to US Law, one of which is to strengthen US measures to prevent and prosecute money laundering and financing of terrorism. Also, the Consumer Financial Protection Bureau (CFPB) was established as part of the Dodd–Frank Wall Street Reform and Consumer Protection Act of 2010. This independent agency is responsible for particularly protecting the financial services consumers. Another measure to regulate, assess and control financial institutions is a regulatory framework introduced by the Fed: The Comprehensive Capital Analysis and Review (CCAR). Besides laws and regulations, enhancement of compliance and risk management as well as reporting standards are standing agenda items for most institutions.

Culp (2015) for instance, sees an opportunity for the once relatively quiet back-office compliance function to play a more central role in helping banks, insurers and capital markets firms effectively deal with disruptive forces. However, he contends that while the financial services industry is experiencing disruptive change, compliance officers remain more focused on the priorities of yesterday. Basing his arguments on a risk study involving leading compliance officers at 150 financial institutions, Culp draws attention to the fact that 70 % of respondents said that managing the firm's reputation among shareholders, the public and the media is critical to their function; however 59 % of respondents said they did not see understanding technology trends as a skill likely to be needed by a compliance officer over the next five years.

Obviously, the financial landscape is changing swiftly, and both, system, service and product enhancement are required next to developed risk management and internal audit systems, proper stress testing, and continued adherence to capital adequacy rules to remain competitive. The increasing pressure to be more accountable (including social and environmental accountability), and more transparent in management and reporting has brought into focus the importance of issues such as corporate governance, integrated risk management, internal audit, and sustainability reporting, all of which go hand in hand to ultimately restore the trust lost in the financial services industry.

2 Background

According to the Internal Compliance Association,[1] the term compliance refers to the ability to act according to an order, a set of rules or a request. Accordingly, in the context of financial services, businesses compliance operates at two levels: (1) compliance with the external rules that are imposed upon an organization as a whole, (2) compliance with internal systems of control that are imposed to achieve compliance with the externally imposed rules.

Generally speaking, compliance, risk management and governance (or "GRC"), has been used as an umbrella term in many organizations. Compliance programs are usually designed to make sure that the businesses' activities do not violate established guidelines, laws and regulations. Risk management practices, on the hand, serve to identify, classify, measure, prevent or mitigate potential risks. Recognized as a distinct risk class requiring dedicated resources, program design, and oversight by senior management, The Basel Committee on Banking Supervision (2005) defines compliance risk as "the risk of legal or regulatory sanctions, material financial loss, or loss to reputation a bank may suffer as a result of its failure to comply with laws, regulations, rules, related self-regulatory organization standards, and codes of conduct applicable to its banking activities" (NYSSA 2010). The governance concept relates to whether the business operates in accordance with its predefined goals. Governance practices typically ensure that critical management information reaching the executive team is sufficiently complete, accurate and timely to enable appropriate management decision-making (Lamm et al. 2010).

Even though the corporate compliance function is said to be better developed in the financial services sector than in other industries, it continues to evolve (PwC 2014). The 2014 PwC Annual Survey on the state of compliance, which includes 222 financial institutions, identifies four themes that are thought to capture important elements w.r.t. compliance in the financial services industry: (1) Financial services organizations are devoting increasing attention and resources to compliance, (2) there is no consensus among financial services organizations as to where the chief compliance officer (CCO) fits in the organizational chart, (3) CCOs and compliance committees are challenged to better understand their organizations' business strategies, activities, and operations, and (4) CCOs are challenged to report compliance matters to the board and senior management in a way that supports their organizations' strategies.

Nowadays, compliance and ethics programs, particularly subsequent to notorious examples, such as Bear Stearns and Lehman Brothers, are integrated in company mission statements. This drive partially stems from the recognition that pure profit-seeking corporate behavior is no longer sustainable and needs to be complemented with societal goals.

---

[1] http://www.int-comp.org

3 Literature Review

Having emerged as "a common practice of 21st-century" (EY and Boston College Center for Corporate Citizenship 2013) sustainability reporting and can be regarded as a more evolved form of the established practices to ensure corporate accountability and transparency.

The consulting firm Ernst and Young[2] reports that 95 % of the Global 250 issue sustainability reports and that firms continuously seek new ways to improve performance, protect reputational assets, and win shareholder and stakeholder trust. And an analysis conducted by the Governance and Accountability Institute, a sustainability consulting firm, shows that, the number of companies in the S&P 500 Index that published a sustainability report, increased from 53 % in 2012 to 72 % percent in 2013 (Jaeger 2014).

For instance, Toyota provides very detailed sustainability reports on its website.[3] There, entire sections are dedicated towards reporting the company's corporate governance, risk management, compliance and environmental activities, among others. As an example, in the compliance section of its 2015 sustainability report, the company explains that, "Toyota will honor the language and spirit of the law of every nation and undertake open and fair corporate activities to be a good citizen of the world." It is through this process that Toyota seeks to fulfill the responsibilities expected of it, which leads to compliance. It also reiterates the Toyota Code of Conduct adopted in 1998 and presents its checking activities that are in place to enhance compliance (see Fig. 1).

Diverse regulations and guidelines seem to be in common agreement that it is senior management, who should be responsible for compliance. For instance, while The FCA Principles of Good Regulation suggest that "a firm's senior management is responsible for…ensuring that its business complies with regulatory requirements", the Basel Committee on Banking Supervision states that "The bank's senior management is responsible for establishing and communicating a compliance policy, for ensuring that it is observed, and for reporting to the board of directors on the management of the bank's compliance risk" (Mills and Haines 2015).

Prominent investment bank Goldman Sachs, divides its 2014 ESG Report[4] into sections such as environment (with risk management being a sub-section) and governance (under which a sub-section is dedicated to responsible and sustainable investing).

Evidently, more and more people and businesses are becoming aware that not only profit-oriented mission statements, but also a corporate picture that embraces social responsibility and sustainability, are critical for the subsistence of companies.

---

[2]http://www.ey.com/US/en/Services/Specialty-Services/Climate-Change-and-Sustainability-Services/Value-of-sustainability-reporting

[3]http://www.toyota-global.com/sustainability/report/sr/

[4]http://www.goldmansachs.com/citizenship/esg-reporting/esg-highlights-2014.pdf

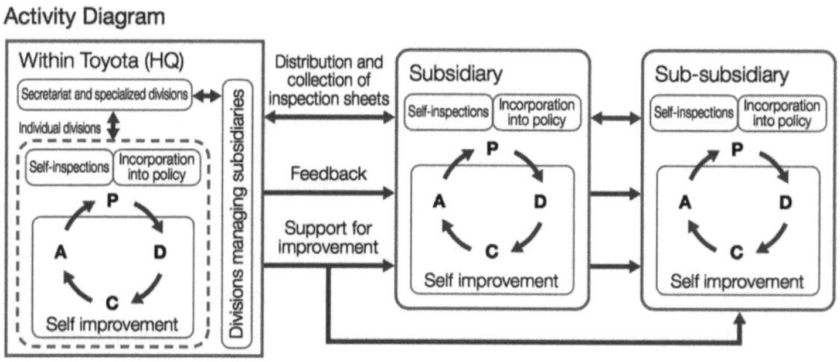

Fig. 1 Activity diagram. Source: Toyota Global, 2015 Sustainability Report 14-01

When the financial services industry is compared to other industries, the creation of a sustainable compliance program maybe even more essential especially due to the basic underlying trust issues, complex transactions and masses of stakeholders, which makes this respective industry relatively more prone to swindle and fraud.

Particularly stakeholders in financial services, and foremost customers and regulatory agencies, require detailed information about whether or not their institutions are meeting required standards and guidelines.

Clearly, the awareness and consequently, demands of customers and investors monitoring social, environmental and governance issues (referred to as "ESG", "sustainability" or "triple bottom-line"), have increased. According to Hohnen (2012), the proposition that organizations, and business organizations in particular, should supplement their financial accounting with accounting on their environmental, social and other 'non-financial' performance ("sustainability reporting"), first emerged in the 1990s, primarily instigated through calls from advocacy groups and investors, as well as business leaders and governments. During its initial years environmental issues were understood and addressed in sustainability reports. The United Nations Conference on Environment and Development (UNCED), also known as the Rio (de Janeiro Earth) Summit that took place in 1992, was a landmark in the history of sustainability reporting, that addressed environmental and climate issues. According to website of the Global Reporting Initiative ("GRI"),[5] sustainability reporting enables organizations to consider their impacts of wide range of sustainability issues, enabling them to be more transparent about the risks and opportunities they face. Sustainability reporting can be considered as synonymous with other terms for non-financial reporting; triple bottom line reporting (economic, social environmental), corporate social responsibility (CSR) reporting, and more.

Some of the providers of sustainability reporting guidance include:

- GRI (Global Reporting Initiative)

[5]https://www.globalreporting.org/information/sustainability-reporting/Pages/default.aspx

- The Organization for Economic Co-operation and Development (OECD Guidelines for Multinational Enterprises)
- The United Nations Global Compact
- The International Organization for Standardization ISO 26000
- International Integrated Reporting Committee

Experts estimate that sustainability oriented investments already account for about 20 % of the global market—with clear indications of continued growth.[6]

According to UNEP,[7] while there is no internationally agreed on definition of corporate sustainability reporting, it is generally understood as being the practice of measuring and disclosing sustainability information alongside, or integrated with, companies' existing reporting practices. Sustainability information can be understood as any information having to do with how companies use and affect financial, natural and human resources, and how their corporate governance is conducted. As explained in Seguis-Mas et al. (2015), since the second half of the twentieth century, a long debate on sustainability has been taking place. The authors argue that since the publication of the seminal book "Social Responsibilities of the Businessman" Bowen (2013), there has been a shift in terminology from the social responsibility of business to sustainability (Garriga and Melé 2004).

In a recent KPMG International global survey of 378 senior executives,[8] conducted in cooperation with the Economist Intelligence Unit, 62 % of companies surveyed have a strategy for corporate sustainability, and just over a third (36 %) have issued at least one public report on sustainability with another 19 % planning to do so soon. Stakeholders (investors, employees, customers, suppliers, and the community) and the capital markets are increasingly demanding better, more transparent communication of nonfinancial sustainability data.

Ernst and Young[9] reports that the wealth and asset management (WAM) industry is in the midst of a permanent global shift in its underlying activities. Firms that fail to adjust will face severe challenges to continued profitability and growth. Consequently, the WAM industry must consider a number of critical sustainability factors. These include the integration of environmental, social and governance factors into investment portfolios, responsible investment practices and sustainable indices and stock exchanges.

Finally, the table below provides a succinct summary of prominent academic research surrounding the theme of this chapter (Table 1).

---

[6]https://www.db.com/cr/en/concrete-Sustainable-banking-business---Ensuring-future-success-today.htm

[7]http://www.unep.org/resourceefficiency/Business/SustainableandResponsibleBusiness/CorporateSustainabilityReporting/tabid/78907/Default.aspx

[8]https://www.kpmg.com/US/en/IssuesAndInsights/ArticlesPublications/Documents/iarcs-sustainability-reporting-what-you-should-know.pdf

[9]http://www.ey.com/Publication/vwLUAssets/ey-fostering-sustainability-in-financial-services/$FILE/ey-emeia-financial-services-sustainability-report-2014.pdf

Table 1 Literature review

Author, year	Subject	Variables	Method of data collection	Research methodology	Findings
Ruf et al. (2001)	An empirical investigation of the relationship between change in corporate social performance and financial performance: A stakeholder theory perspective	Corporate social performance (CSP), financial accounting measures	Questionnaire, secondary data	Regression	Change in CSP is positively associated with growth in sales for the current and subsequent year. Return on sales is significantly positively related to change in CSP for the third financial period, indicating that long-term financial benefits may exist when CSP is improved.
Moore (2001)	Corporate social and financial performance: An investigation in the UK supermarket industry.	Corporate social performance (CSP), corporate financial performance (CFP).	Secondary data	Correlation, regression	There is a negative relationship between the two variables, with CFP deteriorating as CSP improves. Lagged CFP compared with overall CSP, however, shows an opposite trend suggesting positive association.
Konar and Cohen (2001)	Does the market value environmental performance?	Environmental performance, financial performance (intangible asset value), R&D expenditures, market shares	Secondary data	Regression	Poor environmental performance has a significant negative effect on intangible asset value of firms.
Orlitzky et al. (2003)	Corporate social and financial performance: A meta-analysis	Corporate social/environmental performance (CSP), corporate financial performance (CFP)	Survey, secondary data	Correlation	CSP appears to be more highly correlated with accounting-based measures of CFP than with market-based indicators, and CSP reputation indices are more highly correlated with CFP than are other indicators of CSP.

(continued)

Table 1 (continued)

Author, year	Subject	Variables	Method of data collection	Research methodology	Findings
Van Beurden and Gössling (2008)	The worth of values–a literature review on the relation between corporate social and financial performance	Corporate social responsibility (CSR), financial performance	Secondary data	Literature review	The results of the literature study performed here reveal that there is indeed clear empirical evidence for a positive correlation between corporate social and financial performance.
Orlitzky et al. (2011)	Strategic corporate social responsibility and environmental sustainability.	Corporate social responsibility (CSR), financial and economic performance	Secondary data	Archival—theoretical	Economic theories of strategic CSR have the greatest potential for advancing this field of inquiry, although theories of strategic leadership should also be incorporated into this perspective.
Coleman (2011)	Losses from failure of stakeholder sensitive processes: Financial consequences for large US companies from breakdowns in product, environmental, and accounting standards.	Environmental, social, governance (ESG) behavior and financial performance	Secondary data	Regression	Firms' sales margins will be damaged by unethical treatment of stakeholders as evidenced by ESG breaches.
Ettredge et al. (2011)	The effects of firm size, corporate governance quality, and bad news on disclosure compliance	Firm size, corporate governance quality, bad news, compliance with disclosure requirements	Secondary data	Regression	Noncompliant firms have lower quality corporate governance and less need for external financing but are not smaller than compliant control firms. Additional analyses indicate that compliance is negatively associated with bad news

As the table above suggests, adherence to corporate social responsibility standards and behaving ethically towards stakeholders is positively associated with corporate financial performance and firm value.

4 Conclusion

The financial services landscape is changing rapidly due to newer technologies, disruptive forces and the sentiment and demands of its customers, among others. Clearly financial institutions, to remain competitive and continue their subsistence, need to transform themselves in many aspects. Mostly, adherence to increasingly stringent compliance standards as well as voluntary disclosures on their social, environmental and governance practices, in the form of detailed sustainability reports, deem to be crucial in establishing the trust that has been lost in this industry as a result of a history of financial crises and corporate scandals.

References

Basel Committee on Banking Supervision (2005) Compliance and the compliance function in banks. http://www.bis.org/publ/bcbs113.pdf

Bowen HR (2013) Social responsibilities of the businessman. University of Iowa Press, Iowa

Coleman L (2011) Losses from failure of stakeholder sensitive processes: financial consequences for large US companies from breakdowns in product, environmental, and accounting standards. J Bus Ethics 98(2):247–258

Culp S (2015) Confronting disruptive forces, financial services firms need new approach to compliance. 23 Feb 2015. http://www.forbes.com/sites/steveculp/2015/02/23/confronting-disruptive-forces-financial-services-firms-need-new-approach-to-compliance/#74a2e565db04

Ettredge M, Johnstone K, Stone M, Wang Q (2011) The effects of firm size, corporate governance quality, and bad news on disclosure compliance. Rev Acc Stud 16(4):866–889

EY and Boston College Center for Corporate Citizenship (2013) Value of sustainability reporting. Retrieved from http://www.tksolution.net/media/394/Value-of-Sustainability-Reporting.pdf

Garriga E, Melé D (2004) Corporate social responsibility theories: mapping the territory. J Bus Ethics 53(1–2):51–71

Hohnen P (2012) The future of sustainability reporting. EEDP programme paper. Chatham House, London

Jaeger J (2014) Sustainability reporting on the rise. 5 June 2014 https://www.complianceweek.com/blogs/the-filing-cabinet/sustainability-reporting-on-the-rise-0#.VuFVCCSA3dk

Konar S, Cohen MA (2001) Does the market value environmental performance? Rev Econ Stat 83 (2):281–289

Lamm J, Blount S, Boston S, Camm M, Cirabisi R, Cooper N et al (2010) Under control. Apress, New York

Mills A, Haines P (2015) Essential strategies for financial services compliance. Wiley, New Jersey

Moore G (2001) Corporate social and financial performance: an investigation in the UK supermarket industry. J Bus Ethics 34(3–4):299–315

NYSSA (2010) Knowledge of good and evil: a brief history of compliance. 26 May 2010 http://post.nyssa.org/nyssa-news/2010/05/a-brief-history-of-compliance.html#sthash.kYFjrJPi.dpuf

Orlitzky M, Schmidt FL, Rynes SL (2003) Corporate social and financial performance: a meta-analysis. Organ Stud 24(3):403–441

Orlitzky M, Siegel DS, Waldman DA (2011) Strategic corporate social responsibility and environmental sustainability. Bus Soc 50(1):6–27

PwC (2014) State of compliance 2014. Financial services industry brief. Retrieved from https://www.pwc.com/us/en/risk-management/state-of-compliance-survey/assets/pwc-soc-financial-services.pdf

Ruf BM, Muralidhar K, Brown RM, Janney JJ, Paul K (2001) An empirical investigation of the relationship between change in corporate social performance and financial performance: a stakeholder theory perspective. J Bus Ethics 32(2):143–156

Seguis-Mas E, Bollas-Araya HM, Polo-Garrido F (2015) Sustainability assurance on the biggest cooperatives of the world: an analysis of their adoption and quality. Ann Public Coop Econ 86 (2):363–383

Van Beurden P, Gössling T (2008) The worth of values—a literature review on the relation between corporate social and financial performance. J Bus Ethics 82(2):407–424

Semen Son-Turan is an Assistant Professor of Business Administration at MEF University, Department of Business Administration, Istanbul, Turkey. Dr. Son-Turan has a BA in Political Science and International Relations from Bogazici University (1998), an MBA in Finance and Accounting from The Pennsylvania State University—The Smeal College of Business Administration (2000) and holds a PhD in Business Administration with a focus on Finance and Accounting from Yasar University (2014).

Dr. Son-Turan has held various managerial positions at prominent multinational companies and has extensive experience in the financial services industry. Her research interests include behavioral finance, capital markets, financial innovation and higher education finance. She has taught finance, financial and managerial accounting and strategy courses, among others, at US and Turkish institutions.

Developing a Risk Management Framework and Risk Assessment for Non-profit Organizations: A Case Study

Elif Karakaya and Gencay Karakaya

Abstract Risks in the rapidly increasing global business environment began to receive more attention among both researchers and practitioners illuminating the delicate balance between enterprise efficiencies and risk economies. However, Risk Management, in recent years, are becoming more complex to analyze and more challenging to manage and optimize.

Besides that, risk and uncertainty concept have always been a significant concern not only for private sectors and public sectors but also for non-profit organizations (NPOs) sector. In this chapter, the potential risks and their drivers are identified, assessed and ranked for a wide spread and most effective for a non-profit organization which aims to bring together native and foreign students for creating a bridge of humanity and education. After investigating the key control measures of major sources of risk, risk management processes and strategies were developed. To provide analytical results, Analytic Hierarchy Process (AHP) used by utilizing the questionnaire technique.

1 Introduction

With the rapid change in today's environment, risk management became more popular among NPOs with intent to increase the efficiency and besides to mitigate the negative effects of disturbances. Not only business environment and science always attached particular importance to risk issue, but also the concept of NPOs

E. Karakaya (✉)
Logistics Program, Vocational School of Social Science, Istanbul Medipol University, Kavacik Campus, Beykoz 34810, Istanbul, Turkey
e-mail: ekarakaya@medipol.edu.tr

G. Karakaya
Department of International Trade, Istanbul Commercial University, Sutluce Campus, Beyoglu 34445, Istanbul, Turkey
e-mail: gkarakaya@ticaret.edu.tr

H. Dinçer, Ü. Hacioğlu (eds.), *Risk Management, Strategic Thinking and Leadership in the Financial Services Industry*, Contributions to Management Science, DOI 10.1007/978-3-319-47172-3_20

increased its popularity in recent years due to complexity and increase in the amount of global interactions.

Beasley (2011) claims that having significant risk awareness results in better performance while governing an organization as a whole. In other words, executive staffs who realize that organizations, as well as non-profit ones, must assume that the importance of risk can go further their mission goals or objectives being more informed about the types of risks and their effects.

Young (2009) points out the problem clearly by saying that non-profit organizations did not take account of view of risk management into consideration adequately. He also puts forward in his comprehensive study that non-profit organizations are not able to take consequential decisions in a strategic level, even though they appear to take part in some studies concerned with stopping or reducing the negative effects of risks. Besides, Trivunovic et al. (2011) argue that until now, many international benefactors and the NPOs did not apply a comprehensive method to overcome an expected or unexpected corruption of risks. That is why; this study could be proposed as a structural framework in order to ensure that it is beneficial for practitioners or executive staffs of NPO throughout the implementation of the all steps of risk management.

This chapter is organized in the following way. This first section gives a brief overview of the recent history of risk management for NPOs and the second part deals with the potential risks and their drivers in the NPOs are identified. Thirdly, the determined potential risks are scored, assessed and ranked in terms of four objectives which are financial loss, growth, image and profit in order to find the most effective risks. Lastly, the suitable and applicable mitigation-methods are developed for handling the negative consequences of selected risk.

2 Literature Review

There is a large volume of published studies describing the risk management and the role of risk management even in the area of both business and science. So far, however, there were little discussions about application of risk management approach for NPOs. An extensive study in this field was provided by Jackson (2006). Although his book called Risk Management and Contingency Planning includes comprehensive theoretical explanations about risk management for NPOs and planning methods, there are no available empirical case studies.

Mohammed (2007) identifies potential risks and the ways of managing risks for an NPO that provides health and services for mental, intellectual and physical disability individuals. Young (2009) offers a conceptual framework by identifying the kinds of decisions in order to help non-profit organizations when they need to manage their risks in a strategic level.

Wilson-Grau (2004) implements risk management steps in a strategic level in order to help NPOs to achieve their mission or long term purposes. Gaudenzi and Borghesi (2006) provides a method to evaluate supply chain risks by using

Analytical Hierarchy Process (AHP) model. Chen (2010) provides mathematical model for non-profit organizations to compute and compare dysfunction situations. Trivunovic et al. (2011) prepare a comprehensive approach for international donor agencies or international NPOs to manage risks which may result in corruption. Matan and Hartnett (2011) analyze the types of risk which can more likely be seen in non-profit community. Although they support their paper with a case study, the evaluation and assessment steps are not explained comprehensively. Pehlivanli (2012) deals with enterprise risk management which gives a chance to non-profit organization leaders to ensure managing both external and internal risks across the organization. Carter and Demczur (2013) compose a legal risk management checklist for the directors or executive staff of non-profit organizations who desire to take account all required actions in the organization and to protect organization operations as the risks occur.

3 Risk Management for NPOs

Sitkin and Pablo (1992) define risk as "the extent to which there is hesitation whether potentially desired or insignificant/unwanted outcomes of decision will be realized". In other respects, Ritchie and Brindley (2007) formulate a principle of risk to assess (1) the probability of occurrence of certain outcomes (2) severity from the occurrence of event (3) the ability to detect the risk. It is put together in the notation below.

$$\text{Risk} = \text{Likelihood} \times \text{Severity} \times \text{Detection} \tag{1}$$

Boas (2012) defines risk for NPOs as anything that may have a negative impact on achieving your NPO's mission, goals, objectives and strategies if it becomes reality.

Risk Management is defined as "an organized process to identify what can go wrong, to quantify and assess associated risks, and to implement/control the appropriate approach for preventing or handling each risk identified" (INCOSE 2002). Matan and Hartnett (2011) have provided an extensive definition of Risk Management: "the process that is adopted to plan for the possibility that events may cause harm to an organization, focusing specifically on risk associated with board members and volunteers, staff, programs and events, services offered, operations, technology and financial management". Wilson-Grau (2003) claims that in this volatile environment, risk management is a tool for maximizing an NPO's opportunities and minimizing the dangers to success. It enables NPOs' decision-makers to think strategically all the time.

The key aspects of risk management can be listed under four topics, which are identifying and categorizing the risks, evaluating the available risks, deciding how to mitigate them and applying the necessary action.

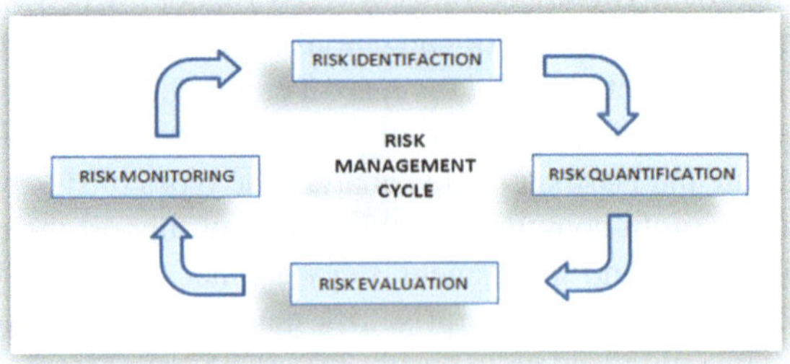

Fig. 1 Risk management steps

The risk management process is shown in Fig. 1 which can be repeated until the risks are kept inside the acceptable corridors. These steps are implemented incrementally within the scope of the study.

4 Case Studies

4.1 Risk Identification

Risk identification is the phase in which the risks are determined. All possible risks are collected in a list, then not only identification of risk conducted but also recognition the source or drivers of potential risks are carried out in this step.

A significant amount of literature published on categorization of possible risks or changes, in other words change drivers. An example of this kind of literature is carried out by Christopher and Peck (2004) who divide source of changes into five classes: environment, supply, demand, control and process. On the other hand, Tang and Tomlin (2008) diversify the classes by adding political, social and behavioural sources of risk. Some other studies attempted to classify the source of change as well, for example Chopra and Sodhi (2004), Harper (2012), Park (2011). Boas (2012) separate possible risks into three levels (1) Risks could be seen in the macro environment such as governmental legislation and regulations or shifting lifestyle, (2) Risks emerge in micro environment level and interruption of energy or required resources and cancelling donation or financial aid can be given as the example, (3) Risks happen inside the organization and effect directly as departure of staff members with high qualifications or poor decision making etc. Matan and Hartnett (2011) list risk as follows: Volunteer risk, financial risk, staffing risk, restricted grants risk, reputation risk.

To identify supply chain risks in our case study, the possible risks are identified through a series of brainstorming sessions with officials at executive level of the firm with guidance from related literature in the background. Within these sessions, six potential risk types are determined and listed with examples as follows.

1. Financial risk (economic crisis, insufficient donation)
2. Other associations risk (negative competition, lack of communication)

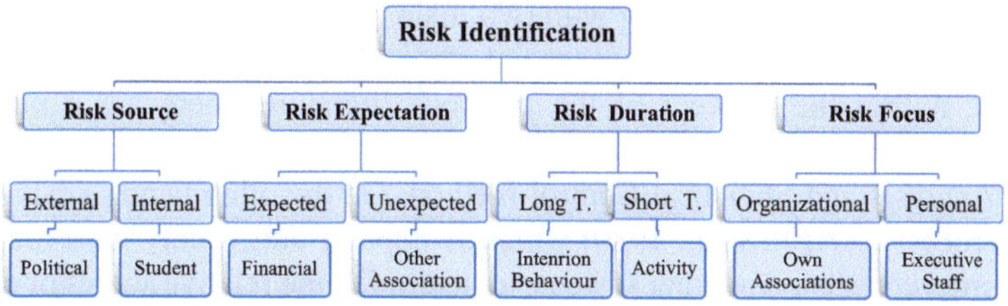

Fig. 2 Structure of potential risks for NPO

3. Own association risk (rapid growth, low performance due to high bureaucracy)
4. Student risk (lack of realizing the real necessary, inefficient student performance)
5. Executive staff risk (management deficiency, overloading)
6. Activity risk (ineffective and non-systematic working, unsuitable meeting place)
7. Political risk (political instability, legislations)
8. Intention and behaviour risk (different aim and purpose)

The identified risks are then put into a hierarchical structure as shown in Fig. 2. The structure of the hierarchy consists of three levels. While the top level represents the essential classification of available risks in terms of different risk properties. It consists of four main classes, which are namely risk source, risk expectation, risk duration and risk focus. The second level consists of two sub-classes of each fundamental risk features, as external and internal, expected and unexpected, long term and short term, organizational and personal. Finally, the bottom level includes one example for each subclass which is chosen from the case study.

In order to provide a better understanding of the above figure, the class of 'Risk Source' is explained in detail. Internal risks mean disruptions or dysfunctions originated from problems inside the bounds of NPOs such as electricity breakdowns or information technologies related problems. Within the concept of the case study, students which are the reason for establishment of the NPO could be accepted as an internal risk. External risks take notice of environmental causes that can implicitly or explicitly lead to disturbances within the NPO. Political risk, legislation or regulations can be given an example for external risk of our case. The probability of occurrence for internal supply chain risks is grater compared to external supply chain risk. On the other hand, external supply chain risks are more dangerous than internal supply chain risks.

4.2 *Risk Quantification*

Risk Quantification phase comes after the risks analyses in order to identify the prioritization of the risks affect. The well-known method is to measure the likelihood and the expected impact on the defined system. In other words, this assessment is essentially dealing with two main questions; first, "how likely a risk is" (i.e., the frequency of risk) and second, "how terrible risk can be" (i.e., severity of risk). Within the concept of the previous literature, there are a number of methods to quantify risks such as the Six Sigma Method, the Failure Modes and Effect Analysis and Statistical Control method. On the other hand, Analytic Hierarchy Process (AHP) (Saaty 1980) which is popular and widely used method for multi- criteria decision making systems to determine the relative scores of each risk factor. The model presented in this study utilizes the AHP to calculate the risks' scores to determine risks efficiently for the NPO.

The following Table 1 shows importance scale for pair wise comparisons of (risk xy) of two risk items (item x and item y). In other words, risk xy represents the comparison between item x and item y. If item y is 7 (very strong importance) times more important than item x, then the comparison of risk yx = 1/7.

4.3 Risk Evaluation

The evaluation objective is determined as a selection of the most effective risk. The evaluation criteria are financial losses, image, growth and quality of organization while the alternative risks are listed as follows:

- Financial risk
- Other associations risk
- Own associations risk
- Student risk
- Executive staff risk
- Activity risk
- Political risk
- Intentional and behaviour risks

As it was stated before that AHP method which is used as an evaluation technique in order to figure out the most significant risk consists of three phases.

1. Comparison of objectives is the first phase in which a matrix is established where columns represent the predetermined alternative risks and rows include the evaluation criterion. The value of pairwise comparisons which are collected from experts of the organization in terms of four main objectives; financial loses, growth, image and profit are input inside the matrix. Table 2 given below shows the compact of the illustration of the matrix.
2. Building normalization matrix phase includes some mathematical calculations to specify the relative weights of the decision criteria. In order to normalize the criteria, each value of paired comparisons divided by the summation of the columns and then the average of rows refer to the relative weight of each risk type. All calculations are presented in Table 3 below.

Table 1 Scale of importance

Intensity of importance	Definition	
1	Equal importance	Two factors contribute equally
3	Moderate importance	1. Factor slightly favours over 2. Factor
5	Strong importance	1. Factor strongly favours over 2. Factor
7	Very strong importance	1. Factor is favoured very strongly over 2. Factor
9	Extreme importance	1. Factor is favoured in the highest possible way
2, 4, 6, 8		Intermediate value

3. Ranking of the weighted alternatives is the last phase in which all calculated scores of each risk factor depending on evaluation criterion are shown in a same chart. To define the most important risk types, firstly, the summation of the risk factors taken in terms of financial losses, image and growth. In the second step, the relative rankings (priorities) of alternatives were determined. It is apparent from the obtained results that the *Financial Risk* is specified as a most effective risk than others in our case study. The final results are summarized in Table 4 below.

   The results can be summarized as follows.

1. The results identify the financial risk as the most important risk factor since the score of financial risk is the highest score for all the tables. The NPO should deal with ways to mitigate this risk. Moreover, lots of interpretations can be made about the results of tables:
2. The financial risk is for sure the most effective risk in financial losses. In other words, if the NPO makes a monetary mistake, the most apparent damage is the cost rather than image and profit.
3. Activity risk and own association risks are more significant from the aspect of the NPO's image. The reason is that the NPO is known with their spectrum of activities; therefore, the impact of activity risk is directly linked with reputation of the company.
4. In order to make company grow, the NPO should arrange the economic situations like fees or donations in a balanced way to decrease the financial risk.
5. In the same way, the financial risk affects the company's quality negatively. Losing benefactors or declining number of students is the unwanted situation for all NPOs. Thus, the company scores significant loss in its quality when an unbalanced situation occurs for financial resources.
6. It can be concluded that internal risks cause more hazard than external risks owing to the fact that the possibility of external risks is much lower.
7. To conclude, considering the whole risk results, the financial risk should be immediately mitigated. It is suggested that the NPO should take precautions and measures for eliminating or at least reducing these risks.

Table 2 The comparison of objectives, using the AHP method

Financial losses	Financial risk	Other associations risk	Own association risk	Student risk	Executive staff risk	Activity risk	Political risk	Intention and Behaviour risk
Financial risk	1	5	3	7	3	8	6	9
Other associations risk		1	5	3	1/5	1/2	1/6	2
Own association risk			1	6	1	4	3	3
Student risk				1	1/6	1/4	1/4	1
Executive staff risk					1	4	3	5
Activity risk						1	1/6	4
Political risk							1	7
Intention and behaviour risk								1

Table 3 An example of "Normalized Matrix" during AHP application procedure

Normalized matrix for financial losses	Financial risk	Other associations risk	Own association risk	Student risk	Executive staff risk	Activity risk	Political risk	Intention & Behaviour risk	Total	Average	Measure (%)
Financial risk	0.41	0.25	0.27	0.22	0.49	0.33	0.44	0.28	2.69	0.34	**34**
Other associations risk	0.08	0.05	0.45	0.09	0.03	0.02	0.01	0.06	0.81	0.10	**10**
Own association risk	0.14	0.01	0.09	0.19	0.16	0.17	0.22	0.09	1.07	0.13	**13**
Student risk	0.06	0.02	0.02	0.03	0.03	0.01	0.02	0.03	0.21	0.03	**3**
Executive staff risk	0.14	0.25	0.09	0.19	0.16	0.17	0.22	0.16	1.37	0.17	**17**
Activity risk	0.05	0.10	0.02	0.13	0.04	0.04	0.01	0.13	0.52	0.06	**6**
Political risk	0.07	0.30	0.03	0.13	0.05	0.25	0.07	0.22	1.12	0.14	**14**
Intention and Behaviour risk	0.05	0.02	0.03	0.03	0.03	0.01	0.01	0.03	0.22	0.03	**3**
Total	1	1	1	1	1	1	1	1	8	1	

Table 4 The weights of risk factors

	Financial losses (%)	Image (%)	Growth (%)	Quality (%)	Total (%)	Priority
Financial risk	34	11	30	30	105	1
Own association risk	13	20	18	18	69	2
Executive staff risk	17	7	14	17	55	3
Activity risk	6	21	11	9	48	4
Intention and behaviour risk	3	19	13	13	48	5
Other associations risk	10	9	3	4	26	6
Political risk	14	4	3	3	25	7
Student risk	3	8	8	5	24	8

4.4 Risk Mitigation

Risk Mitigation is the phase in which mitigation decisions are taken to stop or at least reduce the effects of risks. This phase is composed of many mitigation strategies and new implementation plans for undesired event occurrences.

After evaluation of risk alternatives, the risk management plan is documented, justified and described. Also the chosen treatments are described. During this process allocated responsibilities are recorded, monitored and evaluated, and assumptions on residual risks are made. To handle possible risks, the following suggestions might be offered for the NPO organizations:

- Financial risk
  - Finding new financial resources
  - Effortless and inexpensive transportation vehicles to reach activity location
  - Ensuring the more transparent financial structure for expense awareness
- Activity risk
  - The increased quantity and diversity of activities to support recognisability
  - Announcement of activities by using all social media opportunities
  - Sufficient speakers for the educational activities
  - Academic and systematic education or training
- Student risk
  - Acceptable and appropriate activities for all kind of students
  - Carrying out activities in a harmonized atmosphere
  - Out of town trips for country introduction

The impact of mitigation plans should be monitored. For many reasons, an organization should have a dynamic control system on managing risks in an organization and frequent system updates by applying some other changes within the system or in the environment.

5 Conclusions

This chapter explained the central importance of risk management for NPOs. One of the more significant findings to emerge from this study is that an analytical approach and risk management framework is provided for NPOs. By means of these findings of the study, NPOs will be able to increase the efficiency of its organization and reduce the risk of major possible malfunctions simultaneously.

References

Beasley M (2011) Increasing risk awareness for mission critical objectives of not-for-profit organizations. American Institute of Certified Public Accountants, Durham

Boas K (2012) Building capacity in NGO risk management. Retrieved from http://www.thesustainablengo.org/

Carter TS, Demczur JM (2013) Legal risk management checklist for non- for-profit organizations. Carters Professional Corporation, Ottawa, Toronto

Chen L (2010) Risk management for nonprofit organizations. Oregon State University, Corvallis

Chopra S, Sodhi MS (2004) Managing risk to avoid supply-chain breakdown. MIT Sloan Manag Rev 46(1):53–62

Christopher M, Peck H (2004) Building the resilient supply chain. Int J Logist Manag 2:1–13

Gaudenzi B, Borghesi A (2006) Managing risks in the supply chain using the AHP method. Int J Logist Manag 17(1):114–136

Harper TJ (2012) Agent based modeling and simulation framework for supply chain risk management. Dissertation, Air Force Institute of Technology

INCOSE (2002) What is "Risk". Risk Management Working group, Hall, DC

Jackson P (2006) Nonprofit risk management and contingency planning. Wiley, New Jersey

Matan R, Hartnett B (2011) How nonprofit organizations manage risk. Sobel & Co, Livingston

Mohammed KM (2007) Managing risk: a case study of a non-governmental organization that provides long- term care and support service for people with mental, intellectual and physical disabilities. Massey University, Palmerston North

Park K (2011) Flexible and redundant supply chain practices to build strategic supply chain resilience: contingent and resource-based perspectives. Dissertation, The University of Toledo

Pehlivanli D (2012) Kâr Amacı Gütmeyen Kuruluslarda Kurumsal Risk Yönetimi ve Risk Çalıstayı Vaka Çalısması. Muhasebe ve Finasman Dergisi:117–128

Ritchie B, Brindley C (2007) Supply chain risk management and performance: a guiding framework for future development. Int J Oper Prod Manag 27(3):303–322

Saaty TL (1980) The analytic hierarchy process. St. Louis ua, New York

Sitkin SB, Pablo AL (1992) Reconceptualizing the determinants of risk behavior. Acad Manag Rev 17(1):9–38

Tang C, Tomlin B (2008) The power of flexibility for mitigating supply chain risks. Int J Prod Econ 116(1):12–27

Trivunovic M, Johnsøn J, Mathisen H (2011) Developing an NGO corruption risk management system: considerations for donors. U4 Issue, 2011(9)

Wilson-Grau R (2003) The risk approach to strategic management in development NGOs. Dev Pract 13(5):533–536

Wilson-Grau R (2004) Strategic risk management for development NGOs: the case of a grantmaker. Seton Hall J Dipl and Int'l Rel. 5:125

Young DR (2009) How nonprofit organizations manage risk. In: Musella SD (ed) Paid and unpaid labour in the social economy. Georgia State University, Georgia

Elif Karakaya is a Lecturer in Logistics Program of Vocational School of Social Science at Istanbul Medipol Unıversity. Dr- Ing Karakaya has a BS in Industrial Engineering and Computer Engineering from İstanbul Kültür Unıversity (2008), a MS from Fatih University (2011), a Ph.D. in Industrial Engineering from Dortmund Technical University (2015). Her research areas are Simulation Programming especially Agent- Based Simulation, Manufacturing, Warehouse systems, Statistics Analysis, Supply Chain Management and Logistics. She has taught Statistics, Production Planning, Logistics Management, and Physical Distribution Channels and Planning

Gencay Karakaya is a Research Assistant at Istanbul Commerce University Department of International Trade, Istanbul-Turkey. Karakaya has a BS in Business Administration from Sakarya University (2011), an MBA from Istanbul Commerce University (2014). Karakaya is a Ph.D. student in Accounting and Auditing from Istanbul Commerce University. His research interests; international trade, financial accounting system, auditing, internal control, international financial report system and financial risk.

Part V
Culture and Leadership in Risk Management

Giving Risk Management Culture a Role in Strategic Planning

Tuba Bozaykut-Bük

Abstract Strategically planned and implemented risk management paves the way for competitive advantage and a decisive edge for global financial institutions. The importance of risk management becomes more evident in financial instability periods. The failure of global financial institutions in the recent financial crisis revealed that firms with strong risk management and culture were more prepared and economically less damaged. As financial institutions have been criticized severely about risk management practices, it also becomes clear that most financial institutions have difficulties in developing a risk management culture. To have a clear understanding of risk management culture, the chapter aims to highlight a need to extend our understanding of risk management culture and how it can find a voice in the strategic planning of global financial institutions.

1 Introduction

Risk management has always been a top priority issue for financial institutions in terms of enhancing performance (Krause and Tse 2016), competitive advantage (Fiegenbaum and Thomas 2004) and increasing value provided to the shareholders (Cooper 2000). As it is well proposed, risk management constitutes one of the most important veins of survival, attainment of strategic goals and an important determinant of success in financial turmoil. Along this line of thinking, financial firms approach risk management as a strategic tool both in their daily operations and in crisis preparedness, detection and prevention because of its continuous evaluation of environmental threats.

The one thing researchers reach a consensus on is that doing business means taking risks and risk is a "strategic issue" (Clarke and Varma 1999). As the risk

T. Bozaykut-Bük (✉)
Department of Business Administration, School of Business and Management Sciences, Istanbul Medipol University, Kavacik Campus, Istanbul, Turkey
e-mail: tbozaykut@medipol.edu.tr

H. Dinçer, Ü. Hacioğlu (eds.), *Risk Management, Strategic Thinking and Leadership in the Financial Services Industry*, Contributions to Management Science, DOI 10.1007/978-3-319-47172-3_21

management has a role in gains and losses of the firm, the value created and offered to shareholders is directly linked to risk management practices (Elahi 2013). The shareholders' aim is to have higher returns in lending or investing their capital. They expect managers to take risks, but at the same time; they refrain from making investments in the institutions that would take great risks for these returns. The artistry of risk management comes from the difficulty of satisfying the shareholder demand of higher returns without losing the shareholder trust.

To develop a strong risk management culture is of strategic importance to the success of risk management. According to the worldly accepted regulators of financial markets such as Institute of International Finance (IIF), not having a proper risk management culture strategically set is one of the main reasons why many global banks and other financial institutions faced with the catastrophic economic consequences of the recent crisis. On the other hand, institutions with strong risk management culture had the chance to overcome the crisis and surpass their competitors. Hence, it is now evident that to set, manage and assess the risk management culture is both a challenging issue and a source for competitive advantage for today's financial institutions.

Risk management culture refers to common norms and values related with risk identification, management and assessment within the organization (IIF 2009). Also, risk management culture is an organization-wide issue (Elahi 2013) and has to be designed according to the risk attitudes and behaviors defined strategically in order to attain corporate objectives. Likewise, firms need to introduce analytical and statistical tools for risk assessment as well as they have to make employees get familiar with the common language and the tone of the behavior in identifying and managing risks. Thereby, all these factors make risk management culture a strategic issue. To identify certain attitudes and behaviors related with the risks faced and to embed risk management culture throughout the firm, risk management culture should find its place in strategic planning.

In the chapter, the risk management's significance to financial institutions is firstly discussed. Then, risk management and factors for enhancing risk management are highlighted. The chapter continues through the examination of risk management culture together with strategic planning and ends with final remarks and implications on the topic.

2 Global Financial Institutions and Risk Management

Risk is defined by diverse disciplines with their own unique lenses. The finance theorists approach risk in three manners (Cooper 2000). The first approach evaluates risk as an "opportunity" and asserts that the gain will increase as the risks increase. According to this perspective; for more profit, the institution would have to undertake greater risks. Conversely, risk as "hazard or threat" connotes negative meanings as failure or loss. Approaching risk as something to be avoided, the institution would use techniques to refrain from situations that would put them in a risky position on the sake of benefitting from the potential advantages of risks (March and Shapira 1987). The third approach, namely the futuristic point-of-view, takes risk as "uncertainty" that can bring both positive and negative outcomes. The main point of the approach is to minimize the difference between what is expected and what is attained by the risky operations. In line with the third perspective, researchers associate risk with a decision making process about the future (Cooper 2000). In other words, the notion of future refers to uncertainty and the claim for controlling the uncertainties lies in the essence of risk management (Power 2007; Cooper 2000). Also, to some authors, risk is the various combinations of these approaches. For instance, risk can refer to "uncertainty" with negative consequences (Elahi 2013).

Similar with risk approaches, there is a traditional and a modern way of thought on risk management. Traditional risk management approach risk negatively and propose that risk would harmful or costly effects on the firm (Elahi 2013). Conversely, modern risk management thinking is in the manner of seeing risks as a positive phenomenon that would create improvement and growth as the creativity level of the firm would increase (Bowers and Khorakian 2014). Meanwhile some studies support the notion that firms that have enriched risk capabilities stand one step ahead of its rivals in the market and have greater competitive advantage (Elahi 2013).

Another matter to be mentioned is the dilemma that resides in the risk taking behavior. From time to time under different conditions, the risk appetite of the firms can rise or decline. Being always either on the risk-averse side or on the risk-lover side can also have hazardous effects on the survival and the competitiveness of the firms (Kahneman and Lovallo 1993; Fiegenbaum and Thomas 2004). Whether to take that risk is a big question to answer and requires a detailed analysis in diverse perspectives. In that decision making process, another problem encountered is the bounded rationality issue. From the bounded rationality lenses (Simon 1972; March 1978), the firm cannot control every factor that can affect its operations and has to give decisions depending on its limited knowledge. Although there are statistical and scenario-based methods for measuring risks, it is not possible to estimate every single factor in the market and the results of risk taking behavior can be the Schrodinger's cat paradox for financial institutions.

Through a closer gaze on the global financial institutions (GFIs), it can be proposed that GFIs need to manage diverse risks encountered not only in their constant daily operations but also have to be prepared at the strategic level when faced with crises. To create a risk management culture, a financial firm needs to identify the risks to be encountered. For instance, risks encountered by banks are defined as credit risk, country and transfer risk, market risk, interest rate risk, liquidity risk, operational risk, legal risk and reputational risk by Basel 1998 Framework (Cooper 2000). Basel 1998 Framework also offers an internal control system that would detect and control risks listed for banks. Similarly, Bilal et al. (2013) in their paper on re-modelling of risk management in banking summarizes the process for control mechanisms recommended after the global financial crisis as such: "To ensure the circumvent from potential risks, the Banking Supervisory

Committee has taken up Basel Accord-I in 1988, followed by Basel Accord-II in 2004 and the recent agreement of Basel Accord-III in 2010 in which global regulatory standards are developed on market liquidity risks, capital adequacy and stress testing in order to introduce new regulatory requirements on "leverage" and "liquidity" of financial institutions" (p.469).

The new regulations and new technological tools for assessing market and non-market risks help to prevent the unexpected consequences of the financial instabilities. However; with every crisis it becomes more evident that GFIs need more than technological or analytical control systems and tools for the uncontrolled or unanticipated risks. To overcome the unanticipated risk especially faced at economic crises, risk management culture expressed in the strategic planning of the firm would be a strong hand of mitigation of damages. Besides these standards and analytical techniques, firms should adopt a certain set of norms and common attitude related to risks. When supported by a commonly accepted and implemented risk management culture, risk management practices would reach to a success. Therefore, for the long term success, having a strong risk management culture comes forth as a big asset for GFIs.

3 Risk Management Culture

Like many terms in social sciences, it is difficult to define what "risk management culture" (RMC) is. To have a broad understanding of the meaning of "risk management culture", it would be enlightening to focus firstly on the term, organizational culture. Since Peters and Walterman's (1982) inspiring work, *In Search for Excellence*, organizational culture is approached as something to be managed (Willcoxson and Millett 2000). Peters and Walterman (1982) suggest that if managed well, organizational culture would help organizational performance to be enhanced and competitive advantage would be gained over competitors. After a decade, Schein (1992: 12) with his study entitled *Organizational Culture and Leadership* attracts the attention to the organization's relations to external environment and defines the organizational culture as:

> A pattern of shared basic assumptions that the group learned as it solved its problems of external adaptation and internal integration that has worked well enough to be considered valid and, therefore, to be taught to new members as the correct way to perceive, think, and feel in relation to those problems.

As by internal integration, Schein refers to forming a collective identity among members, and by external integration, the corporate's interaction with others as it strives for achieving its goals. Through his definition, Schein implies that culture is not a closed but dynamic system evolving according to other factors in the environment.

In the finance literature, it is seen that many related terms such as "risk culture", "risk management culture" and "strategic risk management" are referred in the studies. To McConnell (2013) different terms are used for RMC because institutions have different layers of culture related with different risk perceptions. Thereby, to McConnell (McConnell 2013: 36), the 'risk culture' refers to how individuals within an organization approach risk and 'risk management culture' addresses specifically to the culture of the risk management group(s) and its interactions with the organization; and we can also talk about a culture of 'risk-taking' in organizations.

In some other works, authors use the term of risk-oriented culture. The awareness of risks and of the ways to approach risk at all levels of the organization means that organization has a risk-oriented culture. Similarly, to create and develop a risk-oriented culture may require an "organizational paradigm shift" through which the organization revises itself in order to develop risk management and vision as a core competency (Cooper 2000: 19). To achieve this paradigm shift, an awareness of the risk types faced by the institution should be developed (Girling 2013). That's to say, employees and managers at all levels are expected to have the awareness of what risks are encountered, how they are assessed and controlled (Girling 2013).

Although admitting there is no consensus on a definition, IIF (2009) defines risk culture as such: "risk culture is the set of norms and traditions of behavior of individuals and of groups within an organization, that determine the way in which they identify, understand, discuss, and act on the risks the organization confronts and the risks it takes". Along with this definition as with others, it is still difficult to suggest a prescription for developing a risk culture environment when taking into consideration the contingencies specific to each institution (Institute of International Finance 2008). Contingencies do really matter so it would be difficult to define an "ideal risk culture model"; yet it is possible to talk about some common elements that would help to create a RMC. In their studies, many researchers outline some factors that help to flourish a strong risk management culture. As to the studies, for instance, the role of managers is an important facilitator of RMC in the GFIs (McConnell 2013; Girling 2013; Geretto and Pauluzzo 2015). What's more, managers' attitude towards risk is another element that comes to the forefront. Especially the managers who approach risks negatively would definitely affect the development of risk management and culture. March and Shapira's study (1987) is a significant example of this assumption and it empirically indicates that managers mainly focus on the potential losses instead of potential gains.

On the organizational level, RMC is a governance issue strategically designed by top managers (De Marchi and Ravetz 1999). Specially, The Chief Risk Officer (CRO) has an influential part on the cultivation of RMC. CRO has the role to develop and reinforce risk culture by interacting with managers and the Board (IIF 2013). On the individual level, RMC is related with some ethical issues as the bad behavior or showing indifference towards risks. As individuals, members have to detect, speak out loud and document risks, and be responsible about factors threatening the risk management culture of the institution (Ashby et al. 2012; Girling 2013).

As an organization-wide issue, developing a RMC covers all members from top to the bottom. Strictly speaking, the rationale behind RMC is to furnish all members with the mentality to identify, understand, manage and assess the risks. All members should feel responsibility and accountability in managing risks. Hence; risk must be the concern of all at every level of the organization and its presence should be felt from strategic planning to daily operations (IIF 2012; Girling 2013; Geretto and Pauluzzo 2015).

Another important factor for RMC development is to create a language of risk for mutual understanding. The common language is a facilitator for establishing set of values among members and it also can get things done or understood more quickly by not letting managers spend too much time in communicating risk issues within the organization (Espersen 2007). Further, a high quality of information flow is another significant element for an effective RMC. The easiness of asking questions and not hesitating to raise voices are clear signs of a healthy organizational communication. IIF (2009: 31) specifies the importance of communication in such sentences: "...a risk culture depends not only on both formal and informal channels for employees to raise these questions but also on their being accountable for those who do or do not step forward". Similarly in a recent report on risk culture, IIF (2013: 2) points out that the attitude of "bad news must travel faster than good news" should be embedded in the governance of the firm. Along with the issues mentioned in the IIF reports, a need to create awareness about the key concepts and training should be on the agenda to keep members updated about risk related issues within the organization.

The use of incentives and other human resource practices that promote the ethical way of approaching risks also are offered as factors for developing RMC (Geretto and Pauluzzo 2015). Through the use of incentives that would promote ethical working manners, all employees would know how to act in cases of uncertainties or when faced with any type of risks. Besides HR practices, the alignment of organizational goals with the objectives of risk management, the managerial and personal attitudes towards risk, high quality communication, awareness of the significance of a sound risk management are listed as the other facilitating factors of creating and developing a RMC at financial institutions (Geretto and Pauluzzo 2015).

A strong risk management culture has also some positive consequences on firms. To exemplify, Oliver Wyman & RMA (2010) provided empirical evidence that GFIs with strong RMC have better business performance and innovation capability during the financial crisis. IIF (2013: 2) also affirms that strong risk culture in firms is essential to "their safety and soundness and to financial stability".

4 The Role of Risk Management Culture in Strategic Planning

Likewise the term culture, "strategy" is mainly interested with the relation of organization and environment and the basic premise is that organizations develop strategies to cope with the changes in the environment (Mintzberg 1994). For instance, the adaptive model of strategy implies that organizations have to be active and not solely cope with the environment but "change with the environment" (Chaffee 1985: 92). Hence, culture and strategy are two terms propounded as means for dealing with changes in the environment.

Studies suggest that institutions engage more with strategic planning process if the environment is complex and the rate of the change in the environment is increasing (Bird 1991; Steiner 1979; Hopkins and Hopkins 1997). The economic ups and downs are examples of transition periods in which institutions return to their strategic planning and are more deeply concerned with the process. For instance to overcome the economic turmoil of the recent global crisis, top managers have started to develop their strategic plans on the risk governance mechanisms (Cooper 2000).

Strategic planning is "an iterative, comprehensive and systematic approach to developing a firm's overall direction, one that allows 'management to analytically determine an appropriate strategic path for the whole organization'" (Andersen 2000: 185). To Mintzberg (1994), strategic planning has the technical aspect of strategic management and it is associated with analysis. Further mission, vision, goals and values constitute the base of a strategic plan and strategic planning is the "road map of the organization determining where the organization is now to where it would like to be in five or ten years" (Bouhali et al. 2015: 74). With a future projection in mind, strategic planning sets a direction to achieve organizational goals through analysis.

Basically a strategic planning has three main processes (Hopkins and Hopkins 1997: 637): "(1) formulation, which includes developing a mission, setting major objectives, assessing the external and internal environments, and evaluating and selecting strategy alternatives (2) implementation and (3) control". Through these processes, the strategic planning also serves a symbolic function in developing cognitive maps for common understanding (Duncan and Dutton 1987). To some studies, strategic planning also serves a symbolic function in developing cognitive maps for common understanding (Duncan and Dutton 1987). Besides developing mission, vision and objectives; the values and standards of behavior in doing business are also identified and developed in the strategic planning. To illuminate this issue, IIF (2013: 2) implies that the Board has to be sure that culture fits the business model and asks themselves constantly "What is the organization doing to support things that we value? What are we doing to deter things that we don't value? Do we have an organization that is constantly risk aware?"

In the strategic planning, it is critical to determine the major risks faced, determine the risk tolerance level of the firm and how to control these risks through internal and external environment analysis (IIF 2009; Holmquist 2012). Especially the recognition of risks related to the business strategy is of great importance at this stage (IIF 2009). After identifying these major issues of risk management, the manner and behaviors of the employees should be identified as to create mutual understanding of risk and to form a common set of values and attitudes in managing risks. In a RMC, members have the responsibility and accountability of the risks they face and take precautions against not to eliminate but to control these risks (Cooper et al. 2011; IIF 2009). As a consequence, RMC consists of dynamic processes that require the whole organization's participation.

In a dynamic environment, it is expected that the employees of GFIs should internalize the common premises of the risk management culture so as to follow the strategic plans. If financial institutions expect their members to detect and manage risks in their daily operations in an ethical manner, the tools and symbolic actions for a risk-oriented climate should be set in their strategic planning (IIF 2013). Besides the role of CRO, the meetings or forums for discussing risks or introducing analytical tools for managing risks are all to be set up in the strategic planning (IIF 2009; Cooper et al. 2011).

To lighten the significance of RMC in the strategic planning, the global economic crisis of 2007–2009 can be an example. The crisis demonstrated that the risks were not calculated as they had been and firms were not behaving ethically. What's more, many did not adopt sound risk management awareness and culture that should have supported daily operations. Though believed to have efficient risk calculation techniques and methodologies, GFC pointed out that the relevant skills had not been developed to embed risk management in the organizational structure and culture (Girling 2013 Geretto and Pauluzzo 2015). In line with this, regulators of financial markets all around the world such as US Financial Crisis Inquiry Commission or UK Parliamentary Inquiry pointed out the missing link of cultural support as one of the paramount reasons why institutions face the global financial crisis (McConnell 2013). After the crisis, although the problems with the risk modeling have been tried to be solved by the regulations based on Basel standards, yet; it is still a search to how to set up the risk management culture and risk management practices (Bilal et al. 2013). Also recent researches interestingly have showed the fact that GFIs still lack the mentality of risk management culture. For instance, Geretto and Pauluzzo (2015) study the risk management of 50 large banking companies around the world and find out that GFIs still evaluate risk management mainly as "financial trading or insurable risks"; "something negative, or to be avoided without having a clear risk organization responsibilities or culture" (p.313).

As the crisis proved, it is vital to give an effort for developing RMC in the strategic planning of the firm. This would not only provide an alignment of culture and strategy but also help to increase firm performance and value creation to the shareholders in the long run. In brief, to have a strong risk management culture requires a strategic thinking and planning approach for long term success and when strategically formed, RMC would minimize the negative consequences of the economic fluctuations.

5 Conclusion

One of the topics raised by governments and regulators is how financial institutions approach risks and the "criticality" of the implementation and improvement of risk management. The complex and turbulent business environment makes it difficult to manage risks, requiring a more detailed approach for an effective risk management. Thereby, risk management and culture embedded in strategic planning can be be an enhancer of sustainable competitive advantage while firms react to the threats and opportunities in the environment.

The recent global crisis revealed that global financial institutions failed in behaving ethically and the risk management of these firms had many shortcomings. Especially, the banking sector is criticized severely in not having a strong risk management structure and culture supporting the corporate strategies. It is now clear that the risk management has to be supported culturally and GFIs have to approach risk management also as a "cultural phenomenon". All in all, to achieve competitive advantage and create value to shareholders, GFIs have to develop solid risk management culture.

Because of the increased significance risk management attained after the global crisis, banks and other financial institutions aim to form a risk management culture strategically. To do this, in their strategic planning, firms map how to flourish risk management culture on instrumental and symbolic level. On the instrumental level, analytical tools to be used in detecting and controlling risks are introduced. Further to that, the common jargon and attitude in approaching risk has to be implemented throughout the organization for the symbolic level.

As a solution to the problem of how to implement a strong risk management culture, it is suggested that firms have to identify their risks, risk appetite and the tolerance level in their strategic planning. Besides, the articulation of these critical factors to the members by top management is indicated as an important factor to create the base for a mutual risk understanding and behavior. Also, Chief Risk Officer and Board have pivotal roles on the development of risk management culture. The use of analytical tools and the acceptance of common set of norms and values in assessing risks are the main elements of the risk management culture. Yet, for today's managers, it is a highly challenging mission to form the risk management culture within their organizations.

This chapter has set out to attract attention to risk management culture and its place in the strategic planning. Being the compass of the firms, strategic planning process should also cover the cognitive terrains and should direct tools, techniques, attitudes and behaviors for developing risk management culture. The literature is weak in explaining the cultural aspect of risk management. It is hoped that the alignment of risk management culture with strategic thinking and planning would be examined from diverse perspectives in the future studies.

References

Andersen TJ (2000) Strategic planning, autonomous actions and corporate performance. Long Range Plan 33:184–200

Ashby S, Palermo T, Power M (2012) Risk culture in financial organisations: an interim report. Centre for Analysis of Risk and Regulation and The University of Plymouth, London

Bird A (1991) A 1990s twist on strategic planning, March–April. Bank Mag 174(2):66–69

Bouhali R, Mekdad Y, Lebsir H, Ferkha L (2015) Leader roles for innovation: strategic thinking and planning. Procedia Soc Behav Sci 181:72–78

Bowers J, Khorakian A (2014) Integrating risk management in the innovation project. Eur J Innov Manag 17(1):25–40

Chaffee EE (1985) Three models of strategy. Acad Manag Rev 10(1):89–98

Clarke CJ, Varma S (1999) Strategic risk management: the new competitive edge. Long Range Plann 32(4):414–424

Cooper C (2000) How good are banks at managing business risk? Balance Sheet 8(1):15–19

Cooper T, Speh C, Downey A (2011) Creating a culture of risk management. Wolters Kluwer Financial Services, Waltham, MA

De Marchi B, Ravetz JR (1999) Risk management and governance: a post-normal science approach. Futures 31(7):743–757

Dutton JE, Duncan RB (1987) The influence of the strategic planning process on strategic change. Strateg Manag J 8(2):103–116

Elahi E (2013) Risk management: the next source of competitive advantage. Foresight 15(2): 117–131

Espersen D (2007) The language of risk: organizations can improve risk management and audit processes by communicating risks in terms that everyone understands. Intern Audit 64(3): 69–72

Fiegenbaum A, Thomas H (2004) Strategic risk and competitive advantage: an integrative perspective. Eur Manag Rev 1(1):84–95

Geretto EF, Pauluzzo R (2015, September) Knowledge management and risk culture in the banking industry: relations and problems. In: European conference on knowledge management. Academic Conferences International Limited

Girling PX (2013) Operational risk management: a complete guide to a successful operational risk framework. Wiley, New Jersey

Holmquist E (2012) Risk management and business strategy. RMA J 94(10):40–45

Hopkins WE, Hopkins SA (1997) Strategic planning-financial performance relationships in banks: a causal examination. Strateg Manag J 18(8):635–652

Institute of International Finance (2008) Final report of the IIF committee on market best practices: principles of conduct and best practice recommendations

Institute of International Finance (2009) Reform in the financial services industry: strengthening practices for a more stable system. The report of the IIF Steering Committee on Implementation (SCI)

Institute of International Finance (2012) Governance for strengthened risk management

Institute of International Finance (2013) Promoting sound risk culture: lessons learned, challenges remaining and areas for further consideration

Kahneman D, Lovallo D (1993) Timid choices and bold forecasts: a cognitive perspective on risk taking. Manag Sci 39(1):17–31

Krause TA, Tse Y (2016) Risk management and firm value: recent theory and evidence. Int J Account Inf Manag 24(1)

March JG (1978) Bounded rationality, ambiguity, and the engineering of choice. Bell J Econ 9(2): 587–608

March JG, Shapira Z (1987) Managerial perspectives on risk and risk taking. Manag Sci 33(11): 1404–1418

McConnell PJ (2013) A risk culture framework for systemically important banks. J Risk Gov 3(1)

Mintzberg H (1994) The fall and rise of strategic planning. Harv Bus Rev 72(1):107–114

Oliver Wyman Financial Services and RMA (2010) Institutions need to better understand their risk appetite. RMA J, 38–42
Peters T, Waterman R (1982) In search of excellence: lessons from America's best-run corporations. Warner, New York
Power M (2007) Organized uncertainty: designing a world of risk management. Oxford University Press, New York
Raza Bilal A, Bt. Abu Talib N, Noor Azli Ali Khan M (2013) Remodeling of risk management in banking: evidence from the sub-continent and gulf. J Risk Financ 14(5):468–489
Schein EH (1992) Organizational culture and leadership. Wiley, New Jersey
Simon HA (1972) Theories of bounded rationality. Decis Org 1(1):161–176
Steiner GS (1979) Strategic planning. Free Press, New York
Willcoxson L, Millett B (2000) The management of organisational culture. Aust J Manage Organ Behav 3(2):91–99

Dr. Bozaykut-Bük is an Assistant Professor of Management at the School of Business and Management Sciences, Istanbul Medipol University. She received her BA from Bogazici University in 2002 and MA in Management and Organisation from Marmara University in 2009. She earned her PhD in Management and Organisation from Istanbul University in 2014. Her current researches are on organizational identity, organizational legitimacy and organizational sociology.

Agile Intrapreneurship in Volatile Business Environment: Changing Roles of Financial Managers and Risk Takers According to Schumpeterian Approach

Tuna Uslu

Abstract As a result of the economic, social and cultural reflections of the rapidly developing information and communication technologies, a new social reference was developed based on information society which is a an intellectual reformist domain paradigm which can also be called as the information age. In this radical transformation process, where information becomes a strategic resource including information and communication technologies in its center, economic, social, political and cultural lives were deeply affected. The changes and developments in social dynamics also affected the structure of the organizations, their management understanding, the technologies used and the employees while the organizations had to re-design their functions and the managers had to re-design their roles. More importance was given to the intrapreneurship and leadership qualities of the managers who can adapt to the changing competition conditions in the organizational sense in the information society. This destructive change in the operation and management techniques also affected the economy theories and was affective in the development of endogenous growth approach. In this section, we draw a conceptual framework between leadership and managership, discuss personal characteristics of the chief officers and financial managers, the leadership of the time while looking for a place for these concepts within Schumpeter's approaches and endogenous growth theories.

T. Uslu (✉)
Graduate Program of Business Management, Istanbul Gedik University, Kartal, Istanbul, Turkey
e-mail: tuna.uslu@gedik.edu.tr

H. Dinçer, Ü. Hacioğlu (eds.), *Risk Management, Strategic Thinking and Leadership in the Financial Services Industry*, Contributions to Management Science, DOI 10.1007/978-3-319-47172-3_22

1 Introduction

It is observed that the social developments and radical changes taking place throughout the history took place only within a generation with different periods and different characteristics. Human kind experienced one of its most fragile periods throughout the history with the industrial and technological revolution. The technology based developments emerging in the twenty-first century transformed the official borders between countries into imaginary lines while the technology and innovation came to the center point of daily life to become the virtual dome of societies. Technology became to form the dynamism of the social developments of our age. Technology can be considered as a positive reaction in the aspect of cultural interaction between societies and its audience positioning reduced the costs of communication and reaching to information while causing radical transformations in the structures and functions of social dynamics, production structures, social institutions and organizations. With this transformation taking place in the field of technology and communication, a new social structure emerged. The changes and developments taking place social dynamics affected the structure of the organizations, their way of management, the technologies used and the employees while also affecting the functions of organizations and roles of managers.

Today, the ways of business operations which change in parallel to information economy while also increasing the industrial relations and management approaches in organizations. The most important and critical resource of organizations in the rapidly changing environment of business, competition and entrepreneurship is the qualified, knowledgeable and competent man force (Drucker 1986). Hence, organizations aim to strengthen their employees with a positive approach by infusing them with concepts such as autonomy, creativity, and flexibility and supporting them (Uslu 2014: 7). Hierarchical stages are reduced in businesses while two-way communication between stages increases. This whole change created new organizational structures after the third and fourth industrial revolutions, and it is also effective for the employees to become more participating and to develop positive attitudes. Due to the intense communication and interaction between employees and managers, employees are able to have more participation in organization processes and become a part of the management processes in the information economy (Uslu 2015a). According to Castells (2000), information economy has three basic qualities:

(1) In the information economics, the capacity to produce, process and manage information is the main determinant of productivity and competitive power in all economic units in the level of industry, region and country.
(2) Information economics is a global economy; production is carried out locally but for all the world. It is not possible for the products and services that are not globally produced to exist before the high quality products which are produced for global market or the "creative destructive" (Schumpeter 1962) products

which have high competition power. Utterback and Acee (2005: 2) call this kind of technologies as "destructive technologies".

(3) Information economy is a network economy (Juniper 2002: 748). Economic units in the information economy are called as network businesses. Network is a cluster of interconnected ends. Each end has a one-to-one connection to other ends. Therefore, the information sharing possibility and synergy in the network structure are at the highest level. The strategies of the businesses in the information economy are based on developing their own business ecosystems.

The organizations that attempt to exist in the information economy have to ensure continuous renovations by keeping themselves open to information based change and developments as well as developing technology and changing environmental factors. However, with respect to sustainable competition, the leadership profile within the conventional management approaches cannot respond to these needs. The leadership concept of the future will underline the personality features that can rapidly respond to change, adapt to developments, renew itself, has effective communication skill, can take initiative, can rapidly interpret information and turn it to opportunity, has knowledge on the qualities and capacity of the audience it represents, assuring confidence to followers.

The rapid development of information and communication technologies have been changing the organizational structure, business and work methods, manager and employee profile, and in general work life, and have been bringing out new models particularly in communication in inside and outside the organization (Uslu 2014: 290–291). Moreover, methods towards providing a participatory work environment such as accurate decision making from the lower division to the upper division in businesses and establishing communication, empowerment and increasing authority; allow employees to be freer, stronger, and making authoritative decisions, thus identify alternative ways to achieve goals and be motivated (Uslu 2014: 282–283). It was found that the most important factor determining organizational creativity is organizational communication support followed by corporate innovativeness (Uslu and Çubuk 2015).

Information society as well as organizational communication and social networks change paradigms and play a critical role in management approaches in the new age. In our age, organizations and managers systematically develop new methods and approaches to ensure competitive advantage. Product development, product, service and process renewal are the leading innovative methods that are used. Innovation describes the transformation in the business fields and production philosophy. The differences between the countries and regions in terms of management, science, engineering, technology and labour quality have become the factors that explain the complexity dynamics of the twenty-first century. Hence; increasing the international competitive power of the local firms in the framework of regional development politics, improving entrepreneurship and innovation capacity in local area are highly important in this century (Eryiğit and Uslu 2014: 429).

2 Schumpeterian Innovation and Endogenous Growth

In the process of economic development, Schumpeter is the first person to deal with the concept of innovation in the most comprehensive sense (1912). In Schumpeter's approach, it is important to state that innovation and invention don't have the same meaning. It is the innovator who drives development, not the inventor. Hence the invention that doesn't become innovation cannot be the driving force of development. Therefore, for Schumpeter, the dynamics of development turns to the dynamics of innovation. Therefore, innovation causes development in stable economies (Schumpeter 1947: 152–153). Another important concept that Schumpeter added to the literature of economics is the creative destruction in relation to innovation. This term refers to the economic derogation of old things or old technologies by the new technologies or innovations (Aghion and Howitt 1997: 53). Schumpeter argues that innovation is the basic functions of new companies and entrepreneurship and that it takes places after creative destruction. When defining the essence of capitalism, Schumpeter (1962) links initiatives that create new product, service, market and economic enterprises to consecutive revolutions and economic dynamism within the economic structure. This dynamism is a "creative destruction" that continuously destroys what is old and creates new periods instead.

The analysis of Schumpeter gives innovation a basic role. When applied to industrial process, invention becomes an innovation. An entrepreneur is the person who realizes new combinations and who brings innovations. An entrepreneur is always a leader in creating new production processes and new forms business organizations or in entering new markets. Schumpeter believes that economic life will maintain its static balance if it weren't the innovations and that it will continue as a process that repeats itself every year in the same channel. For Schumpeter, innovations emerge as clusters not in a continuous manner. Activities of some entrepreneurs create a convenient environment for the others who follow them. Some others who don't follow innovations are wiped off the market. This approach of Schumpeter is called as "creative destruction". As the innovation process takes year by year, some survive in the market while others are wiped off the market. These processes create periodical movements and bring in economic development.

According to Schumpeter, economic order takes place when a new technology, product, market, production process or organizational structure becomes an open alternative to the existing products and organizational applications with creative destruction. If a new technology, product, market or organization applications don't form open alternatives to the products or organizational applications currently available in the market, then creative destruction doesn't take place (Larson 2000: 306). Today, there is emphasis on the destruction of the competitive structure in the market with the intrinsic change of innovations. However, the power of destroying the current structure in the market also show the contribution of change to economic growth. Therefore, we can also talk about "creative making" instead of "creative destruction" which will take place in the market due to innovations (Lambooy 2005: 1140). Schumpeter's definition of innovation highlights the commercialization of goods. Innovation refers to introduction of a new product to the world, adding a new product to the existing product line by improvement or revision, cost reduction of existing products or re-positioning of the existing products in the market. Among these definitions, only the introduction of a new product to the world addresses to innovation on a radical dimension while the innovation in other dimensions increases little by little (Malaviya and Wadhwa 2005: 2).

2.1 The Relation Between Innovation and Investment

Investment is the most important instrument of growth and development. Investments should be promoted and supported while favourable environments should be provided for the investors. State has limited capacity to do something in this sense and it obliged the private sector to become more effective and guided it to various areas where it can make profits. The increase of businesses operating in the same sector also increased competition and forced businesses to have a difference. Therefore, innovative businesses take advantage in the competition and advance one step ahead.

Businesses have to bear certain costs in order to be able to realize their new and innovative ideas and projects. Realization of an innovative project creates multidimensional effects and any support in this area bears more value than being just a financing as each investment may have different requirements. Today, managers tend to manage the risk by sharing their responsibilities and powers with the employees and teams similar to the rendering of the private sector to be effective by the state. Therefore the need for the internal entrepreneurs increases every day. Entrepreneurs should be supported and the culture of entrepreneurship should be established for a sustainable economic growth and social welfare level.

Innovation appears to be a new phenomenon today while it is based on the works of Schumpeter in 1930s. In his book "Economic Cycles" published in 1939, Schumpeter stated that innovation is an obligation to continue economic activities that an economy which is not dynamic cannot be healthy and that innovation is very important in economy (Schumpeter 1939: 85–86). Schumpeter studied the economic stages in four different parts, i.e. welfare, stagnation, crisis and recovery. Schumpeter followed Kondratieff and defined nearly 50 years of development periods as cycles and periods (Freeman and Soete 1997). The total of the change waves covering all these periods, researches and innovations is called as consecutive industrial revolutions.

What started innovation or how innovation emerged don't matter. What matters is the fact that innovation starts the economic period. Entrepreneur is highlighted as the person who realizes innovations (Schumpeter 1939: 130–131). Innovation requires the emergence of new entrepreneurs. According to Schumpeter, an entrepreneur is in the social structure as an entrepreneur leader and his position in the social structure is determined by his leadership skills (Schumpeter 1934).

Schumpeter (1934) compared entrepreneurs in his book "Economic Development Theory" to the medieval chevaliers and stated that the entrepreneurship activity was such a broad area of activity that cannot be explained by rationality.

The concept of innovation that is required to create a difference in economy has not the same meaning with invention. Innovation doesn't require a scientific work and the desire of a businessman turns an invention into an innovation. Inventions, however, are the products of an intellectual effort (Schumpeter 1939: 84–86). The concept of financial innovation refers to the new things (Frame and White 2004) that allow the development of cost and risk reducing financial products (services/ instruments) as well as to the technological developments (Solans 2003) that enable access to information and that provides comforts in transactions and payments and to the emerging financial instruments, services, new organization forms and developed markets.

Drucker (2008) states that having an entrepreneur management in new enterprises is based on four conditions including market focus, financial prediction, top management team creation and the determination of the role of the founder entrepreneur. The biggest hazard in the next stage of growth for an enterprise is the lack of sufficient financial focus and proper financial policies. In a new enterprise, entrepreneurs usually focus on profits. However, profit is the last thing to consider. The continuity of the enterprise in the current condition is more important. As stated by Drucker, the growth should be fed and what growth needs is more cash and capital.

Innovation is a phenomenon that contains risk and uncertainty by nature. This risk and uncertainty bring some setbacks for investment. Shaping the project by proper measurement of risks and uncertainties is essential for the success of the investment. Various methods are used to provide finance to the innovation works to be carried out by businesses. Financing these activities is ensured by equity, cooperations, incentives and grants.

Xiao and Zhao (2012: 884) mentioned that there might be various reasons behind the limitations experienced in the financing of innovative projects and that the asymmetric information on this matter is an important problem. Inability of the investor to select proper and profitable projects due to asymmetric information causes the increase of risks and uncertainties, increase of costs, delay in the merchandising processes of the projects and thus the extension of the periods of return of investment. Therefore, asymmetric information happens to be an important element that needs to be minimized for the investors and entrepreneurs.

In recent years, that has been a special focus on the need of supporting innovative projects, having a public sector that guides the private sector, and increasing the private sector investments in this sense. One of the policy principles of the OECD innovation strategies is having a good functioning financial system and facilitating the access of companies to financial resources. National Innovation Policies have supported this subject and steps have been taken to increase the competitive powers of enterprise and develop effective innovation strategies. Policy makers added to their goals the plans to ensure particularly financial support and development of innovative activities. First the macroeconomic favourable conditions should be provided so that the financing of investments is no more a problem. Realization of innovative projects is relatively easier than the others in an economy where financial systems and stock exchanges are functional. The reason for it is that the developed financial systems can alleviate the asymmetric information problem in particular, therefore an important step is taken to minimize the assumed risk and incentive possibilities are diversified. The common judgement in several countries is that "innovation" is one of the dynamics of sustainable growth in future years. For example, the report of the British Government for the years between 2004 and 2014 stated that the future growth to be ensured in future years can be possible by the importance assigned to the innovation, research and development activities of today. The report highlighted that the efficiency and production in the information societies of future will be shaped around new ideas and facts and therefore it is essential to have relevant partnerships of public and private sectors (HM Treasury 2004: 15–18).

2.2 From Labourer to Schumpeterian Entrepreneur

In the process of transition to information society that we are currently in, one of the paradigm-changing organizational dynamics in industry is the psychological qualities of this mental change through innovative entrepreneurship as well as information production. Considering with respect to paradigm change, the essence of entrepreneurship theory of Schumpeter (1934) in particular is made of the concept of creative destruction caused by the innovative entrepreneur. Schumpeter (1962) links the enterprises that create new economic organizations to consecutive revolutions and economic dynamism that follow each other in the economy. This dynamism is a creative destruction movement that constantly destroys what is old and creates new periods instead. Creative destruction is the inclusion of new methods to the production process after the elimination of organizations producing old products and services by the organizations that make advance production with new methods (Montgomery and Wascher 1988). From the micro point of view, individuals can act rationally in repeated and familiar processes, while they may not be able to easily grasp a new situation. But in a change process, individuals tend towards the satisfaction of their desires and may go out of patterns. These individual behaviours may functions as the motivating factors of transformation (Schumpeter 1934).

Schumpeter is the first person to define entrepreneurship from a different perspective. According to Schumpeter, the innovation concept underlines the definition of entrepreneurship. He defines an entrepreneur as the person who destroys the current economic order by creating new combinations like producing new goods and services, developing new processes, finding new export markets, and creating a new organization structure. Classical economic point of view defines entrepreneurship focuses on the personality traits like creativity (Schumpeter 1934) and risk taking (Mill 1954).

The entrepreneur is the person who provides financial and personal satisfaction by taking psychological risks and who is in the process of creating anything that has a different value by spending the required time and effort (Hisrich 1985). The entrepreneur is an individual who creates valuable things to obtain results for individual satisfaction like success and independency and for financial satisfaction by assuming the financial and social risk within the process to increase economic efficiency (Hisrich and Peters 2002). Entrepreneurship is the activity of economic mobilizing of resources (Hisrich et al. 2005: 8). An entrepreneur coordinates the production factors, manages the process, audits staff, orders raw material, estimates demand, takes an intermediate role between producers and consumers (Winata 2008: 16). The entrepreneur is the key person, coordinator, modern leader and manager in its own enterprise. An entrepreneur is a risk bearer, innovative, constructive, organizer, maker, industrial leader, project coordinator, employer, arbitrator, financial capital supplier and allocator of resources between alternative uses. The duties of entrepreneurship include especially risk taking. For example, decisions are taken in the uncertainty conditions which include information asymmetry, and therefore they exhibit more risk taking behaviours than managers (Stewart and Roth 2001).

Schumpeter defines the entrepreneur as the person founding new companies, innovative, destroying routines and resisting against the old methods. The entrepreneur of Schumpeter assumes these tasks only become successful. The special leadership skills of the entrepreneur show him the correct way to take action. To meet innovations, an entrepreneur should resist against the deviated behaviour and the opposition of the environment who are hostile to innovation. The entrepreneur of Schumpeter takes pleasure from this opposition. On the other hand, the entrepreneur is a non-conventional creator, not a religious opposition (Brouwer 2002: 89). Moreover, Schumpeter makes a distinction between the types of entrepreneurs as ordinary and economic actor. The entrepreneur in Schumpeter's theoretical system is the driving actor of the economic system. Revealing the innovations is based on the leadership skills of the entrepreneur. Autonomous adaptations are impossible for ordinary actors. Ordinary economic actors need visionary guides to design new production and consumption plans (Ebner 2000). Schumpeter defines the entrepreneur as a leader who has intuition and vision, who can realize new things as well as evaluate old things through new ways. Leadership in Schumpeterian system is not homogenous. Leadership skill is partly caused by the use of information which looks like a public asset. Human movement perceiving and responding to information does it through various ways. Each internalizes public assets through different ways. Leader leaves the manager behind by his skills (Hébert and Link 2006: 101). Schumpeter distinguishes entrepreneur, manager and financier. Entrepreneur usually provides vision and leadership to the organization different from the managers who run the daily works of a company. The main task of the entrepreneur is to decide which goals to pursue not how (Praag 1999: 320). The basic function of the entrepreneur in modern societies is to continuously realize the innovations. In this aspect, the power of the modern entrepreneur is considered by his skill to make innovations and turn them into concrete commercial products.

According to Schumpeter, there may be innovation without having anything that can be called as invention. An entrepreneur chooses the most appropriate inventions that are known but not popular yet and turns them into innovation (Schumpeter 1934). For Schumpeter, one needs desire not intelligence for successful innovations. Innovation is based on leadership, not intelligence, and it shouldn't be confused with invention. Innovation is a difficult job that requires the work of skilful people to work on creative ideas who supplement each other. In addition, innovation is also involved in developing consumer services, reducing costs and creating new profit area within organization within the process of turning creative ideas to concrete products and processes (Rosenfeld and Servo 1994: 29). While there is dominant introversion as a personal trait of creative persons, the dominant personal trait of innovative persons is extroversion. The most important difference between innovative persons and creative persons is the dynamic personal traits. This is related to the characteristics of innovative persons like taking more responsibility, needing to realize ideas, ability to turn ideas to money and more future expectations. In addition, dynamic leadership is the skill of taking initiatives and organization (Heunks 1998: 264).

2.3 Neo-Schumpeterian Approach

The innovation types suggested by the Neo-Schumpeterian school which developed the modern innovation theory are incremental innovations, radical innovations and innovations in technology system. The innovations causing incremental progress in the technological field are the small technological innovations that automatically take place in the daily production process and that are seen in the industry and service sectors. Organized R&D activities and high skill level are not necessary for such innovations to emerge. However, radical innovations are the developments that don't have continuity and that emerge independently from the current products or production processes. The Neo-Schumpeterian approach takes technology from a different perspective with respect to both conceptual level and size (Metcalfe 1997: 270–273).

Creative destruction is the inclusion of new methods into the production process as a result of elimination of old products and services and organizations that produce them by the organizations with higher production with new techniques (Montgomery and Wascher 1988). In this process, organizations cannot create the future if they cannot obtain the ability to get rid of the influence of the past (Drucker 1999: 86). One of methods to accomplish transformation is through removing inhibiting factors in the previous structure or burning one's bridges to prevent returning. Drucker (1986) defines Schumpeter's approach as one of the most important elements of modern economy. Worldwide developments such as the Advanced Manufacturing, Internet of Things, Full Automation, Industry 4.0 and Smart Industries have the potential to make a new form of creative destruction possible. Schumpeterian approach describes new markets in media and the internet much better than traditional markets in manufacturing and services. But as more and more industries become increasingly digitalized and networked, the people can expect the Schumpeterian dynamic to spread (Brynjolfsson and McAfee 2014).

2.4 Endogenous Growth Approach and Human Capital

This destructive change in the production methods also affected the economy theories and were effective in the development of endogenous growth approach. There is consensus in the economy literature (Pack 1994; Solow 1994; Grossman and Helpman 1994; Fine 2000) on the fact that the endogenous growth theory is based on the works of Romer (1986) and Lucas (1988). The study of Romer (1986) on the long term growth dynamics and his new growth theories that are developed as a different view to the neo-classical growth theory consider technology and human capital as an endogenous input of growth (Shaw 1992: 615). Romer incorporated the technological change to the model and stated that the long term growth is actually based on information background. In addition, it was stated that positive externality may be involved in information production depending on the feature of information that it cannot be patented or cannot be kept hidden. New theory uses production functions based on increasing efficiency instead of neo-conventional production function. This controversial assumption that Romer used in his model is based on the argument that it is not only physical production that comes in the investment and production process, but also the new production information. Romer uses in its model the "learning-by-doing" idea of Arrow. Romer uses this idea and assumes that technical information is produced as a side product in the process of production and investment and that this information is used in the new production almost as a free input and the new production is carried out at lower cost and at higher quality.

Romer points out to the existence of increasing income due to the non-competitive nature of creative ideas. Endogenous growth models suggest that every kind of policies that affect physical capital, human capital and intellectual capital will have a positive impact on long term growth (Dowrick 1995). Improvements in the quality of education and workforce as well as the factors like scale economies and technological development (Patrinos 1994). In his studies comparing the growth speeds of countries, Barro (1990) states that the factor preventing poor countries from catching up with rich countries is not the lack of physical capital investment by the lack of investment on human capital. The model of Barro is one of the first endogenous growth models and it regards the public policies as a clear production factor. Lucas (1988) defines the human capital as the physical, intellectual and technical capacity of individuals and emphasizes that it is the driving force of growth. However, the human capital is a production factor like the physical capital and it has increasing profits not decreasing ones. In this context, human capital is a concept that will create internal growth. Those who defend endogenous growth theory highlight different subjects but one of the common points gathering these views in the same group is the idea that growth is determined endogenously in the long term. This is attempted to be explained by Romer (1986) with information background and technical progress, by Lucas (1988) with the education of human capital, by Becker et al. (1990) with workforce growth and productivity, by Yang and Borland (1991) with work force specialization and by Young (1993) with learning-by-doing. This approach has become the basis for the organizations to form human oriented, simpler organizations with their employees and customers.

3 Intrapreneurship from the Perspective of the Contemporary Management and Organization Approach

3.1 *Organizational Intrapreneurship*

Drucker (1984) defined the concept of innovation as "the useful information that provides first chance to ensure efficiency of employees working together in an organization having different knowledge and skills". Innovation is an instrument of entrepreneurship and an action that provides necessary sources in creating a new capacity (Drucker 1984, 1986). In the enterprises, innovation approach increases also psychological ownership of employees and therefore has positive effect on the job satisfaction through emotional commitment to organization (Uslu 2014: 314).

Organizational intrapreneurship refers to the internal market research activities in organizations, provision of improving and innovative employee services, and developments in the internal markets of big organizations and the small and independent units that were designed to expand technologies and methods. This is different than the comprehensive organization entrepreneurship that intends to obtain a profitable position in external markets (Nielsen et al. 1985). Intrapreneurs are the individuals who take responsibility to increase any innovation in the organization. They can be creative and inventive but also dreamers who can always understand how to convert an idea into a profitable reality (Pinchot 1984).

3.2 *Lean Management and Lean Startup*

Lean approach refers to the redefinition and organization of the functions, departments and processes to provide a positive contribution to knowledge and value creation (Womack and Jones 1996). Participation of employees and work groups are also the most important aspect of the lean production practices (Kirkman 1997: 735). This concept involves the integration of the organization structure to make sure faster response to the quality and standards requested by consumers. Lean organizations or enterprises have five qualities. Firstly, entrepreneurs are everywhere. You don't need to work in the garage to establish a business. What matters is the fact the product and service to emerge will meet a need at certain periods. The second quality is the entrepreneurship management which is a new management form. The third quality is the approved learning. Entrepreneurs need approved scientific data that will test the accuracy of their vision. The fourth quality is the cycle of do-measure-learn. The basic activity of the new enterprise is to turn ideas to product, to measure the reactions of customers and to learn whether a new direction will be taken or the same direction will remain. The fifth quality is the innovation accountancy. Outputs of the enterprise should be developed and the recorded progress should be measured which can be possible by innovation accountancy.

Lean startup refers to rapidly setting up and managing enterprises with low cost in line with requests of customers. It directs the entrepreneur to set up the balance of the work progress and prescribes when to move ahead with full speed and with whole resources and when to slow down. It refers to shaping, testing and reporting of product according to the feedback of the customer over the product which is produced at low cost instead of multiplying the features (Ries 2011). According to this point of view, the first thing to do in a new enterprise is to present in the shortest period the simplest product which will do the job for the customer. The entrepreneur may test the accuracy of the assumptions by turning the business idea into testable hypotheses, may continue the business idea he has been doing by small modifications, may pivot the business idea or completely quit the business idea. Lean startup model may be defined as the delivery of product or service under rather uncertain conditions with the least capital. That is, the entrepreneur should produce the simplest product which will meet the need of the customer (minimum viable product) and receive feedback from user as soon as possible. Usually the biggest mistake of the entrepreneur is to focus on the solution too early assuming that he knows the problem. However, if one tries to understand the problem in line with the demands of the customers and users, one may face a very different problem than the assumed problem. At this point, lean start is human oriented contrary to the traditional models and attempts to understand the problems of human from user to product. As a result, this point of view presents a full time feedback particularly at an early stage for the acceptance of an idea by the market.

At lean startup, business model is essential instead of business plan. Instead of losing time on the business plan, it is important to address to the audience called as "early adapters" which is small but can quickly adapt to the system in order to find the correct business model. The main goal is to create the system and platform according to the user demands instead of product development. This approach is based on user experiences and works on the cycle of "build, measure and learn" called as "pivot". The rate of speed in developing product ad user simultaneously with the productivity in the pivot cycle is called agility. That is, making mistakes as early as possible is very good. One needs to measure these mistakes, take lessons and do what is correct in order to rapidly meet the user demand. Exceeding the pivot cycle already refers to finding the correct model and putting the system on the right track with visible user increase.

3.3 Strategic and Agile Management

Until today, strategy and agility are usually considered as opposite poles by the administrators. Strategy is defined as the following of path which is clearly determined over a set of carefully selected action, or in other words, of a previously systematically defined path. On the other hand, agility is regarded as the concrete form of opportunism. In fact, they both need each other. Strategy without agility is merely a central planning and agility without strategy creates chaos.

The matter that is hardly grasped by many organizations is that an effective strategy is encouraging by determining the limits in which the innovation and experimentalism should take place rather than suppressing an agile attitude. Agile strategy approach, however, develops companies from vision to strategy by blending agility and strategy. In this process, agility comes into play iteratively for companies to develop new skills against what they learned and to re-organize and improve their initial strategies. The employees who continuously work through their processes and who can talk to each other about process improvement can establish an agile management. Otherwise, the maintenance of the "present condition" will be considered to be less problematic and troublesome and companies will try to protect the condition and accepted strategies instead of embarking on "new adventures". This attitude will create stationary systems which face increasingly more problems. The system may become more "agile" by the use of system that comprehends the processes in detail and that combines them after the management documents the processes with their details. The management will become more agile if processes get away from stationery as much as possible and transaction periods gets shorter with the information technologies. In conclusion, system should be turned to form that can quickly respond to the changing conditions. This change is possible by well-defined and continuously improved processes. Shortening of the cycle durations, which is another requirement of agile management is possible by the improvement of processes. According to agile management, individuals and the interaction between them are more important than the used process and instruments. Prototype product or service is more important than the comprehensible documentation. Relation with the customer is more important than the text of the customer contract. Adapting to change is more important than strictly sticking to the existing plan.

4 Changing Roles of Managers in Organizations

4.1 Differences Between Leaders and Managers

Leaders are responsible for creating a vision and having this vision embraced in the organization. Leader serves to the goals he sets. However, the management concept is fixed, only concerned with today and is responsible to realize the vision. The manager takes his power from the formal structures like laws and regulations while leader takes his power from the circumstances and personal qualities (Starratt 1995). Managers have authority while leaders have power. A manager is introvert for realizing the goals and only sees the trees in the forest while a leader sees the forest with his extrovert quality. A manager manages and coordinates at the business relations stage while a leader assures confidence and acts to develop his subordinates (Lunenburg 2011). A successful leader manager profile for managerial skills is summarized as the person who is smart, is imaginative, entrepreneur, has the skill to take fast decision and inspires his subordinates (Tannenbaum and Schmidt 1973).

Within the management metaphors based on knowledge, we need leaders who can represent the organizations within increasing competitive environments and who can take organizations forward. At this point, the key leadership qualities of the period to come are defined as follows (Leslie 2009); righteousness and moral courage, self-awareness and modest, empathy skill, transparency and openness, vision, adaptation and flexibility, energy, determination against uncertainty, judgement, consistency and righteousness, inspiration, motivation and resting motivation, respect and trust, knowledge and experience, strategic planning, inspiring commitment, change management and leadership to masses.

Human element is located in the center of the understanding of information society, therefore, leadership projection in the information society is not defined over merely professional knowledge or physical qualities. The future understanding of leadership should take this element into consideration in every stage of management understanding. A leader should give importance to moral values in concentrating on the task without ignoring the human element. The leader of the new century is the person who can turn threats to opportunity by rational approaches and who can present practical solutions. Information age also turned to a more chaotic structure in parallel to the developments in the field of informatics. An effective leader should adopt the collective intelligence/team approach to provide proper respond to the new order which become more complicated under current conditions. This approach also categorizes the decision making mechanism towards the team structure rather than the individual while it will also open the way for the personnel to show their skills to reach their goals.

In line with the modern management approach, organization structures evolved towards the team approach. With the collective intelligence approach, participation of employees in decisions has become a prerequisite in decision making steps which involves the future and success of organization. Within this process management, leadership approach has a key position. For the organization employees to adopt the collective intelligence approach, there should be an environment of confidence where the opinions of the employees are taken into consideration and their opinions are significant and necessary for the organization. Leader should have the self-confidence and representational skill to direct this intellectual infrastructure, to create an environment of confidence and to create an organizational atmosphere.

Different employee oriented leadership styles such as transactional, transformational or relation oriented leadership have different effects on organizational outcomes and employees. Leadership is defined as a process of achieving certain goals in the organization, mobilizing, influencing and guiding individuals in the organization or as the ability to guide employees to achieve the goals of the organization. Especially employee oriented leaders attach importance to the expectations and feelings of employees and act accordingly with regard to the achievement of organizational goals. On the other hand, with the widespread increase in the use of different communication channels and in the ease of access to information, the information age has brought its own leadership requirements (Uslu 2015b).

4.2 Current Leadership Styles

Leadership takes place within a social context. Leadership is a relation taking place between culture and psychology that is informed by individual and social behaviours (Adams 2013). According to the integrated leadership theory, the rules and values of cultural communities affect the behaviours of leaders; leaders affect the organization structure, culture and behaviours; cultural values and customs affect the organization culture; organization culture and customs affect the leadership behaviour. In short, within the light of this theory, culture, leader and organization structure are continuously affected from each other. This shows us, within the light of the data obtained from these researches, that cultural differences are affective on the leadership behaviours (House et al. 2004: 17–18). As a result of a comprehensive study, there are six definitions of global leadership behaviour. Charismatic leadership characterized by demonstrating integrity, decisiveness, and performance oriented by appearing visionary, inspirational and self-sacrificing; team oriented leadership characterized by supporting team collaboration and integration; participative leadership characterized by managerial skills; human orientated leadership; characterized by modesty; autonomous leadership characterized by autonomy, independence and individuality as a concept being recently defined; self-protective leadership characterized by self-centered, procedural, conscious of status and position which is also being recently defined (House et al. 2004: 14).

Today, organizations systematically develop new methods and approaches to provide competitive advantage. The innovative methods being employed particularly include the renewal of Production Development, product, service and processes. Together with the information society, the organization communication and social networks change the paradigms and play a critical role in the management approaches in the new age. The open and relation oriented approach of leadership which is the particularly effective in increasing the positive behaviour and psychological capitals of employees are therefore effective for the employees to develop proactive behaviours beyond their both work related performances and roles. Employees are positively strengthened thanks to the managers who are sincere, honest and have mutual relation and their desire to contribute to the organization increases. In addition, it is seen that such a leadership approach is effective in perceiving the innovativeness and entrepreneurship of the organization. Further, it is understood that an open and relation oriented leadership approach has a great effect for the innovativeness of the institution and for the participation of employees by developing their psychological capital (Uslu 2015a). The qualities of positive leader are listed as having communication with others with the awareness that they are "human", being reliable and honest, helping to the development of others, prudential, sincere and authentic, focusing on opportunities rather than obstacles, solving the problems for others, smiling and rarely straight-faced, modest and expressing satisfaction, flexible and open to the ideas of others, not selfish and team player (Cameron 2014). The effect of positive leadership is mainly perceived through the management of organization and has an effect on the evaluation of employees about their quality levels at work (Uslu 2014: 314). Open and ethical communication of leader has a role on the organizational commitment of employees especially through process management (Uslu 2014: 310). The researches show that open leadership is an approach that directly supports entrepreneurship and innovativeness in organizations (Uslu et al. 2015).

4.3 Expanding Roles of Financial Risk Takers and Chief Financial Officers

Today, the most important personal characteristics to be possessed by Chief Financial Officers (CFOs) in organizations (KPMG 2016: 27) are the leadership ability, command of processes and details, execution ability, ability to cope with shareholders and analysts, ability to see the big picture, strategic approach, being open to transformation and innovation, partnerships with parties out of the company, network establishment, curiosity and knowledge on all business sectors, ability to establish partnership with the parties in the company (top management, management board etc).

However, the Y generation of today has different requirement and expectations which is challenging for the CFOs who originate from the X generation. Now the popular qualities are to work side by side by the other departments as "business partner", acting as an indivisible part of the decision making mechanism, comprehending and embracing the activities of the company as the operational units, taking the role of guiding and problem solving in the company. Such that the most important qualities of the new competence set defined for the finance professionals are the leadership skills. In such an environment, communication skills and managerial abilities are especially important (Deloitte 2010: 3). The CFOs today are trying to manage an ecosystem which gets more sophisticated every day and includes global operations to create a competitive environment, use of financial data and analyses for profitable growth, realization of company strategies and coping with a dynamic regulatory environment. On the other hand, CFOs are expected to find and retain skilful human resource and to communicate with a broad group of stakeholders. Such people who can do all of the above, use the wisdom of the past and technology of the present and imagine the innovation of the future can be called (KPMG 2016: 24) as "Renaissance CFO".

5 Conclusion

Today, entrepreneurship is a new way of management the infrastructure of which is defined by Schumpeter. Now investors invest on entrepreneurs who break previous cycles and start to grow business with team. New managers in this paradigm should be positive, autonomous, agile, simple and dynamic, innovative and transformative, protective and participating, supporting entrepreneurship and including all stakeholders into the process, human and team oriented. The researches show that the leadership and governance as well as top-down communication effectiveness are understood to increase innovation. Improvement of management skills and increase of entrepreneurs with employees in small enterprises have also important effects to create an environment which cause the emergence of new ideas in the organization (Uslu and Çubuk 2015). In the enterprises, entrepreneurial spirit dimensions are passion, internal eco-systems, organizational climate, internal cooperation, organizational support, management support, strategic human resources and availability of rewards and resources (Aned and Alya 2013).

An open and relation oriented leadership approach which is particularly effective in increasing the positive behavior and psychological capital of employees has also an effect for the employees to develop job related performance and proactive behaviour beyond their jobs. Employees are positively empowered and have more desire to contribute to their institutions owing to managers that establish sincere, honest and mutual relations. In addition, it is found that such a leadership approach is also effective for the perception of innovation and entrepreneurship of the institution. It is further understood that an open and relation oriented leadership approach has great influence on the innovation of institution and on the inclusion of employees by developing their psychological capital (Uslu 2015a). Compared to the other leadership styles, open leadership is suggestive of stronger links with organizational outcomes such as organizational innovativeness and corporate entrepreneurship (Uslu et al. 2015).

The agile intrapreneurship process of the leaders could be defined as depending on the information gathered from the customers, agents and shareholders, the methodology of supporting new business process designs of employees which are effective, integrated and optimized. The basic activity of the intrapreneur leaders and innovative managers are to transform ideas to product, to measure customer reactions, to find out whether to change direction or to persist on the same path. This experience should be also based on scientific methods and a clean hypothesis. The prediction of this hypothesis should conform to what is expected to occur in reality. Then, the empirical predictions and the product should be successfully tested, be inspected by special customers and employees, be presented to focus groups and then the production should be started. During the course of time, product/service is distributed to a wider environment and becomes an output created by the customers where problems, if any, are solved. The agile and intrapreneur manager follows the development process and the achieved progress in these outputs. Employee oriented activities of these managers are hiring, training, and promoting the right people, providing a participatory work environment such as accurate decision making from the lower division to the upper division in businesses and establishing communication, empowerment and increasing authority; creating an open culture and removing barriers, thus identify alternative ways to achieve goals and be motivated, encouraging employees for rational risk taking and speed recovery from failure.

References

Adams EA (2013) Context, culture, and cognition: the significant factors of global leadership research. Int Leadersh J 5(2):94

Aghion P, Howitt P (1997) Endogenous growth theory. MIT Press, Cambridge, MA

Aned OAM, Alya OAM (2013) Invigorating entrepreneurial spirit among workforce. Int J Manage Sustain 2(5):107–112

Barro R (1990) Government spending in a simple model of endogenous growth. J Polit Econ 98:103–125

Becker GS, Murphy KM, Tamura R (1990) Human capital, fertility, and economic growth. J Polit Econ 98:12–37

Brouwer MT (2002) Weber, Schumpeter and Knight on entrepreneurship and economic development. J Evol Econ 12:83–105

Brynjolfsson E, McAfee A (2014) The second machine age. Work, progress, and prosperity in a time of brilliant technologies. W.W. Norton, New York

Cameron KS (2014) Positive leadership requires positive energy. The Wheatley Institution, http://wheatley.byu.edu/fellow_notes/individual.cfm?id=35&gt

Castells M (2000) Materials for an exploratory theory of the network society. Br J Soc 51(1):5–24

Deloitte (2010) CFO after the millennium: the 10 essential elements marked the last 10 years, Deloitte CFO Series 2, September 3

Dowrick S (1995) Innovation and endogenous growth: the new theory and evidence. Economic approaches to innovation. Edward Elgar, Cheltenham

Drucker PF (1984) Our entrepreneurial economy. Harvard Bus Rev 62(2):59–64

Drucker PF (1986) Innovation and entrepreneurship: practice and principles. Simon and Schuster, New York

Drucker PF (1999) Management challenges for the 21st century. Harper Collins, New York

Drucker PF (2008) Management, revised edn. Harper Collins, New York

Ebner A (2000) Schumpeterian theory and the sources of economic development: endogenous, evolutionary or entrepreneurial? In: The International Schumpeter Society conference on

"Change, development and transformation: transdisciplinary perspectives on the innovation process", Manchester
Eryiğit N, Uslu T (2014) Human resource and knowledge management in industrial clusters within the framework of international technology transfer and regional development. In: Proceedings of 14th Production researches symposium, Bahçeşehir University, pp 429–438
Fine B (2000) Endogenous growth theory: a critical assessment. Cambr J Econ 24(2):245–265
Frame WS, White LJ (2004) Empirical studies of financial innovation: lots of talk, little action? J Econ Lit 42(1):116–144
Freeman C, Soete L (1997) The economics of industrial innovation, 3rd edn. MIT Press, Cambridge, MA
Grossman GM, Helpman E (1994) Endogenous innovation in the theory of growth. J Econ Perspect 8(1):23–44
Hébert RF, Link AN (2006) Historical perspectives on the entrepreneur. Found Trends Entrepreneursh 2(4):1–152
Heunks JF (1998) Innovation, creativity and success. Small Bus Econ 10:263–272
Hisrich RD (1985) The woman entrepreneur in the United States and Puerto Rico: a comparative study. Leadersh Org Dev J 5:3–8
Hisrich RD, Peters PM (2002) Entrepreneurship. McGraw-Hill Irwin, London, UK
Hisrich RD, Peters MP, Shepherd DA (2005) Entrepreneurship. McGraw-Hill, New York
HM Treasury (2004) Science and innovation investment framework 2004–2014. Department for Work and Pensions, Department for Education and Skills, The Stationery Office, HMSO, London
House RJ, Hanges PJ, Javidan M, Dorfman PW, Gupta V (2004) GLOBE culture, leadership and organizations. Sage, London
Juniper J (2002) Universities and collaboration within complex, uncertain knowledge-based economies. Crit Perspect Acc 13:747–778
Kirkman B (1997) The impact of cultural values on employee resistance to teams: toward a model of globalized self-managing work team effectiveness. Acad Manage Rev 22(3)
KPMG (2016) Are you renaissance CFO? KPMG Turkey Agenda Magazine, No. 25, Winter
Lambooy J (2005) Innovation and knowledge: theory and regional policy. Eur Plann Stud 13 (8):1137–1152
Larson AL (2000) Sustainable innovation through an entrepreneurship lens. Bus Strateg Environ 9:304–317
Leslie JB (2009) The leadership gap; what you need, and don't have, when it comes to leadership talent. Center for Creative Leadership, 9
Lucas RE (1988) On the mechanics of economic development. J Monet Econ 22(1):3–42
Lunenburg FC (2011) Leadership versus management: a key distinction-at least in theory. Int J Manage Bus Admin 14(1):2
Malaviya P, Wadhwa S (2005) Innovation management in organizational context: an empirical study. Glob J Flex Syst Manage 6(2):1–14
Metcalfe S (1997) Technology systems and technology policy in an evolutionary framework. Technology, globalisation and economic performance. Cambridge University Press, Cambridge, pp 270–273
Mill JS (1954) Principle of political economy with some of their application to social philosophy. In: Schumpeter JA (ed) History of economic analysis. Oxford University Press, New York
Montgomery E, Wascher W (1988) Creative destruction and the behavior of productivity over the business cycle. Rev Econ Stat 70(1):168–172
Nielsen R, Peters MP, Hisrich RD (1985) Intrapreneurship strategy for internal markets - corporate non-profit and government institution cases. Strateg Manage J 6:181–189
Pack H (1994) Endogenous growth theory: intellectual appeal and empirical shortcomings. J Econ Perspect 8(1):55–72
Patrinos HA (1994) Notes on education and economic growth: theory and evidence. Human Resources Development and Operations Policy Working Papers, no. HRO 39. World Bank, Washington, DC

Pinchot G (1984) Who is the intrapreneur? In: Intrapreneuring: why you don't have to leave the corporation to become an entrepreneur. Harper & Row, New York, pp 28–48
Praag CM (1999) Some classic views on entrepreneurship. The Economist 147(3):311–335
Ries E (2011) The Lean startup: how today's entrepreneurs use continuous innovation to create radically successful businesses. Crown Publishing, New York
Romer PM (1986) Increasing returns and long-run growth. J Polit Econ 94(5):1002–1037
Rosenfeld R, Servo JC (1994) Facilitating innovation in large organization. In: Henry J, Walker D (eds) Managing innovation. Sage Publication, London
Schumpeter JA (1934) The theory of economic development. Oxford University Press, New York
Schumpeter JA (1939) Business cycles: a theoretical, historical and statistical analysis of the capitalist process. McGraw-Hill Book, New York
Schumpeter JA (1947) The creative response in economic history. J Econ Hist 7(2):149–159
Schumpeter JA (1962) Capitalism, socialism, and democracy, Harper perennial, 3rd edn. Harper Collins, New York
Shaw GK (1992) Policy implication of endogenous growth theory. Econ J 102:590–620
Solans ED (2003) Financial innovations and monetary policy. In: 38th SEACEN Governors conference on structural change and growth prospects in Asia - challenges to central banking, Manila, 13 Feb 2003. https://www.ecb.europa.eu/press/key/date/2003/html/sp030213.en.html
Solow RM (1994) Perspectives on growth theory. J Econ Perspect 8(1):45–54
Starratt RJ (1995) Leaders With vision the quest school renewal. Corwin Press, Thousand Oaks, CA
Stewart WH, Roth PL (2001) Risk propensity differences between entrepreneurs and managers: a meta-analytic review. J Appl Psychol 86(1):145–153
Tannenbaum R, Schmidt WH (1973) How to choose a leadership pattern. Harvard Bus Rev 36:162–180
Uslu T (2014). Perception of organizational commitment, job satisfaction and turnover intention in M&A process: a multivariate positive psychology model. Unpublished PhD Thesis, Department of Business Administration, Marmara University
Uslu T (2015a) Current leadership approaches and the maintenance of the fourth industrial revolution from a Schumpeterian point of view. In: International congress on economy administration and market surveys, Istanbul, 4–5 Dec 2015, pp 110–111
Uslu T (2015b) The comparison of contemporary leadership styles in organizational context according to employees. In: Proceedings of international conference on modern research's in management, economics and accounting, Istanbul, 27 Jul 2015. ISBN: 978-9944-0203-10-2
Uslu T, Çubuk D (2015) The effects of knowledge management and self-organization on organizational creativity: the mediating roles of corporate innovativeness and organizational communication. Int J Org Leadersh 4(4):403–412
Uslu T, Bülbül IA, Çubuk D (2015) An investigation of the effects of open leadership to organizational innovativeness and corporate entrepreneurship. Els Proc Soc Behav Sci 195:1166–1175. doi:10.1016/j.sbspro.2015.06.169
Utterback JM, Acee HJ (2005) Disruptive technologies: an expanded view. Int J Innov Manage 9 (1):1–17
Winata S (2008) The economic determinants of entrepreneurial activity: evidence from a Bayesian approach. Massey University, Palmerston North
Womack JP, Jones DT (1996) Lean thinking. Simon & Schuster, New York
Xiao S, Zhao S (2012) Financial development, government ownership of banks and firm innovation. J Int Money Fin 31(4):880–906
Yang X, Borland J (1991) A microeconomic mechanism for economic growth. J Polit Econ 99:460–482
Young A (1993) Invention and bounded learning by doing. J Polit Econ 101(3):443–472

Tuna Uslu is an Assistant Professor at Istanbul Gedik University, Graduate Program of Business Management, Istanbul, Turkey. He is also head of the Sport Management Department. Dr. Uslu has a BS in Economics and Business Administration from Istanbul Bilgi University, an MSc in Total Quality Management from Dokuz Eylul University and a PhD in Organizational Behavior from Marmara University. His research interests lie into fields including micro-economics, strategic management, sport management, cognitive psychology, industrial and organizational psychology. He has taught Business Management, Entrepreneurship and Facility Planning, Strategies and Methods of International Trade, Quality Management Systems, International Transportation and Logistics, Social Psychology, Management and Organization courses, among others, at both graduate and undergraduate levels. He has several articles, awards and book chapters, joined more than hundred national and international conferences. He is in the editorial board of International Journal of Business and Management, Management and Organizational Studies, Journal of Management and Sustainability, International Journal of Economic Behavior and Organization, International Journal of Psychological Studies and has been an ad hoc reviewer for journals such as Information Resources Management Journal and Review of Innovation and Competitiveness.

Emerging Trends in the Post-Regulatory Environment: The Importance of Instilling Trust

Semen Son-Turan

Abstract The financial services industry is one of the most critical pillars of economic growth and sustainable development in any country. As such, the findings of the 2016 Edelman Trust Barometer, that measures trust in institutions with more than 33,000 respondents in 28 countries over the last 15 years, are highly alarming. Accordingly, the financial services industry is ranked among the lowest with a mere 51 % on a global basis. Despite this darkened outlook, areas exist that seem to be promising: Sustainability management, responsible innovation and the organized and systemic efforts to increase transparency, comparability, accountability and reliability. Although the recent crises in financial markets have led regulators to come to a general agreement that a mutual effort is needed to develop procedures for increased compliance standards, and increase the pace of harmonization in accounting and financial reporting standards, the industry is faced with an imminent challenge: The low levels of trust in financial services. In this chapter, the author discusses how to re-build trust and reputation of the industry.

1 Introduction

There are some industries in which trust, confidence, the feeling to be in "good hands", a gut instinct that the particular company is "the right one" for you, weigh relatively more heavily as a decision factor when considering to start or continue working with that specific institution. Financial services institutions are intermediaries with whom most people entrust their nest eggs and rely on these financial "trustees" to keep them safe and ready to be returned with an "interest" when asked to do so. Be it for investing or even speculating rather than saving purposes, risk-

S. Son-Turan (✉)
Department of Business Administration, MEF University, Ayazaga Cad. No. 4, Maslak Sariyer, Istanbul, Turkey
e-mail: semen.son@mef.edu.tr

H. Dinçer, Ü. Hacioğlu (eds.), *Risk Management, Strategic Thinking and Leadership in the Financial Services Industry*, Contributions to Management Science, DOI 10.1007/978-3-319-47172-3_23

savvy investors, too, do exercise judgment over whether their financial institution is worthy the opportunity cost of not working with an alternative competitor.

The study of trust has been attracting diverse groups of researchers for long. Hence, various measures, definitions and drivers of trust depending on the discipline of the scholar, the types of stakeholders and the industry specifics (Huberman 2001; Tyler and Stanley 2007; Guiso et al. 2008), have thus far been determined.

The concept of trust in relation to financial services can be addressed in a systemic context (w.r.t. financial markets and their instruments), or on an institutional basis (ie. the confidence customers have in local banks, their stock brokers or insurance agents). Clearly, the financial system is comprised of markets, institutions, instruments and stakeholders, who all interact and create chain reactions, causing spillover effects and are even contagious on international levels. However, this chapter focuses on the institutional perspective and how financial institutions, in specific, can and do tackle customer trust, confidence and reputation-related issues.

Without the existence of risk or uncertainty about the outcomes of certain actions, trust would not be needed. Trust inherently is associated with vulnerability and individuals are potentially willing to accept such on basis of positive expectations about the intentions or behavior of another in a situation of interdependence and risk (Ennew and Sekhon 2007).

The financial services industry is, by far, one of the most versatile industries, which also determines its risk and return potential. In that sense it is uniquely fragile as it mostly relies on human sentiment. What makes it so unique, and, volatile at the same time, can easily be understood by examining the size and scope of financial innovations, some of which are shown in Fig. 1. As trade began to flourish, so did the financial system. In ancient Greece and during the Roman Empire, lenders based in temples made loans and deposits, and changed money. Archeology from this period in ancient China and India also shows evidence of money lending activity. Whereas the medieval and Renaissance Italy and particularly the affluent cities and wealthy merchants of Florence, Venice and Genoa are attributed the greatest role of the development of the modern banking system. Seventeenth century Amsterdam set the stage for many financial innovations such as the first joint stock company in history, the Dutch East India Company. It is often considered to have been the first multinational corporation in the world and the first company to issue stock. Undoubtedly, the invention of the automated teller machine (ATM) at the end of the 1960s, the advent of telephone banking by the mid 1980s, and the bloom of Internet banking in the 1990s laid the foundation of today's "modern" financial services industry with concurrent regulatory gaps either paving the way to misuse of innovation or constraints opening up the stage for disruptive competitors, such as new generation financial intermediaries, like crowdfunding platforms, or cryptocurrencies, like Bitcoin.

Marked by global macroeconomic instability and increased disruption, the financial services landscape clearly needs to restore trust and boost its clientele's confidence, which is comprised of retail banks, insurance companies, investment banks, accounting, audit and consumer finance companies, among others.

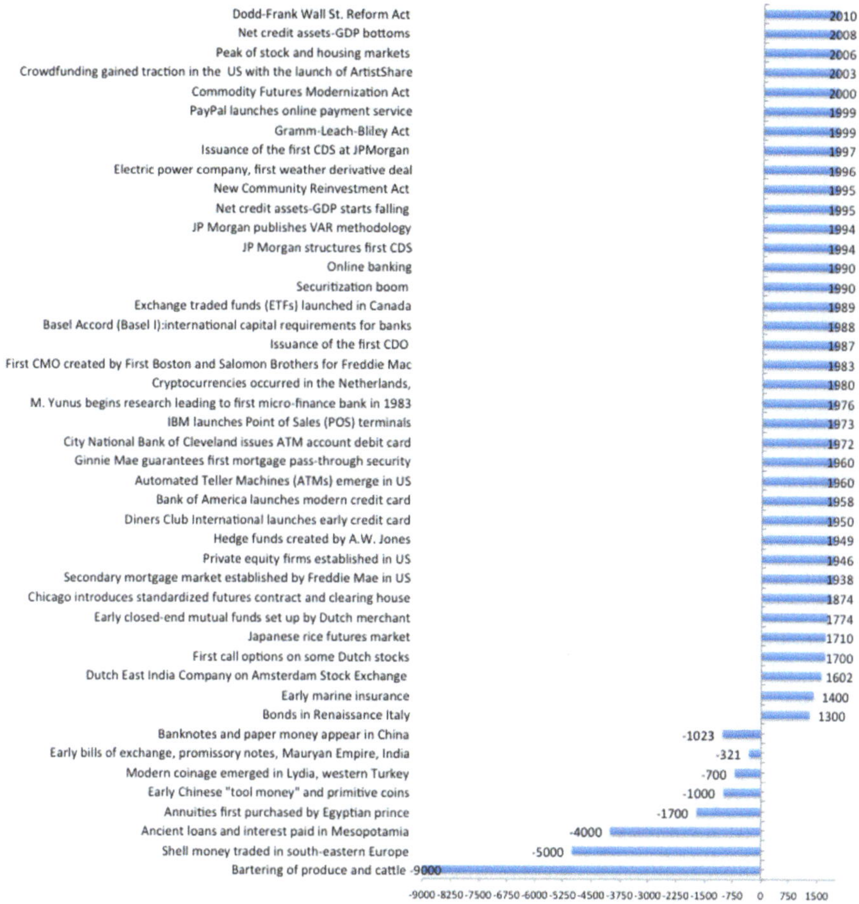

Fig. 1 A short account of financial services history. Source: Author's own elaboration, information is drawn from various sources (http://www3.weforum.org/docs/WEF_FS_RethinkingFinancialInnovation_Report_2012.pdf, https://bitcoinmagazine.com/articles/quick-history-cryptocurrencies-bbtc-bitcoin-1397682630, http://www.money-zine.com/investing/investing/collateralized-mortgage-obligations/, https://www.imf.org/external/pubs/ft/wp/2010/wp10164.pdf, http://w4.stern.nyu.edu/research/technological_change_and_fin_innovation_in_banking.pdf, http://www.freedman-chicago.com/ec4i/History-of-Crowdfunding.pdf)

The 2016 Edelman Trust Barometer[1] reveals that the financial services industry, although being on an upward trend since 2012 with an eight-point increase, ranked last in the 28-country survey of the general population with a trust rating of 51 %.

[1]Source: http://www.edelman.com. The 2016 Edelman Trust Barometer surveyed more than 33,000 respondents with an oversample of 1150 general population respondents ages 18 and over and 500 informed public respondents in the U.S. and China and 200 informed public respondents in all other countries representing 15 % of the total population across 28 countries.

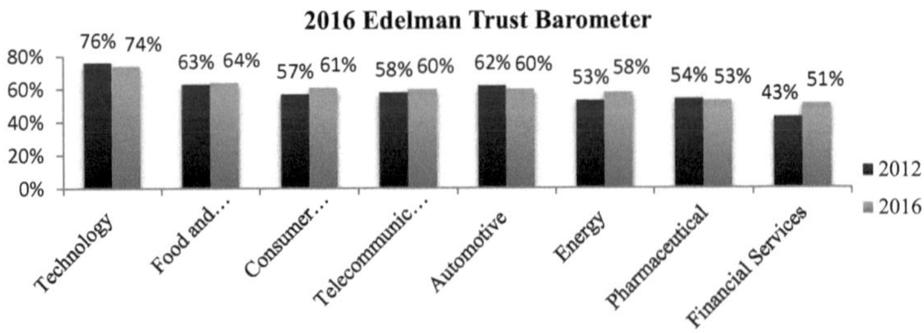

Fig. 2 2016 Edelman Trust Barometer. Source: http://www.edelman.com/insights/intellectual-property/2016-edelman-trust-barometer/

According to the results, the public is not only interested in adherence to profit-related goals but is also perceptive towards the societal contributions of firms. Integrity and engagement are among the potential drivers of lower trust levels. The previous, 2015 Edelman Trust Barometer, on the other hand, pointed out that only technology-related innovation in the financial services industry, that is electronic and mobile payments, garnered more trust than the industry itself.

According to a PwC report (PwC 2014),[2] the problem the industry faces, is bigger than trust. It is about the apathy and frustration of its clients who feel that all financial services institutions are the same. Anxieties have multiple drivers, (except for the investment banking sector that is most influenced by press coverage), personal experience is the most significant factor determining the trust level followed by press coverage, transparency of price and terms/conditions and word of mouth. According to the said report, among the factors that might improve consumer trust comes greater transparency on products and services (46 %), stricter codes of conduct for employees (41 %), changes to remuneration rules (40 %) and improved internal governance (37 %) (Fig. 2).

Reputation and trust are closely related. Jaffer et al. (2014), assert that strong trustworthiness, willingness and competence in keeping commitments, requires that the responsible institutions for delivering an obligation both, render an account of their performance, and be held accountable for such. To that end, informed and objective performance appraisal (what has been done and clearly communicated and enforceable standards of what ought to be done) and clear accessible communication of such is necessary.

Kindleberger and Aliber (2005) explain that the history of the financial services industry has been the stage for a multitude of bubbles, scandals, crashes, panics and fraudulent activity. Clearly, recent financial crises, such as the 2008 US Housing Bubble resulting in the sub-prime mortgage crisis (the financial crisis of 2008), the 2001 US Internet stock crash, the 1985–1989 bubble in real estate and stocks in

[2]The report is based on analysis of a survey of over 2000 people across the UK.

Finland, Norway and Sweden, and the bubble in real estate and stocks in Thailand, Malaysia, Indonesia and several other Asian countries have not contributed positively to customers' perceptions of financial services institutions. Kindleberger and Aliber differentiate between bubbles that are swindles and those that are not. According to the scholar, the Mississippi Bubble was not a swindle; the South Sea Bubble was. A bubble is said to generally start with an apparently legitimate or at least legal purpose. Accordingly, what became the Mississippi Bubble initially started as the Compagnie d'Occident, to which the Law system added the farming-out of national tax collections and the Banque. In the South Sea Bubble on the other hand, the monopoly of trade in the South Atlantic is said to be purely incidental (Kindleberger and Aliber 2005: 190).

Whether or not investors in financial markets can differentiate between purposeful and incidental financial tragedy though is a different concern.

2 Background

Be it retail or wholesale finance, the sources and drivers of trust (or distrust) are more or less the same across the globe.

Llewellyn (2014) discusses the importance of trust in financial services, with particular emphasis on the UK. According to the author, some of the several structural and behavioral elements as a result of which trust has been lost include: (1) Succession of high-profile scandals, the (complex) nature of financial products and services and the vulnerability of retail customers' trust is an important issue, (2) numerous episodes of mis-selling of some financial products, (3) a lack of diversity w.r.t. ownership structure of financial firms, corporate governance arrangements, capital structure and primarily business models, the latter reducing consumer choice and effective competition, (4) the fact that relationship banking has given way to transactional banking, which in turn has promoted a sales culture and potentially hazardous incentive structures within banking and other financial firms, (5) a serious erosion in the application of the principles of the "Treating Customers Fairly" regime, which was imposed on the retail financial services industry by the then regulator—the Financial Services Authority (FSA) (in the UK), (6) low priority given to ethical standards within financial firms, (7) the existence of perverse incentive structures inherent in the shareholder value maximization model and within financial firms in forms such as bonuses and salaries, (8) Opportunistic cross-subsidization by life assurance firms, who offer new customers better returns than existing ones, (9) unjustifiably high and complex charges in a complex intermediation setting and the lack of transparent pricing, (10) the lack of truly effective competition in some retail markets, (11) the lack of access to financial products and services for some consumers (financial inclusion issues), and (12) the fact that independent advisory market is weak due to the exit of several retail banks as a result of regulatory changes.

A survey (IPSOS 2013), conducted on 19 financial institutions measured across 25 countries, identifies key drivers of trust in financial services as: (1) experience/aspiration, (2) commitment to customers, (3) personal relationship, (4) the value of products and services, (5) transactional care, and (6) expertise/authority. According to this survey, payment-processing companies enjoy a much better reputation than do banks. Furthermore, the study determines that in nearly all emerging markets, domestic banks receive very high net trust scores—widely larger than do non-local banks on average.

Llewellyn (2014) furthermore argues for diversity in the financial system, in a way that promotes risk-diversification and states that there are clear economic, systemic and welfare benefits to be derived from a successful mutual or cooperative sector in the financial system. He further argues that a financial system populated by diversity of ownership and governance structures, and with contrasting business models, is likely to be more competitive and systemically less risky than one populated by a single dominant model, whatever that model might be. What follows from these arguments is that there is a public policy interest in fostering diversity in the financial system.

Herman (2015) reports that JPMorgan Chase launched The Financial Solutions Lab, in partnership with the Center for Financial Services Innovation (CFSI) to specifically address the issue of diversity. The motivation for this endeavor is the manifestation that low-income American families spend the same share of their yearly income on interest and fees as the average American household spends yearly on food. Moreover, low-income households are said to face financial literacy and infrastructure challenges at a much higher rate than the average American household. Consequently, it is implied that access to financial products and services is necessary to achieve full participation in the global economy. Thus, thus the accessibility of innovations can help increase savings, improve credit, and build assets.

Accenture consulting explains how technology can be used to rebuild consumer confidence, by not only being fast and flexible in their innovative banking application roll-outs, but also by being more responsive to customer needs with new products and services. This necessitates devising new ways of interaction with customers and investing more to learn about details of consumer attitudes to be able to separate hype from reality.[3] In that sense, big data analytics and, proper use of such, can provide key insights to trends and fads in consumer behavior. Academic literature, too, has already acknowledged the importance of big data analytics in understanding consumer confidence (Choi and Varian 2012) and investor sentiment (Son-Turan 2014).

In an effort to understand how consumer trust in financial services can be restored, the Social Market Foundation (2011) underscores that consumer trust and strong economies run in tandem and determines in its report that introducing 'simple products' may be one method of achieving this, but advises that the industry

[3]https://www.accenture.com/us-en/insight-financial-services-technology-rebuild-consumer-confidence.aspx

should also adopt a more sophisticated approach that explores how innovation and new technologies can simplify the consumer experience and enhance their interaction with financial services. According to the report, this would enable the delivery of faster, safer and more convenient ways for consumers to handle their finances, independent of government intervention. Furthermore, with regards to the proposition that financial crises have been the major cause of declining trust, the findings show that more long-term drivers, such as the distinctive nature of consumer finance products, are more instrumental in defining the concept of trust. Finally, the report proposes two interventions: First, the regulator should create a kite-mark for a wide range of privately provided 'trusted financial products', from current accounts to pensions, which would conform to mandated standards and act as market norms against which all other products could be compared. Second, having secured product quality through the 'trusted product' kite-mark, competition between providers should be strengthened.

However, whether regulation is a substitute for reputation is another issue and beyond the scope of this article.

A Global Consumer Banking Survey (EY 2014), which includes responses from over 32,000 retail banking consumers across 43 countries, explores the role of trust in creating customer advocates and how valuable trust is to the overall banking relationship. To that end, it established that the one most sought after benefit that needs improvement is the transparency of fees and simplicity of offers and communication. Secondly, while customers are satisfied with the convenience of traditional banking, their expectations are constantly rising as new technologies and consumer benefits develop. The findings of the report suggest that trust is mostly associated with the customers' experience of how they are being treated, followed by communication and problem solving.

3 Literature Review

The role of trust, confidence and reputation in financial services has been addressed frequently in academic literature. Tyler and Stanley (2007), in their qualitative research based on 147 in-depth interviews with corporate bankers and their clients, find that small companies are more trusting than large corporates. Furthermore the authors establish that, bankers use calculative and operational trust and were cynical about their counterparts' trustworthiness. Pi et al. (2012), propose a framework of intention to continuously adopt online financial services and suggest that (1) website trust influences on the intention to continuous adoption of online financial services, (2) cognitive trust of online customers influences on affective trust, (3) factors of transaction security, website and company awareness, prior Internet experience, and navigation functions directly influence on cognitive trust of online customers, and; (4) transaction security is the only factor that influences on affective trust of online customers. Bejou et al. (1998), examining the relationship between trust, ethics and relationship satisfaction establish that from the customer's perspective, the determinants of relationship satisfaction are thought to include factors such as customer orientation, trust, length of relationship, expertise and ethics. Nguyen and LeBlanc (1998), using data collected from 1224 customers in the banking service industry satisfaction and service quality are positively related to value and that quality exerts a stronger influence on value than satisfaction. Howcroft et al. (2007), suggest that the financial services and products market consists of distinctive customer segments and that the majority of bank customers are still essentially "passive" and there appears to be an overwhelming customer need for more product information and more involvement with banks. Gill (2008) explores how consumer trust can be restored in financial services and provides financial services marketers some insight into the future of online advertising and explains the benefits of adopting a dual approach of both brand advertising and search marketing to restore consumer confidence. Prahalad and Ramaswamy (2004) pose the questions whether financial services firms should have a "consumer bill of rights"? and Ogrizek (2002) looks into the effect of corporate social responsibility on the branding of financial services.

On the other hand, the financial services loss-of-reputation literature seems to be more populated after 2008, coinciding with the global financial crisis. Brown and Whysall (2010) for instance, explore the perceived paradox whereby companies in Britain's financial services sector were externally promoted as "world class" yet on a major peer survey of company reputations performed relatively weakly. The authors mention of the possibility that recent events are seen as somewhat resolving the paradox in that low reputation has apparently been justified by crises in the sectors. Mintz (2016) discusses the disagreement on who was to blame for the sub-prime mortgage crisis and argues that ethical lapses in the financial services industry were an important cause. The author also draws attention to the fact that technology and better use of big data could also allow banks to use nontraditional standards for lending.

4 Conclusion

Compliance, especially starting with the Sarbanes Oxley Act, has been thought to be an effective tool, not only in hindering potential fraudulent activity, but also thereby instilling the trust lost in financial services. However, surveys like the Edelman Trust Barometer mentioned previously, imply that these measures have not been enough and the public, and especially the millennials, which form a huge percentage of the near future financial services customer base, cares about social responsibility rather than simple control and compliance, which are more or less de facto mechanisms nowadays.

The mind of a typical member of Generation Z ("Gen Z"[4]) is a crowded place (Holland 2013). Gen Z-ers are already the biggest generational group in the U.S.,

[4]Individuals born between 1995 and 2012, according to http://www.socialmarketing.org/newsletter/features/generation3.htm

having overtaken the millennials in what Sparks & Honey describe as a coming "demographic tsunami" (Bershidsky 2014). An article by the Wall Street Journal (WSJ 2016) reports that the first wave of Gen Z's 1.8 million job candidates will enter the labor force in May 2016 and, like preceding generations, they come weighted with unique characteristics determined partly by the events and technology that helped shape their formative years. The same article highlights findings of a study from Randstad Holdings and Millennial Branding that portrays the digital dependency of this generation: 84 % of Gen Z sleep with their phones. More and more do we see headlines in popular media such as; "Gen Z is about to rock the banking industry" (WSJ 2016), "Generation Z' is entrepreneurial, wants to chart its own future" (Northeastern News 2014), and "The money mind-set of Generation Z" (Holland 2013).

To conclude, this chapter has portrayed a major concern for the financial services industry: the declining trust of customers and investors, and the concurrent loss of reputation. Understanding the dynamics underlying these developments will help financial services companies revamp their product and service offerings by adapting to the changing social, environmental and economic conditions. It is advised to particularly gain a deep understanding of the needs and demands of the newer generations and embrace their values. Secondly, transparency in management and reporting, with universally agreed upon rules and regulations, should be a de facto understanding across the industry.

References

Bejou D, Ennew CT, Palmer A (1998) Trust, ethics and relationship satisfaction. Int J Bank Mark 16(4):170–175

Bershidsky L (2014) Here comes generation Z. 18 Jun 2014. http://www.bloombergview.com/articles/2014-06-18/nailing-generation-z

Brown M, Whysall P (2010) Performance, reputation, and social responsibility in the UK's financial services: a post-'credit crunch' interpretation. Serv Ind J 30(12):1991–2006

Choi H, Varian H (2012) Predicting the present with Google Trends. Econ Rec 88(s1):2–9

Ennew C, Sekhon H (2007) Measuring trust in financial services: the trust index. Consum Policy Rev 17(2):62

EY (2014) Winning through experience. EY Global Consumer Banking Survey 2014. http://www.ey.com/Publication/vwLUAssets/EY_-_Global_Consumer_Banking_Survey_2014/$FILE/EY-Global-Consumer-Banking-Survey-2014.pdf

Gill C (2008) Restoring consumer confidence in financial services. Int J Bank Mark 26(2):148–152

Guiso L, Sapienza P, Zingales L (2008) Trusting the stock market. J Fin 63(6):2557–2600

Herman J (2015). Innovators improve consumer confidence in the Financial Solutions Lab. 30 Mar 2015. https://www.uschamberfoundation.org/blog/post/innovators-improve-consumer-confidence-financial-solutions-lab/42924

Holland K (2013) The money mind-set of Generation Z. 13 Sep 2013. http://www.cnbc.com/id/101026186

Howcroft B, Hamilton R, Hewer P (2007) Customer involvement and interaction in retail banking: an examination of risk and confidence in the purchase of financial products. J Serv Mark 21(7):481–491

Huberman G (2001) Familiarity breeds investment. Rev Fin Stud 14(3):659–680
IPSOS (2013) Global reputation of the financial services industry: 2013 Snapshot. http://www.ipsos.com/public-affairs/sites/www.ipsos.com.public-affairs/files/Global%20Reputation%20of%20the%20Financial%20Services%20Industry%202013%20Snapshot%20INTL.pdf
Jaffer S, Morris N, Sawbridge E, Vines D (2014) How changes to the financial services industry eroded trust. In: Morris N, Vines D (eds) Capital failure: rebuilding trust in financial services. Oxford University Press, Oxford, p 32
Kindleberger C, Aliber RM (2005) Panics, and crashes: a history of financial crises. Wiley, Hoboken, NJ
Llewellyn DT (2014) Reforming the culture of banking: restoring trust and confidence in banking. J Fin Manage Mark Inst 2(2):221–235. doi: 10.12831/78760
Mintz SL (2015) Ethics and financial services, 16 Mar 2015. doi:10.1177/2374556815579661. http://businessresearcher.sagepub.com/sbr-1645-95217-2661757/20150316/ethics-and-financialservices. Sage, Thousand Oaks, CA
Nguyen N, LeBlanc G (1998) The mediating role of corporate image on customers' retention decisions: an investigation in financial services. Int J Bank Mark 16(2):52–65
Northeastern News (2014) 'Generation Z' is entrepreneurial, wants to chart its own future. 18 Nov 2014. http://www.northeastern.edu/news/2014/11/generation-z-survey/
Ogrizek M (2002) The effect of corporate social responsibility on the branding of financial services. J Fin Serv Mark 6(3):215–228
Pi SM, Liao HL, Chen HM (2012) Factors that affect consumers' trust and continuous adoption of online financial services. Int J Bus Manage 7(9):108
Prahalad CK, Ramaswamy V (2004) Co-creating unique value with customers. Strateg Leadersh 32(3):4–9
PwC (2014) Financial services industry faces bigger problem than lack of trust – apathy. 2 Oct 2014. http://pwc.blogs.com/press_room/2014/10/pwc-research-financial-services-industry-faces-bigger-problem-than-lack-of-trust-apathy.html
Social Market Foundation (2011) A confidence crisis? Restoring trust in financial services. http://www.smf.co.uk/wp-content/uploads/2011/07/Publication-A-Confidence-Crisis-Restoring-trust-in-financial-services.pdf
Son-Turan S (2014) Internet search volume and stock return volatility: the case of Turkish companies. Inf Manage Bus Rev 6(6):317
Tyler K, Stanley E (2007) The role of trust in financial services business relationships. J Serv Mark 21(5):334–344
WSJ (2016) Onboarding the always-on generation. 20 Jan 2016. http://blogs.wsj.com/cio/2016/01/20/onboarding-the-always-on-generation/

Semen Son-Turan is an Assistant Professor of Business Administration at MEF University, Department of Business Administration, Istanbul-Turkey. Dr. Son-Turan has a BA in Political Science and International Relations from Bogazici University (1998), an MBA in Finance and Accounting from The Pennsylvania State University—The Smeal College of Business Administration (2000) and holds a PhD in Business Administration with a focus on Finance and Accounting from Yasar University (2014).

Dr. Son-Turan has held various managerial positions at prominent multinational companies and has extensive experience in the financial services industry. Her research interests include behavioral finance, capital markets, financial innovation and higher education finance. She has taught finance, financial and managerial accounting and strategy courses, among others, at US and Turkish institutions.

The Effect of National Culture on Corporate Financial Decisions

Emin Huseyin Cetenak, Ayse Cingoz, and Elif Acar

Abstract Recently, studies on the effects of cultural factors on corporate financial decision-making have emerged in the finance literature. Culture shapes behaviors of people and distinguishes members of one group or category from another. The decision-making process depends greatly on cultural background. Executives' financial decisions show variance from society to society as a result of their cultural differences. The objective of this study is to point out the effects of national culture on financial decision-making. We examined Hofstede's cultural dimensions among 20 countries around the world to explain the variation of financial decisions based on cultural differences. According to our results, power-distance has an effect on all financial decisions included in the study, except for the capital structure. Individualism also has an influence on all the financial decisions we analyzed, except for Research & Development (R&D) expenditures. Uncertainty avoidance is found to have an effect on all of the financial decision parameters included here, except for discretionary accruals, which are an indication of a firm's earnings-management decisions and can be considered as a clue for manipulation of earnings. Masculinity is found to have an effect only on capital structure and working capital level.

1 Introduction

Culture is the entirety of values, norms, beliefs and assumptions that govern individuals' attitude and behavior. Circumstantially, culture causes individuals' attitudes and behaviors to represent similarities and at the same time allows

E.H. Cetenak (✉) • A. Cingoz
Department of Business Administration, Faculty of Economics and administrative Sciences, Nevsehir Haci Bektas Veli University, Nevsehir, Turkey
e-mail: cetenak@gmail.com; acingoz@nevsehir.edu.tr

E. Acar
Department of Management Information Systems, Faculty of Business, Adana Science and Technology University, Adana, Turkey
e-mail: eacar@adanabtu.edu.tr

H. Dinçer, Ü. Hacioğlu (eds.), *Risk Management, Strategic Thinking and Leadership in the Financial Services Industry*, Contributions to Management Science, DOI 10.1007/978-3-319-47172-3_24

differentiating between individuals. At this point, the concept of national culture becomes important. National culture can be defined as the totality of behavioral norms, traditional beliefs, and values that are formative influences on the majority of individuals that live in a given country.

Culture, not only influences the attitude and behavior of individuals in a country, but also impacts on the country's institutions, policies and processes. National culture especially impresses the organizational culture by affecting institutional applications, policies and norms. One of the most important processes that national culture affects is the decision-making process. Decision-makers are affected by the culture in which they perform and make preferences according to cultural characteristics. Culture also influences the way official institutions function in a country, which in turn affects decision-making. In any organization financial decisions, like most other functional decisions, are affected by culture. Managers' and investors' decisions, preferences and economic conduct are affected by not only certain individual traits and organizational characteristics, but also by the national culture.

The national culture and its sub dimensions in which an organization operates affect the organizational decision-making process and entail dissimilar managerial course action across cultures. The most widely used classifications employed in analyzing the national culture and its sub dimensions are the cultural dimensions developed by Hofstede. Hofstede, specified four main cultural dimensions in his studies and identified them as: individualism, power distance, uncertainty-avoidance and masculinity (1983, 1998). These cultural dimensions, by their various aspects, have an effect on a diverse array of financial decisions such as risk taking, cash holdings, R&D expenditures, and general and administrative expenditures.

In this regard, the aim of this study is to determine the effect of national culture on financial decisions. Firstly, we have given some information on the concepts of culture and national culture. Then, we have theoretically discussed the effects of culture and national culture dimensions, as defined by Hofstede, on the financial decisions. Finally, we examined the empirical evidence of the effect of national culture on various financial decisions by utilizing multilevel models. The number of multilevel studies in finance is limited. Our results are discussed in the conclusion section.

2 The Role of Culture/National Culture in Corporate Decision Making

Several studies in the management, financial, and accounting literatures have explored the importance of culture in decision-making (Jaggi and Low 2000; Kurtz 2003; Griffin et al. 2009; Nolder and Riley 2013; Rehbein 2014). These studies found that culture can explain the institutional, legal, and economic environments of a country at the macro level, which can influence corporate decisions (Mihet 2013).

The decision-making process depends on cultural background and choice of "the right way"—decision-making processes are dependent on the values and beliefs of the people who are involved in the decision-making process (Podrug 2011). In this regard, it can be said that firms' policies and processes are affected by their country's cultural environment since managers' and investors' views and choices are impressed by the national culture (Chen et al. 2015). According to some past research, culture is a major and overlooked key to understanding decision-making processes (Kurtz 2003).

Culture is something that is shared by almost all members of a social group (Podrug 2011). Similarly, Hofstede defines culture as "the collective programming of the mind that distinguishes the members of a group from another" (Chang and Noorbakhsh 2009). National culture is the behavioral norm and traditional beliefs of the majority of people in a certain country (Chang and Lin 2015).

It is essential to have knowledge of other cultures, cultural values and their impact on the types of organizations that emerge and behaviors that take place within them. A different cultural environment requires different managerial behavior (Podrug 2011). National culture may explain several corporate decisions. For example, various financial decisions of executives show variance from society to society as a result of their cultural differences (Mihet 2013). Particularly, culture effects perceptions of decision-makers that are related to cost and risk-taking decisions in business (Chang and Noorbakhsh 2009). Griffin et al. (2009) expressed that managers from different cultural backgrounds will differ in their preferences for risk-taking, and hence, that firms operating in different countries will differ systematically and predictably on their level of corporate risk-taking. Culture affects corporate risk-taking both through its influence on managerial decision-making and through its influence on a country's official institutions (Li et al. 2013). Also, culture may cause exhibition of similar investment strategies of managers or financial preferences of investors in the same country (Chang and Lin 2015).

3 Hofstede's Dimensions of National Culture and Financial Decision-Making

Recently finance and international business scholars have studied cultural factors as legitimate variables in explaining financial decision making processes at individual and institutional levels. Since culture might have an important role in economic behavior such as financial decisions (Chang and Noorbakhsh 2009), researchers tried to determine the dimensions of culture and contribute to understanding national culture dimensions.

Hofstede's cultural dimensions provided researchers with the most comprehensive framework to analyze the effects of cultural values on business organizations and decision-making (Chang and Noorbakhsh 2009). Hofstede's dimensions of national culture were determined by a survey. Data was collected from IBM employees in different countries (53 countries and regions of the World). Hofstede carried out a research in the period from 1967 to 1969, with over 60,000 respondents, employees in IBM's branches in 53 countries, and repeated the research in 71 countries in the period from 1971 to 1973 with a modified questionnaire on 60,000 respondents of which 30,000 respondents were from the first study, 20,000 respondents recently employed by IBM, and 10,000 respondents who did not participate in the first study (Podrug 2011). By factor analysis Hofstede identified four of the national culture dimensions (1) individualism/collectivism, (2) uncertainty avoidance, (3) power distance, and (4) masculinity/femininity (Chang and Noorbakhsh 2009; Dimitratos et al. 2011; Podrug 2011). These dimensions together cannot be assumed to exhaust the universe of differences between national cultures, but they have substantial face validity and have been empirically demonstrated to have an influence on many aspects of management and organizations.

Individualistic cultures emphasize individual freedom and achievement rather than group cohesion-loyalty/dependence (Griffin et al. 2009; Li et al. 2013). Also self-actualization is very important. People in Individualistic cultures have "I-conscious" behavior. Furthermore, they tend to overestimate their own abilities, and be overly optimistic about the precision of their predictions (Chen et al. 2015). In Individualistic cultures, people value their personal freedom. The significance of "I-conscious" behavior and personal freedom causes individuals to demand their wishes.

In collectivist cultures personal identity is based on the social systems where people belong. People in such cultures exhibit higher self-monitoring than people in individualistic cultures (Chen et al. 2015). As can be seen, in collectivist cultures, belonging to a group is important. In this sense, individuals feel associated with the organization, company or family they belong to and make collectivist decisions being influenced by these groups. Individualism stands for "a society in which the ties between individuals are loose—everybody is expected to look after him/herself and his/her immediate family only" while collectivism stands for "a society in which people from birth onwards are integrated into strong, cohesive in-groups, which throughout people's lifetimes continue to protect them in exchange for unquestioning loyalty." (Podrug 2011).

Hofstede defined uncertainty-avoidance as the extent fear of uncertain and unknown situations that are felt by members of a culture (Chang and Noorbakhsh 2009; Mihet 2013). In these cultures individuals perceive ambiguous situations as a threat. Members of uncertainty-avoidant cultures prefer clear rules of conduct (Li et al. 2013). People in uncertainty-avoiding cultures emphasize short-run reactions to short-run feedback rather than anticipation of long-run uncertainty and solve pressing problems rather than developing long-run strategies (Chen et al. 2015).

Uncertainty-avoidance indicates the extent to which a society feels threatened by ambiguous situations and the extent to which a society tries to avoid these situations by adopting strict codes of behavior, a belief in absolute truths, establishing formal rules, and intolerance toward deviant ideas and actions (Hofstede 1980; Podrug 2011). People in uncertainty-avoidant cultures favor an orderly structure in their organizations, institutions, and personal relations and prefer well-anticipated events (Mihet 2013). Uncertainty avoidance is also linked to preferences such as rules, stability, uniformity, and especially closely related to psychological characteristics widely discussed in behavioral financial economics such as conservatism and risk aversion (Chen et al. 2015). These cultural properties influence attitude of people towards risk at micro-level (Mihet 2013). Expectedly, people don't want to take risks in uncertainty-avoidant societies.

The opposite holds for people with a high tolerance for uncertainty. People in low uncertainty-avoidant cultures often exhibit a low sense of urgency in ambiguous, surprising, or unstructured situations. In contrast, people in high uncertainty-avoiding cultures feel more anxious in such situations, and therefore tend to take immediate action to reduce the level of ambiguity (Chen et al. 2015).

The power-distance dimension measures "the extent to which less powerful members of institutions and organizations within a country expect and accept that power is distributed unequally" (Hofstede 1983, 1998; Dimitratos et al. 2011; Mihet 2013). In high power-distance countries, organizations and institutions, individuals know whom to obey. Formal communication channels work from upper levels towards lower levels. In these systems, uncertainty is reduced by power-distance. Institutions and all units have clearly defined processes (Sargut 2001). On the contrary, decision-making is more likely to be decentralized in low power-distance countries. Thus, organizational structures are fairly decentralized with flat hierarchical pyramids in such countries. Further, management in low power-distance countries is more likely to delegate decision-making power (Dimitratos et al. 2011).

Masculinity stands for a society in which social gender roles are clearly distinct: men are supposed to be assertive, tough and focused on material success, and women are supposed to be modest, tender, and concerned with quality of life; while Femininity indicates a society in which social gender roles overlap: both men and women are supposed to be modest, tender and concerned with quality of life (Hofstede 1983; Podrug 2011). In high masculinity societies, such propensities as competition, money-making, audacity stand in the forefront; while humanitarian propensities may lack behind. In feminine societies human interaction is important and there is great emphasis on the quality of life (Sargut 2001).

In addition to individual and organizational variables, cultural background is an effective criterion in decision making process. According to Li et al. (2013) individualism has a positive and a significant association, whereas uncertainty avoidance has a negative and significant association with corporate risk-taking. Cultural values such as individualism and uncertainty avoidance may cause different legal frameworks as well as different laws concerning investor protection and creditor rights, which in turn may affect corporate risk taking. For example, more individualistic countries have legal systems that support individual freedom and autonomy, which may encourage corporate risk taking (Rehbein 2014).

Griffin et al. (2012) examined the effects of culture on firms in the manufacturing sector in the period 1997–2006. They are the only ones who use a hierarchical linear mixed model to analyze the impact of culture on corporate risk-taking. According to the results of their study, individualism has positive and significant direct effects, while uncertainty avoidance has negative and significant direct effects on corporate risk-taking (Mihet 2013). Chen et al. (2015) shows that cash holdings that are an important financial decision, are negatively related to individualism and positively related to uncertainty-avoidance. Also individualism is positively associated with the firm's capital expenditures and acquisition decisions, while uncertainty-avoidance is negatively associated. According to Mihet (2013), culture impacts corporate risk taking directly. Moreover corporate risk-taking is higher in societies with low uncertainty avoidance, low tolerance for hierarchical relationship and in societies that value individualism over collectivism. Kanagaretnam et al. (2011) state that banks in high-uncertainty avoidance countries tend to take less risk, whereas banks in high individualism countries take more risk.

As can be seen, national culture has an effect on a number of financial decisions varying from cash holdings to risk taking and investment decisions. At this point, we can argue that various other financial decisions of a firm can also be affected by national culture. To conclude, based on the above literature review we will test the following hypotheses:

Hypothesis 1:	Culture of a country effects capital structure choices
Hypothesis 2:	Culture of a country effects risk taking of firm
Hypothesis 3:	Culture of a country effects R&D consumption of firm
Hypothesis 4:	Culture of a country effects SG&A expenses of firm
Hypothesis 5:	Culture of a country effects Working Capital level of firm
Hypothesis 6:	Culture of a country effects Retained Earnings of firm
Hypothesis 7:	Culture of a country effects earnings management practices of firm

Additionally, we also test effect of firm specific (Return on Assets and Size) and country specific variables (Ease of Doing Business and Total Credits Provided by Financial Sector) on these financial decisions.

4 Methodology and Data

In this study we examined the relationship between cultural dimensions and certain fundamental financial decisions by using multilevel mixed models which are basically statistical models of parameters that vary at more than one level (Raudenbush and Bryk 2002). Multilevel modelling (namely hierarchical linear models, nested models or mixed models) is a generalization of regression methods, and as such can be used for a variety of purposes, including prediction, data reduction, and causal inference from experiments and observational studies (Gelman 2012).

Multilevel data structures used in multilevel models are very common in the social sciences (Albright and Marinova 2010), e.g. students may be nested within schools, voters within districts, firms within industry or country. This type of multilevel data structure may cause several violations when using standard OLS regression (Kayo and Kimura 2011: 363) such as correlated errors, biased estimates of coefficient standard errors and wrongfully interpreting the results and significance of the predictor variables (Mihet 2013).

Within multi-level framework, Multilevel Models allow to test multilevel (industry or country level) theories simultaneously. Secondly, with multilevel models we can control unbalanced data easily. For example, if the number of firms varies widely across industries or countries, with multi-level fixed model approach we can detect all of those multilevel effects separately. Furthermore, via multilevel mixed models we can add cross-level interactions into a model and by doing so we can see not only firm, industry or country effects but also their cross-level interactions (Mihet 2013).

When considering financial decisions of a firm; it might be affected by its own industry or its home country characteristics beside its own individual characteristics. Thus, in order to explain behaviour of a firm properly, each level should be considered in the analysis. In recent years, statistical methods that take into account multilevel data have gained popularity (Albright and Marinova 2010).

In this study, we analyze three levels of financial decision determinants in 20 selected countries for the year 2014 (for the list of countries, please see Appendix). Most of the countries are OECD countries. We excluded some of the European countries because they exhibit cultural similarities with each other and may have caused the study to be biased. We only included firms quoted in the NYSE for U.S.A. with SIC codes varying from 2000 to 3999, to avoid heterogeneity problems caused by industry diversity. We conducted the analyses only on non-financial firms.

First level in our study is 'firm', while the second level is 'industry', and third level is 'country'. By applying multilevel models, we assume that observations across industries and countries are correlated amongst themselves. Similarly, it is rational to suppose that firms working in the same industry and in the same country have similar behaviour regarding financing decisions. Also we assume all of our firm level independent variables have random slope which effected by both industry and country factors. Our basic model we fit in this study is below:

$$\begin{aligned}\textit{\textbf{FINANCIAL DECISION}}_{i,j,k} = {} & \beta_0 + \beta_1 \mathrm{UAI}_{\mathrm{i,j,k}} + \beta_2 \mathrm{MAS}_{i,j,k} \\ & + \beta_3 \mathrm{IDV}_{i,j,k} + \beta_4 \mathrm{PDI}_{i,j,k} + \beta_{5i,j} \mathrm{SIZE}_{i,j,k} \\ & + \beta_{6i,j} \mathrm{ROA}_{i,j,k} + \beta_7 \mathrm{EDB}_{i,j,k} \\ & + \beta_8 \mathrm{CREDIT}_{i,j,k} + u_{i,} + r_{i,j} + e_{i,j,k}\end{aligned}$$

Where *i* denotes country, *j* industry and *k* denotes firm. Additionally $u_{i,}$, $r_{i,j}$ and $e_{i,j,k}$ random error terms representing the variance respectively across country, industry-country and firm-industry-country which are normally distributed with zero mean and σ^2 variance.

We have identified seven dependent variables from seven different models. Our dependent variables are the leverage ratio, Altman Z score, R&D expenses, SG&A expenses, working capital investment, retained earnings and discretionary accruals. The data used in the analysis are given in Table 1. In order to calculate firm level

Table 1 Definition of variables and descriptive statistics

Variables	Description	Source	Mean	SD
Dependent variables				
Leverage	Firm's leverage was calculated by dividing total debt to total assets. Leverage is proxy for firm's capital structure	Datastream	0.2391	0.3629
Z score	Risk or distance from bankruptcy score was calculated by following Mackie-Mason's (1990) modified Altman's Z score formula where $Z = 3.3(\text{EBIT}/\text{Total Assets}) + 1.0(\text{Sales}/\text{Total Assets}) + 1.4(\text{Retained Earnings}/\text{Total Assets}) + 1.2(\text{Working Capital}/\text{Total Assets})$	Datastream	1.415	8.122
R&D	Firm's R&D expenditures scaled dividing by firm's total assets	Datastream	0.0442	0.1275
Selling and general administrative costs	Firm's SG&A costs scaled dividing by firm's total assets	Datastream	0.2018	0.3134
Working capital	Working capital was calculated by dividing the difference between a firm's current assets and accounts payable to the firm's total asset	Datastream	0.3909	0.3241
Retained earnings	Firm's retained earnings scaled dividing by firm's total assets	Datastream	0.2339	22.96
Discretionary accruals (absolute value)	Discretionary Accruals calculated based on Adjusted Jones model (Jones 1991) which was modified by Dechow et al. (1995). Discretionary accruals are residual of modified Jones model that obtained from year-industry-country estimation. We considered absolute value of discretionary accruals because magnitude of residuals is more important than its direction.	Calculated by Authors	0.082	0.1831
Hofstede culture indexes				
Uncertainty avoidance	Uncertainty aversion index. Higher values indicate higher uncertainty aversion	Hofstede	63.92	24.71
Masculinity vs femininity	Higher values indicate higher masculinity	Hofstede	52.52	10.76
Individualism vs collectivism	Higher values indicate higher individualism	Hofstede	49.90	28.39
Power distance index	Higher values indicate higher power distance	Hofstede	60.21	22.62
Firm-level control variables				
Return on asset	Profitability of the firm was calculated by dividing EBIT to total assets	Datastream	0.0290	0.3265
Firm size	Natural logarithm of total assets	Datastream	14.60	3.685

(continued)

Table 1 (continued)

Variables	Description	Source	Mean	SD
Country-level control variables				
Ease of doing business	Economies are ranked on their ease of doing business, from 1–189. A high ease of doing business ranking means the regulatory environment is more conducive to the starting and operation of a local firm.	World Bank	32.09	35.68
Credit from private sector	Domestic credit provided by the financial sector includes all credit to various sectors on a gross basis (% of GDP)	World Bank	143.7	58.39

variables, income statement and balance sheet items were used by the authors. Ease of doing business and credit from private sector variables were obtained from World Bank, Hofstede's cultural dimension variables were obtained from Hofstede's web site. Table 1 also presents definition, source and descriptive statistics of each variable used.

Leverage was calculated as total debt to total assets ratio and used as proxy for firms' capital structure. The mean of Leverage was 0.24, which indicates an overall low leverage ratio for the sample. The Altman Z score is used as proxy for risk or distance from bankruptcy and was calculated by following Mackie-Mason's (1990) modified Altman Z score formula (see Table 1). The average of the Z scores is 1.415. R&D, SG&A expenses, working capital and retained earnings were all scaled dividing by total assets. The average of R&D was 0.04, the average of SG&A was 0.20 and the average of working capital and retained earnings were 0.39 and 0.23, respectively. Discretionary Accruals was calculated based on Modified Jones model (Jones 1991) which was adjust by Dechow et al. (1995). Discretionary earnings are an indication of a firm's earnings management decisions and can be considered as a clue for manipulation of earnings. The average was 0.08.

Hofstede's four dimension indexes are independent variables in our analysis: uncertainty-avoidance, masculinity, individualism and power-distance. The average of the uncertainty score was 63.92. Higher scores denote higher avoidance of uncertainty. The average of masculinity score was 52.52, and the averages of individualism and power-distance indexes were 49.90 and 60.21, respectively.

5 Results

Table 2 presents the results. Our dependent variables are leverage ratio, Altman z score, R&D and SG&A expenses, working capital investment, retained earnings and discretionary accruals. Size and return on assets are firm level control variables. Ease of doing business and credit from private sector are country level control variables. Most of the cultural variables have a significant effect on financial decisions. On the other hand, the firm-level control variable 'size' has an effect

Table 2 Effect of national culture on corporate financial decisions

Variables	LEV	Z	RD	SG&A	WC	RETND	DA
Uncertainty avoidance index (UAI)	**0.002119** (0.000)	**0.017854** (0.051)	**−0.000935** (0.001)	−0.001251 (0.065)	**−0.001692** (0.007)	**0.012438** (0.012)	0.00042 (0.202)
Masculinity vs femininity (MAS)	**0.004063** (0.004)	−0.007947 (0.761)	0.001213 (0.251)	−0.000548 (0.779)	**−0.00469** (0.007)	0.014958 (0.336)	0.00063 (0.521)
Individualism vs collectivism (IDV)	**−0.002029** (0.021)	**0.052732** (0.053)	−0.00065 (0.530)	**0.002144** (0.072)	**−0.00212** (0.045)	0.014954 (0.085)	**−0.00189** **(0.000)**
Power distance index (PDI)	−0.000762 (0.259)	**0.042429** (0.001)	**−0.00143** (0.000)	**−0.002860** (0.002)	**−0.002532** (0.003)	**0.026606** (0.000)	**−0.00097** **(0.006)**
Intercept	**−0.549612** (0.006)	**−9.0665** (0.001)	**0.23232** (0.004)	**0.48938** (0.001)	**0.914332** (0.000)	**6.74059** (0.000)	**0.1801** **(0.014)**
Firm-level control variables							
Size	**0.01594** (0.000)	**0.22736** (0.001)	**−0.00653** (0.006)	**−0.02355** (0.000)	**−0.03108** (0.000)	**0.17665** (0.000)	**−0.01657** **(0.000)**
Return on asset	**−0.63525** (0.000)	**10.440** (0.000)	−0.06257 (0.291)	−0.09282 (0.217)	**0.45397** (0.001)	**4.3159** (0.000)	−0.01028 (0.851)
Country-level control variables							
Ease of doing business	**0.00096** (0.042)	0.00250 (0.735)	**0.0002067** **(0.005)**	0.00072 (0.245)	0.00075 (0.190)	−0.00509 (0.282)	**0.00137** **(0.000)**
Credit from private sector	**0.00083** (0.011)	0.01010 (0.127)	−0.00005 (0.837)	−0.000057 (0.893)	**0.000758** (0.058)	**0.000476** (0.046)	**0.00065** **(0.002)**
LR test vs. linear regression: (chi^2)	1612.20 (0.000)	1619.38 (0.000)	240.18 (0.000)	874.08 (0.000)	343.57 (0.000)	9.49 (0.0500)	56.58 (0.000)
Number of obs	2711	2711	2680	2465	2703	2709	1579
Wald $chi^2(8)$	102.170 (0.000)	97.53 (0.000)	102.17 (0.000)	165.16 (0.000)	229.63 (0.000)	269.29 (0.000)	36.08 (0.000)

Note: Firm level control variables (size and roa) have both fixed and random coefficients according to firm, industry and country level; p values are in parenthesis. Significant coefficients at %1 and %5 levels are bolded on all financial decisions while ROA has an effect on most of them. Similarly as can be seen from the table, 'ease of doing business' and 'credit from private sector' variables have an effect on most of the financial decisions. The models are meaningful as a whole.

6 Conclusion

In this study, we have aimed to determine the effect of national culture on financial decisions. Firstly, we have given some information on the concepts of culture and national culture. Then, we have theoretically discussed the effects of culture and national culture dimensions, as defined by Hofstede, on the financial decisions. Finally, we examined the empirical evidence of the effect of national culture on various financial decisions by utilizing multilevel models.

Our first dependent variable was leverage ratio, which is a proxy for capital structure. Leverage ratio denotes how extensively a company uses debt. It is sometimes directly associated with the riskiness of the firm, hence risk-taking. However, it would be inadequate to say that the lower the leverage ratio, the less risky the business is. In general, if a firm's leverage ratio is too high, it's a signal that the firm may be in financial distress. But, at the same time a leverage ratio that is too low may be a sign that the firm is over-relying on equity to finance its business, which can be costly and inefficient. In our findings, leverage ratio is positively and significantly correlated with both uncertainty avoidance and masculinity, while it is negatively and significantly correlated with individualism. Masculinity, which denotes such traits as money-making and competition, also affects risk-taking behavior. The tax advantage obtained by using debt financing may encourage managers who are keen on increasing profits to use leverage as a tool to do so. As individualism increases, leverage ratio decreases.

Altman Z Score's gives an indication of risk or distance from bankruptcy as well as financial performance. A higher Z score denotes lower riskiness for the firm. Based on our results, uncertainty avoidance, individualism and power distance are positively and significantly correlated with the Z score. As uncertainty avoidance increases, risk avoidance increases. Higher individualism and power-distance also denote risk avoidance and a better financial performance.

R&D expenditures are instrumental on future earnings rather than short-term earnings. Thus, there is a trade-off for firms. A firm with high R&D expenditures takes on a certain level of risk. Our findings indicate that the R&D expenditure is negatively and significantly correlated with uncertainty avoidance and power-distance. Risk avoiding managers prefer not to spend too much on R&D and similarly an authoritative management culture (high power distance) that prefers clearly defined rules isn't expected to promote R&D expenditures.

SG&A expenditures include management salaries, bonuses, marketing and even some R&D expenses. We can interpret the results based on these expenses similar to R&D expenditures. These are expenses made not only for today's earning but also for future benefits. These expenses are correlated positively with individualism and negatively with power-distance, which indicates that as individualism increases

SG&A expenses increase and as power-distance becomes higher these expenses get lower.

Working capital investments usually follow three main motivations: operations, financial prudence and/or speculation. Working capital investments are significantly and negatively correlated with all cultural dimensions examined here. The negative relationship with uncertainty avoidance can be explained by risk avoidance (higher working capital means financial flexibility and lower risk of cash constraint). At the same time, results also suggest that masculine, authoritative and individualistic management style prefer lower working capital investment. This implies lower accounts receivable, lower cash flow and inventory and higher accounts payable levels.

The variable retained earnings represent the portion of profits that the firm chose not to distribute as dividend to the shareholders, rather retain for the firm, with various motives. It has positive and significant correlation with uncertainty avoidance and power-distance at the 5 % level, while a positive and significant correlation with individualism at the 10 % level. This finding suggests that risk avoiding firms retain more earning. At the same time, as individualism and authoritative management levels increase, management prefers not to distribute dividends and have higher retained earnings.

Discretionary Accruals were calculated based on Adjusted Jones model (Jones 1991) which modified by Dechow et al. (1995). Discretionary accruals are residual of modified Jones model that obtained from year-industry-country estimation. We considered absolute value of discretionary accruals because magnitude of residuals is more important than its direction. Discretionary accruals are an indication of a firm's earnings management decisions and can be considered a clue for manipulation of earnings. As individualism and power-distance increases, such earnings management practices become less. An interpretation may be that as individualism increases, managers become avoidant of unethical behavior. At the same time, because power-distance reduces agency conflict, this results in lower discretionary accruals.

As a whole, the findings in our study suggest that firms' financial decisions cannot be explained only by the risk-return formula. Cultural influences like power, control, individualism and such play a crucial role in the financial-decision making process.

Appendix

Table 3 List of countries analyzed

Country		
Argentina	Indonesia	Romania
Brazil	Israel	Singapore
Chile	Korea (South)	South Africa
Egypt	Malaysia	Turkey
France	Mexico	United Kingdom
Germany	Philippines	United States (NYSE)
Greece	Poland	

References

Albright JJ, Marinova DM (2010) Estimating multilevel models using SPSS, Stata, SAS, and R. Indiana University, Bloomington, IN

Chang CH, Lin SJ (2015) The effects of national culture and behavioral pitfalls on investors' decision-making: herding behavior in international stock markets. Int Rev Econ Fin 37:380–392

Chang K, Noorbakhsh A (2009) Does national culture affect international corporate cash holdings? J Multinatl Fin Manage 19(5):323–342

Chen Y, Dou PY, Rhee SG, Truong C, Veeraraghavan M (2015) National culture and corporate cash holdings around the world. J Bank Fin 50:1–18

Dechow PM, Sloan RG, Sweeney AP (1995) Detecting earnings management. Acc Rev 70:193–225

Dimitratos P, Petrou A, Plakoyiannaki E, Johnson JE (2011) Strategic decision-making processes in internationalization: does national culture of the focal firm matter? J World Bus 46 (2):194–204

Gelman A (2012) Multilevel (hierarchical) modeling: what it can and cannot do. Technometrics 48:432–435

Griffin D, Li K, Yue H, Zhao L (2009) Cultural values and corporate risk-taking. University of British Columbia and Peking University Working Paper

Griffin DW, Li K, Yue H, Zhao L (2012) How does culture influence corporate risk-taking? doi:10.2139/ssrn.2021550. Available at SSRN: http://ssrn.com/abstract=2021550

Hofstede G (1980) Motivation, leadership, and organization: do American theories apply abroad? Organ dyn 9(1):42–63

Hofstede G (1983) National culture in four dimension: a research-based theory of cultural differences among nations. Int Stud Manage Org XIII(1–2):46–74

Hofstede G (1998) Attitudes, values and organizational culture: disentangling the concepts. Org Stud 19(3):477–498

Jaggi B, Low PY (2000) Impact of culture, market forces, and legal system on financial disclosures. Int J Acc 35(4):495–519

Jones JJ (1991) Earnings management during import relief investigations. J Acc Res 29:193–228

Kanagaretnam K, Lim CY, Lobo GJ (2011) Effects of national culture on earnings quality of banks. J Int Bus Stud 42(6):853–874

Kayo EK, Kimura H (2011) Hierarchical determinants of capital structure. J Bank Fin 35 (2):358–371
Kurtz RS (2003) Organizational culture, decision making, and integrity: the National Park Service and Exxon Valdez. Public Integr 5(4)
Li K, Griffin D, Yue H, Zhao L (2013) How does culture influence corporate risk-taking? J Corp Fin 23:1–22
Mackie-Mason JK (1990) Do taxes affect corporate financing decisions? J Fin 45(5):1471–1493
Mihet R (2013) Effects of culture on firm risk-taking: a cross-country and cross-industry analysis. J Cult Econ 37(1):109–151
Nolder C, Riley TJ (2013) Effects of differences in national culture on auditors' judgments and decisions: a literature review of cross-cultural auditing studies from a judgment and decision making perspective. Auditing 33(2):141–164
Podrug N (2011) Influence of national culture on decision-making style. SE Eur J Econ Bus 6 (1):37–44
Raudenbush SW, Bryk AS (2002) Hierarchical linear models: applications and data analysis methods, vol 1. Sage, London
Rehbein K (2014) Does culture influence corporate risk taking? Acad Manage Perspect 28(1):1–3
Sargut AS (2001) Kültürler Arası Farklılaşma ve Yönetim. İmge Kitabevi, Ankara

Emin Huseyin Cetenak is an Assistant Professor of Accounting and Finance at Nevsehir Haci Bektas Veli University Department of Management, Nevsehir-Turkey. Dr. Cetenak has both BS and MBA degrees in Business Administration from Cukurova University and PhD in Finance from Cukurova University (2012) as well. His research fields are corporate finance, corporate governance, working capital management etc. He has taught Financial Management, Corporate Finance, International Finance, Working Capital Management, Financial Risk Management courses, among others, at both graduate and undergraduate levels.

Ayşe Cingöz is Associate Professor in Management and Organization at Nevşehir University. She has Ph.D. of Management and Organization at Erciyes University (2011). She has taught organization theory, strategic management, human resource management, strategic human resource management, and contemporary management at the undergraduate, graduate and doctorate levels. Her research areas are strategic human resource management, strategic management, organizational downsizing, and innovation management.

Elif Acar, is an instructor of finance at Adana Science and Technology University Department of Management Information Systems, Adana–Turkey. Ms. Acar has a BA in Economics from Boğaziçi University (1994), an MBA from University of Hartford, CT (USA, 1998) with an academic excellence scholarship, and is currently pursuing her PhD in finance at Çukurova University in Adana. MS. Acar has extensive working experience in the finance field prior to her academic studies. She worked in the banking sector in Turkey during 1995–1997, then at Standard & Poor's credit rating agency in New York and in London for a total of 12 years as a corporate and project finance rating analyst with managerial responsibilities. She has conducted corporate credit analyses on many projects in the energy and utilities sector, alternative energy projects, public private partnerships, and infrastructure projects. Her research interests are corporate finance, capital structure, capital markets, information technology risk, and financial decision making process. She has taught international finance, banking and financial markets at the undergraduate level. She also gives seminars to entrepreneurs and mentors of entrepreneurs through the university's continuing education center and various university-industry partnership organizations. Ms. Acar is bilingual in Turkish and English.

Human Side of Strategic Alliances, Cooperations and Manoeuvrings During Recession and Crisis

Tuna Uslu

Abstract Together with the globalizing economy, it is no more possible for any system to survive by ignoring the market changes and transformations. A change taking place anyhow in any place of the world triggers complex processes and affects everyone by growing in waves. Successful ways of business conduct of today is based on predicting the growth speed of these waves and on the ability to carry out strategic cooperations and manoeuvres accordingly. Sometimes these fluctuations also trigger serious crises. Apart from the shocks created in organizational structures, periods of crisis have complex effects on people. Some people approach to these events in hesitation, while other people or organizations happen to have skills to turn these processes into opportunity. The practical examples show that the organizations that adapt to new condition by getting simpler and getting rid of burdens in the constriction process are able to come out in a better condition before the crisis. This section discusses the way of organizations to become human oriented when acting strategically during strategic alliances, cooperations and manoeuvrings.

1 Introduction

The changing ways of doing business and organizational development process, within the globalization period, has been moving towards managing the intangible abstract assets more than physical resources, and must focus on managing the processes instead of concrete outputs. While the standardization process that started with the reconstruction and quality assurance systems has been silhouetting for the organizations, in the following years, approaches such as transformation engineering, organization learning have been moving towards differentiation and creating

T. Uslu (✉)
Graduate Program of Business Management, Istanbul Gedik University, Kartal, Istanbul, Turkey
e-mail: tuna.uslu@gedik.edu.tr

H. Dinçer, Ü. Hacioğlu (eds.), *Risk Management, Strategic Thinking and Leadership in the Financial Services Industry*, Contributions to Management Science, DOI 10.1007/978-3-319-47172-3_25

competition advantage. During this transformation process, organizations learn just like the living entities, change and chart out their own course. From this perspective, organizations have been transforming into organisms that the human abilities are attributed to. They are born, they learn, develop, however if unable to ensure their continuity, they die as all the people do. With the total quality movement in the organizations, this made it necessary for the employees to take part in the process both mentally, physically and psychologically. The organizations, being more than organisms that possess a certain structure, are now abstract fields that continuously change and transform with their employees and structures. These abstract fields, beyond the economical and physical resources, host social and psychological interactions (Uslu 2014: 288).

Another aspect of globalization is economic and financial crises other than international competition. The increase of expansion speed of crises and their impact areas causes it to affect its region and all other countries during the course of time, which supports the chaos theory. Market changes and transformations among the factors that create financial inconsistency also cause employment issues, social trends, fluctuations and constrictions in money markets and therefore crisis (Silver 2014). On the other hand, the strategic cooperations in the process of globalization is a popular expansion and management strategy chosen by the businesses in present world of competition (Elmuti and Kathawala 2001). Strategic cooperations take place in various ways. However, the most widespread cooperations are company mergers, company acquisitions and assignments, joint venture and licence agreements. It is highly remarkable that these strategies take place particularly during and after crisis periods. For example, the 2001 crisis in Turkey had a positive incentive for the company mergers. The post-crisis increase trend in company mergers had a wary progress in 2002 and 2003 and reached to a significant level in 2004. There was an almost booming increase in 2005 (Deloitte 2010). This process has a significant impact on the social environment and human relations, particularly the employees.

Today, organizations try to survive in a continuously changing dynamic environment. In this process, trends are set by the organizations that keep pace with innovation and create transformation and only the organizations that are able to follow change trend can adapt to this new environment, whereas organizations that are left out of this field cannot survive. The leading factor that ensures transformation of businesses is the ability of top management to change and to manage change (Romanelli and Tushman 1994). On the other hand, strategies used transformation processes like mergers and acquisitions usually focus on profitability and sustainability (Cartwright and Schoenberg 2006). However, the works for acquiring companies, stocks and assets should not be considered merely as a process of tendering and contracting (Bruner 2004) but dealt with as change and transformation processes that should be managed. In addition, change processes like mergers and acquisitions have socio-cultural aspects that have individual and organizational impacts on employees (Marks 1982; Buono and Bowditch 2003). The failure to accomplish set goals in many attempts of organizational change makes one think that focus should be on how employees think, feel and behave during the transformation period (Ngyuen and Kleiner 2003). From the psychological perspective, the integration strategies and plans of organizations should be reviewed in relation to moods of managers, supervisors and personnel (Mirvis and Marks 1992).

The company mergers are a desired incident for the company stakeholders while it is a little different for employees. The company acquisitions and mergers are infections and it is normal that the fever of the organization increases and the body of the organization starts a resistance order (deGeus 1997). The mistakes that cause failure of mergers are usually experienced in the post-merger integration process (Simpson 2000). Particularly, the failure to assign the required importance to the human factor during the integration process can be shown among the significant causes of failure (Hutchinson 2002). It is emphasized that the emotions and personal contributions of the members of organization should be taken into consideration for a new formation to succeed (Syrjala and Tuomo 2007). The management reorganizes the human resources of the merging businesses in this period to make sure that the personnel not fitting to the structure of the new business are discharged or leave voluntarily (O'Rourke 1989). If we study mergers by taking human factor into consideration, every year thousands of people lose or change their jobs upon mergers. This obviously may cause psychological traumas. Individuals losing their jobs or those who cannot adapt to their new work environment are negatively affected by the mergers activities (Kusstatscher and Cooper 2005).

During crisis periods, business may realize a series of options that have direct or indirect negative effect on the rights, health and security of their employees in order to ensure compliance. The leading elements of the crisis adaptation strategy are reducing the costs, decreasing the scale, closing down some businesses and units and narrowing the employment. Shrinking is the first option chosen by the businesses to reduce their expenses and it can be defined as a passage from the current organization structure to the required organization structure. In this sense, businesses reduce their productions in the event of crisis, avoid from creating new employment, fire several employees, widespread temporary employment and transfer certain parts of production to supplier relations and subcontractors (ILO 2009). Economic crises may increase the inequality between income groups as well as the death rates among both adults and children. Suicide rates among low-income young men may increase. It was determined that the geographical and ethnic inequality with respect to life expectation and death rate increased during crisis periods (Mills 2010). Suicide based deaths increase in periods when economic growth is reduced and there is shrinkage (Bezruchka 2009). As there are such big and serious reflections of economic crises and shrinkage on human psychology, the effects on individuals and employees should be managed by the public and organization managers. It can be said that the crisis period start in a business when disputes among employees increase, the effect of business operations decreases, the business image is hurt and it becomes gradually impossible for the business to achieve its goals (Fink 1986).

2 Effects of Crises on Organizations and Employees

The word crisis is a concept that is used in daily life and in almost every part of life. Crisis is a very delicate issue that takes place in all organizations like non-profit organizations, state organizations, service organizations, small partnerships, strategic cooperations and international organizations (King 2002). An important feature of crisis is that it is a circumstance including events that may cause significant organization losses and involve time pressure for making decisions (Mitrof 1992). Organizational crises affect each unit and individual of the organization in waves and leave significant destruction behind. Crises are the circumstances that threaten the priority goals of the business, involve limited time to prevent, shock decision makers when take place and therefore cause high stress. Another essential feature that distinguishes crises from ordinary circumstances is that it involves the requirement of immediate intervention to the emergency. One needs to act quickly in crisis periods. In this sense, a crisis period can be defined as the changes that require urgent response and rapid adaptation (Puchan 2001). As the response to crisis to be given by the organization is determined and guided by individuals, one should study first the managerial, then the individual and then the organization reactions (Milburn et al. 1983). In addition, the effects of crisis on employees are very important for the organization and organizational activities (Podolok 2002).

In the crisis period, there may be shocking stress reactions, symptoms of violence, distress from problems, depression, exposure to assault and sadness. The concerned stress may cause long term mental and physical diseases as well as family problems. In such periods, the management of the organization should have its personnel feel that it cares about them (Persons 1995). In crisis periods, people experience "hidden anger", "accusations of each other" and "communication disorder". These feelings rapidly spread in the work places and employees start to think that they are the ones who are wronged the most instead of sharing and thus reducing their feelings. The variables that affect the thoughts of an employee about his job include salary, promotion chances, social benefits, managers, colleagues, working conditions, communication, security, efficiency and quality of job. Each of these variables has various effects on the job satisfaction (Berry 1997). In the crisis, the only factor that motivates the employees to do their job is the fear of being unemployed. Employees may show the tendency to work extra hours because of fear of losing their jobs (Uslu 2012).

Corporate strategies and crisis intervention plans affect the employees in different ways. They may play a role in making the employees to develop positive or negative attitudes. For this reason, managers get into new paths of seeking new structure and transformations which will bring the advantage of competitiveness to their organization and will make their institutions to survive. In the same time, this change also affects the relations between the employee and the organization. With regard to the employees, not having information about the future and being nervous about the uncertainty may lead to the tendency of resisting the intervention process (Uslu 2012).

3 Human Factor in Crisis Management

Crisis management refers to the management activities in a critical time period where the management decisions would decide the future of the organization (Weisaeth et al. 2002: 37). Crisis management involves the activities like analyzing the possible or on-going crisis process in businesses, solving the problems behind the crises and overcoming the crisis period with the least damage. Crisis management refers to "the internally connected evaluation or inspection to be carried out in a series with respect to crises that pay causes a significant danger to the basic processes of the business, employees and managers and external environment". The crisis management is a process involving series of activities like crisis prediction, prevention, preparation, determination of priorities, planning and implementing the improvement and learning mechanisms (Mitrof 1992). The categories of an ideal crisis management program include strategic activities, technical and structural activities, evaluation and diagnosis activities, communication activities, psychological and cultural activities (Pearson and Mitroff 1993).

Taking human element and human resources into consideration for crisis management is as important as the system design and integration is for the organization (Pearson and Clair 2003). Strategic cooperations have become a decisive feature on the basis of new industrial relations. Partnership in the broader sense refers to "cooperation of employers and unions to achieve joint goals like equality and competitiveness" (Lucio and Stuart 2004). Indeed, the turbulent and uncertain markets, competition environment, changing political status, transformations in business strategies and innovative methods require a new interaction based on the contribution of parties. In the narrow framework, the human resources management understanding and policies based on technical and completely profit based idea cause significant problem for the organization at times of organizational crisis (Sheaffer and Negrin 2003). Today, businesses obtain their competitive superiority through functional flexibility provided by various qualified workers with multidimensional skills in addition to their new production systems (de Silva 1997). Therefore, what shocks the organization worse than the crisis is the misuse of human resources and ignoring many human qualities with respect to crisis management and solution (Weisaeth et al. 2002). It is believed that the most important element for a successful merger and acquisition process is the human factor (Carey and Ogden 2004). Therefore, one needs to diagnose the qualities and psychological responses of employees, to exhibit a leadership skill to channel them for the solution of crisis and to show it in human resources policies (Burnett 1998). As a result, it becomes possible to implement cooperation based strategic human resources management in organizations.

3.1 Developing Resistance Against Crisis

Crisis management is not a discipline that can be learnt in the middle of a storm during an organizational work. Crisis management should be learnt when there is no cloud in the horizon (Hesselbein 2002). The manager should be able to have good estimation of long term circumstances to avoid from the possible future crises. However, many organizations evaluate short term conditions quickly while ignoring the long term conditions (Schleh 1974: 19). According to the literature, this approach constitutes the basis for unpreparedness and failure in crisis.

According to one view, the failure in crisis actually makes us prepared for both the present and future crises. Particularly, a business which didn't have a crisis before will be caught unprepared to the crisis if it gets wrong signals from the market (Silver 1992: 13). The studies didn't show a significant relation of crisis experience and technological risk in the industry with crisis preparedness while organizations with high performance in the market were found to be more prepared to crisis (Carmeli and Schaubroeck 2008). Some companies do not panic at the crisis environment but develop various product and production processes by avoiding excessive reactions and creating different tactics and crisis plans for alternative possibilities. It is attempted not to reflect the increases in production costs to the product prices thus the expected inflation rate is taken into consideration in determining the prices. In sales, it is attempted to increase the sales volume by presenting attractive price offers to customers (Barton 1994; Mitrof 1988). In a sense, the businesses that turn crises to opportunity are the organizations that use proactive approaches in their operations and that constantly learn, improve and develop themselves even in normal times beyond being prepared.

Organizations use certain methods to achieve their strategic, tactical and operational goals. These methods they use are also perceived and explained by the society somehow. There is a relation between the rules applied by the organization, way of behaviour, perception of the organization by the society and the performance of the organization. If the behaviours and applications are accepted, the image will increase and this will bring financial support to the sales of the organization and investment opportunities. The benefits obtained by the employees in this case will result in more work, protection of institution and integration with the institution (Bromley 1993). Particularly the human resources policies of the institution are the factors that configure the image to be provided by the employees with respect to their own organizations, culture structure, vision and the image taking place out of the institution (Dowling 1993). In order to create an image of a strong organization, the needs of the employees and their expectations from their organization should be covered. Employees generally need a vision and be proud of their jobs. Again, the employees expect a shared organization culture, a communication climate operated by all aspects and career opportunities (Schutz and Cook 1986). Employees will be able to experience an internal transformation in compliance with the process. Structural premises interact with personality traits and empower employees while they also ensure development of attitude against the condition.

Fig. 1 Internal transformation and external representation process of employees

As a result of this transformation, they will be able to acquire a role where they can express and represent themselves in this uncertain atmosphere or newly established balance. These effects lead to social identity formation of individuals and are reflected to observable and organizational outputs through an external representation process (Uslu 2014). The employees in the process first experience an internal transformation and get repositioned and then externally describe themselves through this new identity and move towards outcomes (Fig. 1).

3.2 The Role of Employees in Strategic Crisis Planning

Employees want to make sure that they are safe particularly at periods of crises. They need to trust in their leaders and experience internal peace caused by loyalty to leaders. It is only this way that employees can take an effective role for the organization to overcome short term circumstances and resolve the crisis in a short time (Mitroff 2001: 19). The most important issue to give priority in preparing the crisis plan is to ensure maximum safety of the employees and to present them a psychological peaceful environment (Perra and Morrison 1997).

Other than that, the crisis plans should be able to root causes of crisis and what can one or more possible factors are. In addition, they should be able to prevent aggravation of emergency case and to cover possible serious outcomes (Harris 1996). Good management of crisis period refers to determining the factors of crisis in a restrained manner, to create crisis teams, to take corrective measures to avoid long term problems and to make flexible emergency plan against a possible future crisis (Allen 1986).

In crisis conditions, creating an independent crisis team becomes useful in achieving a more effective solution. In addition to normal operations, tasks to be carried out with new groups to manage the crisis period become useful in reducing tension of employees and encouraging drive for success. These temporary and even independent working groups are the process of temporary coordination of managers at different units. These groups try to solve a distorted structure or a certain problem (Knowles and Saxberg 1988).

3.3 *Effectiveness of Organizational Communication in Recession and Re-organization*

Considering the fact that there may be conflict of authority at times of recession and the managers controlling the behaviours of employees may be changed or reduced, it is seen that trust and authorization at such times have critical role for the company to perform its essential functions. On the other hand, there feeling of trust between management and employees decreases at times of recession. The main cause of it that the employees start to doubt about the openness of the top management, and to think that the management is concerned about its own needs, doesn't do its job well and that the company is no more reliable (Mishra 1998). Conflicts between employees, their thoughts on decisions made in the organization, concerns regarding work related problems, hesitating to speaking out about neglect and improprieties could do serious damage to the institutions (Morrison and Milliken 2000). How the employees perceive the institutional management and communication methods are the determining factors in terms of job satisfaction and performance (Zhui et al. 2004).

When reducing the management expenses, one should be careful not to damage the basic function of the organization and not to create an excessive opposition among the employees (Chang and Campo-Flores 1980). The way of coping with recession is more critical for the success of the operation rather than the recession itself. The studies showed that the recession actions merely for reducing the number of employees usually ended up with failure. On the other hand, considering the criteria of increasing quality and minimum impact to employees, it is observed that the more success is achieved by the company by reducing its expenses in more comprehensive recession actions for changing the strategies, processes, control, product and services of company (Mishra 1998).

The fact that there is a widespread perception among the employees that equality and justice are not observed in the relation environment and applications in the work places during process like crisis, narrowing or strategic cooperations causes an environment that has negative effect on the health of employees (Wilkinson 2001). Similarly, it is seen that many studies on mergers and acquisitions only deal with the financial function and strategy selection of mergers but ignore the ethical problems in this process (Lin and Wei 2006). This has a negative effect on employees. There are two ethical problems in the mergers and acquisition operations (Werhane 1988). One of them is the violation of the rights of employees as the employees lose their jobs after mergers. Another ethical problem is the violation of the shareholders. Although the shareholders are the people who are affected the most by the operation, they are little informed about their liabilities, obligations and benefits they will obtain from the merger.

An important element to prevent the formation of organization crisis is to ensure the flow of correct and sufficient information. Depending on the ability of the system, quality information within the decision process includes an effective information flow to avoid excessive loading in the system (Smart and Vertinsky

1977: 640). In order to obtain information on a crisis, one needs to hear all people in an organization. It is necessary to benefit at the period of determination of the crisis from the independent observer out of the business just like the people in the business (Augustine 1995, 2000: 29). The most important issue during the crisis is communication and exchange of information. Hence, most of the conflicts and problems in the process are caused by misunderstandings. When the case becomes problematic, the words to use should be selected more carefully and the actions to take should be more meticulous (Coombs 2001; Goldsmith 2002). In addition, the crisis should be explained to employees with all causes of it during the process. Information should be given on how the management will run the crisis and the measures to be taken should be explained (Mishra 1998). If the employees cannot receive replies to eliminate their personal concerns, they cannot show the performance expected from themselves in the crisis. The management should use the "mobile management" technique during the crisis period. The leader should speak to the employees and colleagues face to face and one to one. In addition, employees should be able to feel that the management cares about their expectations. The concerns of employees should be noticed by the management and their views should listened and appreciated (Sherman 2001: 30–31). If the management acts with the feeling of responsibility and cares about internal communication, the employees will be the most willing and effective advocate of the organization. This will enable them to easily overcome the problems they face (Cohn 1991: 20). In addition, the communication between these people after the crisis feeds the roots of innovation (Hurst 1995).

4 Capacities and Strategic Manoeuvres that Provide Adaptation to Sudden Changes by Organizational Learning

The skill of an organization to expand its capacity to determine its own future has a very big importance during the crisis which is an unplanned development. The resistance of organizations that constantly improve themselves against sudden changes is higher. For this, however, the learning in the organization should be continuous or one needs to start a process of cultural change which will radically change the learning approach. The learning organization is centered first of all on the change of mentality. A learning organization is a place that allows people to form and discover their own realities. How to change or reorganize is based on the constant expansion and organization of the capacity of a learning organization to determine its own future (Solomon 1994).

4.1 Reactions of Employees During Re-Organization Process

Re-organization refers to re-arrangement of physical and psychological areas of a business (Uslu 2015). It requires a comprehensive re-organization work to close the strategic gap caused by not following the innovations brought by change and to eliminate the destruction caused by crisis. If, in the present process of fast change, the organizations cannot show this sensitivity while they are required to be sensitive as an open system against every change, there will be strategic gaps and irreversible expansion of the strategic gaps refers to the stage of crisis. The priority activity by an organization at this level is to bring a new structure and understanding to the organization according to the changing conditions so that the organization can achieve its goals and objectives. In a sense, this is the process of re-organizing and addressing the management functions according to the external conditions (Dessler 1986). Re-organization refers to the radical transformation and redesign of work processes in order to realize radical improvements in the most important performance criteria of our age like cost, quality, service and speed (Hammer 1990; Hammer and Champy 1993). Re-organization may cause both negative and positive reactions according to circumstances. The employees who do not have the access to the information about the process tend to have negative feelings and loss of trust to their organizations, managers and themselves together with uncertainty. On the other hand, the employees who participate in the decision processes judge the negative changes more rationally and easily (Uslu 2012). Re-organization process also affects the relations between the employee and organization. Lack of information by the employees about future and their fear of uncertainty may cause a tendency of resistance against the transformation process. Employees may channel their energy to defend themselves and to swim against the stream by responding to this process instead of participating in and adapting to change (Uslu 2015). Therefore, it is critically important to make them a part of the process by informing and including for reducing the resistance by aligning the wheels of the organization to the same direction.

4.2 From Classical Management to Lean Organizations for Adaptation to Sudden Changes

Lean organization concept is another concept that is closely related with and emerging in practice as a result of the concepts like level reduction, zero hierarchy, shrinking and reorganization. Lean organization refers to the redefinition and organization of the functions, departments and processes to provide a positive contribution to value creation (Womack and Jones 1996). This concept involves the integration of the organization structure to make sure faster response to the quality and standards requested by consumers. In lean organizations, the prior objective is to exclude the activity and positions for creating added value and to make the decision maker and the one doing the job as close as possible. This is a structure that is free from details, not delaying works and able to give prompt reaction. The most import differences between "Lean" and "Fordist" production include a the creation of a working organization to make more use of the intellectual knowledge of the work force which is one of the principles of lean management (Lewchuk and Robertson 1997). Team works also involve the most important aspect of the lean production practices (Kirkman 1997: 735). The importance of lean organizations is increased due to the narrowing of time, necessity to take quick decisions and to show prompt reactions to the circumstances particularly during the periods of crisis. The lean organization model is an organization model that can promptly response to change and that is away from centralization and hierarchy which supports the structural functionality of organizations for preventing or observing crises.

4.3 The Behaviours of Employees During the Stages of Strategic Alliances, Merger and Acquisition Process

Psychological problems during and after the structural transformations of strategic alliances like mergers and acquisitions cannot be known adequately as well as the differences in attitudes and behaviours of employees. In fact, mergers and acquisitions are a destruction process (Bruner 2004: 85). Researchers (Marks and Mirvis 1992; Cartwright and Cooper 1993; Schraeder 2001; Buono and Bowditch 2003) designate human resources problems, human and social dynamics during and after the change process as an important determinant of the success or failure of mergers. In addition, it is understood that low cultural adaption is an important cause of failure (Schoenberg 2000). The organization atmosphere (Schneider and Reichers 1983; Rousseau 1988; Ruppel and Harrington 2000) as an indicator of corporate practices, quality processes, employee practices, innovation and organizational factors (Hansen and Wernerfelt 1989) are important descriptors of business performance.

Mergers have many direct impacts on employees. Because of temporary lay-offs, uncertainty, new company culture, management and job roles, mergers and acquisition affect millions of employees every year (O'Shaughnessy and Flanagan 1998; Griffen et al. 2007) and this reduces the performance and competitiveness of the newly structured organization (Weber 1996). Negative factors in the process are mostly felt in the departments or sub-divisions that are discharged or divided the most (Uslu 2014: 310). The most frequent negative outcome of merger and acquisition process is the increase in employees' intention to leave (Krug and Aguilera 2004). Some of the other negative outcomes of change process are reduction in job satisfaction and organizational commitment one hand and increase of job stress, mistakes and restraints of employees (Latack 1986; McHugh 1997).

Employees are bound to be seized by negative feelings mainly when their organizations are divided or their departments are discharged. The difference between positive organizational behaviours and emotional commitment to organization is in favour of organizations that undergo mergers and acquisitions rather than those that are divided or discharged. The reason is that when the department is divided, positive feelings and commitment to organization of employees may disappear (Uslu 2014: 315). Commitment to change and organization can be ensured as long as the executions during the process are managed fairly, organization has a positive approach to the reactions of participants to change and is able to integrate employees to the process (Wanberg and Banas 2000). In the process, the innovative approach of the management has an important role on employee psychology. At this point, what matters is that the innovative organizations have the ability to better manage the processes. Especially, the contribution of innovation to process management appears to be more than organization management and positive leadership approach (Uslu 2014: 317).

During the merger and acquisition process, employees become bound to face the increase of different approaches, systems and objectives in the post-acquisition integration stage where organizational transformation starts (Chakrabarti and Mitchell 2005). If the perceptions and expectations of employees on the process are negative, it is possible that they have negative attitude towards administration and start to work less efficiently as a result of reduction in their job satisfaction (Covin et al. 1996). In this period, more attention is needed for the requirements and requests of employees (De Cock and Rickards 1996; Bijlsma-Frankema 2001). In order to be able to reach the real value to be created by merger, it is understood that administrators need to manage the human aspect of change (Gertsen et al. 1998; Olie 1994; Buono and Bowditch 2003). Leadership approach is an important premise with respect to adaptation to change (Kavanagh and Ashkanasy 2006). In the process of merger, leaders should focus on creating openness, cooperation, moral and commitment by developing sense of belonging among employees. This leadership approach requires direction towards human resources, socio-cultural problems and humane issues in order to be able to improve individual competencies and empower organization climate. Quinn and colleagues (1996) who put emphasis on developing, empowering and committing employees define this approach as a "human relations" point of view characterized by flexible guidance of individuals and focusing on the inner circle of organization. They advocate that leaders should feature mentorship and facilitating qualities during the process. A proper management of the process has positive effect on psychological ownership, emotional commitment to organization and job satisfaction of employees while it has a negative effect on their intention to leave. In this process, the period with the most negative effect on employees is understood to be post-merger integration. Especially in this period, the positive effect of the ability of organization to manage the process and of the psychological ownership of employees is heavily noticed on job satisfaction (Uslu 2014: 7).

5 Conclusion

The most widespread strategic cooperations are mergers, acquisitions and assignments, joint venture and licence agreements. It is highly remarkable that these strategies take place particularly during and after crisis periods. As mentioned in the literature, the process of mergers and acquisitions may be a threat for the employees to maintain their organizational identities. Therefore, the operations of mergers and acquisitions need to be carried out specifically by pre-planning, support and improve positions of employees in the workplace. Employees will be able to experience an internal transformation in compliance with the process. Structural premises interact with personality traits and empower employees while they also ensure development of attitude against the condition (Uslu 2014: 278). It is seen that structured innovations in the process empower process management activities and reduces the organizational cynicism and intention to leave of employees (Uslu 2014: 309). Open and ethical communication of leader has also an important role on the organizational commitment of employees through process management (Uslu 2014: 310). As a result of the transformation, employees will be able to acquire a role where they can express and represent themselves in this uncertain atmosphere or newly established balance. These effects lead to social identity formation of individuals and are reflected to observable and organizational outputs through an external representation process (Uslu 2014: 270).

In general, the biggest negativities for employees in organizations that undergo critical processes like strategic cooperations are experienced in the post-merger integration process. Employees perceive weakening with respect to positive guidance within the framework of positive leadership and with respect to open and ethical communication especially in this period. Therefore, their work enthusiasm and target oriented hopes can be broken. This causes a reduction in benefitting from the sources of the organization during the process of negotiation and contracting as well as a reduction of psychological ownership in the following integration process. In this period, organizational cynicism levels of employees increase and their organizational commitments and job satisfactions get weaker (Uslu 2014: 316). Change and crisis management is also not a discipline that can be learnt in the middle of a storm. It should be learnt when there is no cloud in the horizon. Structural transformations are operations that need to be carried out by planning on the levels of organization, division and individuals before the process by the top management. Therefore, regardless of the fact that there is a merger, acquisition, assignment or discharge, it is observed that transformations, that are attempted without determining procedure, innovation and process stages, corporate infrastructure, organizational communication instruments, leadership approach, human resources practices, would fail (Uslu 2014: 318).

The priority activity of the management at the first stage of the transformation is to bring a new structure and understanding to the organization according to the changing conditions so that the organization can achieve its goals and objectives. In a sense, this is the process of re-organizing and addressing the management functions according to the environmental conditions. The leader of the change needs to create a program characterized by flexible guidance of individuals and focusing on the inner circle of organization and separate sub-plans for each period beginning from the first stage. These plans need to include the corporate and cultural transformation of the organization step by step as well as the compliance of employees with this transformation (Uslu 2014: 318). The categories of the program include strategic activities, technical and structural activities, evaluation and diagnosis activities, communication activities, psychological and cultural activities. The strategies and plans of organizations should be reviewed in relation to moods of managers, supervisors and employees. Lack of information by the employees about future and their fear of uncertainty may cause a tendency of resistance against the transformation process. Employees may channel their energy to defend themselves and to swim against the stream by responding to this process instead of participating in and adapting to change (Uslu 2015). Therefore, it is critically important to make collaborators and employees a part of the process by informing and including for reducing the resistance by aligning the wheels of the organization to the same direction. In the process, leaders should focus on creating openness, cooperation, moral and commitment by developing sense of belonging among employees. This leadership approach requires direction towards human resources, socio-cultural problems and humane issues in order to be able to improve individual competencies and empower organization climate.

References

Allen JE (1986) Beyond time management: organizing the organization, 1st edn. Addison-Wesley, Boston, MA. ISBN 0-201-15793-4

Augustine NR (1995) Managing the crisis you tried to prevent. Harvard Bus Rev 1(4):147–158

Augustine NR (2000) Managing the crisis you tried to prevent. Harvard business review on crisis management. Harvard Business School, Boston, pp 1–32

Barton L (1994) Crisis management: preparing for and managing disasters. Cornell Restaurant Admin Q 35(2):63

Berry LM (1997) Psychology at work. McGraw Hill, San Francisco, CA

Bezruchka S (2009) The effect of economic recession on population health. Can Med Assoc J 181 (5):281–282

Bijlsma-Frankema K (2001) On managing cultural integration and cultural change processes in mergers and acquisitions. J Eur Ind Train 25(4):192–207

Bromley BD (1993) Reputation image and impression management. Wiley, London

Bruner RF (2004) Applied mergers and acquisitions. Wiley, New York

Buono AF, Bowditch JL (2003) The human side of mergers and acquisitions: managing collisions between people, cultures, and organizations. Beard Books, Washington, DC

Burnett JJ (1998) A strategic approach to managing crises. Public Relat Rev 24(4):475–488

Carey DC, Ogden D (2004) The human side of M & A: how CEOs leverage the most important asset in deal making. Oxford University Press, Oxford. ISBN 978-0-19-514096-5

Carmeli A, Schaubroeck J (2008) Organizational crisis-preparedness: the importance of learning from failures. Long Range Plann 41:177–196

Cartwright S, Cooper CL (1993) The psychological impact of mergers and acquisition on the individual: a study of building society managers. Hum Relat 46:327–347
Cartwright S, Schoenberg R (2006) Thirty years of mergers and acquisitions research: recent advances and future opportunities. Br J Manage 17(1):1–5
Chakrabarti A, Mitchell W (2005) A corporate level perspective on acquisitions and integration. In: Cooper CL, Finkelstein S (eds) Advances in mergers and acquisitions, 4th edn. Elsevier, Oxford
Chang YN, Campo-Flores F (1980) Business policy and strategy. Goodyear, Santa Monica, CA
Cohn RJ (1991) Pre-crisis management. Exec Excell 8(10):20
Coombs TW (2001) Teaching the crisis management/communication course. Public Relat Rev 27 (1):89–101
Covin TJ, Sightler KW, Kolenko TA, Tudor RK (1996) An investigation of post-acquisition satisfaction with the merger. J Appl Behav Sci 32:125–136
De Cock C, Rickards T (1996) Thinking about organizational change: towards two kinds of process intervention. Int J Org Anal 4(3):233–251
de Silva SR (1997) The changing focus of industrial relations and human resources management. In: Paper presented at Industrial Labour Organization in Asia-Pasific in the Twenty-First Century, Turin, Italy, 5–13 May 1997. ILO, ACT/EMP Publications
deGeus A (1997) The living company. Longview Publishing, Chicago, IL
Deloitte (2010). Deloitte M&A Reports, Deloitte Turkey
Dessler G (1986) Organization theory integrating structure and behavior, 2nd edn. Prentice-Hall, Englewood Cliffs, NJ, p 449
Dowling GR (1993) Developing your company image into a corporate asset. Long Range Plann 26 (2):101–109
Elmuti D, Kathawala Y (2001) An overview of strategic alliances. Manage Decis 39(3):205–217
Fink S (1986) Crisis management: planning for the inevitable. Amacom Press, New York
Gertsen MC, Soderberg AM, Torp JE (1998) Different approaches to understanding of culture in mergers and acquisitions, cultural dimensions of international mergers and acquisitions. de Gruyter, Berlin, pp 17–38
Goldsmith B (2002) Leadership in crisis: best practice from people who've been there. Am Water Works Assoc J 94(1):32–34
Griffen MA, Neal A, Parker SK (2007) A new model of work role performance: positive behavior in uncertain and interdependent contexts. Acad Manage J 50:327–347
Hammer M (1990) Reengineering work: don't automate, elaborate. Harvard Bus Rev Jul–Aug:104–112
Hammer M, Champy J (1993) Reengineering the corporation. Nicholas Brealy, London
Hansen G, Wernerfelt B (1989) Determinants of firm performance: the relative importance of economic and organizational factors. Strateg Manage J 17:399–411
Harris J (1996) Sharpen your team's skills in project management. McGraw-Hill Education, London
Hesselbein F (2002) Crisis management: a leadership imperative. Acad Manage J 34(2):63
Hurst DK (1995) Crisis & renewal: meeting the challenge of organizational change. In: Tushman ML, de Ven AHV (eds) From the management of innovation and change series. Harvard Business School Press, Boston, MA
Hutchinson S (2002) Managing the people side of mergers, why communication is critical for the success of mergers and acquisitions. Melcrum 6(5):26
ILO (2009) Health and life at work: a basic human right, 28 April World Day for safety and health at work. International Labor Organization, Geneva, pp 7–8
Kavanagh M, Ashkanasy N (2006) The impact of leadership and change management strategy on organizational culture and individual acceptance of change during a merger. Br J Manage 17:83–105
King G (2002) Crisis management and team effectiveness: a closer examination. J Bus Ethics 41 (3):235–250

Kirkman B (1997) The impact of cultural values on employee resistance to teams: toward a model of globalized self-managing work team effectiveness. Acad Manage Rev 22(3):730–757
Knowles HP, Saxberg BD (1988) Organization leadership of planned and unplanned change. Future 20(3):258–259
Krug JA, Aguilera RV (2004) Top management team turnover in mergers & acquisitions. Adv Merge Acquis 4:121–149
Kusstatscher V, Cooper CL (2005) Managing emotions in mergers and acquisitions. Edward Elgar, Cheltenham, p 31
Latack JC (1986) Coping with job stress: measures and future decisions for scale development. J Appl Psychol 71(3):377–385
Lewchuk W, Robertson D (1997) Production without empowerment: work reorganization from the perspective of motor vehicle workers. Capital Class 63:37–64
Lin YY, Wei YC (2006) The role of business ethics in merger and acquisition success: an empirical study. J Bus Ethics 69:95–109
Lucio M, Stuart M (2004) Swimming against the tide: social partnership, mutual gains and the revival of tired HRM. Int J Hum Resour Manage 15(2):410–422
Marks ML (1982) Merging human resources: a review of current research. Mergers Acquis 17:50–55
Marks ML, Mirvis PH (1992) Track the impact of mergers and acquisitions. Pers J 71:70–79
McHugh M (1997) The stress factor: another item for the change management agenda? J Org Change Manage 10(4):345–362
Milburn TW, Schuler RS, Watman KH (1983) Organizational crisis. Part I: Definition and conceptualization. Hum Relat 36(12):1141–1160; Part II: Strategies and responses. Hum Relat 36(12):1161–1180
Mills C (2010) Health, employment and recession the impact of the global crisis on health inequities in New Zealand. Policy Q 6(4)
Mirvis PH, Marks ML (1992) Managing the merger: making it work. Prentice Hall, Upper Saddle River, NJ
Mishra EK (1998) Preserving employee morale during downsizing. Sloan Manage Rev 18
Mitrof II (1988) Crisis management: cutting through the confusion. Sloan Manage Rev 1 (Winter):1820
Mitrof II (1992) Effective crisis management. Acad Manage Exec 1(4):283–292
Mitroff II (2001) Crisis leadership. Exec Excell 18(8):19–20
Morrison EW, Milliken FJ (2000) Organizational silence: a barrier to change and development in a pluralistic world. Acad Manage Rev 25:706–725
Ngyuen H, Kleiner BH (2003) The effective management of mergers. Leadersh Org Dev J 24:447–454
O'Rourke JT (1989) Post-merger integration: the Ernst & Young management guide to mergers and acquisitions. Wiley, New York, pp 220–221
Olie R (1994) Shades of culture and institutions in international mergers. Org Stud 15(3):381–405
O'Shaughnessy KC, Flanagan DJ (1998) Determinants of layoff announcements following M&As: an empirical investigation. Strateg Manage J 19:989–999
Pearson C, Clair JA (2003) Refarming crisis management. Acad Manage Rev 23(1):61–62
Pearson C, Mitroff II (1993) From crisis prone to crisis prepared: a framework for crisis management. Acad Manage Exec 7(1):48–59
Perra RD, Morrison S (1997) Preparing for a crisis. Educ Leadersh 55(2):43
Persons W (1995) Crisis management. Career Dev Int 1(5):27
Podolok A (2002) Crisis management teams. Risk Manage 49(9):56
Puchan H (2001) The Mercedes-Benz A-class crisis. Corp Commun 6(1)
Quinn RE, Spreitzer GM, Hart SL (1996) Becoming a master manager: a competency framework. Wiley, New York
Romanelli E, Tushman ME (1994) Organizational transformation as punctuated equilibrium: an empirical test. Acad Manage J 37(5):1145

Rousseau DM (1988) The construction of climate in organization research. Int Rev Ind Org Psychol 3:139–159
Ruppel CP, Harrington SJ (2000) The relationship of communication, ethical work climate, and trust to commitment and innovation. J Bus Ethics 24(4):313–328
Schleh EC (1974) Management tactician. McGraw-Hill Education, New York
Schneider B, Reichers AE (1983) On the etiology of climates. Pers Psychol 36:19–39
Schoenberg R (2000) The influence of cultural compatibility within cross-border acquisitions: a review. Adv Merge Acquis 1:43–59
Schraeder M (2001) Identifying employee resistance during the threat of a merger: an analysis of employee perceptions and commitment to an organization in a pre-merger context. Mid-Atlantic J Bus 37:191–203
Schutz P, Cook J (1986) Porsche on nichemanship. Harvard Bus Rev Mar–Apr:98–106
Sheaffer Z, Negrin RM (2003) Executives' orientation as indicators of crisis management policies and practices. J Manage Stud 40(2):577–578
Sherman R (2001) How to communicate during times of crisis (Professionals at work). Bus Credit 103(10):30–34
Silver AD (1992) The turnaround survival guide: strategies for the company in crisis. Kaplan Publishing, London
Silver AD (2014) Managing corporate communications in the age of restructuring, crisis, and litigation: revisiting groupthink in the boardroom. J Ross, Plantation, FL
Simpson C (2000) Integration framework supporting successful mergers. Merge Acquis Can 12 (10):3
Smart C, Vertinsky I (1977) Designs for crisis decision units. Admin Sci Q 22:640–657
Solomon CM (1994) HR facilitates the learning organization concept. Pers J 59
Syrjala J, Tuomo T (2007) Ethical aspects in Nordic business mergers: the case of electro-business. J Bus Ethics 80:531–545
Uslu T (2012) Investigation of the effects of the structural changes in organizations on employees. In: 20th National management and organization congress, May 24–26. Proceedings Book. Dokuz Eylul University, pp 45–49
Uslu T (2014) Perception of organizational commitment, job satisfaction and turnover intention in M&A process: a multivariate positive psychology model. Unpublished PhD Thesis, Marmara University, Department of Business Administration
Uslu T (2015) Study of the effect of re-organization process on the employee performance through qualitative and quantitative methods. In: International congress on economy administration and market surveys, Istanbul, p 107, 4–5 Dec 2015
Wanberg CR, Banas JT (2000) Predictors and outcomes of openness to changes in a reorganizing workplace. J Appl Psychol 85(1):132–142
Weber Y (1996) Corporate cultural fit and performance in mergers and acquisitions. Hum Relat 49:1181–1193
Weisaeth L, Knudsen O, Tomessen A (2002) Technological disasters, crisis management and leadership stress. J Hazard Mater 93(1):36–37
Werhane PH (1988) Two ethical issues in mergers and acquisitions. J Bus Ethics 7:41–45
Wilkinson C (2001) Fundamentals of health at work: the social dimensions. Taylor & Francis, London, pp 9–10
Womack JP, Jones DT (1996) Lean thinking. Simon & Schuster, New York
Zhui Y, May SK, Rosenfeld LB (2004) Information adequacy and job satisfaction during merger and acquisition. Manage Commun Q 18(2):241–270

Tuna Uslu is an Assistant Professor at Istanbul Gedik University, Graduate Program of Business Management, Istanbul, Turkey. He is also head of the Sport Management Department. Dr. Uslu has a BS in Economics and Business Administration from Istanbul Bilgi University, an MSc in Total Quality Management from Dokuz Eylul University and a PhD in Organizational Behavior from Marmara University. His research interests lie into fields including micro-economics, strategic management, sport management, cognitive psychology, industrial and organizational psychology. He has taught Business Management, Entrepreneurship and Facility Planning, Strategies and Methods of International Trade, Quality Management Systems, International Transportation and Logistics, Social Psychology, Management and Organization courses, among others, at both graduate and undergraduate levels. He has several articles, awards and book chapters, joined more than hundred national and international conferences. He is in the editorial board of International Journal of Business and Management, Management and Organizational Studies, Journal of Management and Sustainability, International Journal of Economic Behavior and Organization, International Journal of Psychological Studies and has been an ad hoc reviewer for journals such as Information Resources Management Journal and Review of Innovation and Competitiveness.

MIX
Papier aus verantwortungsvollen Quellen
Paper from responsible sources
FSC® C105338

If you have any concerns about our products,
you can contact us on
ProductSafety@springernature.com

In case Publisher is established outside the EU,
the EU authorized representative is:
Springer Nature Customer Service Center GmbH
Europaplatz 3, 69115 Heidelberg, Germany

Printed by Libri Plureos GmbH
in Hamburg, Germany